PRAISE FOR THE *MANGA GUIDE* SERIES

"Highly recommended."
—CHOICE MAGAZINE ON *THE MANGA GUIDE TO DATABASES*

"The *Manga Guides* definitely have a place on my bookshelf."
—SMITHSONIAN MAGAZINE

"The art is charming and the humor engaging. A fun and fairly painless lesson on what many consider to be a less-than-thrilling subject."
—SCHOOL LIBRARY JOURNAL ON *THE MANGA GUIDE TO STATISTICS*

"Stimulus for the next generation of scientists."
—SCIENTIFIC COMPUTING ON *THE MANGA GUIDE TO MOLECULAR BIOLOGY*

"The series is consistently good. A great way to introduce kids to the wonder and vastness of the cosmos."
—DISCOVERY.COM

"Absolutely amazing for teaching complex ideas and theories . . . excellent primers for serious study of physics topics."
—PHYSICS TODAY ON *THE MANGA GUIDE TO PHYSICS*

"A great fit of form and subject. Recommended."
—OTAKU USA MAGAZINE ON *THE MANGA GUIDE TO PHYSICS*

"I found the cartoon approach of this book so compelling and its story so endearing that I recommend that every teacher of introductory physics, in both high school and college, consider using it."
—AMERICAN JOURNAL OF PHYSICS ON *THE MANGA GUIDE TO PHYSICS*

"This is really what a good math text should be like. Unlike the majority of books on subjects like statistics, it doesn't just present the material as a dry series of pointless-seeming formulas. It presents statistics as something *fun* and something enlightening."
—GOOD MATH, BAD MATH ON *THE MANGA GUIDE TO STATISTICS*

"A single tortured cry will escape the lips of every thirty-something biochem major who sees *The Manga Guide to Molecular Biology*: 'Why, oh why couldn't this have been written when I was in college?'"
—THE SAN FRANCISCO EXAMINER

WOW!

"A lot of fun to read. The interactions between the characters are lighthearted, and the whole setting has a sort of quirkiness about it that makes you keep reading just for the joy of it."
—HACKADAY ON *THE MANGA GUIDE TO ELECTRICITY*

"The *Manga Guide to Databases* was the most enjoyable tech book I've ever read."
—RIKKI KITE, LINUX PRO MAGAZINE

"*The Manga Guide to Electricity* makes accessible a very intimidating subject, letting the reader have fun while still delivering the goods."
—GEEKDAD

"If you want to introduce a subject that kids wouldn't normally be very interested in, give it an amusing storyline and wrap it in cartoons."
—MAKE ON *THE MANGA GUIDE TO STATISTICS*

"A clever blend that makes relativity easier to think about—even if you're no Einstein."
—STARDATE, UNIVERSITY OF TEXAS, ON *THE MANGA GUIDE TO RELATIVITY*

"This book does exactly what it is supposed to: offer a fun, interesting way to learn calculus concepts that would otherwise be extremely bland to memorize."
—DAILY TECH ON *THE MANGA GUIDE TO CALCULUS*

"Scientifically solid . . . entertainingly bizarre."
—CHAD ORZEL, SCIENCEBLOGS, ON *THE MANGA GUIDE TO RELATIVITY*

"Makes it possible for a 10-year-old to develop a decent working knowledge of a subject that sends most college students running for the hills."
—SKEPTICBLOG ON *THE MANGA GUIDE TO MOLECULAR BIOLOGY*

"*The Manga Guide to the Universe* does an excellent job of addressing some of the biggest science questions out there, exploring both the history of cosmology and the main riddles that still challenge physicists today."
—ABOUT.COM

"*The Manga Guide to Calculus* is an entertaining comic with colorful characters and a fun strategy to teach its readers calculus."
—DR. DOBB'S

THE MANGA GUIDE™ TO MICROPROCESSORS

THE MANGA GUIDE™ TO
MICROPROCESSORS

MICHIO SHIBUYA,
TAKASHI TONAGI, AND
OFFICE SAWA

THE MANGA GUIDE TO MICROPROCESSORS.

Copyright © 2017 by Michio Shibuya, Takashi Tonagi, and Office sawa.

The Manga Guide to Microprocessors is a translation of the Japanese original, *Manga de wakaru CPU*, published by Ohmsha, Ltd. of Tokyo, Japan, © 2014 by Michio Shibuya, Takashi Tonagi, and Office sawa.

This English edition is co-published by No Starch Press, Inc. and Ohmsha, Ltd.

Printed in USA
First printing

21 20 19 18 17   1 2 3 4 5 6 7 8 9

ISBN-10: 1-59327-817-9
ISBN-13: 978-1-59327-817-5

Publisher: William Pollock
Production Editor: Serena Yang
Author: Michio Shibuya
Illustrator: Takashi Tonagi
Producer: Office sawa
Developmental Editors: Jan Cash and Tyler Ortman
Translators: Fredrik Lindh and Akino Lindh
Technical Reviewer: Dan Romanchik
Copyeditor: Paula L. Fleming
Compositors: Max Burger and Serena Yang
Proofreader: Shannon Waite
Indexer: BIM Creatives, LLC

For information on distribution, translations, or bulk sales, please contact No Starch Press, Inc. directly:
No Starch Press, Inc.
245 8th Street, San Francisco, CA 94103
phone: 1.415.863.9900; info@nostarch.com; http://www.nostarch.com/

Library of Congress Cataloging-in-Publication Data
A catalog record of this book is available from the Library of Congress.

CONTENTS

3
CPU ARCHITECTURE

4
OPERATIONS

PREFACE

Ever since the 1950s, when computers saw their debut in markets all over the world, interest in information technology (IT) has seen a steady rise. The core that supports this technology is a semiconductor known as the CPU, or central processing unit. Since the start of the 21st century, advancements in circuit design theory and manufacturing technology have led to rapid progress in both processing speed and chip size, allowing us to embed them in most of the electronics we use on a daily basis. In addition to personal computers, smartphones, and tablets, you'll even find CPUs in things like air conditioners, refrigerators, washing machines, and other major appliances, just to name a few.

It's worth noting that the CPUs found in modern PCs are extremely powerful, and many of their applications are outside the scope of this book. We also will not delve into computer architecture which has had a research boom in recent years. Instead, I think that the best way to give insight into what CPUs are—and, by extension, how programs work—is to go back and analyze how the first CPUs worked and examine the concepts and principles by which they were designed.

Let me share an allegory with you. It's been quite some time since we first started taking automobiles for granted in our daily lives, but despite their ubiquity, very few people today can explain how an engine works or how the energy generated by the engine gets translated into forward momentum for the car. In the 1950s, you had to answer engine design questions on your driver's license examination, but no such questions remain in today's tests. Essentially, this means that to learn things about the internals of a car engine today, you really have to be an incredibly curious person.

In that vein, my wish is that this book will not only act as a platform to teach readers a range of different topics but also to sate their curiosity on the subject by having them learn some of the deeper principles of the CPUs that have so nonchalantly permeated our daily lives.

In regards to the publication of this book, I would like to thank Sawako Sawada of Office sawa, who thought up the fun story, and Takashi Tonagi for the illustration work.

MICHIO SHIBUYA
NOVEMBER 2014

1

WHAT DOES THE CPU DO?

SS
AYUMI

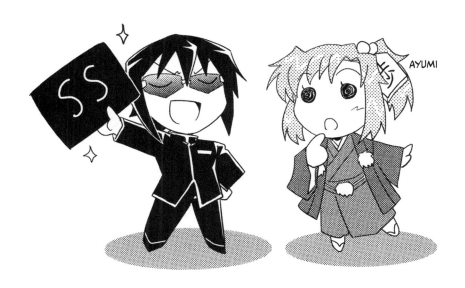

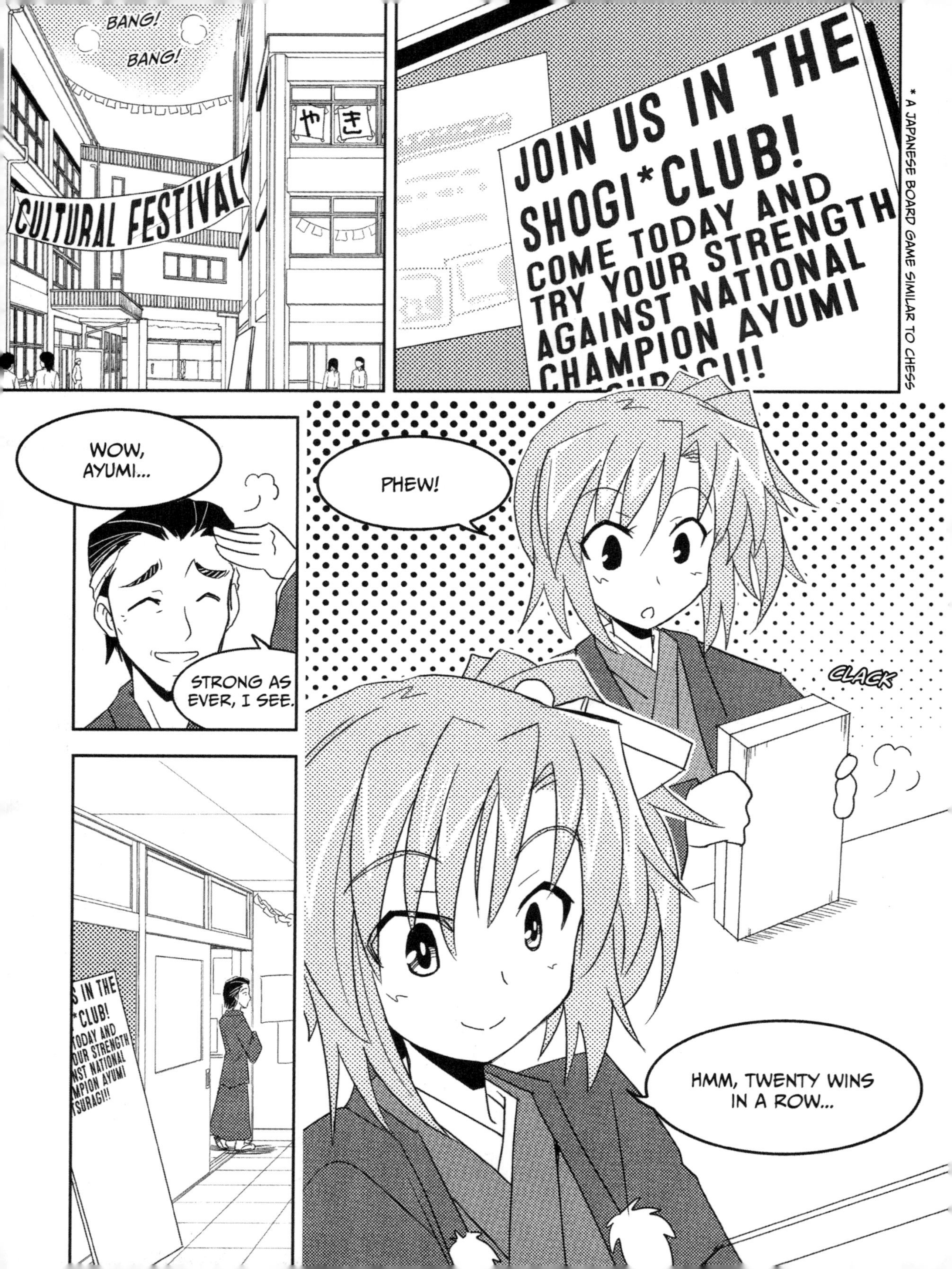
BANG!
BANG!
CULTURAL FESTIVAL
やき
JOIN US IN THE SHOGI*CLUB!
COME TODAY AND TRY YOUR STRENGTH AGAINST NATIONAL CHAMPION AYUMI
WOW, AYUMI...
STRONG AS EVER, I SEE.
PHEW!
CLACK
HMM, TWENTY WINS IN A ROW...

* A JAPANESE BOARD GAME SIMILAR TO CHESS

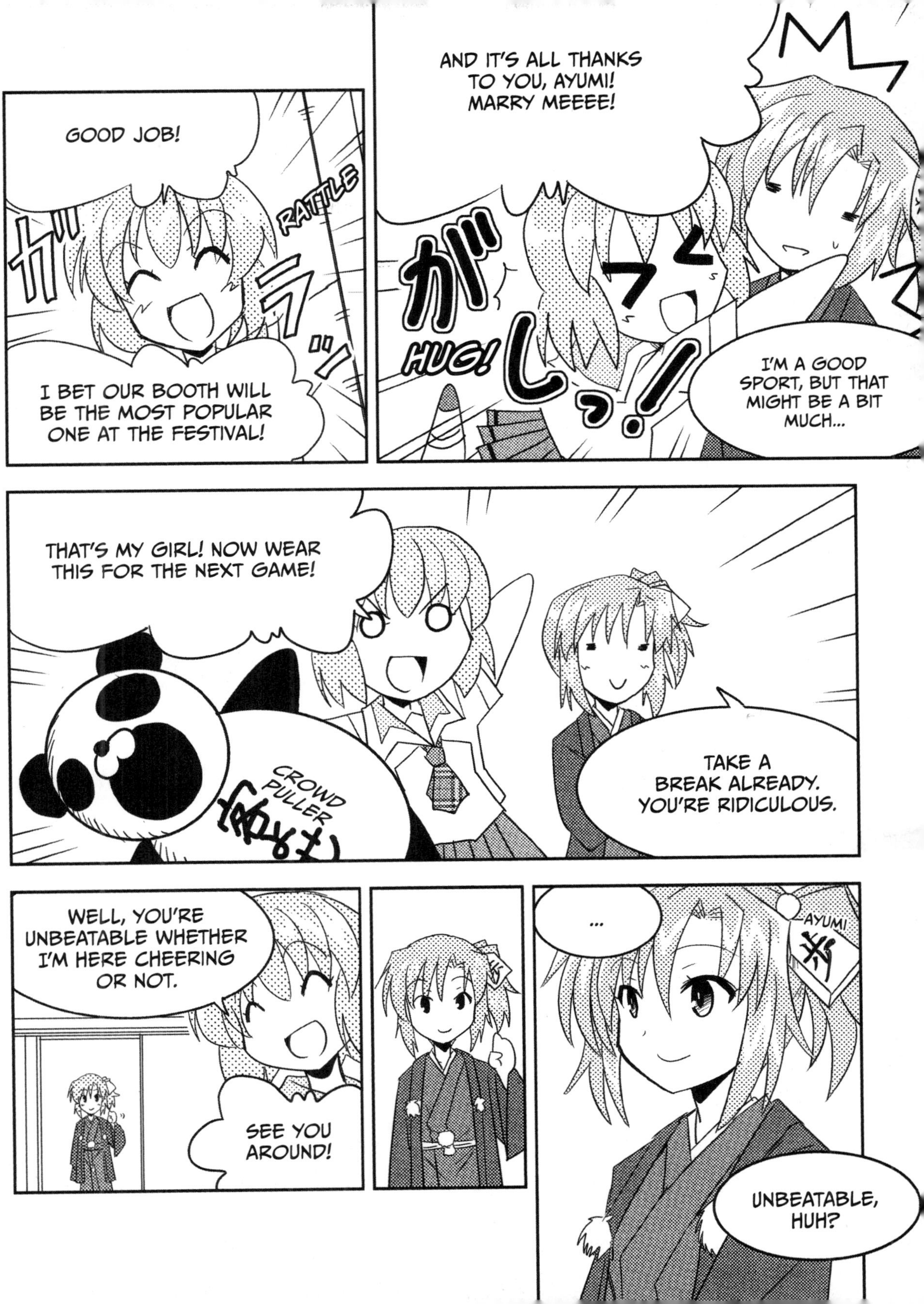
GOOD JOB!
RATTLE
ガラッ
I BET OUR BOOTH WILL BE THE MOST POPULAR ONE AT THE FESTIVAL!
AND IT'S ALL THANKS TO YOU, AYUMI! MARRY MEEEE!
HUG!
がしっ
I'M A GOOD SPORT, BUT THAT MIGHT BE A BIT MUCH...
THAT'S MY GIRL! NOW WEAR THIS FOR THE NEXT GAME!
CROWD PULLER
TAKE A BREAK ALREADY. YOU'RE RIDICULOUS.
WELL, YOU'RE UNBEATABLE WHETHER I'M HERE CHEERING OR NOT.
SEE YOU AROUND!
...
AYUMI
UNBEATABLE, HUH?

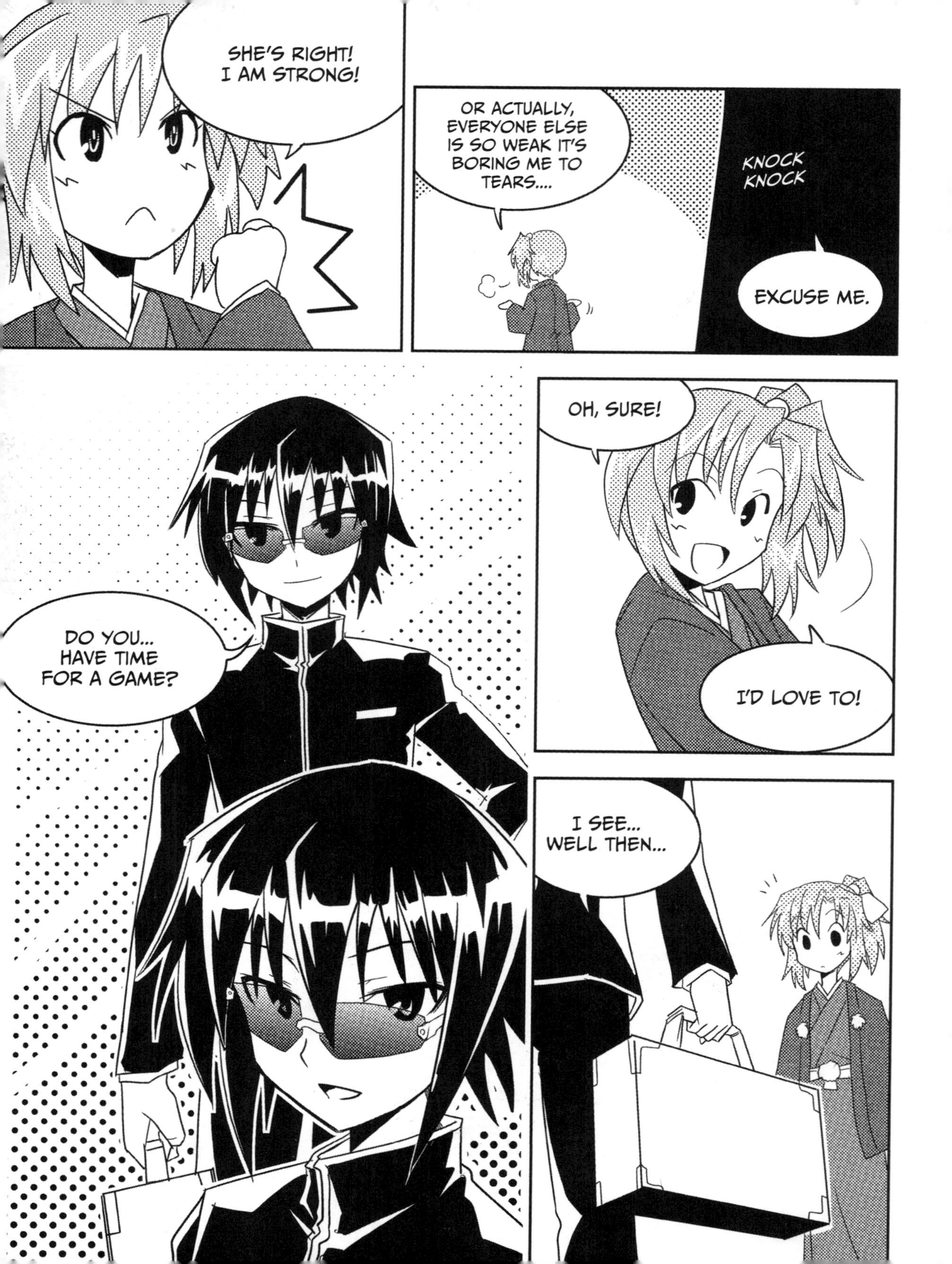
SHE'S RIGHT! I AM STRONG!
OR ACTUALLY, EVERYONE ELSE IS SO WEAK IT'S BORING ME TO TEARS....
KNOCK KNOCK
EXCUSE ME.
DO YOU... HAVE TIME FOR A GAME?
OH, SURE!
I'D LOVE TO!
I SEE... WELL THEN...

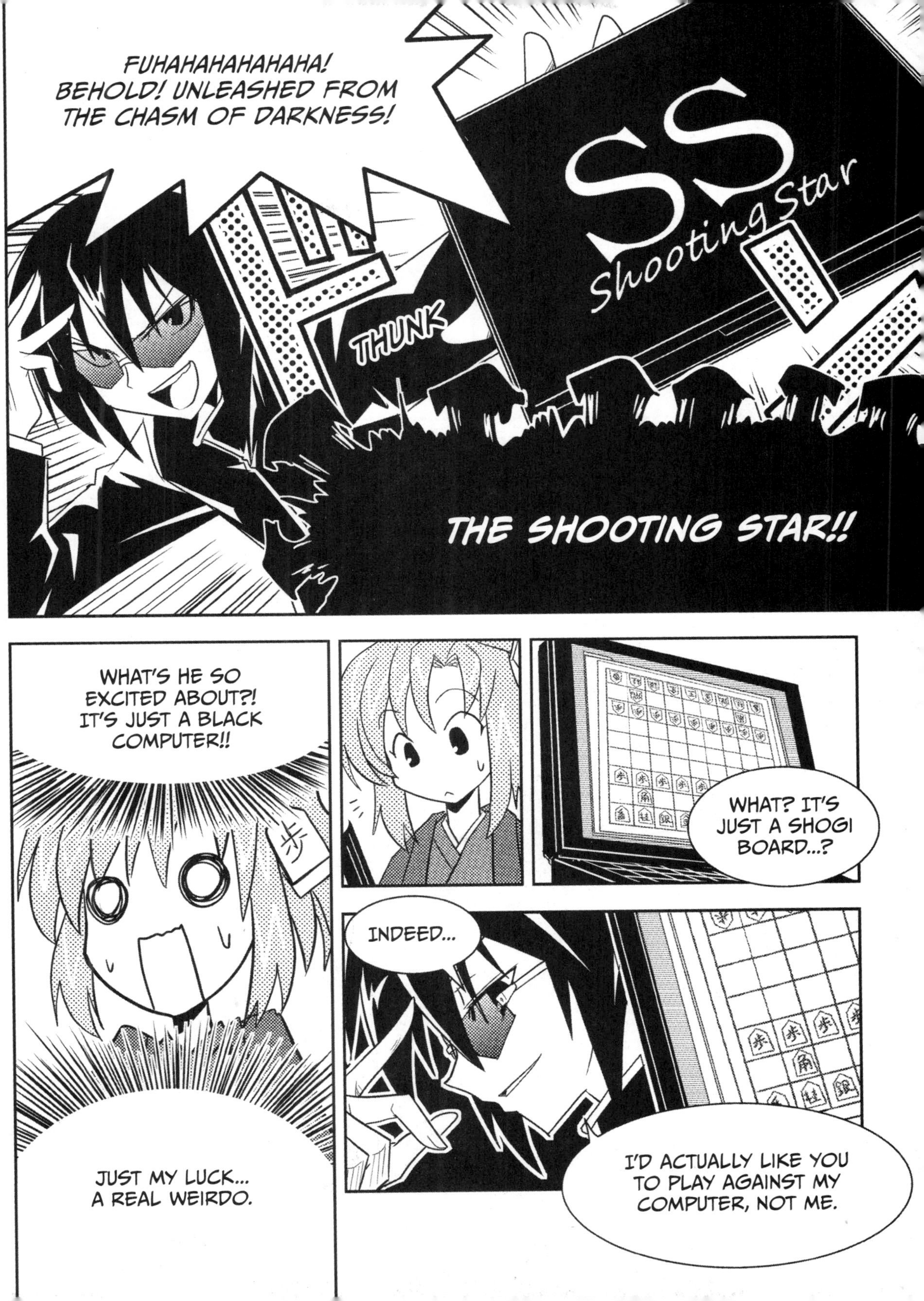
FUHAHAHAHAHAHA! BEHOLD! UNLEASHED FROM THE CHASM OF DARKNESS!
THUNK
SS
Shooting Star
THE SHOOTING STAR!!
WHAT'S HE SO EXCITED ABOUT?! IT'S JUST A BLACK COMPUTER!!
JUST MY LUCK... A REAL WEIRDO.
WHAT? IT'S JUST A SHOGI BOARD...?
INDEED...
I'D ACTUALLY LIKE YOU TO PLAY AGAINST MY COMPUTER, NOT ME.

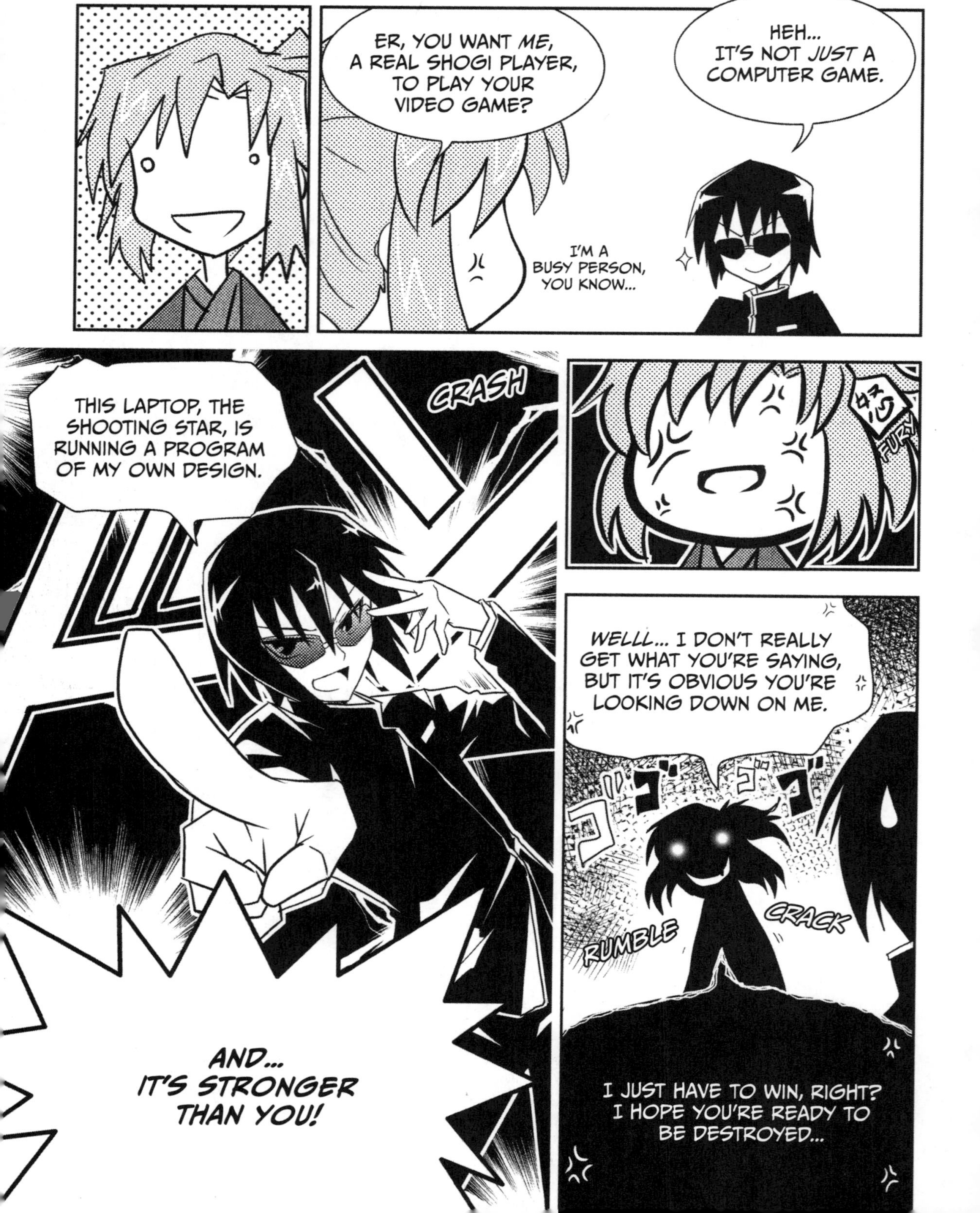
ER, YOU WANT *ME*, A REAL SHOGI PLAYER, TO PLAY YOUR VIDEO GAME?
I'M A BUSY PERSON, YOU KNOW...
HEH... IT'S NOT *JUST* A COMPUTER GAME.
THIS LAPTOP, THE SHOOTING STAR, IS RUNNING A PROGRAM OF MY OWN DESIGN.
CRASH
AND... IT'S STRONGER THAN YOU!
怒 FURY
WELLL... I DON'T REALLY GET WHAT YOU'RE SAYING, BUT IT'S OBVIOUS YOU'RE LOOKING DOWN ON ME.
RUMBLE
CRACK
I JUST HAVE TO WIN, RIGHT? I HOPE YOU'RE READY TO BE DESTROYED...

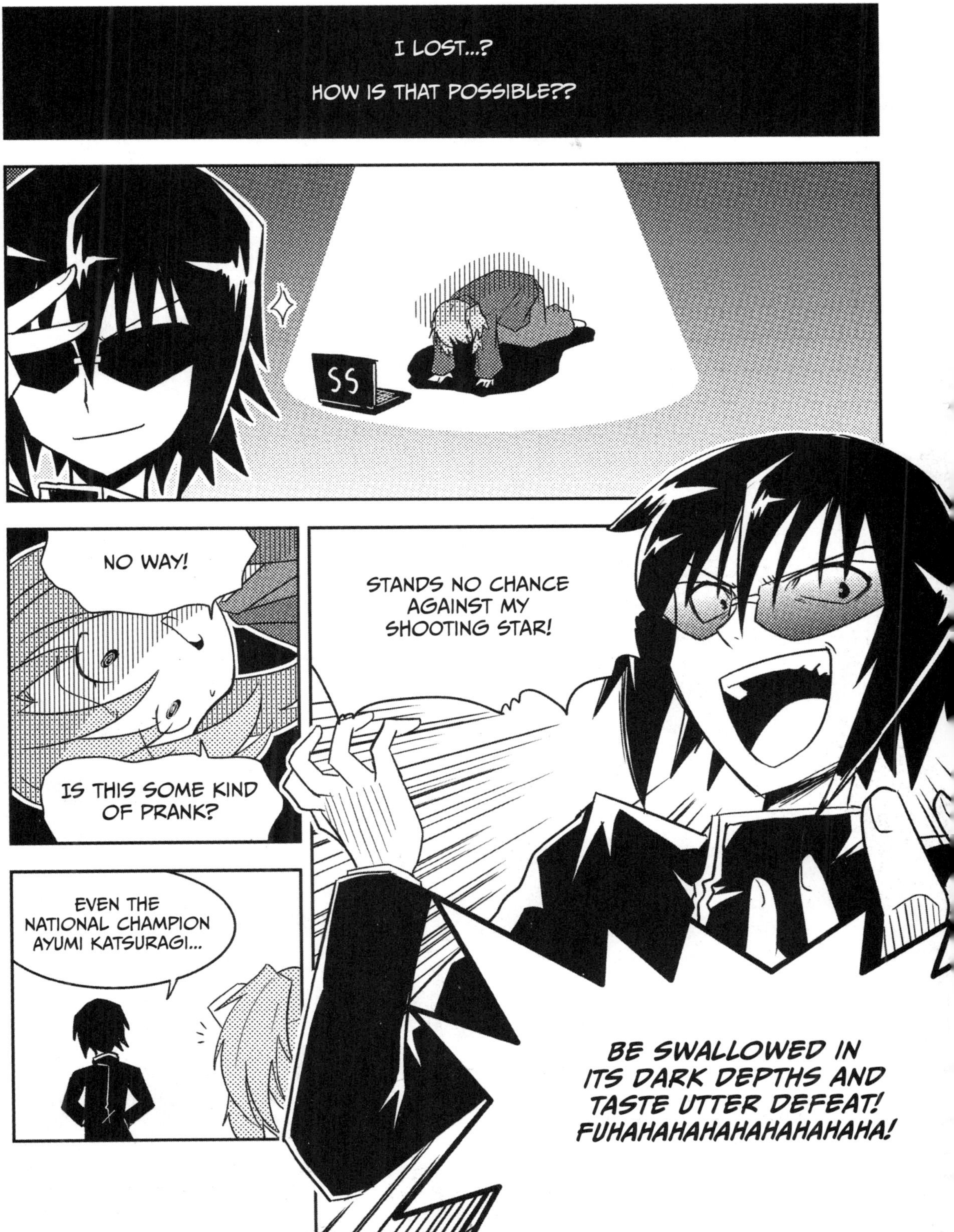
I LOST...?
HOW IS THAT POSSIBLE??
NO WAY!
IS THIS SOME KIND OF PRANK?
EVEN THE NATIONAL CHAMPION AYUMI KATSURAGI...
STANDS NO CHANCE AGAINST MY SHOOTING STAR!
BE SWALLOWED IN ITS DARK DEPTHS AND TASTE UTTER DEFEAT! FUHAHAHAHAHAHAHAHAHA!

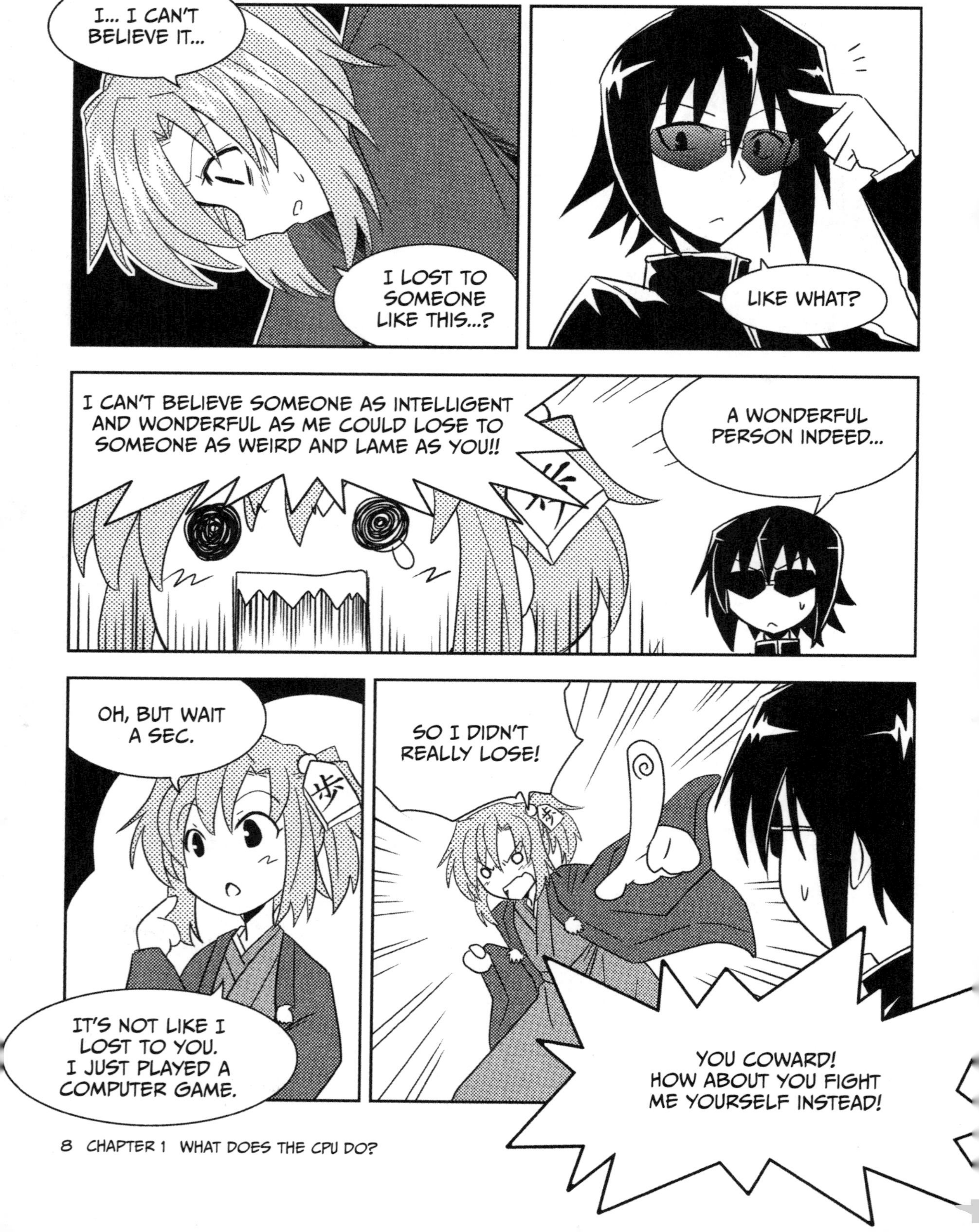

I... I CAN'T BELIEVE IT...
I LOST TO SOMEONE LIKE THIS...?
LIKE WHAT?
I CAN'T BELIEVE SOMEONE AS INTELLIGENT AND WONDERFUL AS ME COULD LOSE TO SOMEONE AS WEIRD AND LAME AS YOU!!
A WONDERFUL PERSON INDEED...
OH, BUT WAIT A SEC.
IT'S NOT LIKE I LOST TO YOU. I JUST PLAYED A COMPUTER GAME.
SO I DIDN'T REALLY LOSE!
YOU COWARD! HOW ABOUT YOU FIGHT ME YOURSELF INSTEAD!

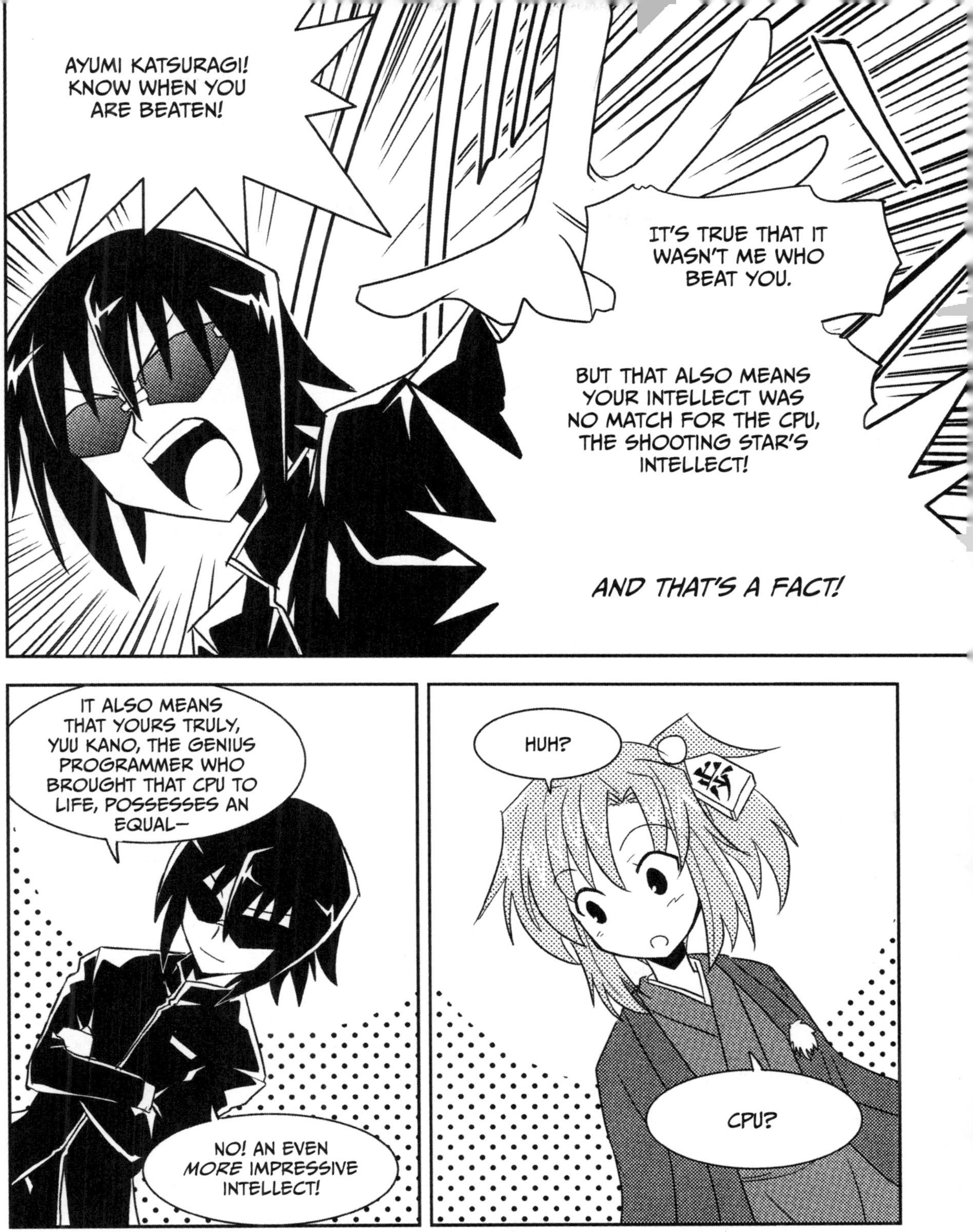
AYUMI KATSURAGI! KNOW WHEN YOU ARE BEATEN!
IT'S TRUE THAT IT WASN'T ME WHO BEAT YOU.
BUT THAT ALSO MEANS YOUR INTELLECT WAS NO MATCH FOR THE CPU, THE SHOOTING STAR'S INTELLECT!
AND THAT'S A FACT!
IT ALSO MEANS THAT YOURS TRULY, YUU KANO, THE GENIUS PROGRAMMER WHO BROUGHT THAT CPU TO LIFE, POSSESSES AN EQUAL—
NO! AN EVEN *MORE* IMPRESSIVE INTELLECT!
HUH?
CPU?

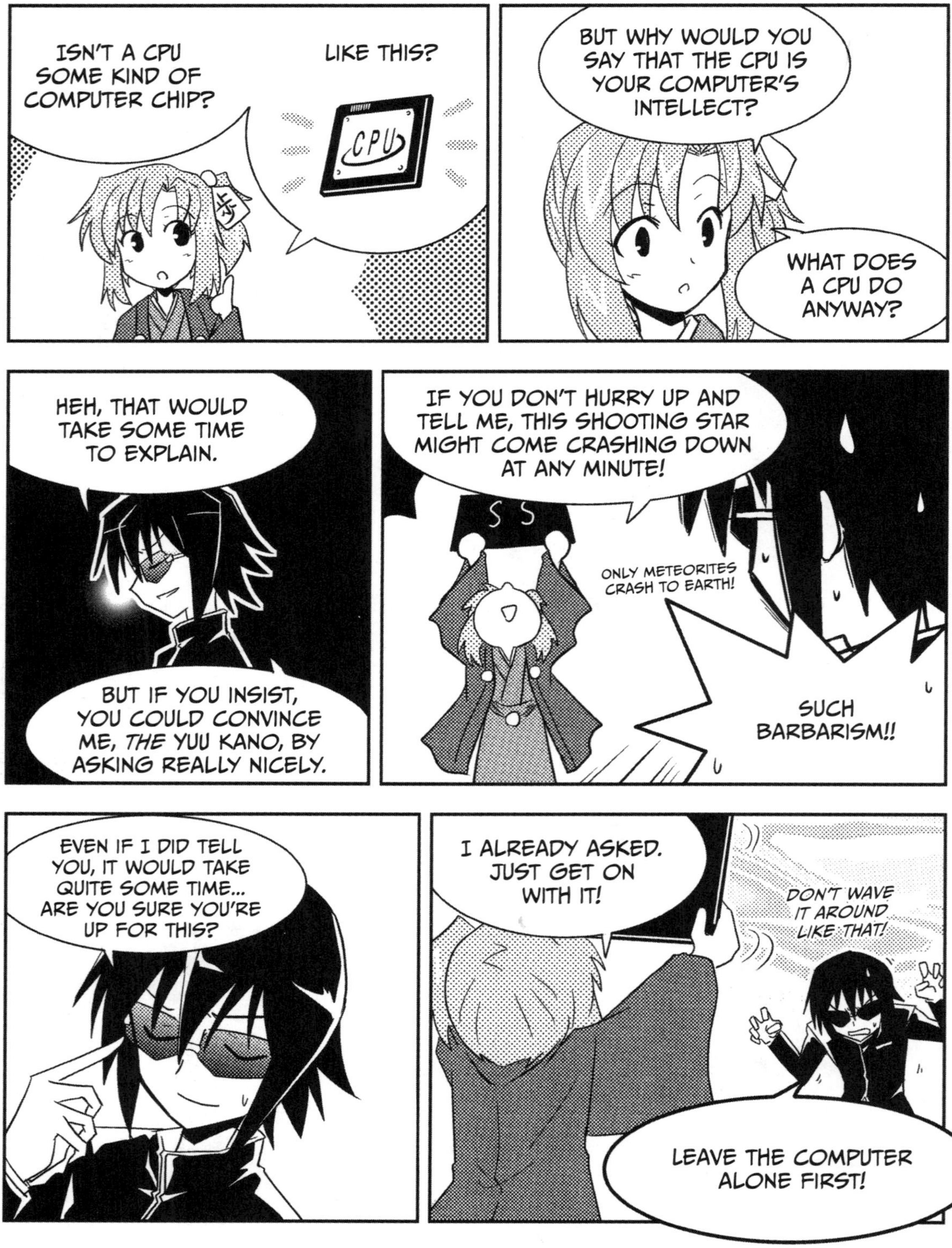
ISN'T A CPU SOME KIND OF COMPUTER CHIP?
LIKE THIS?
CPU
BUT WHY WOULD YOU SAY THAT THE CPU IS YOUR COMPUTER'S INTELLECT?
WHAT DOES A CPU DO ANYWAY?
HEH, THAT WOULD TAKE SOME TIME TO EXPLAIN.
BUT IF YOU INSIST, YOU COULD CONVINCE ME, *THE* YUU KANO, BY ASKING REALLY NICELY.
IF YOU DON'T HURRY UP AND TELL ME, THIS SHOOTING STAR MIGHT COME CRASHING DOWN AT ANY MINUTE!
ONLY METEORITES CRASH TO EARTH!
SUCH BARBARISM!!
EVEN IF I DID TELL YOU, IT WOULD TAKE QUITE SOME TIME... ARE YOU SURE YOU'RE UP FOR THIS?
I ALREADY ASKED. JUST GET ON WITH IT!
DON'T WAVE IT AROUND LIKE THAT!
LEAVE THE COMPUTER ALONE FIRST!

COMPUTERS CAN PROCESS ANY TYPE OF INFORMATION

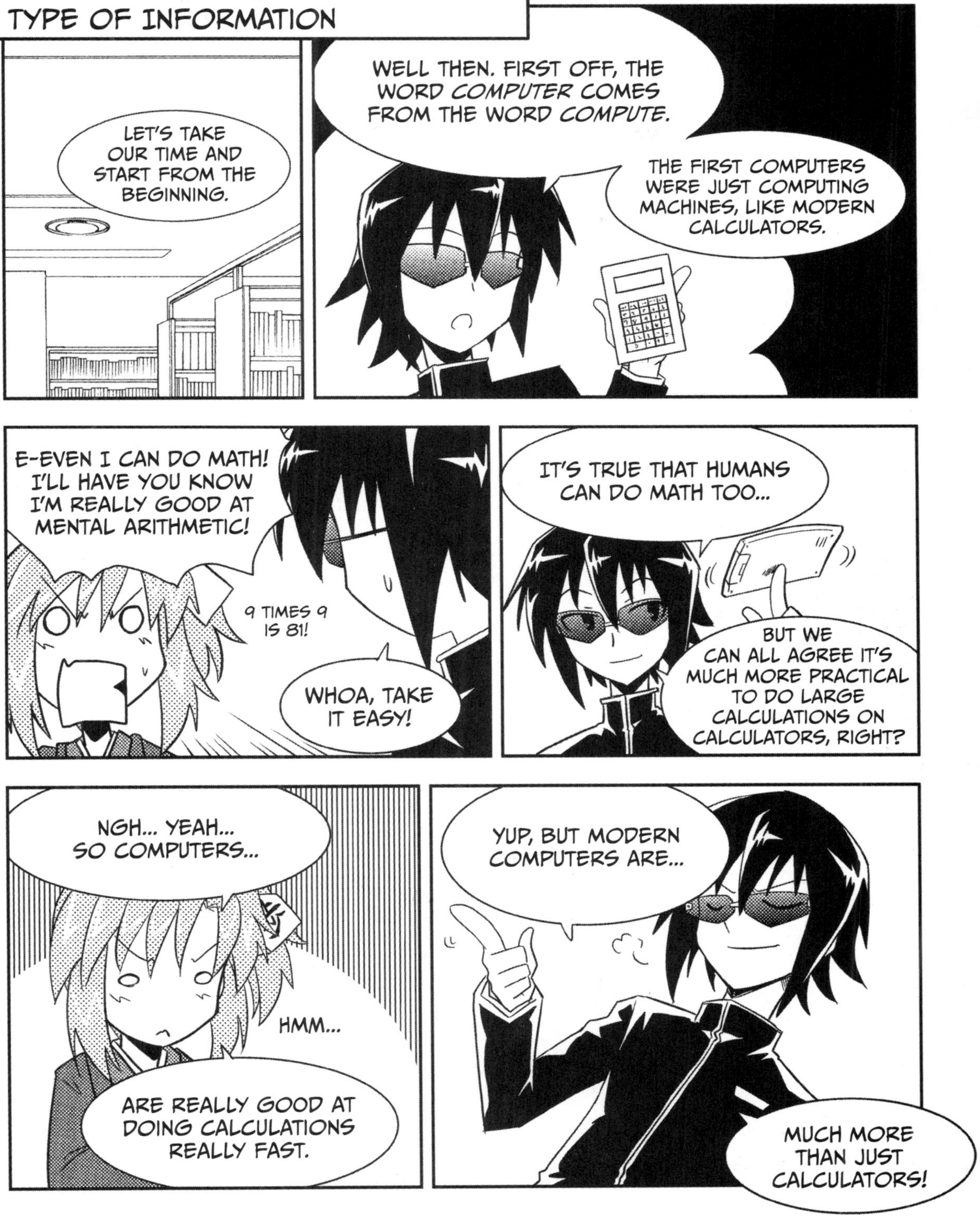
LET'S TAKE OUR TIME AND START FROM THE BEGINNING.
WELL THEN. FIRST OFF, THE WORD *COMPUTER* COMES FROM THE WORD *COMPUTE*.
THE FIRST COMPUTERS WERE JUST COMPUTING MACHINES, LIKE MODERN CALCULATORS.
E-EVEN I CAN DO MATH! I'LL HAVE YOU KNOW I'M REALLY GOOD AT MENTAL ARITHMETIC!
9 TIMES 9 IS 81!
WHOA, TAKE IT EASY!
IT'S TRUE THAT HUMANS CAN DO MATH TOO...
BUT WE CAN ALL AGREE IT'S MUCH MORE PRACTICAL TO DO LARGE CALCULATIONS ON CALCULATORS, RIGHT?
NGH... YEAH... SO COMPUTERS...
HMM...
ARE REALLY GOOD AT DOING CALCULATIONS REALLY FAST.
YUP, BUT MODERN COMPUTERS ARE...
MUCH MORE THAN JUST CALCULATORS!

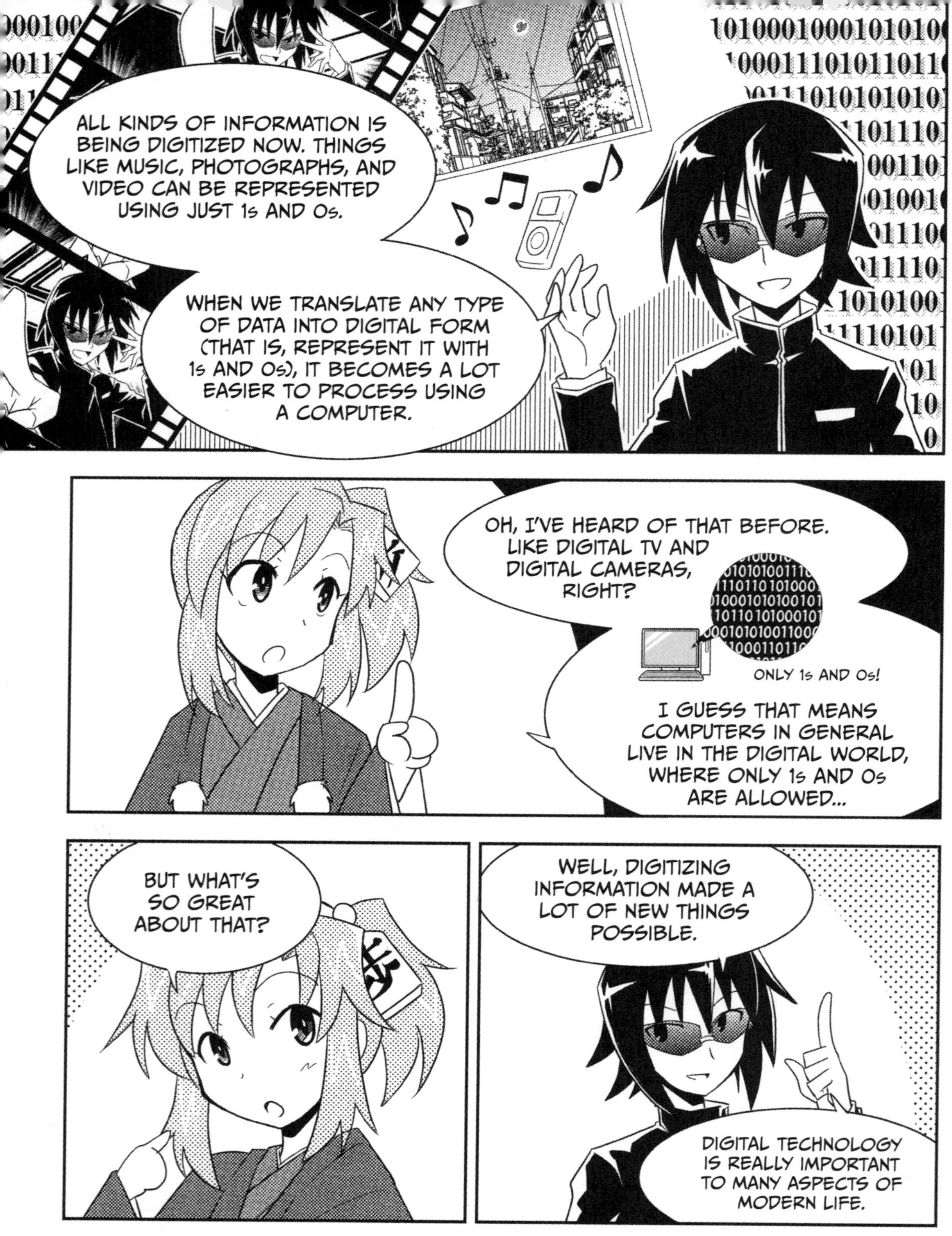
ALL KINDS OF INFORMATION IS BEING DIGITIZED NOW. THINGS LIKE MUSIC, PHOTOGRAPHS, AND VIDEO CAN BE REPRESENTED USING JUST 1s AND 0s.
WHEN WE TRANSLATE ANY TYPE OF DATA INTO DIGITAL FORM (THAT IS, REPRESENT IT WITH 1s AND 0s), IT BECOMES A LOT EASIER TO PROCESS USING A COMPUTER.
OH, I'VE HEARD OF THAT BEFORE. LIKE DIGITAL TV AND DIGITAL CAMERAS, RIGHT?
ONLY 1s AND 0s!
I GUESS THAT MEANS COMPUTERS IN GENERAL LIVE IN THE DIGITAL WORLD, WHERE ONLY 1s AND 0s ARE ALLOWED...
BUT WHAT'S SO GREAT ABOUT THAT?
WELL, DIGITIZING INFORMATION MADE A LOT OF NEW THINGS POSSIBLE.
DIGITAL TECHNOLOGY IS REALLY IMPORTANT TO MANY ASPECTS OF MODERN LIFE.

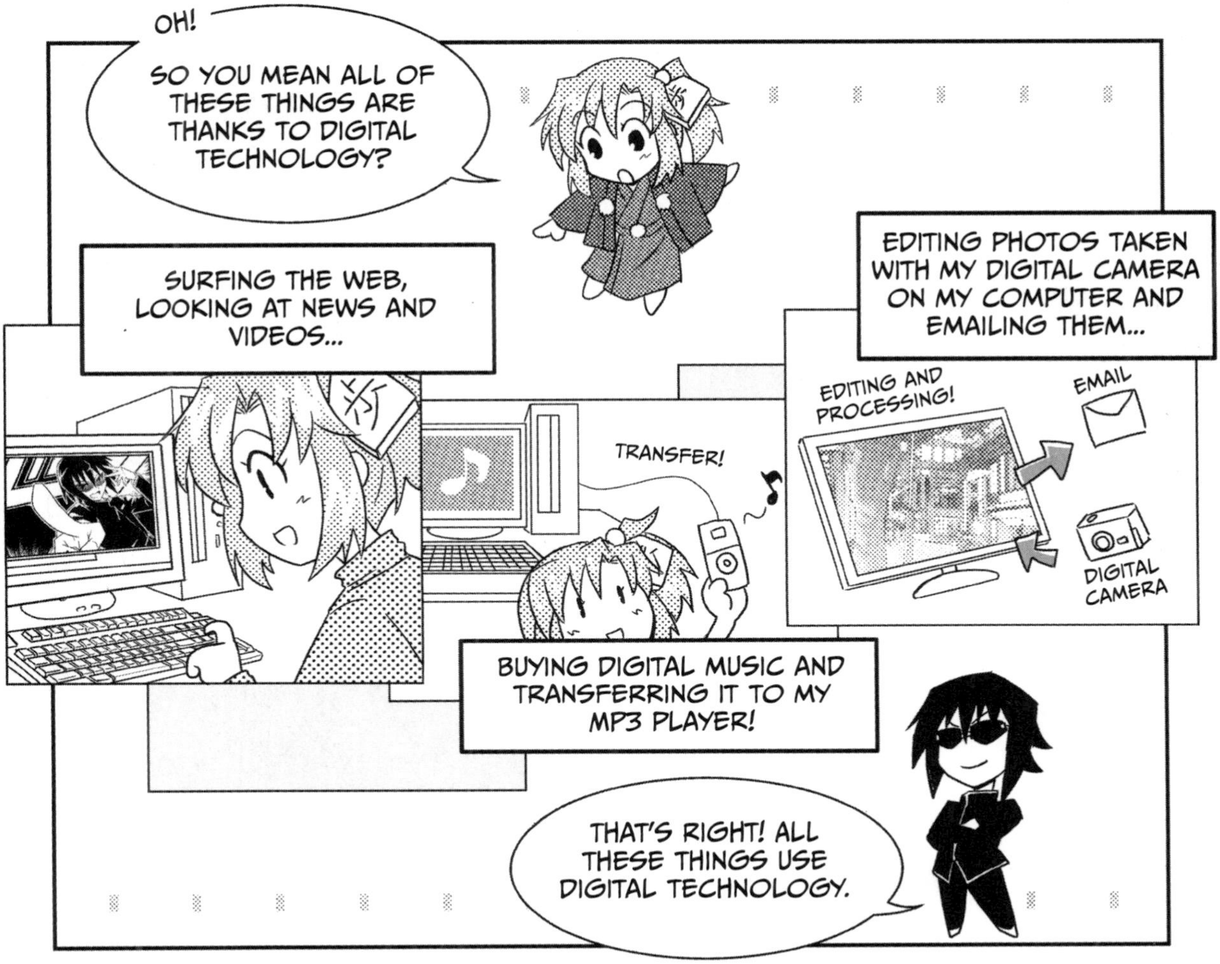
OH!
SO YOU MEAN ALL OF THESE THINGS ARE THANKS TO DIGITAL TECHNOLOGY?
SURFING THE WEB, LOOKING AT NEWS AND VIDEOS...
TRANSFER!
BUYING DIGITAL MUSIC AND TRANSFERRING IT TO MY MP3 PLAYER!
EDITING PHOTOS TAKEN WITH MY DIGITAL CAMERA ON MY COMPUTER AND EMAILING THEM...
EDITING AND PROCESSING!
EMAIL
DIGITAL CAMERA
THAT'S RIGHT! ALL THESE THINGS USE DIGITAL TECHNOLOGY.

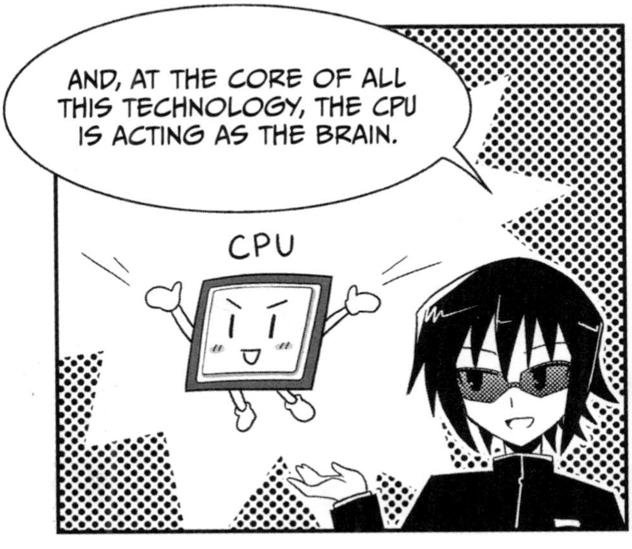
AND, AT THE CORE OF ALL THIS TECHNOLOGY, THE CPU IS ACTING AS THE BRAIN.
CPU

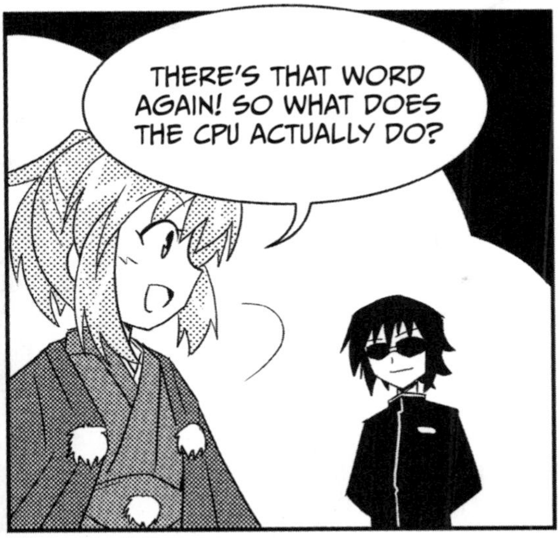
THERE'S THAT WORD AGAIN! SO WHAT DOES THE CPU ACTUALLY DO?

THE CPU IS THE CORE OF EACH COMPUTER

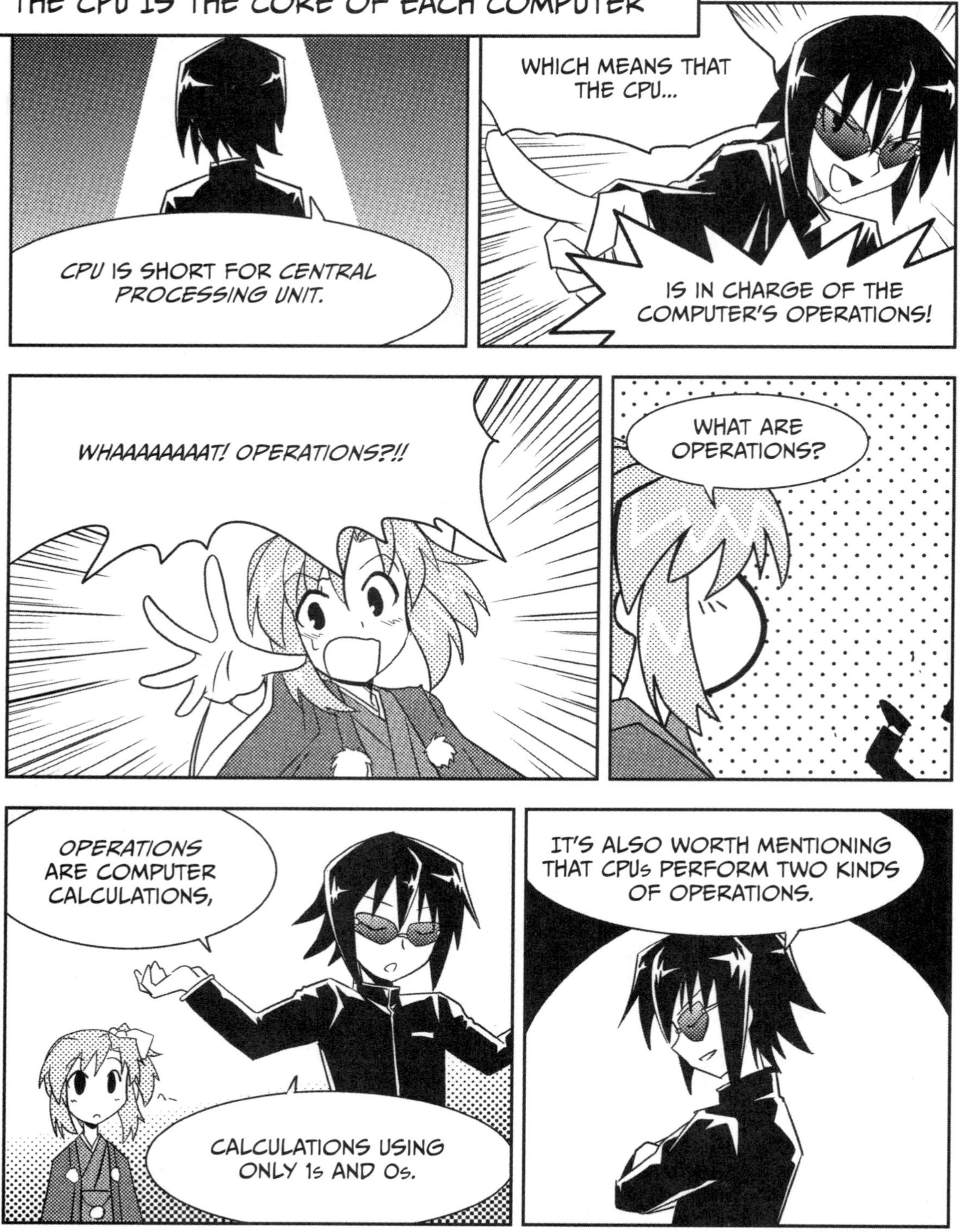
CPU IS SHORT FOR CENTRAL PROCESSING UNIT.
WHICH MEANS THAT THE CPU...
IS IN CHARGE OF THE COMPUTER'S OPERATIONS!
WHAAAAAAAAT! OPERATIONS?!!
WHAT ARE OPERATIONS?
OPERATIONS ARE COMPUTER CALCULATIONS,
CALCULATIONS USING ONLY 1s AND 0s.
IT'S ALSO WORTH MENTIONING THAT CPUs PERFORM TWO KINDS OF OPERATIONS.

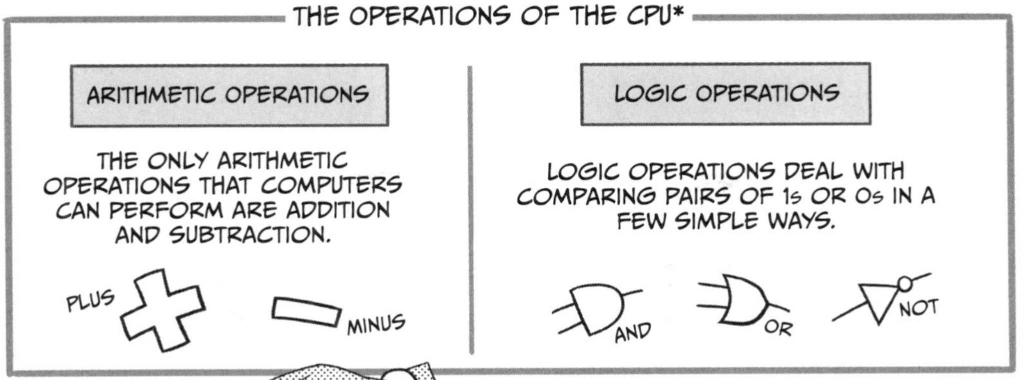
THE OPERATIONS OF THE CPU*
ARITHMETIC OPERATIONS
THE ONLY ARITHMETIC OPERATIONS THAT COMPUTERS CAN PERFORM ARE ADDITION AND SUBTRACTION.
PLUS
MINUS
LOGIC OPERATIONS
LOGIC OPERATIONS DEAL WITH COMPARING PAIRS OF 1s OR 0s IN A FEW SIMPLE WAYS.
AND
OR
NOT

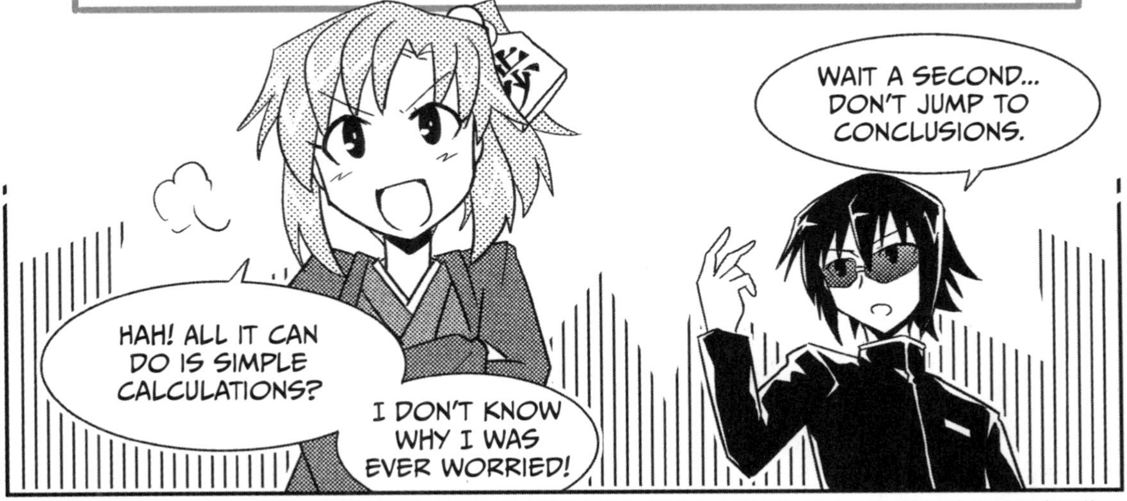
HAH! ALL IT CAN DO IS SIMPLE CALCULATIONS?
I DON'T KNOW WHY I WAS EVER WORRIED!
WAIT A SECOND... DON'T JUMP TO CONCLUSIONS.

* IN ADDITION TO THESE OPERATIONAL UNITS, MODERN CPUs ALSO CONTAIN FPUs (FLOATING POINT UNITS) THAT CAN HANDLE MULTIPLICATION AND DIVISION. BUT THIS BOOK JUST STICKS TO THE BASICS.

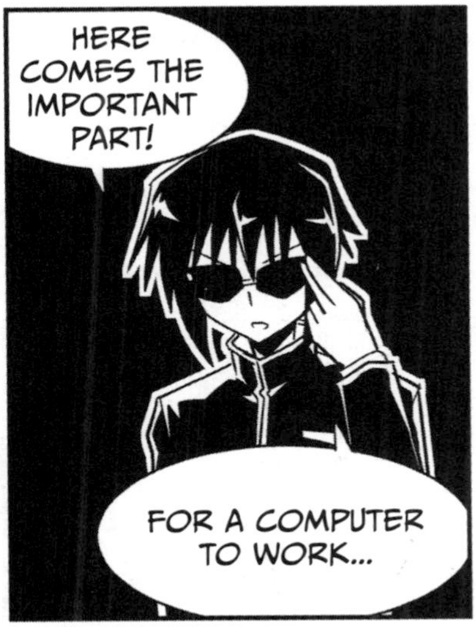
HERE COMES THE IMPORTANT PART!
FOR A COMPUTER TO WORK...

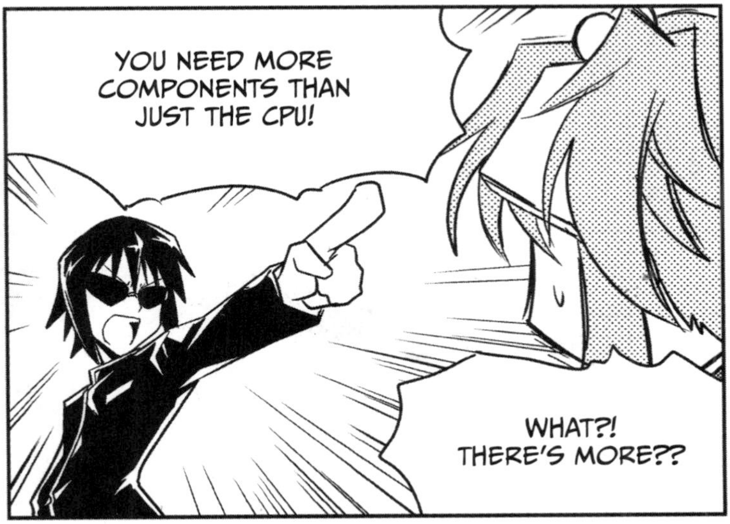
YOU NEED MORE COMPONENTS THAN JUST THE CPU!
WHAT?! THERE'S MORE??

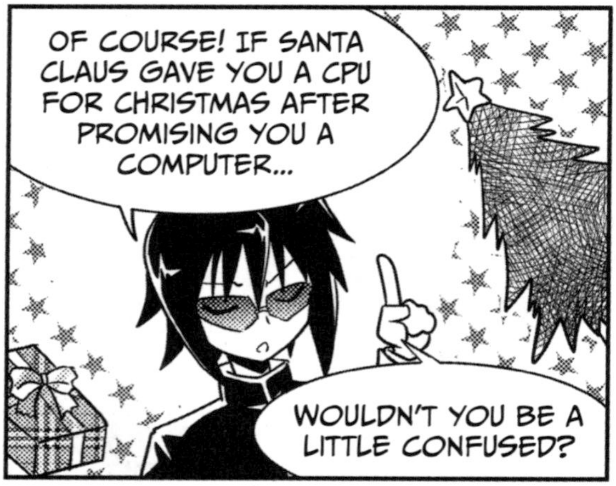
OF COURSE! IF SANTA CLAUS GAVE YOU A CPU FOR CHRISTMAS AFTER PROMISING YOU A COMPUTER...
WOULDN'T YOU BE A LITTLE CONFUSED?

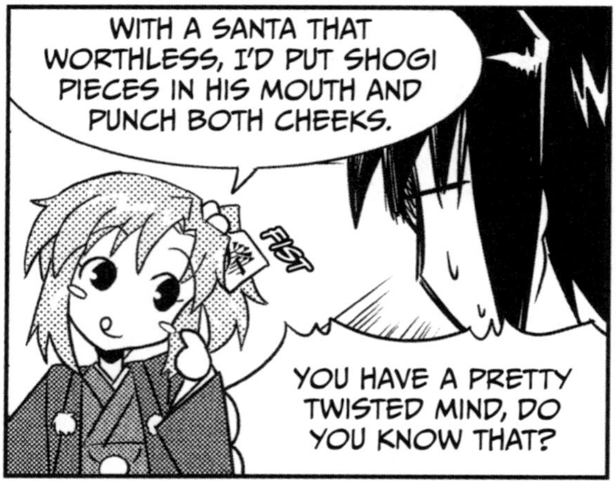
WITH A SANTA THAT WORTHLESS, I'D PUT SHOGI PIECES IN HIS MOUTH AND PUNCH BOTH CHEEKS.
FIST
YOU HAVE A PRETTY TWISTED MIND, DO YOU KNOW THAT?

THE FIVE COMPONENTS OF A MODERN COMPUTER

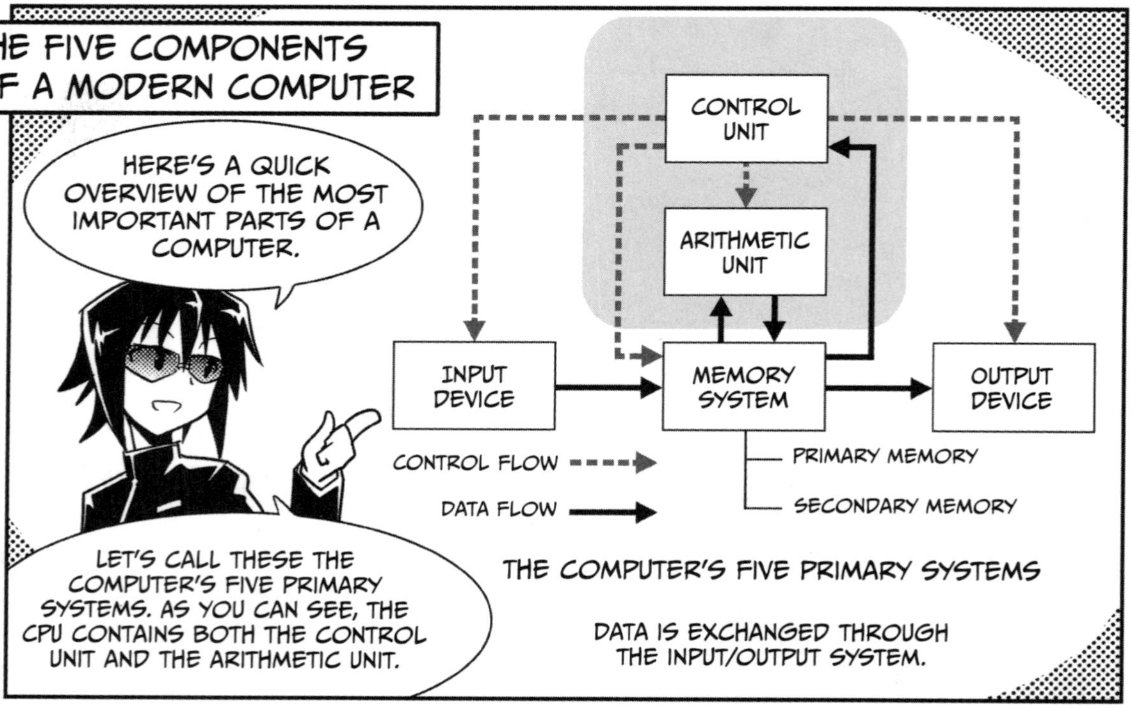
HERE'S A QUICK OVERVIEW OF THE MOST IMPORTANT PARTS OF A COMPUTER.
CONTROL UNIT
ARITHMETIC UNIT
INPUT DEVICE
MEMORY SYSTEM
OUTPUT DEVICE
CONTROL FLOW
DATA FLOW
PRIMARY MEMORY
SECONDARY MEMORY
THE COMPUTER'S FIVE PRIMARY SYSTEMS
LET'S CALL THESE THE COMPUTER'S FIVE PRIMARY SYSTEMS. AS YOU CAN SEE, THE CPU CONTAINS BOTH THE CONTROL UNIT AND THE ARITHMETIC UNIT.
DATA IS EXCHANGED THROUGH THE INPUT/OUTPUT SYSTEM.

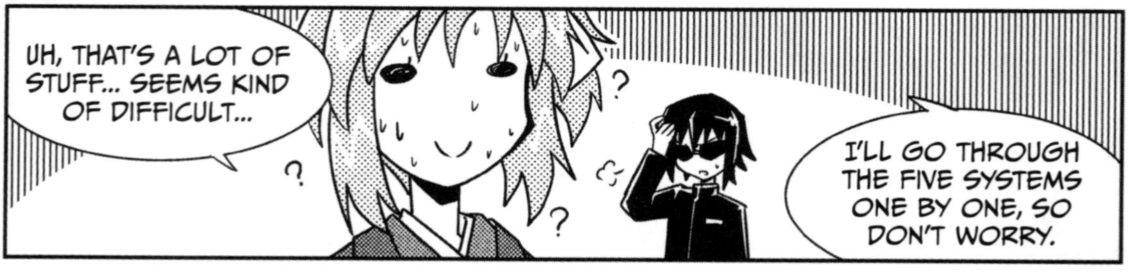
UH, THAT'S A LOT OF STUFF... SEEMS KIND OF DIFFICULT...
?
?
?
I'LL GO THROUGH THE FIVE SYSTEMS ONE BY ONE, SO DON'T WORRY.

FIRST OFF, *INPUT DEVICES* ARE SYSTEMS FOR SUPPLYING THE COMPUTER WITH INSTRUCTIONS AND INPUT DATA.

THE KEYBOARD AND MOUSE FOR YOUR HOME COMPUTER ARE GREAT EXAMPLES.

OUTPUT DEVICES, ON THE OTHER HAND, ARE SYSTEMS THAT TRANSLATE INTERNAL DATA INTO AN EXTERNAL REPRESENTATION.

MONITORS AND PRINTERS ARE GOOD EXAMPLES OF HOME COMPUTER OUTPUT DEVICES.

I GUESS IT'S TRUE THAT I INPUT INFORMATION USING MY KEYBOARD AND ACCESS INFORMATION BY LOOKING AT MY MONITOR.

FURTHERMORE, WE TALKED ABOUT THE *ARITHMETIC UNIT* BEFORE, WHICH IS THE SYSTEM THAT PERFORMS OPERATIONS (OR CALCULATIONS).

THE NAME IS KIND OF SELF-EXPLANATORY.

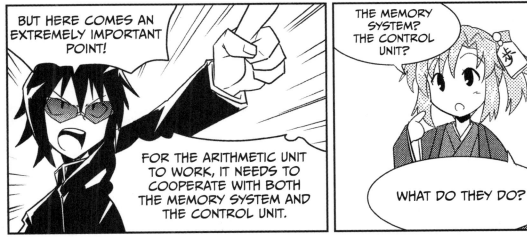

BUT HERE COMES AN EXTREMELY IMPORTANT POINT!

FOR THE ARITHMETIC UNIT TO WORK, IT NEEDS TO COOPERATE WITH BOTH THE MEMORY SYSTEM AND THE CONTROL UNIT.

THE MEMORY SYSTEM? THE CONTROL UNIT?

WHAT DO THEY DO?

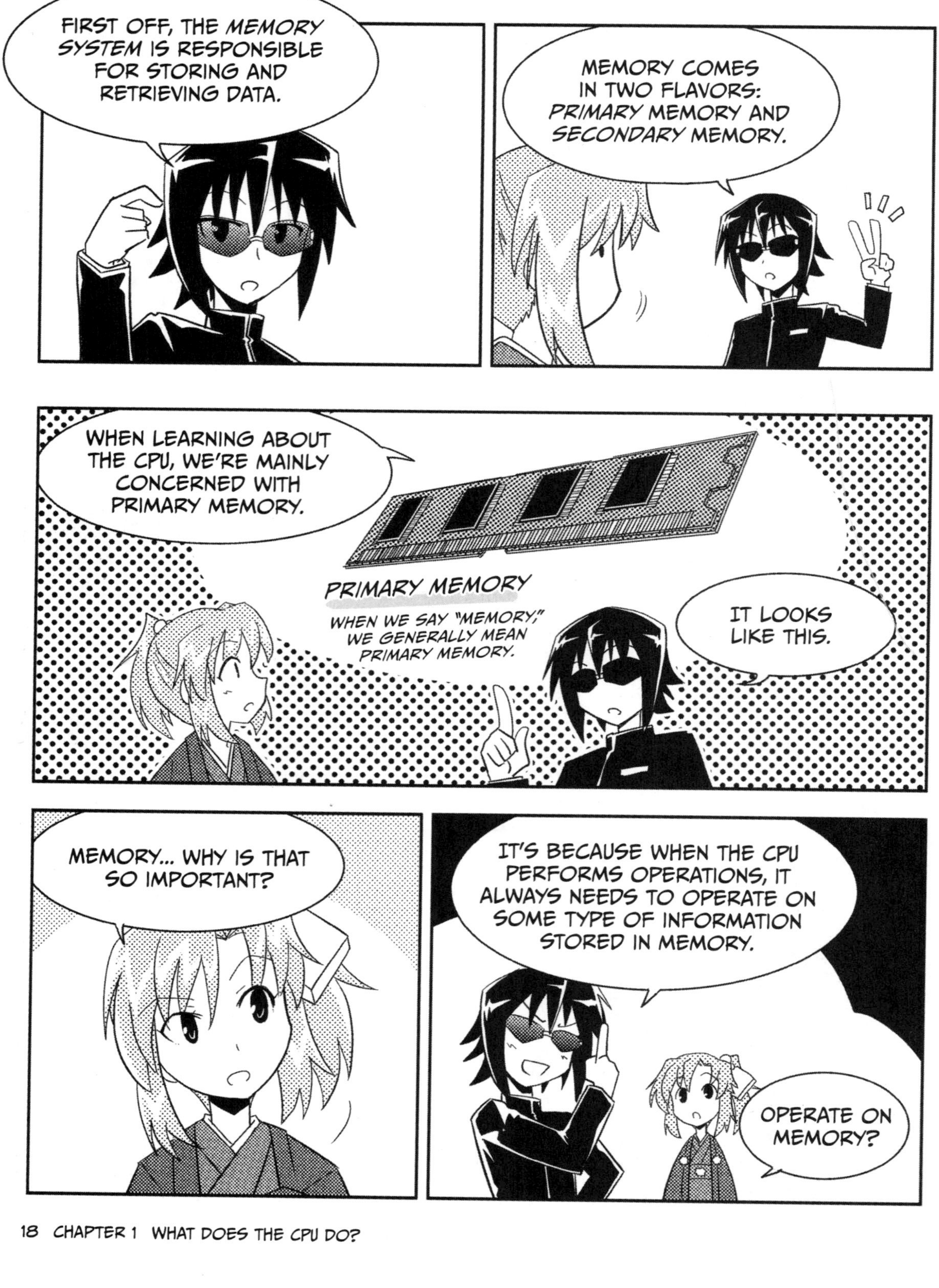
FIRST OFF, THE MEMORY SYSTEM IS RESPONSIBLE FOR STORING AND RETRIEVING DATA.
MEMORY COMES IN TWO FLAVORS: PRIMARY MEMORY AND SECONDARY MEMORY.
WHEN LEARNING ABOUT THE CPU, WE'RE MAINLY CONCERNED WITH PRIMARY MEMORY.
PRIMARY MEMORY
WHEN WE SAY "MEMORY," WE GENERALLY MEAN PRIMARY MEMORY.
IT LOOKS LIKE THIS.
MEMORY... WHY IS THAT SO IMPORTANT?
IT'S BECAUSE WHEN THE CPU PERFORMS OPERATIONS, IT ALWAYS NEEDS TO OPERATE ON SOME TYPE OF INFORMATION STORED IN MEMORY.
OPERATE ON MEMORY?

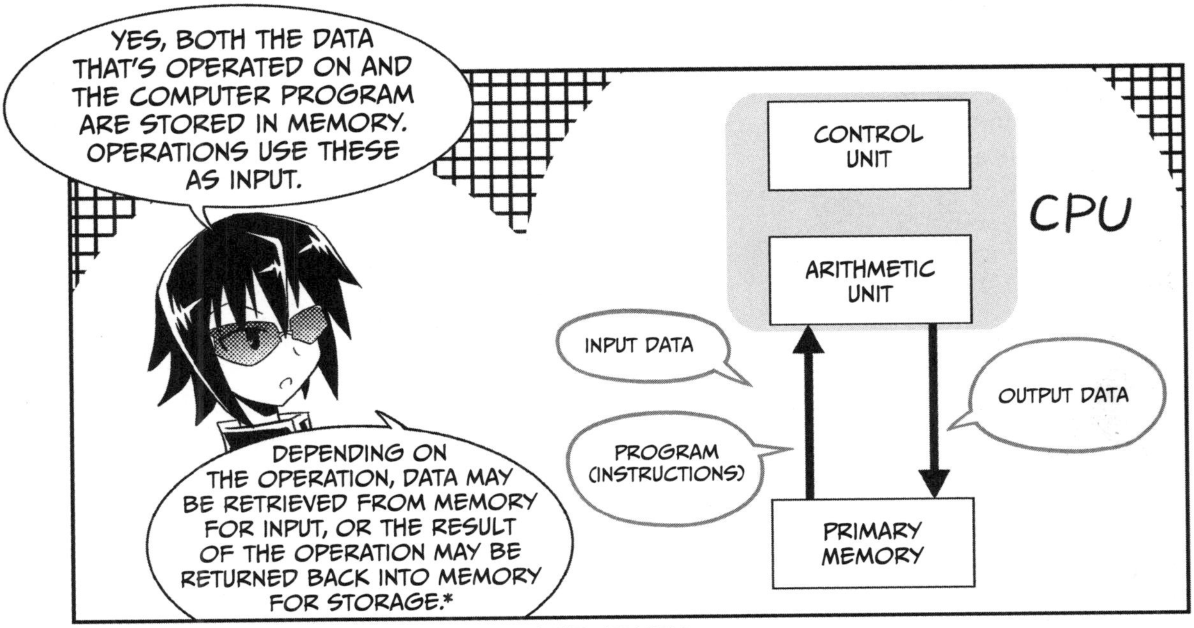
YES, BOTH THE DATA THAT'S OPERATED ON AND THE COMPUTER PROGRAM ARE STORED IN MEMORY. OPERATIONS USE THESE AS INPUT.
CONTROL UNIT
CPU
ARITHMETIC UNIT
INPUT DATA
OUTPUT DATA
PROGRAM (INSTRUCTIONS)
PRIMARY MEMORY
DEPENDING ON THE OPERATION, DATA MAY BE RETRIEVED FROM MEMORY FOR INPUT, OR THE RESULT OF THE OPERATION MAY BE RETURNED BACK INTO MEMORY FOR STORAGE.*

* THE CPU MAY USE EITHER REGISTERS OR CACHE MEMORY.

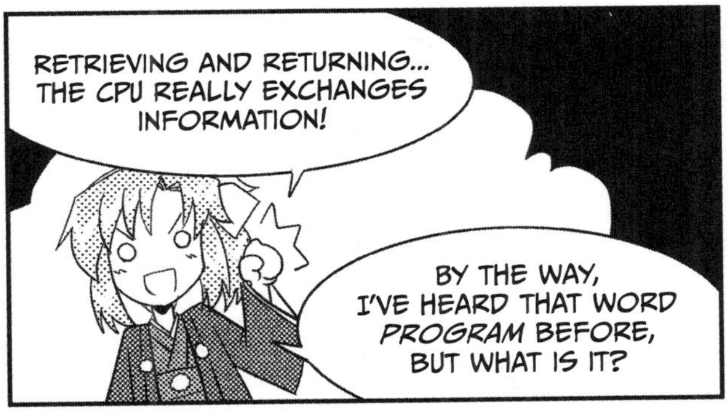
RETRIEVING AND RETURNING... THE CPU REALLY EXCHANGES INFORMATION!
BY THE WAY, I'VE HEARD THAT WORD *PROGRAM* BEFORE, BUT WHAT IS IT?

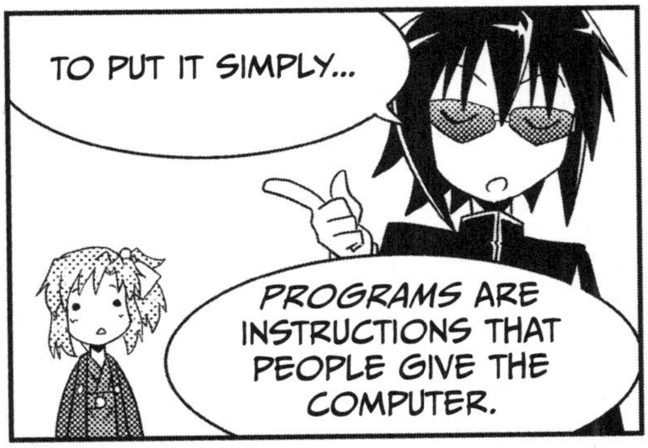
TO PUT IT SIMPLY...
PROGRAMS ARE INSTRUCTIONS THAT PEOPLE GIVE THE COMPUTER.

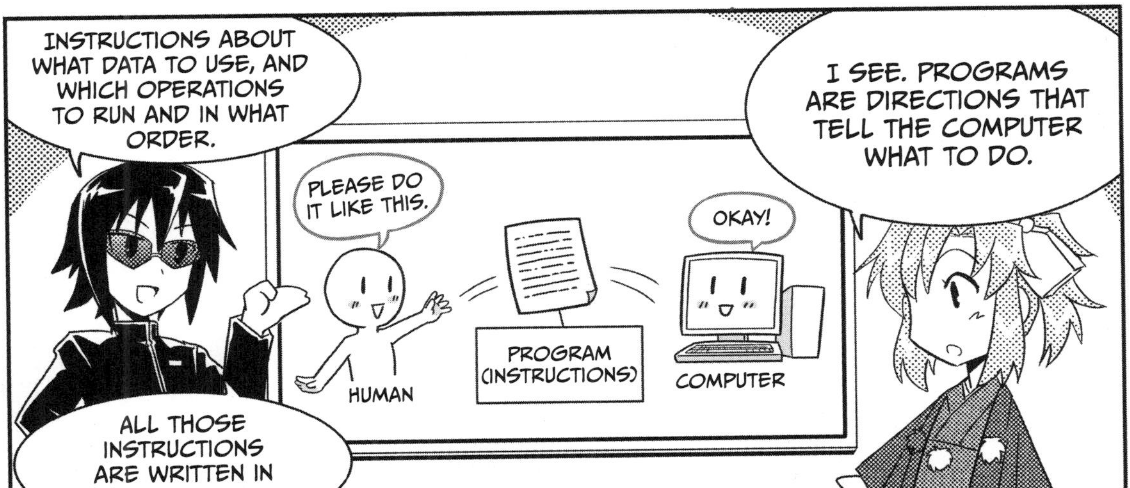
INSTRUCTIONS ABOUT WHAT DATA TO USE, AND WHICH OPERATIONS TO RUN AND IN WHAT ORDER.
PLEASE DO IT LIKE THIS.
OKAY!
HUMAN
PROGRAM (INSTRUCTIONS)
COMPUTER
ALL THOSE INSTRUCTIONS ARE WRITTEN IN PROGRAMS.
I SEE. PROGRAMS ARE DIRECTIONS THAT TELL THE COMPUTER WHAT TO DO.

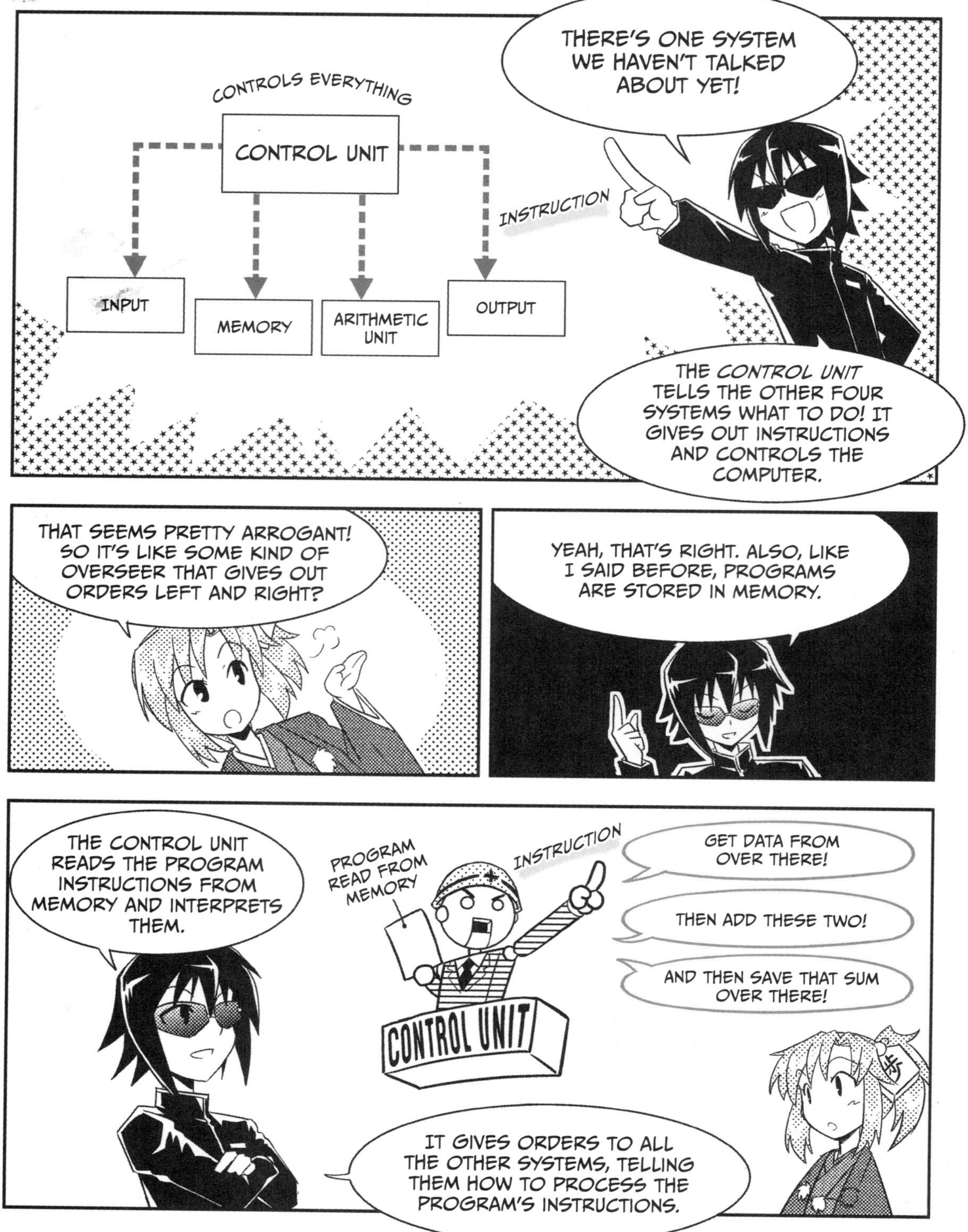
THERE'S ONE SYSTEM WE HAVEN'T TALKED ABOUT YET!
CONTROLS EVERYTHING
CONTROL UNIT
INSTRUCTION
INPUT
MEMORY
ARITHMETIC UNIT
OUTPUT
THE *CONTROL UNIT* TELLS THE OTHER FOUR SYSTEMS WHAT TO DO! IT GIVES OUT INSTRUCTIONS AND CONTROLS THE COMPUTER.
THAT SEEMS PRETTY ARROGANT! SO IT'S LIKE SOME KIND OF OVERSEER THAT GIVES OUT ORDERS LEFT AND RIGHT?
YEAH, THAT'S RIGHT. ALSO, LIKE I SAID BEFORE, PROGRAMS ARE STORED IN MEMORY.
THE CONTROL UNIT READS THE PROGRAM INSTRUCTIONS FROM MEMORY AND INTERPRETS THEM.
PROGRAM READ FROM MEMORY
INSTRUCTION
GET DATA FROM OVER THERE!
THEN ADD THESE TWO!
AND THEN SAVE THAT SUM OVER THERE!
CONTROL UNIT
IT GIVES ORDERS TO ALL THE OTHER SYSTEMS, TELLING THEM HOW TO PROCESS THE PROGRAM'S INSTRUCTIONS.

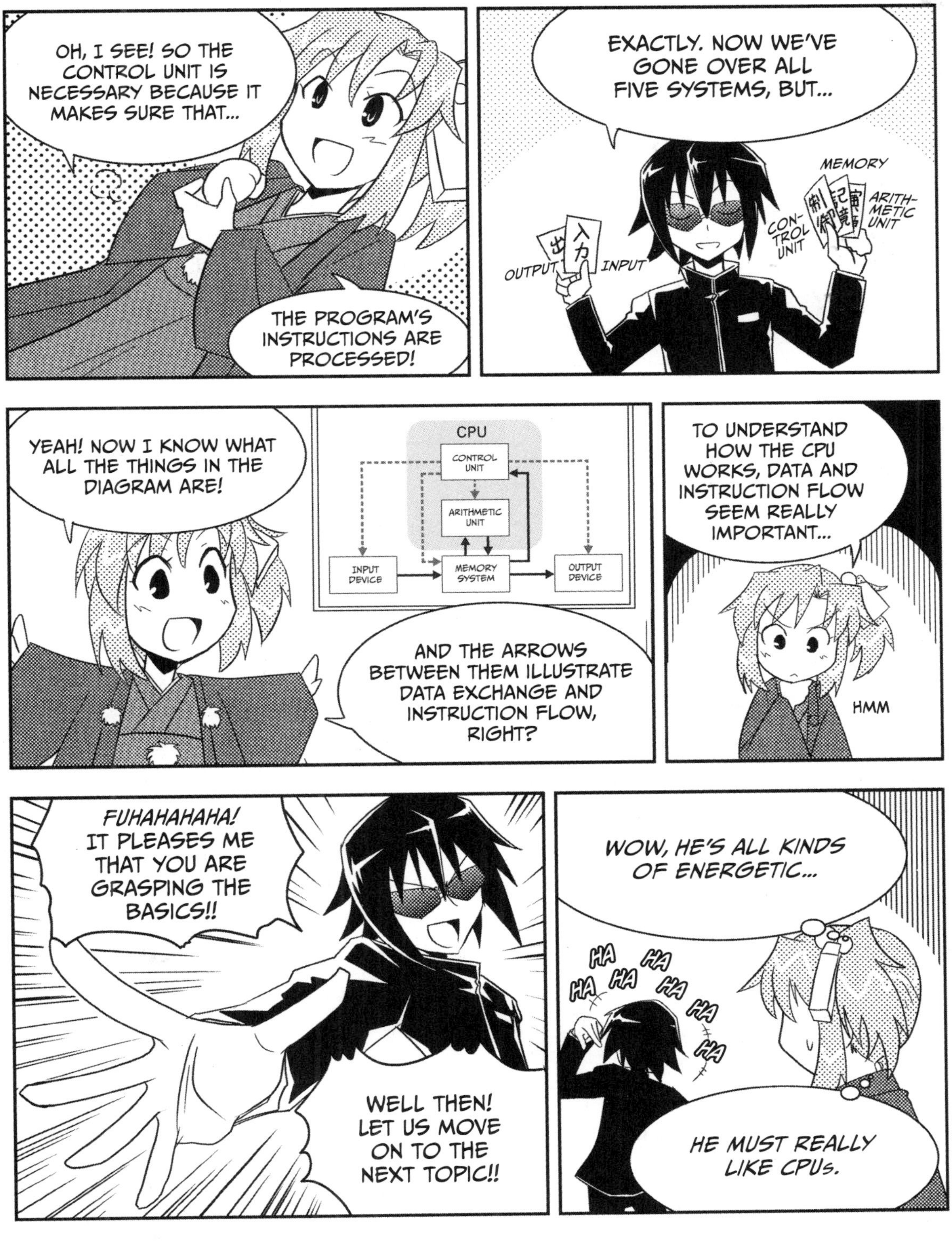

OH, I SEE! SO THE CONTROL UNIT IS NECESSARY BECAUSE IT MAKES SURE THAT...
THE PROGRAM'S INSTRUCTIONS ARE PROCESSED!
EXACTLY. NOW WE'VE GONE OVER ALL FIVE SYSTEMS, BUT...
OUTPUT
INPUT
CONTROL UNIT
MEMORY
ARITHMETIC UNIT
YEAH! NOW I KNOW WHAT ALL THE THINGS IN THE DIAGRAM ARE!
CPU
CONTROL UNIT
ARITHMETIC UNIT
INPUT DEVICE
MEMORY SYSTEM
OUTPUT DEVICE
AND THE ARROWS BETWEEN THEM ILLUSTRATE DATA EXCHANGE AND INSTRUCTION FLOW, RIGHT?
TO UNDERSTAND HOW THE CPU WORKS, DATA AND INSTRUCTION FLOW SEEM REALLY IMPORTANT...
HMM
FUHAHAHAHA! IT PLEASES ME THAT YOU ARE GRASPING THE BASICS!!
WELL THEN! LET US MOVE ON TO THE NEXT TOPIC!!
WOW, HE'S ALL KINDS OF ENERGETIC...
HA HA HA HA HA HA HA HA
HE MUST REALLY LIKE CPUs.

ALUs: THE CPU'S CORE

YOU'RE CATCHING ON PRETTY QUICKLY, IT SEEMS.

SO LET'S TALK A BIT ABOUT ALUs.

ALUs? NOT CPUs? WHAT'S THE DIFFERENCE?

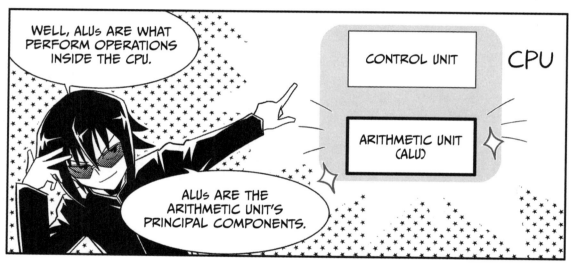

WELL, ALUs ARE WHAT PERFORM OPERATIONS INSIDE THE CPU.

ALUs ARE THE ARITHMETIC UNIT'S PRINCIPAL COMPONENTS.

CONTROL UNIT

CPU

ARITHMETIC UNIT (ALU)

OH! THAT SEEMS LIKE IT'S SUPER IMPORTANT!

YES, ALU IS SHORT FOR *ARITHMETIC LOGIC UNIT*.

IT PERFORMS THE ARITHMETIC AND LOGIC OPERATIONS WE TALKED ABOUT BEFORE.

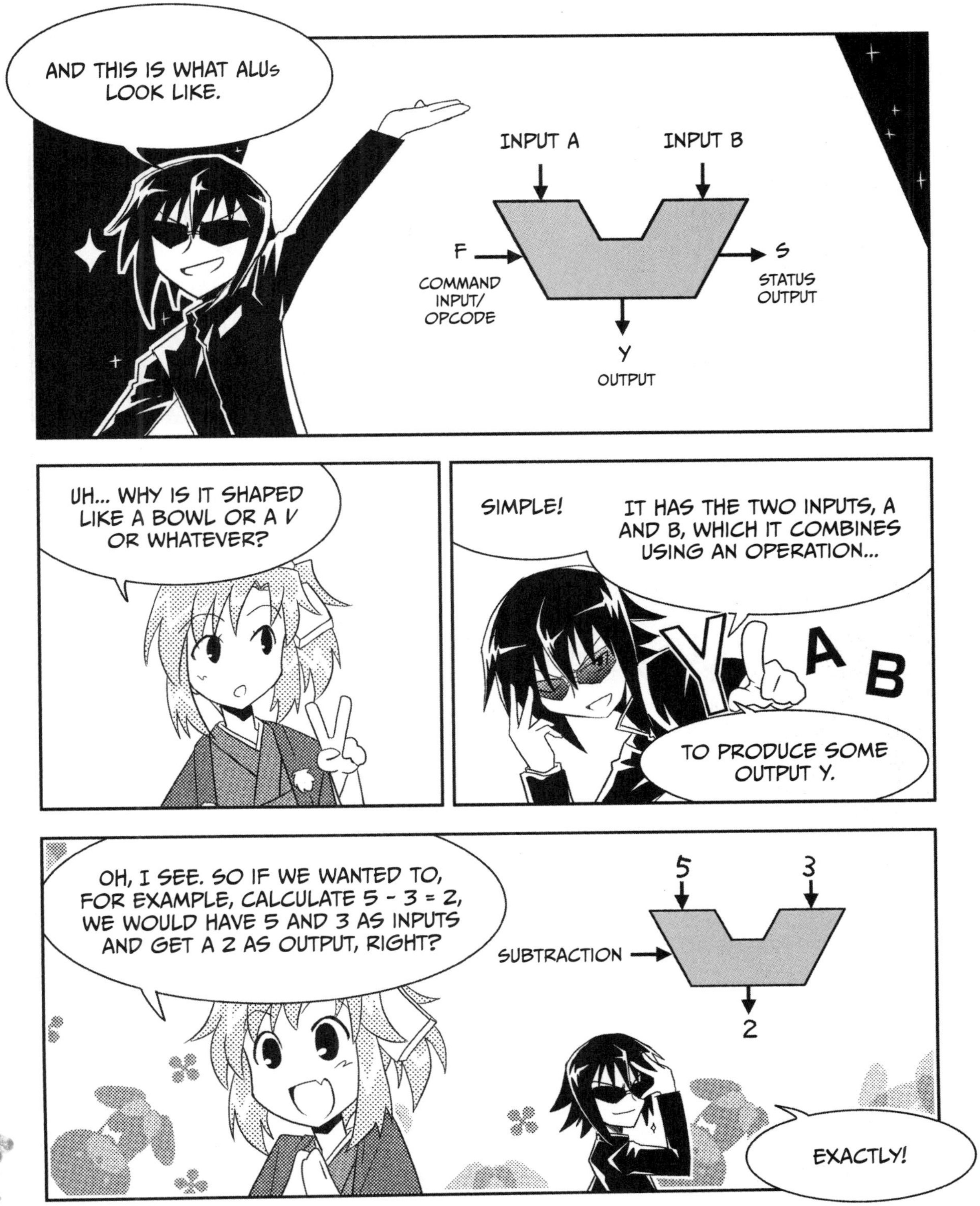
AND THIS IS WHAT ALUs LOOK LIKE.
INPUT A
INPUT B
F
COMMAND INPUT/ OPCODE
S
STATUS OUTPUT
Y
OUTPUT
UH... WHY IS IT SHAPED LIKE A BOWL OR A V OR WHATEVER?
SIMPLE!
IT HAS THE TWO INPUTS, A AND B, WHICH IT COMBINES USING AN OPERATION...
Y
A
B
TO PRODUCE SOME OUTPUT Y.
OH, I SEE. SO IF WE WANTED TO, FOR EXAMPLE, CALCULATE 5 - 3 = 2, WE WOULD HAVE 5 AND 3 AS INPUTS AND GET A 2 AS OUTPUT, RIGHT?
5
3
SUBTRACTION
2
EXACTLY!

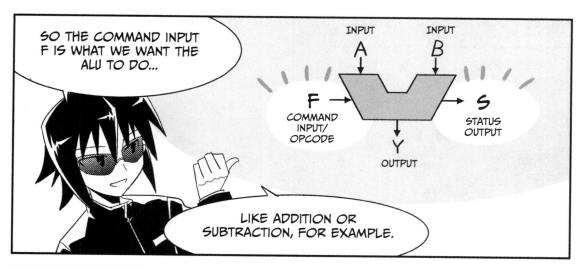

SO THE COMMAND INPUT F IS WHAT WE WANT THE ALU TO DO...
INPUT A
INPUT B
F COMMAND INPUT/ OPCODE
S STATUS OUTPUT
Y OUTPUT
LIKE ADDITION OR SUBTRACTION, FOR EXAMPLE.
AND THE STATUS OUTPUT S TELLS US HOW THE OPERATION WENT.
THIS COULD BE INFORMATION ON WHETHER OUR OUTPUT VALUE WAS POSITIVE OR NEGATIVE, FOR EXAMPLE.
5
3
COMMAND INPUT SUBTRACTION
POSITIVE VALUE
2
STATUS OUTPUT
SO IN THE CASE OF 5 − 3 = 2, SINCE THE RESULT OF THE CALCULATION IS 2, THE STATUS OUTPUT SHOULD SAY IT'S A POSITIVE VALUE, RIGHT?
BUT WHY DOES ANYONE NEED TO KNOW WHETHER THE OUTPUT WAS POSITIVE OR NEGATIVE?
THAT'S A GOOD QUESTION. AS A MATTER OF FACT, THE STATUS OUTPUT CAN BE USED TO MAKE DECISIONS BASED ON WHETHER THE OUTPUT SATISFIES SOME GIVEN CONDITION.
DECISIONS? CONDITIONS?

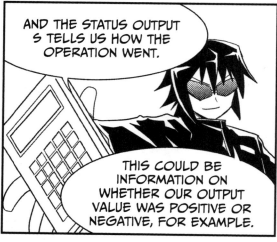

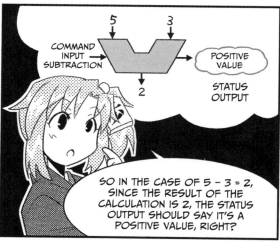

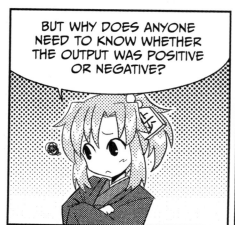

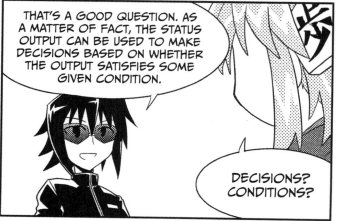

CPUs PROCESS OPERATIONS AND MAKE DECISIONS

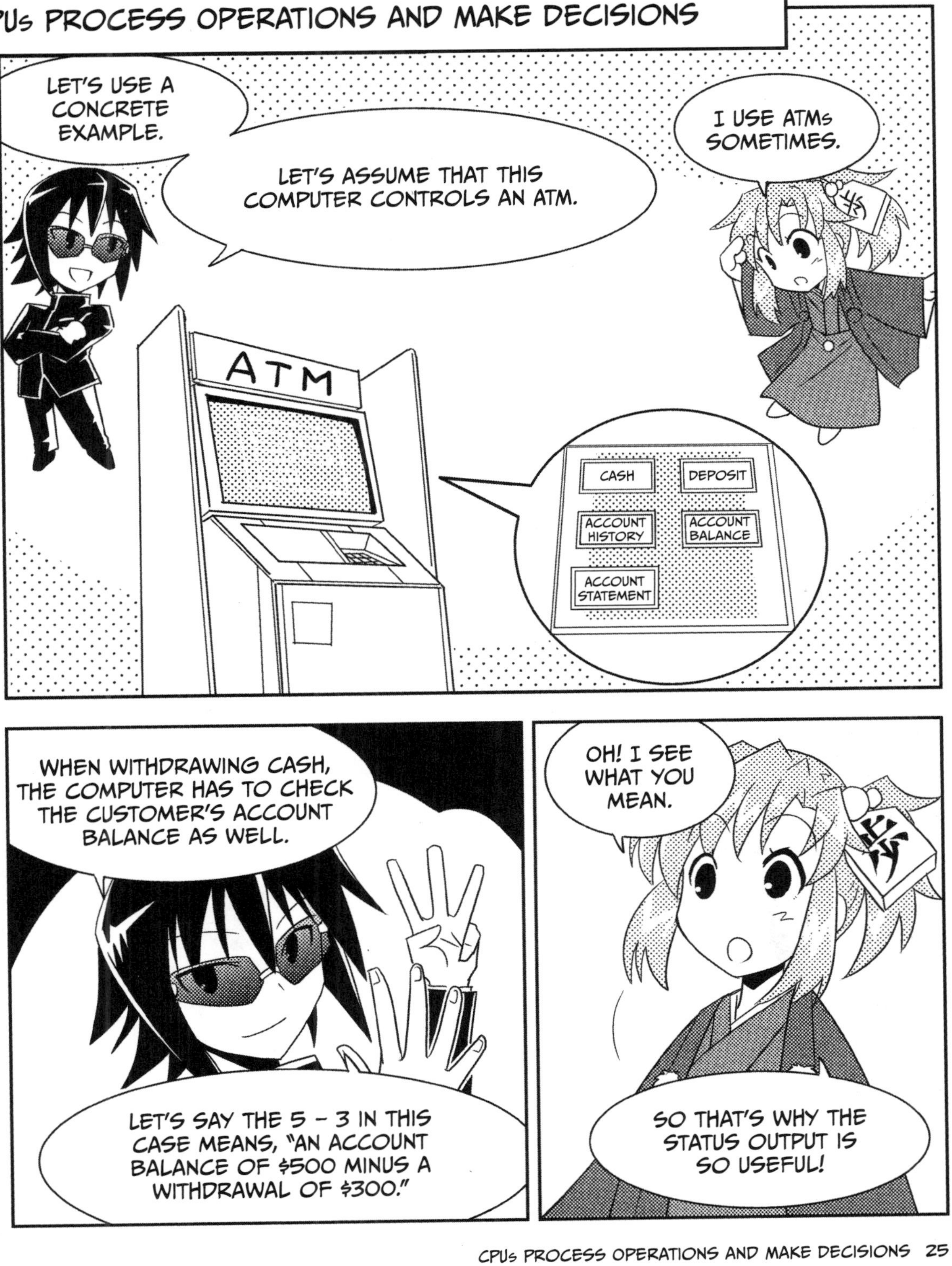
LET'S USE A CONCRETE EXAMPLE.
LET'S ASSUME THAT THIS COMPUTER CONTROLS AN ATM.
I USE ATMs SOMETIMES.
ATM
CASH
DEPOSIT
ACCOUNT HISTORY
ACCOUNT BALANCE
ACCOUNT STATEMENT
WHEN WITHDRAWING CASH, THE COMPUTER HAS TO CHECK THE CUSTOMER'S ACCOUNT BALANCE AS WELL.
LET'S SAY THE 5 – 3 IN THIS CASE MEANS, "AN ACCOUNT BALANCE OF $500 MINUS A WITHDRAWAL OF $300."
OH! I SEE WHAT YOU MEAN.
SO THAT'S WHY THE STATUS OUTPUT IS SO USEFUL!

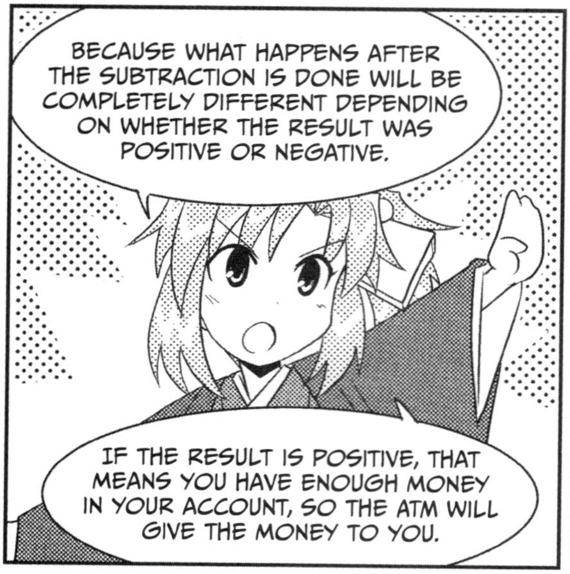
BECAUSE WHAT HAPPENS AFTER THE SUBTRACTION IS DONE WILL BE COMPLETELY DIFFERENT DEPENDING ON WHETHER THE RESULT WAS POSITIVE OR NEGATIVE.
IF THE RESULT IS POSITIVE, THAT MEANS YOU HAVE ENOUGH MONEY IN YOUR ACCOUNT, SO THE ATM WILL GIVE THE MONEY TO YOU.

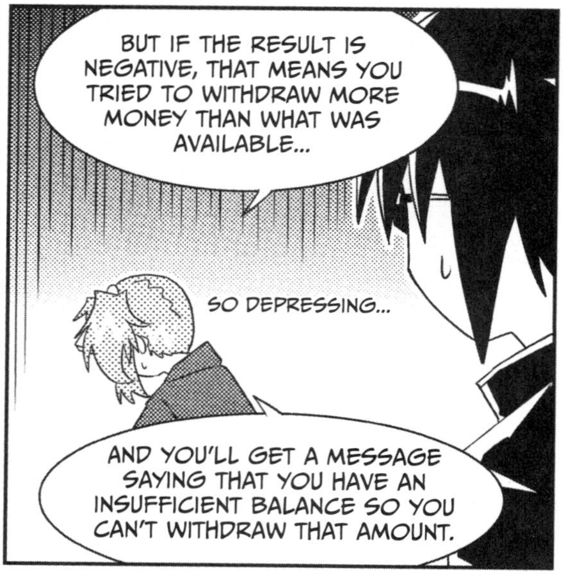
BUT IF THE RESULT IS NEGATIVE, THAT MEANS YOU TRIED TO WITHDRAW MORE MONEY THAN WHAT WAS AVAILABLE...
SO DEPRESSING...
AND YOU'LL GET A MESSAGE SAYING THAT YOU HAVE AN INSUFFICIENT BALANCE SO YOU CAN'T WITHDRAW THAT AMOUNT.

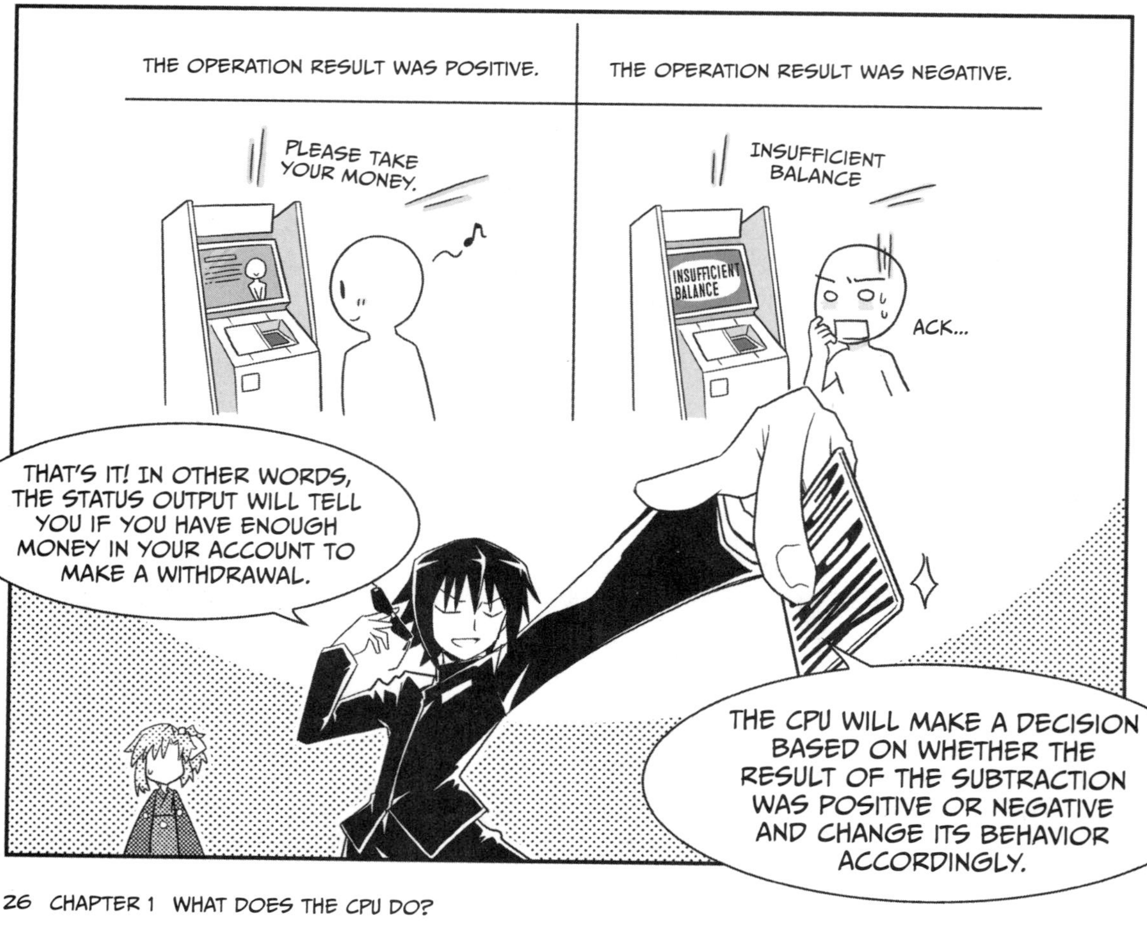
THE OPERATION RESULT WAS POSITIVE.
PLEASE TAKE YOUR MONEY.
THE OPERATION RESULT WAS NEGATIVE.
INSUFFICIENT BALANCE
INSUFFICIENT BALANCE
ACK...
THAT'S IT! IN OTHER WORDS, THE STATUS OUTPUT WILL TELL YOU IF YOU HAVE ENOUGH MONEY IN YOUR ACCOUNT TO MAKE A WITHDRAWAL.
THE CPU WILL MAKE A DECISION BASED ON WHETHER THE RESULT OF THE SUBTRACTION WAS POSITIVE OR NEGATIVE AND CHANGE ITS BEHAVIOR ACCORDINGLY.

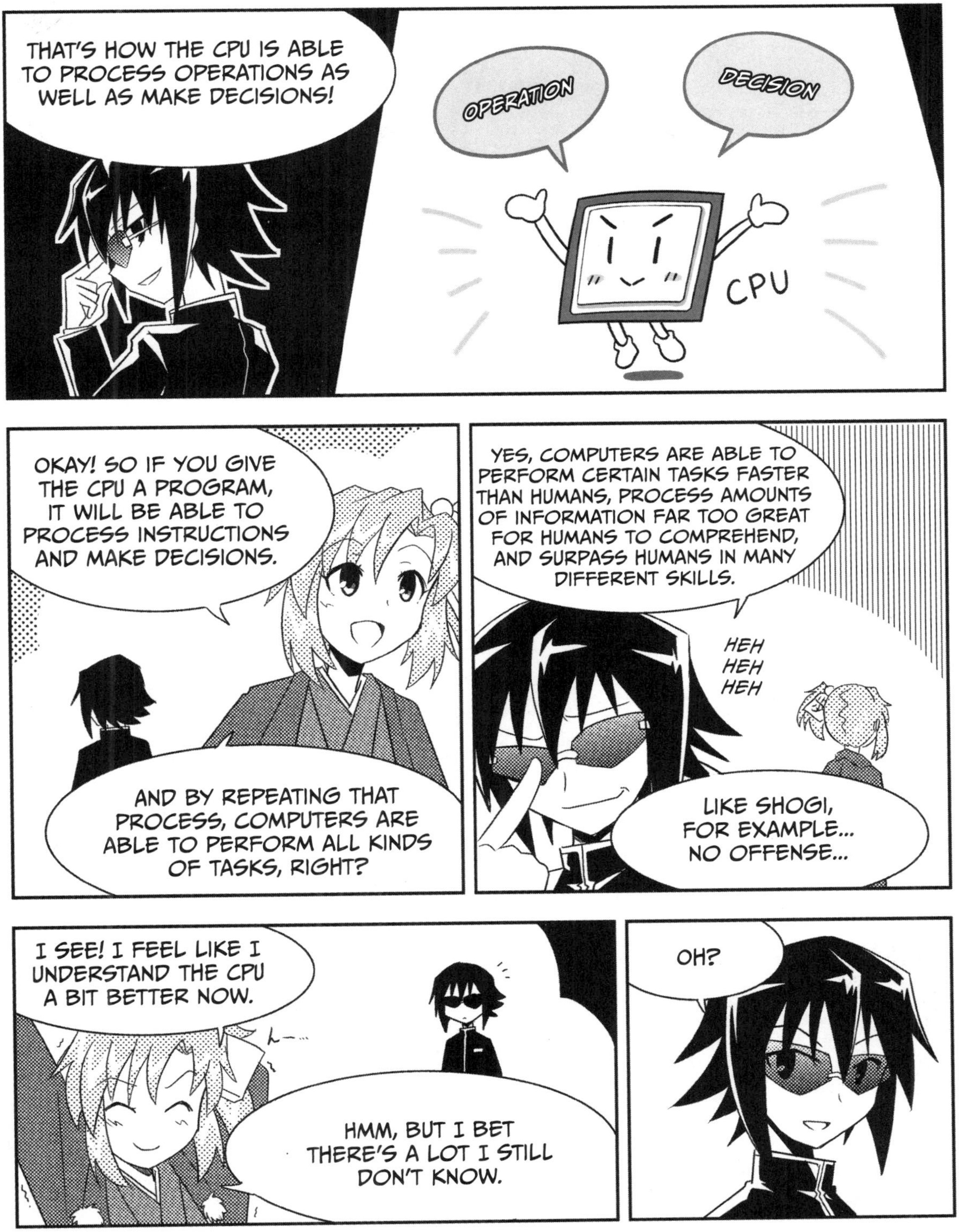
THAT'S HOW THE CPU IS ABLE TO PROCESS OPERATIONS AS WELL AS MAKE DECISIONS!
OPERATION
DECISION
CPU
OKAY! SO IF YOU GIVE THE CPU A PROGRAM, IT WILL BE ABLE TO PROCESS INSTRUCTIONS AND MAKE DECISIONS.
AND BY REPEATING THAT PROCESS, COMPUTERS ARE ABLE TO PERFORM ALL KINDS OF TASKS, RIGHT?
YES, COMPUTERS ARE ABLE TO PERFORM CERTAIN TASKS FASTER THAN HUMANS, PROCESS AMOUNTS OF INFORMATION FAR TOO GREAT FOR HUMANS TO COMPREHEND, AND SURPASS HUMANS IN MANY DIFFERENT SKILLS.
HEH HEH HEH
LIKE SHOGI, FOR EXAMPLE... NO OFFENSE...
I SEE! I FEEL LIKE I UNDERSTAND THE CPU A BIT BETTER NOW.
HMM, BUT I BET THERE'S A LOT I STILL DON'T KNOW.
OH?

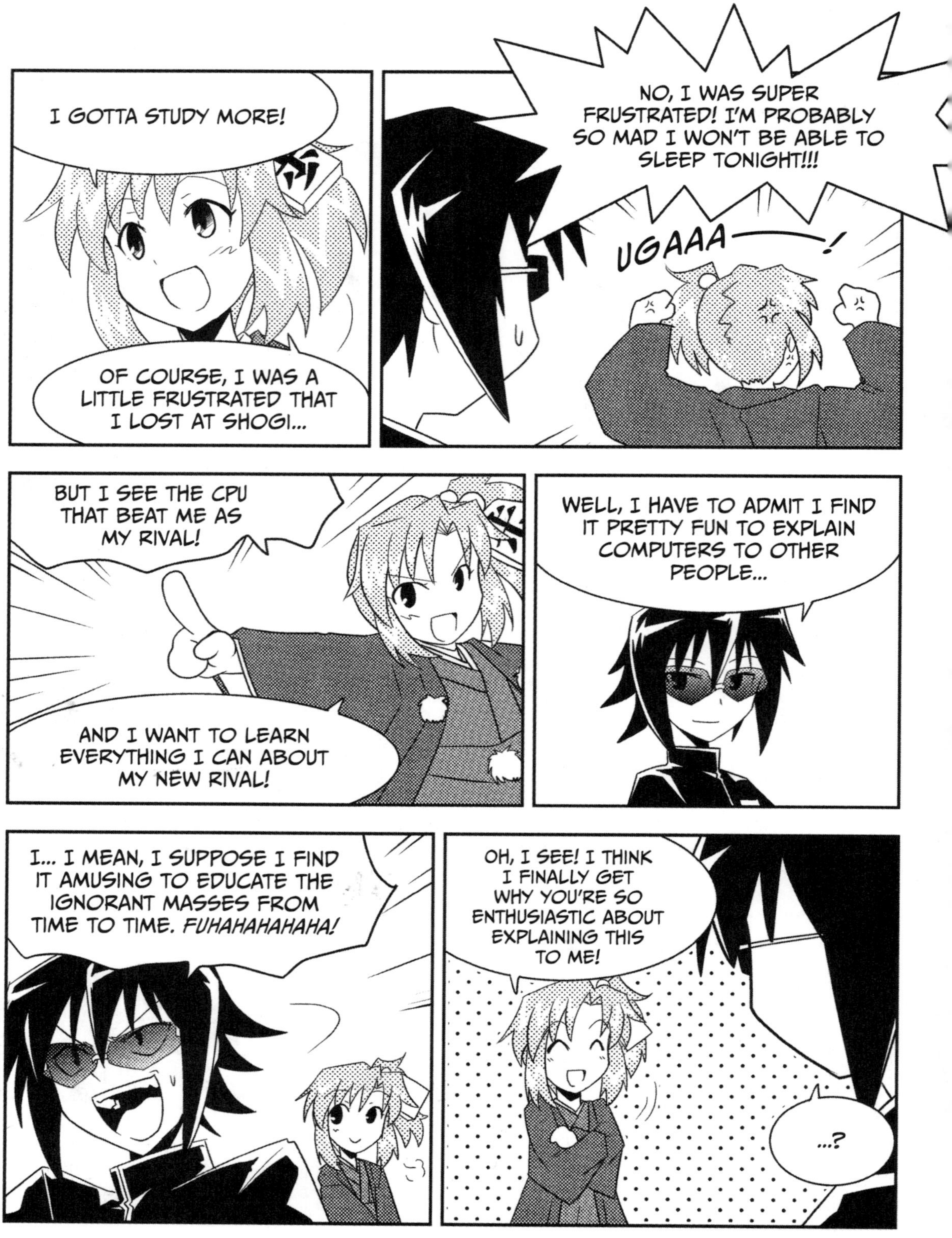
I GOTTA STUDY MORE!
OF COURSE, I WAS A LITTLE FRUSTRATED THAT I LOST AT SHOGI...
NO, I WAS SUPER FRUSTRATED! I'M PROBABLY SO MAD I WON'T BE ABLE TO SLEEP TONIGHT!!!
UGAAA——!
BUT I SEE THE CPU THAT BEAT ME AS MY RIVAL!
AND I WANT TO LEARN EVERYTHING I CAN ABOUT MY NEW RIVAL!
WELL, I HAVE TO ADMIT I FIND IT PRETTY FUN TO EXPLAIN COMPUTERS TO OTHER PEOPLE...
I... I MEAN, I SUPPOSE I FIND IT AMUSING TO EDUCATE THE IGNORANT MASSES FROM TIME TO TIME. FUHAHAHAHAHA!
OH, I SEE! I THINK I FINALLY GET WHY YOU'RE SO ENTHUSIASTIC ABOUT EXPLAINING THIS TO ME!
...?

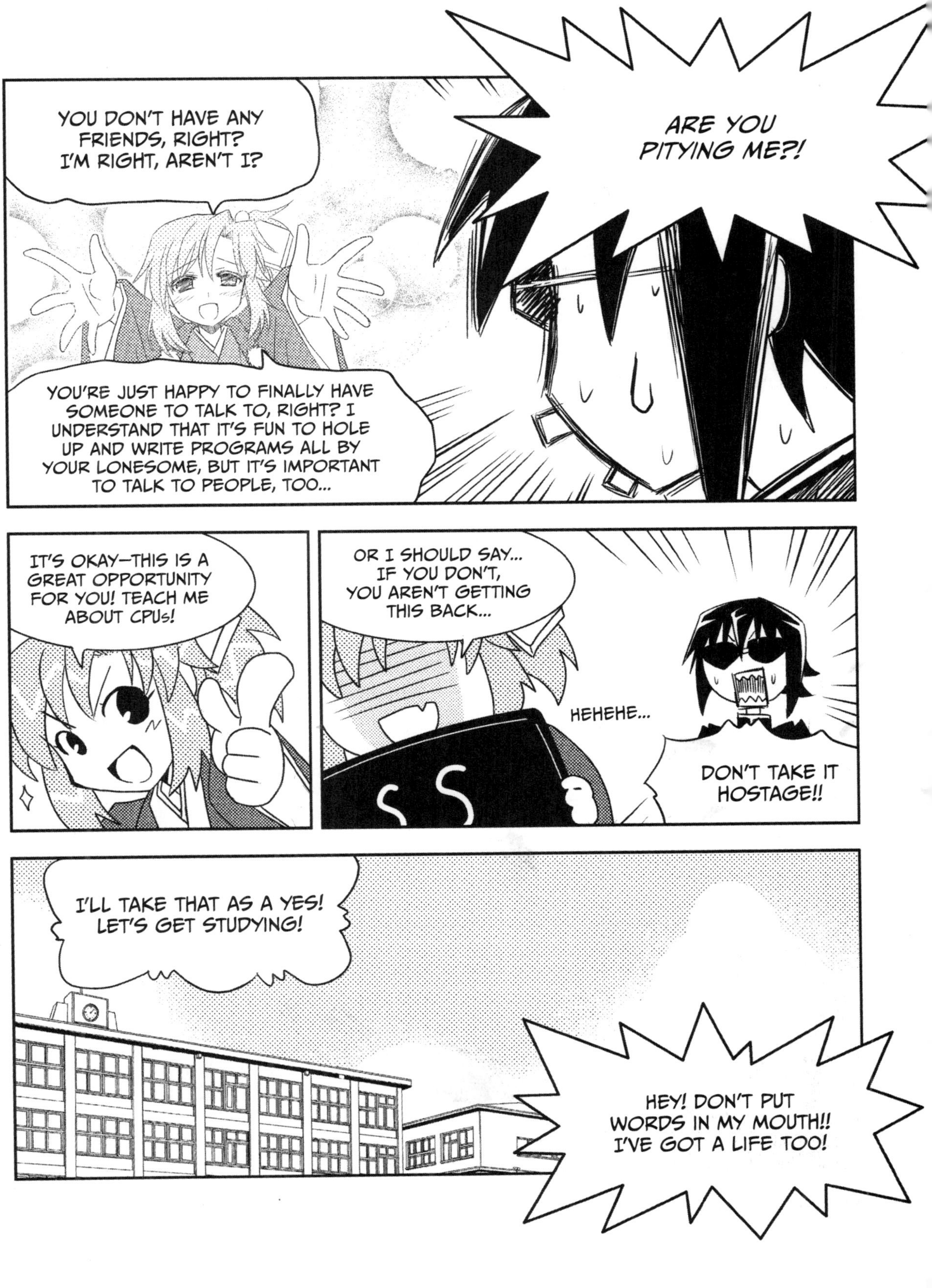
YOU DON'T HAVE ANY FRIENDS, RIGHT? I'M RIGHT, AREN'T I?
YOU'RE JUST HAPPY TO FINALLY HAVE SOMEONE TO TALK TO, RIGHT? I UNDERSTAND THAT IT'S FUN TO HOLE UP AND WRITE PROGRAMS ALL BY YOUR LONESOME, BUT IT'S IMPORTANT TO TALK TO PEOPLE, TOO...
ARE YOU PITYING ME?!
IT'S OKAY—THIS IS A GREAT OPPORTUNITY FOR YOU! TEACH ME ABOUT CPUs!
OR I SHOULD SAY... IF YOU DON'T, YOU AREN'T GETTING THIS BACK...
HEHEHE...
DON'T TAKE IT HOSTAGE!!
I'LL TAKE THAT AS A YES! LET'S GET STUDYING!
HEY! DON'T PUT WORDS IN MY MOUTH!! I'VE GOT A LIFE TOO!

WHAT IS INFORMATION ANYWAY?

Information technology (IT) became an everyday phrase back in the 20th century. The term is frequently heard when people talk about the internet and other computer technology, but it's worth noting that this term predates the use of computers.

First off, what does the word *information* actually mean?To put it simply, information is everything in our environment that can be registered with any of our five senses.

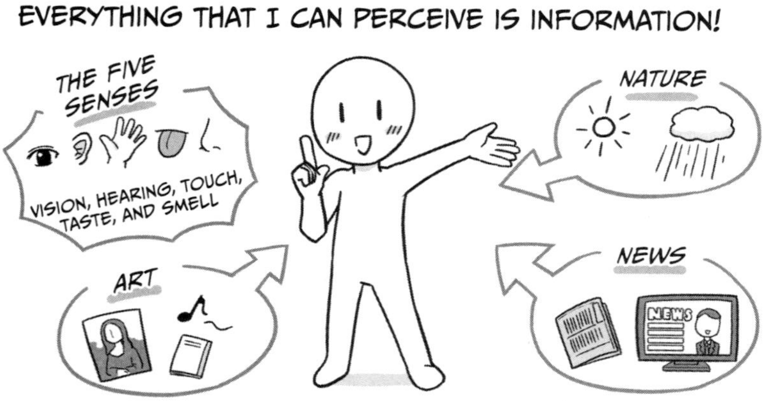
EVERYTHING THAT I CAN PERCEIVE IS INFORMATION!
THE FIVE SENSES
VISION, HEARING, TOUCH, TASTE, AND SMELL
NATURE
ART
NEWS
NEWS

Everything that occurs in nature or in paintings, photographs, music, novels, news, radio, TV broadcasts, and so on is an example of information. Most of these things have been around for a lot longer than our society has had access to electricity. As information spreads throughout society, it affects our lives.

Every day, people and organizations value useful information while trying to filter out everything else. Information that is not important is called *noise*, and important information is called *signal*. Finding ways to maximize the *signal-to-noise ratio*—that is, the amount of signal in an output compared to the amount of noise—without accidentally losing necessary information is important.

One type of information that historically has been important both to people and organizations is information about food—what's safe or healthy to eat, how to find or grow it, and how far away it is or how much it costs to buy. Related information, such as climate and weather forecasts, is also vital. Obviously, information like this was valued long before the rise of the internet. For example, merchants like Bunzaemon Kinokuniya from Japan's Edo period specialized in products such as citrus and salmon and thrived because they valued this type of information. Indeed, the value of information has been respected for as long as people have needed to eat.

However, the digital age has affected many aspects of life. How has it affected our access to information? Well, thanks to the digitization of data, we are now able to process diverse data like text, audio, images, and video using the same methods. It can all be transmitted the same way (over the internet, for example) and stored in the same media (on hard drives, for example).

DIFFERENT TYPES OF INFORMATION
IN THE PAST, ★ DIFFERENT MEDIA WERE USED FOR EACH.
STORAGE!
THE INTERNET
EXCHANGING DATA!
COMPUTER
ANOTHER DEVICE

Computers that are connected to the same network can exchange digitized information. By using computers to match and analyze large sets of data instead of analyzing each instance or type of data individually, people can discover otherwise hidden trends or implications of the information.

Like the storage of data, information transmission has made incredible advances, thanks to important discoveries in electronics and electrical engineering. Commercial applications of this technology in devices such as telephones, radio, and television have played a role in accelerating this development. Today, almost all of Japan enjoys digital television, which uses digital transmission and compression technologies. CPUs play a central part in these applications by performing countless operations and coordinating the transfer of information.

THE DIFFERENCE BETWEEN ANALOG AND DIGITAL INFORMATION

We have been talking about digitizing data into 1s and 0s so that information can be processed by a CPU. But before they are digitized, text, audio, video, and so on exist as analog data.

What is the difference between these two types of data? An example that illustrates the difference is thermometers. Analog thermometers contain a liquid that expands as it heats up, such as mercury or alcohol, in a gradated capillary tube that is marked with lines indicating the temperature. To determine the temperature, we look at the level of the liquid in the tube and compare it to the markings on the tube. We say that the analog thermometer has a *continuous* output because the temperature reading can fall anywhere between the marks on the tube.

Digital thermometers use a sensor to convert temperature into voltage* and then estimate the corresponding temperature. Because the temperature is represented numerically, the temperature changes in steps (that is, the values "jump"). For instance, if the initial temperature reading is 21.8 degrees Celsius and then the temperature increases, the next possible reading is 21.9 degrees Celsius. Because 0.1 is the smallest quantity that can be shown by this thermometer, changes in temperature can only be represented in steps of 0.1 and the value could never be between 21.8 and 21.9 degrees. Thus, digital output is said to be *discrete*.

* *Voltage* is a way of measuring electric currents and is expressed in volts.

ANALOG

EVEN SMALL CHANGES ARE VISIBLE.

ATTENTION!

°C
30
20

HMM, IT'S A BIT LESS THAN 22°C, I THINK...

DIGITAL

A DISCRETE VALUE IS EXPRESSED IN A CERTAIN NUMBER OF DIGITS.

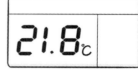

21.8°C

I SEE...

AFTER 21.8°C COMES 21.9°C. THERE ARE NO VALUES IN BETWEEN.

The word *digital* comes from the act of counting off numbers using our fingers—or digits. This tends to lead people to believe that digital computers can only work with data comprised of integers (whole numbers), which is not necessarily true.

In the digital world, everything is expressed in 1s and 0s. Indeed, they are not even what the CPU works with. Note that these are not actually numbers in this context. Instead, a 1 and a 0 are merely symbols. The CPU consists of transistors that transmit or inhibit electrical signals and consequently output either low or high voltages. It is these voltages that we represent as 1 or 0. A high voltage is represented with a 1, since the transistor's state is "on," and a low voltage, or an "off" transistor, is represented with a 0. In text, you could illustrate this by using the symbols ● and ○. The 1s and 0s are called *primitives*, meaning they are basic data types. Computers can work with decimal numbers as long as the value has a finite number of digits. Values such as these are also digital. The important thing to remember is that for any digital number, you can never add or remove a quantity smaller than the smallest possible value expressible.

Let's compare some analog data and its digitized version to better understand how they are alike and how they differ by looking at the figure on the next page. The first pair of images shows audio data, and the second pair shows image data.

As you can see, every time we translate analog data into digital data, some information is lost. But as you've undoubtedly experienced, most modern digitization processes are so good that humans can't tell the difference between the original and the digital copy, even when they are presented side by side.

To store and transmit digital data of a quality such that our senses can't detect any loss of information, we use special compression techniques. These techniques always involve trade-offs among how much space is used, how much information is lost during compression, and how much processing time is needed to compress and decompress the data.

AUDIO WAVEFORM

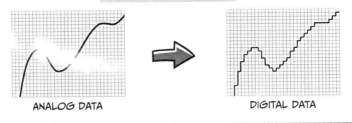

ANALOG DATA

DIGITAL DATA

GRAPHIC OR VIDEO

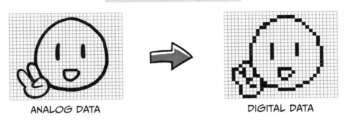

ANALOG DATA

DIGITAL DATA

When color information is translated into digital form, it is split into three base component colors, most often red, green, and blue (known as RGB). These colors are combined to create a composite color on a screen. Each component color can be represented by a number, with larger numbers indicating there's more of that color.

When heavily compressing audio or video data, we often use *lossy* techniques that change and simplify the data in such a way that we usually do not notice a difference. While this approach saves a lot of space, as the name implies, reconstructing the original data perfectly is impossible since vital information is missing. Other techniques—most notably all text compression techniques—use *lossless* compression, which guarantees that the original data can be completely reconstructed.

In any case, with the appropriate arithmetic and logic operations, as long as the data is digital, a CPU can use any compression technique on any form of information. Although digitizing data can involve the loss of some information, a major advantage of digital data over analog data is that it allows us to control noise when transmitting the data.

AS LONG AS THE INFORMATION IS MADE UP OF 1s AND 0s, I'LL KEEP APPLYING OPERATIONS!

2

DIGITAL OPERATIONS

AND
NOT
OR

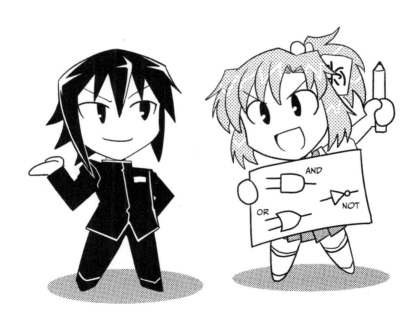

The Computer's World Is Binary

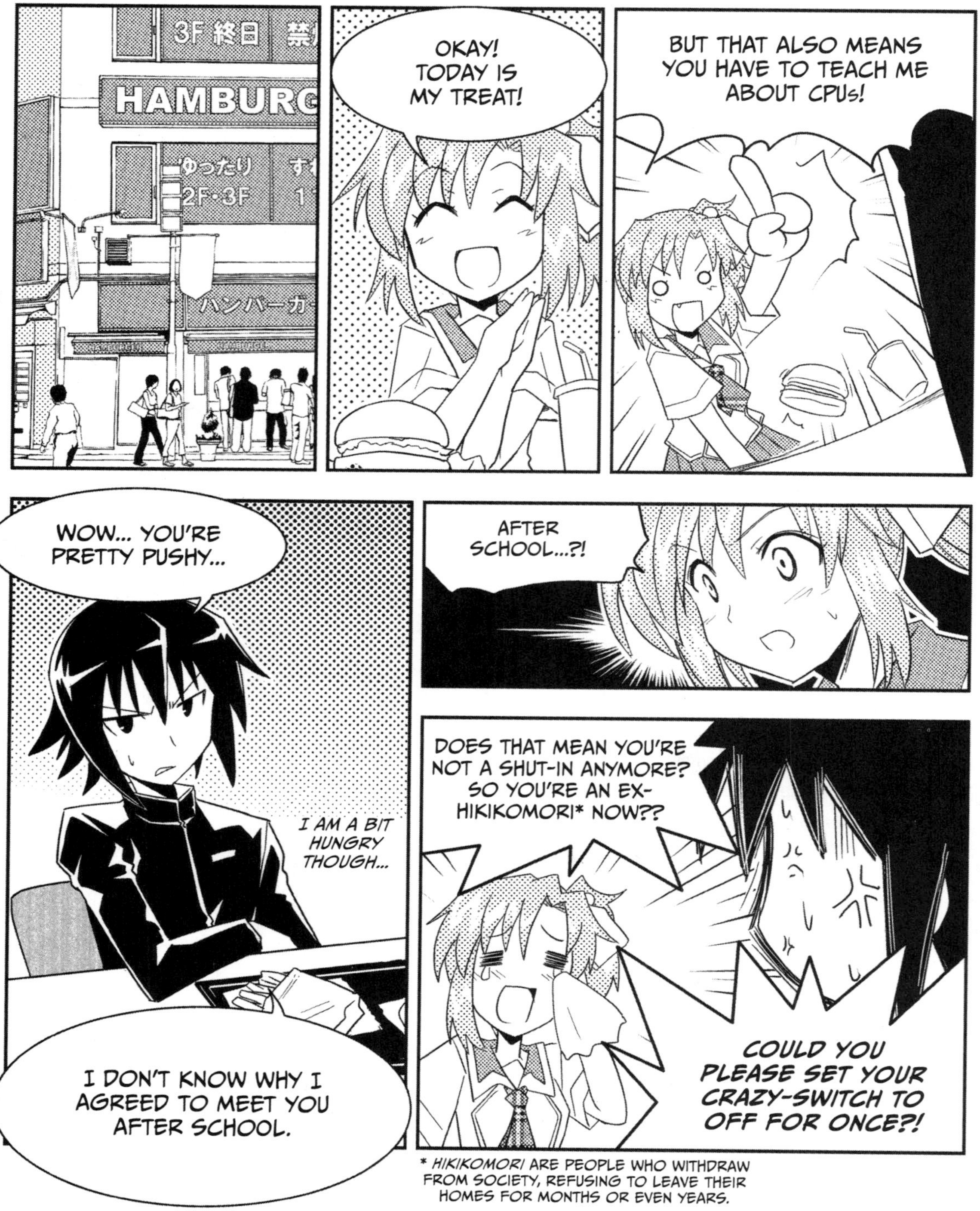

OKAY! TODAY IS MY TREAT!
BUT THAT ALSO MEANS YOU HAVE TO TEACH ME ABOUT CPUs!
WOW... YOU'RE PRETTY PUSHY...
I AM A BIT HUNGRY THOUGH...
I DON'T KNOW WHY I AGREED TO MEET YOU AFTER SCHOOL.
AFTER SCHOOL...?!
DOES THAT MEAN YOU'RE NOT A SHUT-IN ANYMORE? SO YOU'RE AN EX-HIKIKOMORI* NOW??
COULD YOU PLEASE SET YOUR CRAZY-SWITCH TO OFF FOR ONCE?!

* *HIKIKOMORI* ARE PEOPLE WHO WITHDRAW FROM SOCIETY, REFUSING TO LEAVE THEIR HOMES FOR MONTHS OR EVEN YEARS.

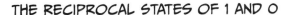

THE RECIPROCAL STATES OF 1 AND 0
OKAY, LET ME START OFF WITH A QUESTION!
LAST TIME, YOU SAID, "COMPUTERS LIVE IN A WORLD OF 1s AND 0s," BUT THAT WAS ALL PRETTY ABSTRACT.
AYUMI
WHAT DO YOU MEAN BY 1s AND 0s ANYWAY?
GOOD QUESTION... YOU CAN THINK OF 1s AND 0s AS TWO RECIPROCAL STATES THAT ARE OPPOSITES.
0
1
THEY'RE MORE LIKE INDICATORS THAN NUMBERS, REALLY.
TWO RECIPROCAL STATES...
YOU MEAN LIKE LIGHT AND DARK, LIFE AND DEATH, OR ON AND OFF?
PRECISELY!
VOLTAGE
HIGH
H
LOW
L
TIME
VOLTAGE CHANGES WITH TIME
TO PUT IT ANOTHER WAY, THE VOLTAGES IN COMPUTER CIRCUITS GENERALLY FALL INTO TWO BANDS. HIGH VOLTAGES ARE CLOSE TO THE SUPPLY VOLTAGE, AND LOW VOLTAGES ARE CLOSE TO GROUND.*

* *GROUND* IS THE REFERENCE POINT FOR VOLTAGE AND IS EQUIVALENT TO ZERO VOLTS.

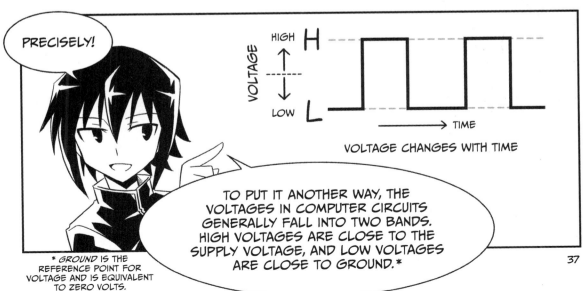

I SEE! IF IT'S JUST TWO VOLTAGES, IT'S ALL PRETTY CLEAR THEN.

THE VOLTAGE IS EITHER LOW (0) OR HIGH (1). IT'S REALLY SIMPLE!

YEAH.

ALL COMPUTERS USE THESE TWO VALUES (0 AND 1, OR LOW AND HIGH*) WHEN PERFORMING OPERATIONS.

* IN THIS BOOK, WE'LL TREAT LOW AS 0 AND HIGH AS 1, BUT IT'S POSSIBLE TO DO IT THE OTHER WAY AROUND AS WELL. IT'S UP TO THE SYSTEM DESIGNER AS TO WHICH ASSIGNMENT TO USE.

DECIMAL VS. BINARY NUMBER SYSTEMS

HMM... BUT WHAT CAN YOU REALLY DO WITH JUST 1s AND 0s?

WOULDN'T YOU ONLY BE ABLE TO DO VERY SIMPLE CALCULATIONS?

HEHEHE! NARROW-MINDED, FOOLISH HUMAN!

COMPUTERS AND HUMANS THINK IN DIFFERENT WAYS!

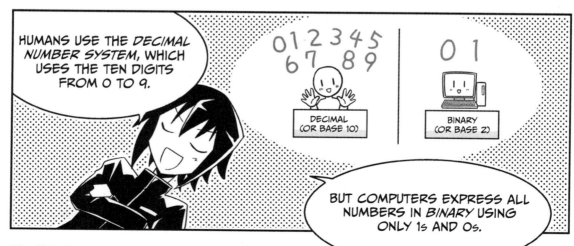

HUMANS USE THE *DECIMAL NUMBER SYSTEM*, WHICH USES THE TEN DIGITS FROM 0 TO 9.

DECIMAL (OR BASE 10)

BINARY (OR BASE 2)

BUT COMPUTERS EXPRESS ALL NUMBERS IN *BINARY* USING ONLY 1s AND 0s.

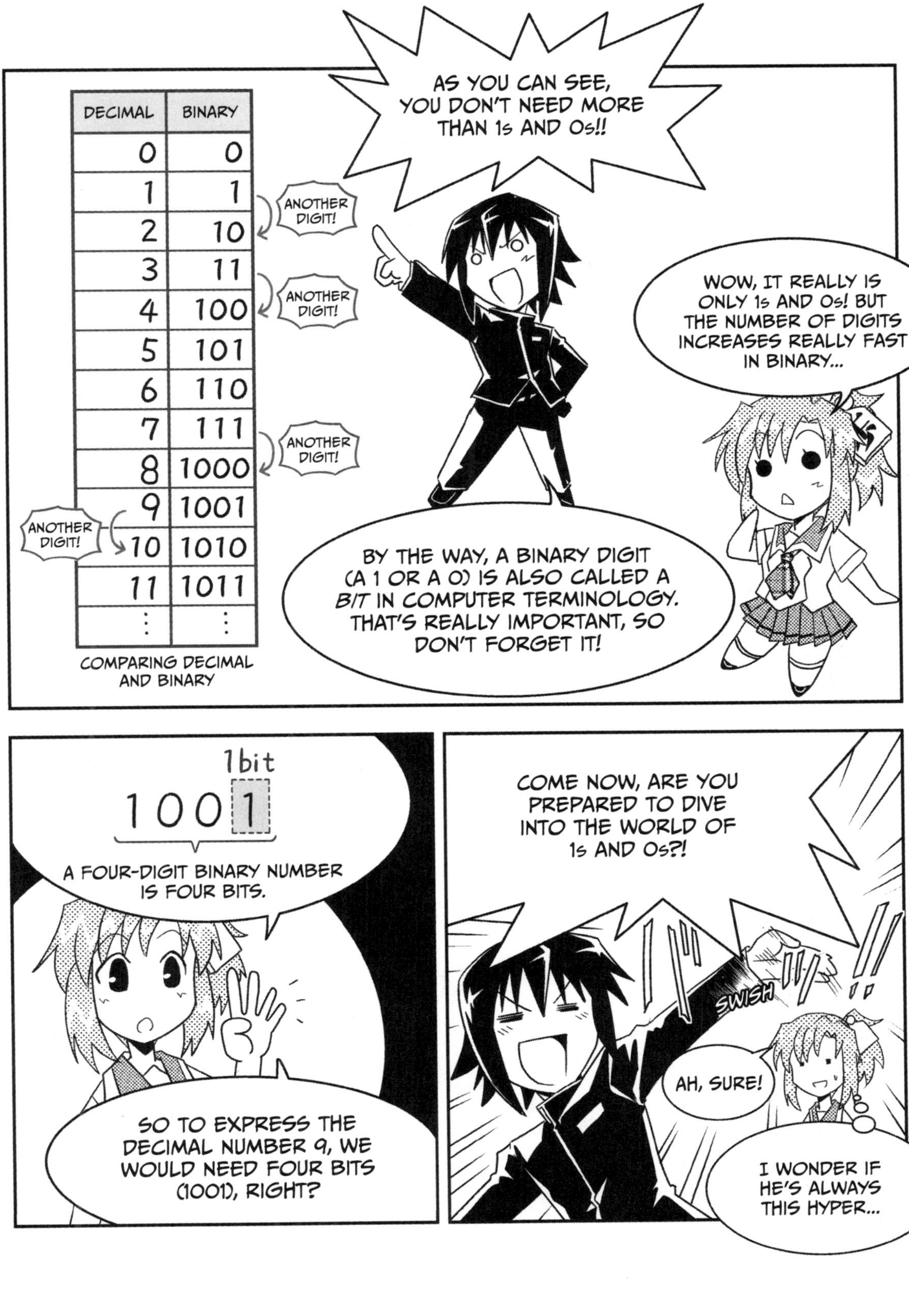

DECIMAL	BINARY
0	0
1	1
2	10
3	11
4	100
5	101
6	110
7	111
8	1000
9	1001
10	1010
11	1011
⋮	⋮

ANOTHER DIGIT!
ANOTHER DIGIT!
ANOTHER DIGIT!
ANOTHER DIGIT!
COMPARING DECIMAL AND BINARY
AS YOU CAN SEE, YOU DON'T NEED MORE THAN 1s AND 0s!!
WOW, IT REALLY IS ONLY 1s AND 0s! BUT THE NUMBER OF DIGITS INCREASES REALLY FAST IN BINARY...
BY THE WAY, A BINARY DIGIT (A 1 OR A 0) IS ALSO CALLED A *BIT* IN COMPUTER TERMINOLOGY. THAT'S REALLY IMPORTANT, SO DON'T FORGET IT!
1bit
1001
A FOUR-DIGIT BINARY NUMBER IS FOUR BITS.
SO TO EXPRESS THE DECIMAL NUMBER 9, WE WOULD NEED FOUR BITS (1001), RIGHT?
COME NOW, ARE YOU PREPARED TO DIVE INTO THE WORLD OF 1s AND 0s?!
SWISH
AH, SURE!
I WONDER IF HE'S ALWAYS THIS HYPER...

EXPRESSING NUMBERS IN BINARY

 Well then, let's learn the basics of binary, or *base 2*, math! Let's start by thinking about the decimal, or *base 10*, system that we use every day. For example, the number 356 is divided up, and then each digit is multiplied by successive powers of ten to get the final value.

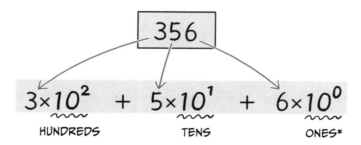

$$3 \times 10^2 + 5 \times 10^1 + 6 \times 10^0$$

HUNDREDS   TENS   ONES*

 Okay! It's really easy if I think of the digits like different coin denominations: 356 yen is just three 100-yen coins (10^2), five 10-yen coins (10^1), and six 1-yen coins (10^0) added together.

 That's right. The next step is to apply that same logic to binary. We just swap the 10 in our decimal calculations for a 2 in the binary case to get the appropriate factors for each digit. Take a look at the following illustration.

---

* Any number to the power of zero is equal to one. For example, $10^0 = 1$, and $2^0 = 1$.

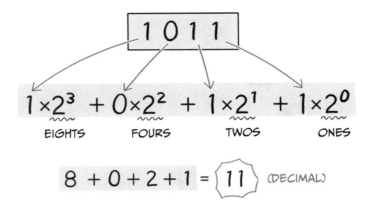

$$1 \times 2^3 + 0 \times 2^2 + 1 \times 2^1 + 1 \times 2^0$$

EIGHTS   FOURS   TWOS   ONES

$$8 + 0 + 2 + 1 = \boxed{11} \text{ (DECIMAL)}$$

Uh-huh! I don't think anyone uses coins like this, though. But if someone did, I would just take either 1 or 0 of each of the 8-yen, 4-yen, 2-yen, and 1-yen coins, right?

So the binary 1011 translates to 8 + 0 + 2 + 1 = 11 in decimal. As soon as you understand the basic principle, it's easy!

By the way, this calculation also works for fractional expressions. Take a look at this.

$$0.14$$

$$0 \times 10^0 + 1 \times 10^{-1} + 4 \times 10^{-2}$$

ONES   ONE-TENTHS   ONE-HUNDREDTHS

In decimal, each digit after the decimal point has factors using negative powers. One-tenth (0.1) is 10^{-1}, one-hundredth (0.01) is 10^{-2}, and so on.

So, it's the same reasoning with binary, right? We would use 2^{-1}, 2^{-2}, 2^{-3} and so on as we add more digits after the decimal point. So the factors would be one-half (0.5), one-fourth (0.25), one-eighth (0.125), and so on. It seems a bit cumbersome, but I think I get it.

FIXED-POINT AND FLOATING-POINT FRACTIONS

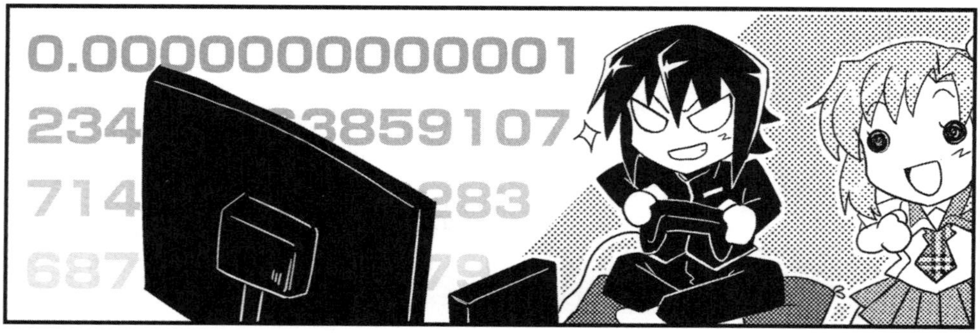

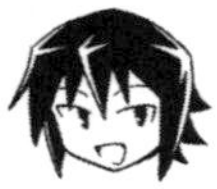

Next up, I'll teach you a really important concept. In computers, there are two ways to store fractions—either fixed point or floating point.

When using extremely small values like 0.00000000000000 . . . 001 or very large values like 1000000000000000 . . . , it's a lot more practical to use floating-point fractions.

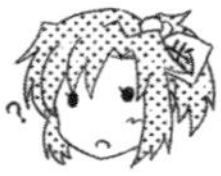

Hmm . . . why is that? What's the difference?

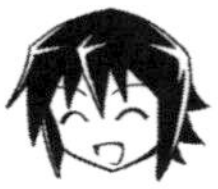

Well, for example, instead of writing a billion in decimal as 1,000,000,000, you could write it as 10^9 to save some space, right? And if you had a number like 1,230,000,000, you could represent it as 1.23×10^9 instead. We call this form *scientific notation* or *standard form*, where the *n* in 10^n is called the *exponent* and the 1.23 is called the *significand*. *Floating-point* numbers use scientific notation when storing values.

In contrast, *fixed-point* numbers express values the way we're used to, with a decimal point. When expressing integers with this method, you can imagine the decimal point being at the far right of the number. Here's a comparison of the two.

FIXED POINT	FLOATING POINT
123. ← DECIMAL POINT	1.23×10^2
1230000.	1.23×10^6
0.0000123	1.23×10^{-6}

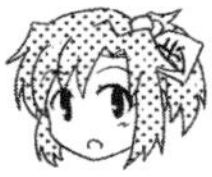

Oh, okay. So if you're using fixed-point fractions to express really large or really small numbers, the number of digits you need increases by a lot. But if you're using floating-point, only the exponent gets bigger or smaller while the number of digits stays the same. Yeah, that's really useful!

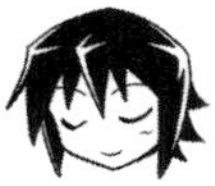

That's right. That last example was in decimal, but since computers use binary, the principle becomes even more relevant. The most common variant used is this one.

AN EXAMPLE SIGNIFICAND

$$1.69 \times 2^{n}$$

SIGNIFICAND (1.69) · BASE (2) · EXPONENT (n)

An example of floating-point representation inside a computer (using a base 10 number as the significand for illustration)

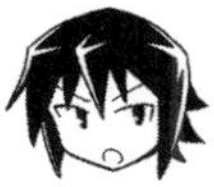

I used the decimal 1.69 just to make it easier to understand. The number would be in binary in a computer. The important part here is that this significand always has to be greater than 1 and less than 2.

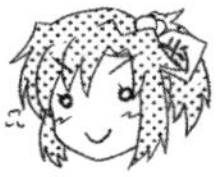

Hm . . . so this representation makes it easy for computers to handle extremely small and extremely large numbers. They're also easy to use in calculations, right?

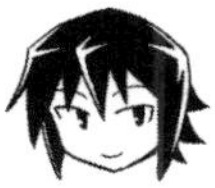

Yes! And it's also important to understand that the speed with which you can calculate using floating-point numbers is critical to CPU performance. Gaming systems that process real-time, high-fidelity graphics also use floating-point arithmetic extensively. (See "CPU Performance Is Measured in FLOPS" on page 137 for a more detailed explanation.)

Generally, scientific calculations require an accuracy of only around 15 digits, but in some cases, 30 are used. Some modern encoding algorithms even use integers of up to 300 digits!

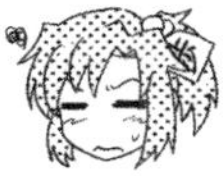

Ugh . . . I don't think I could do those calculations in my head. I hate to lose to computers, but I hope they're at least advancing some fields of science!

ADDITION AND SUBTRACTION IN BINARY

It's finally time to talk about binary arithmetic. Let's start by thinking about addition. First off, adding two bits works like this!

$0 + 0 = 0, \quad 0 + 1 = 1, \quad 1 + 0 = 1, \quad 1 + 1 = 10$

Okay, that's easy! The last equation, 1 + 1 = 10, means that we carried the 1 to the next place value and the first digit became 0, right?

$$\begin{array}{r} 1 \\ +\ 1 \\ \hline 10 \end{array}$$

CARRIED TO THE NEXT PLACE VALUE

Yeah. If you understand how to add one bit to another, you should be able to understand calculations with more digits, as well. For example, when adding the binary numbers $(1011)_2 + (1101)_2$,* you just need to start from the right and work your way to the left, carrying digits as you go. Take a look here.

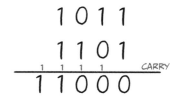

$$\begin{array}{r} 1011 \\ 1101 \\ {\scriptstyle 1\,1\,1\,1\ \ \ \text{CARRY}} \\ \hline 11000 \end{array}$$

1
DON'T FORGET TO CARRY THE 1s!

Uh-huh, I just have to be careful with the carries, right? Binary addition is pretty simple! Or, it might just be my genius shining through.

Hey! Okay then, let's take a look at subtraction next. When doing subtraction, it is important to learn how to create negative values using a technique called *two's complement*.

Adding the two's complement (a number that corresponds to the negative version of a number) of a binary number A to another binary number B is the same as subtracting A from B!! What do you think—pretty cool, right?

* $()_2$ means the number is in binary representation, and $()_{10}$ means it's in decimal representation.

Ahh . . . I'm sorry to stop you when you're on a roll, but I didn't understand that at all. What are you talking about?

 Let's start out slow in decimal. First off, let's agree that subtracting 15 is the same as adding –15. But what would you do if you weren't allowed to use the minus sign at all? Is there some other number that we can use to represent the number –15?

 I . . . I have no idea. Stop putting on airs and just teach me already!

 Where did your genius go? Well, have a look at these two equations then.

EQUATION A	EQUATION B
$\begin{array}{r} 15 \\ +(-15) \\ \hline 0 \end{array}$	$\begin{array}{r} 15 \\ +(\ 85) \\ \hline \textcircled{1}00 \end{array}$
	IGNORE!

Looking at just the final two digits of these equations, we see that the result of equation A is 0 and the result of equation B is 00. We could therefore say that for the last two digits, the results of 15 + (-15) and 15 + 85 are the same!

 Whaaa . . . ? You're right, 0 and 00 are the same! But what happens to the 1 in the equation B result of 100?

 Hah! Since we're doing two-digit math at the moment, we don't care about digits that carry over beyond those two. Just pretend you can't see them! We call those *overflow*, and we just ignore them.

 What kind of twisted reasoning is that? Is that even allowed?

Heh heh heh! Surprised? In situations like this, we say that 85 is the ten's complement of 15. In other words, we say that a number's *complement* in some base is the smallest number you have to add to the original number to make the number's digits overflow. As the name suggests, you can think of the numbers as "complementing" each other to reach the next digit. And this complement corresponds to the original value's negative form. So in this case, 85 is essentially equal to -15.

> Let's take another example. When calculating 9647 – 1200 = 8447, we might as well calculate 9647 + 8800 = 18447 and ignore the carry. That's because in the result we see that the lower four digits are the same. Therefore, we can use 8800 as the ten's complement of 1200 during addition to get the same result as we would get using subtraction.

Uhh . . . this is getting pretty hard to grasp! So using complements, we can perform subtraction by adding instead. I suppose that might be useful. So what happens if we try this far-fetched solution with binary numbers?

It's not far-fetched—it's awesome! It's logical!! Let me show you how to do it in binary.

```
          1010 1000
      +   0101 1000
IGNORE! (1)0000 0000
```

ADD THE TWO NUMBERS: IF THE RESULT IS 0 (IGNORING THE OVERFLOW), IT MEANS THE NUMBERS ARE COMPLEMENTARY.

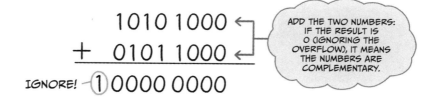

As you can see, when you add two binary numbers and ignore the overflow, the two numbers are complementary if the result equals 0. To subtract a number, simply add its complement instead.

Okay, but finding the complement seems kinda hard. . . .

Don't worry, there is a really easy way to find a two's complement. Just follow these steps.

LET'S FIND THE TWO'S COMPLEMENT TO DO SUBTRACTION!

Step 1: Invert all the digits of the first number from 1 to 0 and vice versa. (This is also called finding the one's complement.)

Step 2: Add 1 to this inverted version of the number, and you'll end up with the two's complement!

Sweet! I tried finding the complement of that last example. Using this method, it was easy.

STEP1
10101000
FLIP ALL THE DIGITS!
01010111
STEP2
01010111
+ 1
ADD 1!
1 1 1
01011000
COMPLEMENT

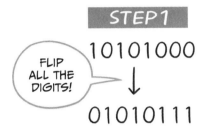

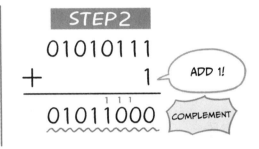

Computers (actually the ALUs) use these two steps all the time for arithmetic operations (addition and subtraction). The only difference is that most ALUs perform subtraction by adding the first number and the inverted second number. Then, they add 1 to that sum. The order of operations is different, but the end result is the same, right?

And since computer calculations only deal with 1s and 0s, this method is both really simple and incredibly fast at the same time.

I see. So there are some merits to binary, I suppose!

BY THE WAY... DON'T FRENCH FRIES KINDA LOOK LIKE 1s AND ONION RINGS KINDA LOOK LIKE 0s?
THIS MUST BE LIKE... BINARY IN THE FRIED-FOOD WORLD!
A GREAT DISCOVERY!
...

What Are Logic Operations?

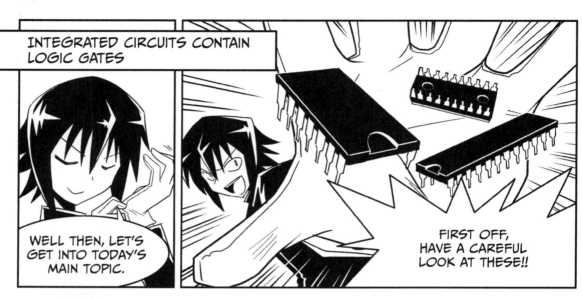

INTEGRATED CIRCUITS CONTAIN LOGIC GATES

WELL THEN, LET'S GET INTO TODAY'S MAIN TOPIC.

FIRST OFF, HAVE A CAREFUL LOOK AT THESE!!

DON'T BRING BUGS INTO RESTAURANTS!!

THEY'RE NOT BUGS!

THIS IS AN EXTREMELY IMPORTANT ELECTRONIC COMPONENT CALLED AN *INTEGRATED CIRCUIT (IC)*.

THEY'RE INSIDE MANY DIFFERENT ELECTRONICS...

LONG TIME, NO SEE!

CPU

EVEN CPUs ARE JUST VERY ADVANCED AND COMPLICATED INTEGRATED CIRCUITS.

EVEN SO, THIS BUG... THIS IC... SURE HAS A LOT OF SILVERY LEGS...

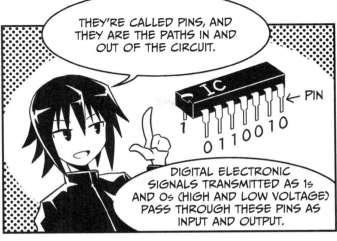

THEY'RE CALLED PINS, AND THEY ARE THE PATHS IN AND OUT OF THE CIRCUIT.

PIN

0110010

DIGITAL ELECTRONIC SIGNALS TRANSMITTED AS 1s AND 0s (HIGH AND LOW VOLTAGE) PASS THROUGH THESE PINS AS INPUT AND OUTPUT.

OH, SO THEY'RE NOT JUST DECORATIONS THEN.

AND HERE'S THE IMPORTANT PART!

LOGIC OPERATIONS!

WOW——!!

LO AND BEHOLD! INSIDE, THE CIRCUIT PERFORMS LOGIC OPERATIONS ON THE 1s AND 0s ON THE INPUT PINS AND PRODUCES THE APPROPRIATE 1s AND 0s ON THE OUTPUT PINS!!

LOGIC OPERATIONS...? THAT SEEMS EVEN MORE COMPLICATED THAN THOSE ARITHMETIC OPERATIONS...

NO, I'VE DECIDED TO THINK LOGICALLY, SO THAT'LL MAKE UNDERSTANDING THEM A BREEZE!!

...I THINK?

THERE'S NO NEED TO GET SO DEFENSIVE ABOUT IT. LOGIC OPERATIONS ARE REALLY SIMPLE AND EASY TO UNDERSTAND.

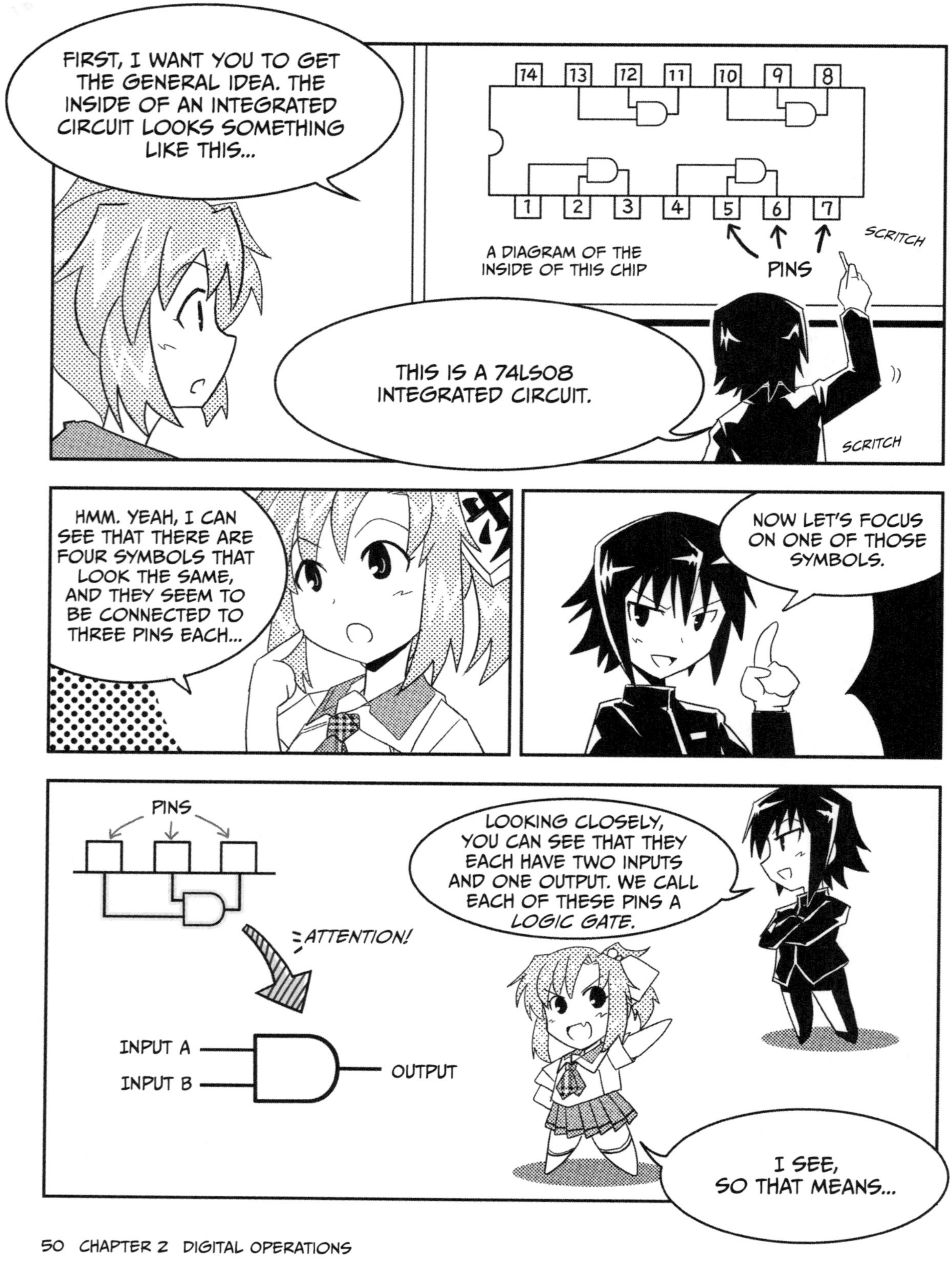
FIRST, I WANT YOU TO GET THE GENERAL IDEA. THE INSIDE OF AN INTEGRATED CIRCUIT LOOKS SOMETHING LIKE THIS...
14 13 12 11 10 9 8
1 2 3 4 5 6 7
A DIAGRAM OF THE INSIDE OF THIS CHIP
PINS
SCRITCH
THIS IS A 74LS08 INTEGRATED CIRCUIT.
SCRITCH
HMM. YEAH, I CAN SEE THAT THERE ARE FOUR SYMBOLS THAT LOOK THE SAME, AND THEY SEEM TO BE CONNECTED TO THREE PINS EACH...
NOW LET'S FOCUS ON ONE OF THOSE SYMBOLS.
PINS
ATTENTION!
INPUT A
INPUT B
OUTPUT
LOOKING CLOSELY, YOU CAN SEE THAT THEY EACH HAVE TWO INPUTS AND ONE OUTPUT. WE CALL EACH OF THESE PINS A *LOGIC GATE*.
I SEE, SO THAT MEANS...

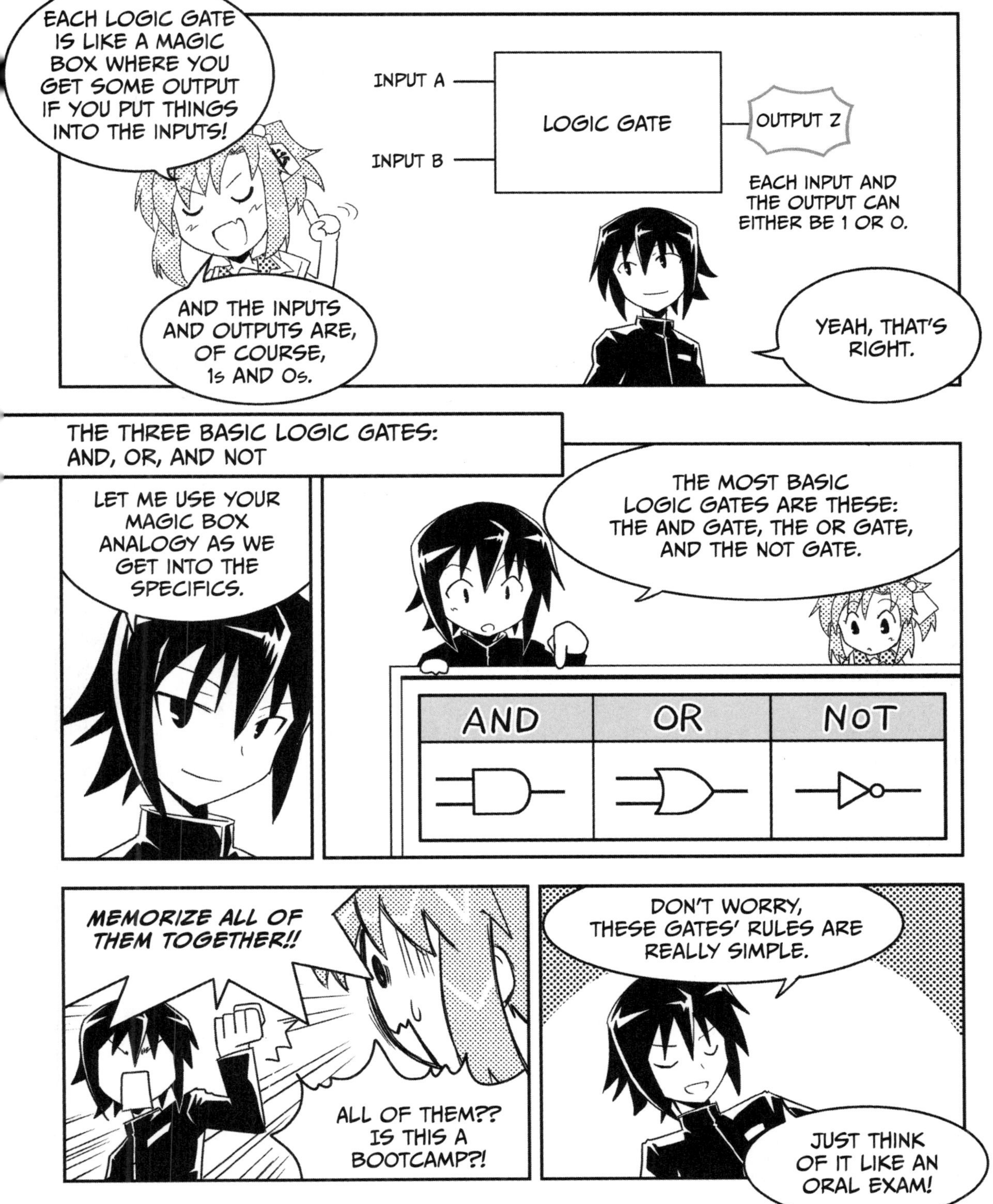
EACH LOGIC GATE IS LIKE A MAGIC BOX WHERE YOU GET SOME OUTPUT IF YOU PUT THINGS INTO THE INPUTS!
INPUT A
INPUT B
LOGIC GATE
OUTPUT Z
EACH INPUT AND THE OUTPUT CAN EITHER BE 1 OR 0.
AND THE INPUTS AND OUTPUTS ARE, OF COURSE, 1s AND 0s.
YEAH, THAT'S RIGHT.
THE THREE BASIC LOGIC GATES: AND, OR, AND NOT
LET ME USE YOUR MAGIC BOX ANALOGY AS WE GET INTO THE SPECIFICS.
THE MOST BASIC LOGIC GATES ARE THESE: THE AND GATE, THE OR GATE, AND THE NOT GATE.
AND
OR
NOT
MEMORIZE ALL OF THEM TOGETHER!!
ALL OF THEM?? IS THIS A BOOTCAMP?!
DON'T WORRY, THESE GATES' RULES ARE REALLY SIMPLE.
JUST THINK OF IT LIKE AN ORAL EXAM!

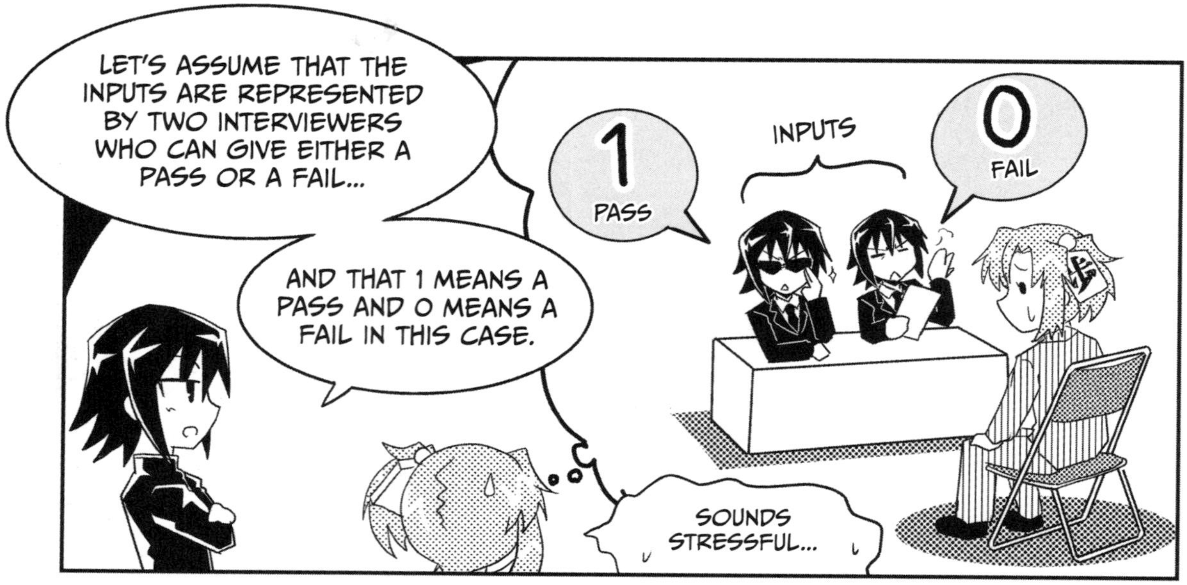
LET'S ASSUME THAT THE INPUTS ARE REPRESENTED BY TWO INTERVIEWERS WHO CAN GIVE EITHER A PASS OR A FAIL...
1
PASS
INPUTS
0
FAIL
AND THAT 1 MEANS A PASS AND 0 MEANS A FAIL IN THIS CASE.
SOUNDS STRESSFUL...

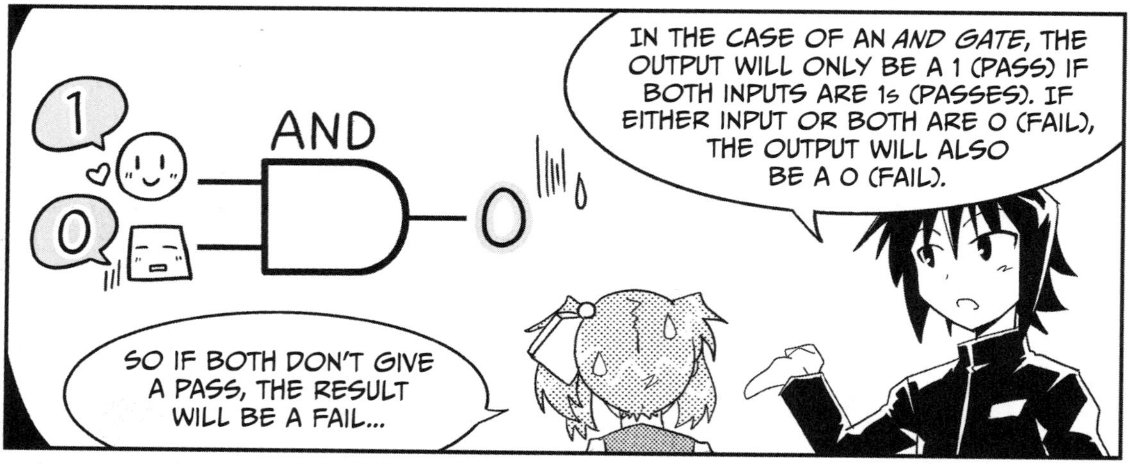
1
0
AND
0
IN THE CASE OF AN *AND GATE*, THE OUTPUT WILL ONLY BE A 1 (PASS) IF BOTH INPUTS ARE 1s (PASSES). IF EITHER INPUT OR BOTH ARE 0 (FAIL), THE OUTPUT WILL ALSO BE A 0 (FAIL).
SO IF BOTH DON'T GIVE A PASS, THE RESULT WILL BE A FAIL...

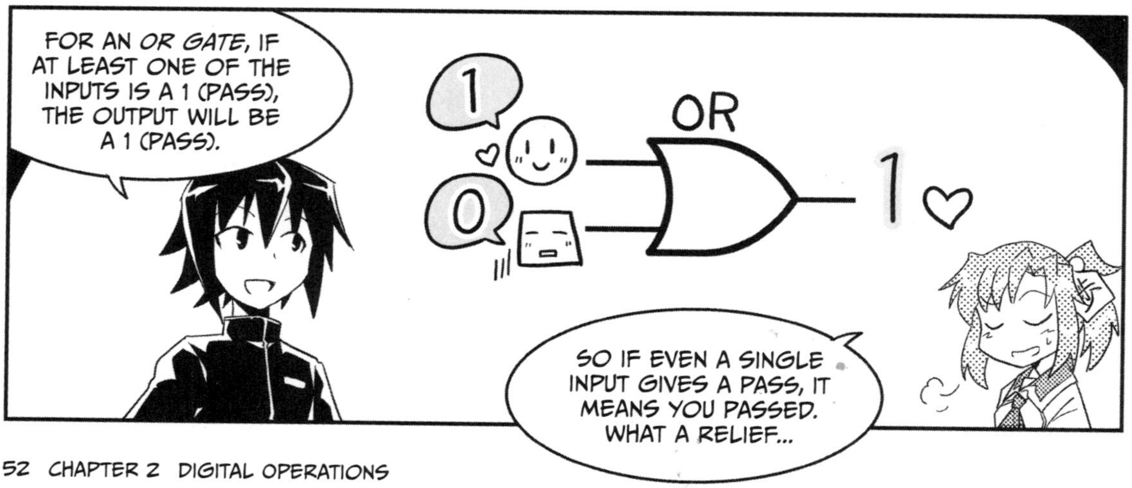
FOR AN *OR GATE*, IF AT LEAST ONE OF THE INPUTS IS A 1 (PASS), THE OUTPUT WILL BE A 1 (PASS).
1
0
OR
1
SO IF EVEN A SINGLE INPUT GIVES A PASS, IT MEANS YOU PASSED. WHAT A RELIEF...

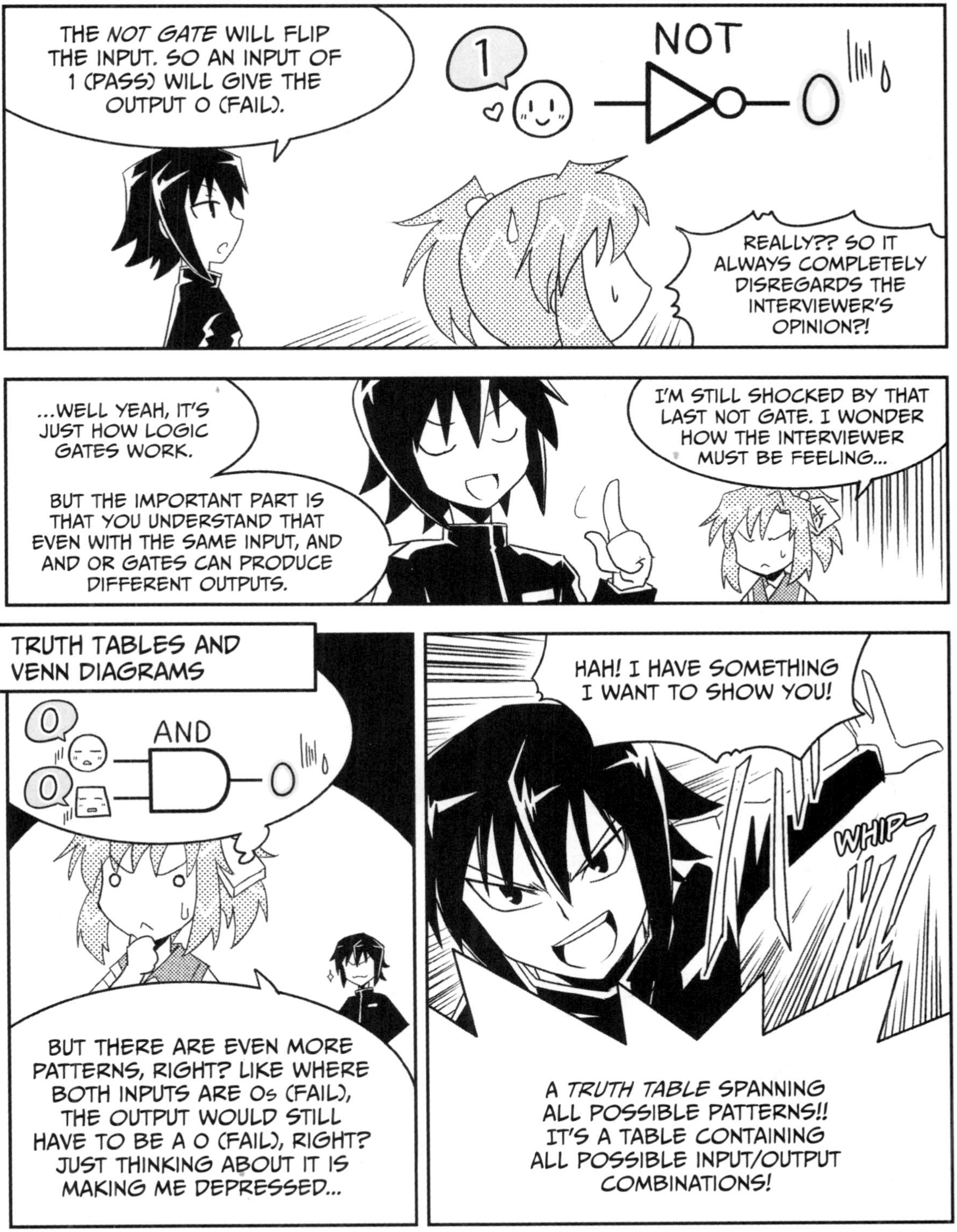

THE *NOT GATE* WILL FLIP THE INPUT. SO AN INPUT OF 1 (PASS) WILL GIVE THE OUTPUT 0 (FAIL).
1
NOT
0
REALLY?? SO IT ALWAYS COMPLETELY DISREGARDS THE INTERVIEWER'S OPINION?!
...WELL YEAH, IT'S JUST HOW LOGIC GATES WORK.
BUT THE IMPORTANT PART IS THAT YOU UNDERSTAND THAT EVEN WITH THE SAME INPUT, AND AND OR GATES CAN PRODUCE DIFFERENT OUTPUTS.
I'M STILL SHOCKED BY THAT LAST NOT GATE. I WONDER HOW THE INTERVIEWER MUST BE FEELING...
TRUTH TABLES AND VENN DIAGRAMS
0
0
AND
0
BUT THERE ARE EVEN MORE PATTERNS, RIGHT? LIKE WHERE BOTH INPUTS ARE 0s (FAIL), THE OUTPUT WOULD STILL HAVE TO BE A 0 (FAIL), RIGHT? JUST THINKING ABOUT IT IS MAKING ME DEPRESSED...
HAH! I HAVE SOMETHING I WANT TO SHOW YOU!
WHIP—
A *TRUTH TABLE* SPANNING ALL POSSIBLE PATTERNS!! IT'S A TABLE CONTAINING ALL POSSIBLE INPUT/OUTPUT COMBINATIONS!

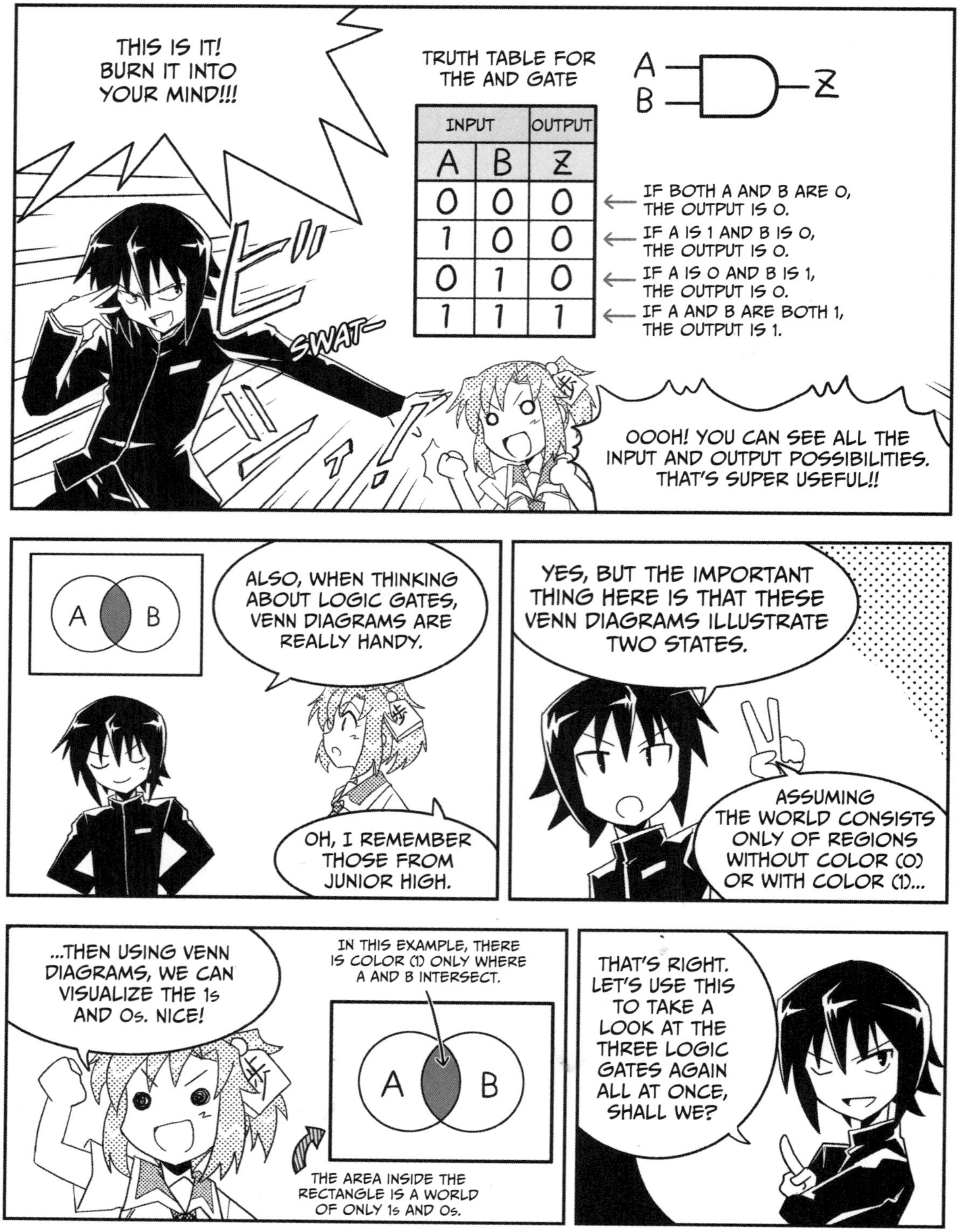
THIS IS IT! BURN IT INTO YOUR MIND!!!
TRUTH TABLE FOR THE AND GATE

INPUT		OUTPUT
A	B	Z
0	0	0
1	0	0
0	1	0
1	1	1

A
B
Z
IF BOTH A AND B ARE 0, THE OUTPUT IS 0.
IF A IS 1 AND B IS 0, THE OUTPUT IS 0.
IF A IS 0 AND B IS 1, THE OUTPUT IS 0.
IF A AND B ARE BOTH 1, THE OUTPUT IS 1.
SWAT—
OOOH! YOU CAN SEE ALL THE INPUT AND OUTPUT POSSIBILITIES. THAT'S SUPER USEFUL!!
A
B
ALSO, WHEN THINKING ABOUT LOGIC GATES, VENN DIAGRAMS ARE REALLY HANDY.
OH, I REMEMBER THOSE FROM JUNIOR HIGH.
YES, BUT THE IMPORTANT THING HERE IS THAT THESE VENN DIAGRAMS ILLUSTRATE TWO STATES.
ASSUMING THE WORLD CONSISTS ONLY OF REGIONS WITHOUT COLOR (0) OR WITH COLOR (1)...
...THEN USING VENN DIAGRAMS, WE CAN VISUALIZE THE 1s AND 0s. NICE!
IN THIS EXAMPLE, THERE IS COLOR (1) ONLY WHERE A AND B INTERSECT.
A
B
THE AREA INSIDE THE RECTANGLE IS A WORLD OF ONLY 1s AND 0s.
THAT'S RIGHT. LET'S USE THIS TO TAKE A LOOK AT THE THREE LOGIC GATES AGAIN ALL AT ONCE, SHALL WE?

A SUMMARY OF THE AND, OR, AND NOT GATES

 Let's summarize the first three basic gates. Let's look at the symbols, truth tables, and Venn diagrams as sets!

AND GATE (LOGIC INTERSECTION GATE)

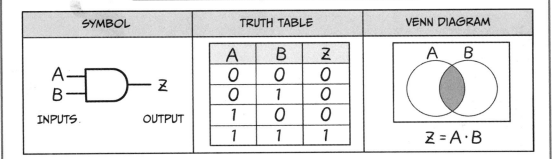

SYMBOL	TRUTH TABLE	VENN DIAGRAM
A — B — Z INPUTS. OUTPUT	A B Z / 0 0 0 / 0 1 0 / 1 0 0 / 1 1 1	A B $Z = A \cdot B$

AND gates output 1 only when both inputs are 1, and they are sometimes expressed in equation form as $Z = A \cdot B$. The symbols used to represent AND are those for logical intersections: $\cdot$ or $\cap$.

OR GATE (LOGIC UNION GATE)

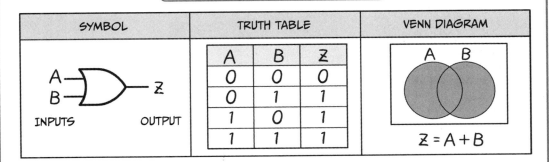

SYMBOL	TRUTH TABLE	VENN DIAGRAM
A — B — Z INPUTS OUTPUT	A B Z / 0 0 0 / 0 1 1 / 1 0 1 / 1 1 1	A B $Z = A + B$

OR gates output 1 when either input or both is 1, and they are sometimes expressed in equation form as $Z = A + B$. The symbols used to represent OR are those for logical unions: $+$ or $\cup$.

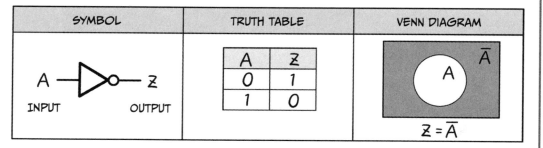

NOT GATE (LOGIC NEGATION GATE)

SYMBOL	TRUTH TABLE	VENN DIAGRAM

A	$\overline{Z}$
0	1
1	0

$Z = \overline{A}$

NOT gates output 0 only when the input is 1, and they are sometimes expressed in equation form as $Z = \overline{A}$. The symbol used to represent NOT is the one for logical negation (complement): ‾.

THIS WHITE CIRCLE
INDICATES THAT 0 AND 1
SHOULD BE FLIPPED!

 Ohh! So you can also write them as A · B, A + B, or $\overline{A}$. I think I understand all these forms now.

 Good. Be extra careful about this though! In the examples here, we showed AND and OR gates having only the two inputs A and B, but it's not uncommon for these gates to have three or more inputs.

SOMETIMES
MORE THAN
THREE!

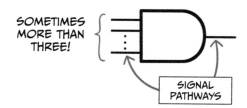

SIGNAL
PATHWAYS

In these cases, we require that all inputs of the AND gate be 1 for the output to be 1. In the case of OR gates, we require that at least one input be 1 for the output to be 1.

 So these input and output lines are called *signals* and can either be a 1 or 0. That's easy to remember.

OKAY, LET'S TAKE A LOOK AT NAND, NOR, AND XOR* GATES NEXT.

NAND	NOR	XOR

WHAT?!

* XOR IS WRITTEN AS EOR OR EXOR IN SOME CASES.

YOU JUST SAID THAT AND, OR, AND NOT WERE THE THREE BASIC GATES...

TOTTERING

ARE YOU JUST GOING TO TAKE THAT BACK? LIAR! THERE'S EVEN MORE OF THEM?!

STOP WHINING AND CALM DOWN!!

YOU SHOULD KNOW ABOUT NAND, NOR, AND XOR, TOO.

AND THE REASON IS...

SOMETHING YOU'LL REALIZE AFTER YOU LEARN ABOUT THEM!!!

EVEN MORE ZEALOUS THAN USUAL!

LET'S DO IT!

A SUMMARY OF THE NAND, NOR, AND XOR GATES

 Okay, let's talk about the other basic gates. These gates are really just *combinations* of AND, OR, and NOT gates!

NAND GATE (LOGIC INTERSECTION COMPLEMENT GATE)

SYMBOL	TRUTH TABLE	VENN DIAGRAM
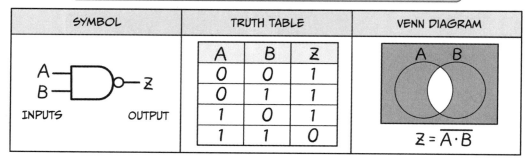		

TRUTH TABLE:

A	B	Z
0	0	1
0	1	1
1	0	1
1	1	0

$$Z = \overline{A \cdot B}$$

THE SAME!

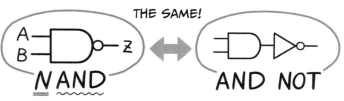

$$\underline{N}AND \quad \Longleftrightarrow \quad AND \; NOT$$

The NAND gate is an AND gate wired to a NOT gate. The NAND gate's output is therefore the output of an AND gate run through a NOT (negation) gate. It's sometimes written as the equation $Z = \overline{A \cdot B}$.

NOR GATE (LOGIC UNION COMPLEMENT GATE)

SYMBOL	TRUTH TABLE	VENN DIAGRAM

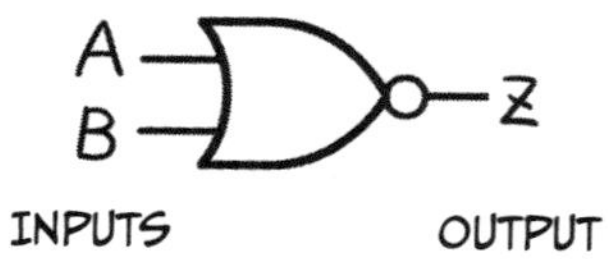

TRUTH TABLE:

A	B	Z
0	0	1
0	1	0
1	0	0
1	1	0

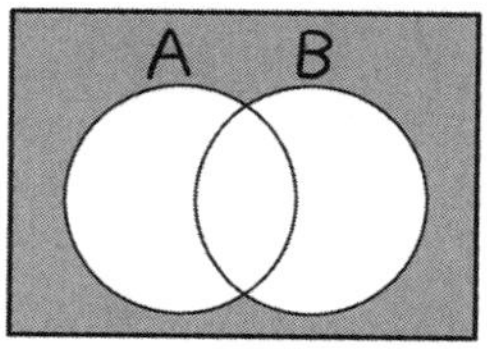

$$Z = \overline{A + B}$$

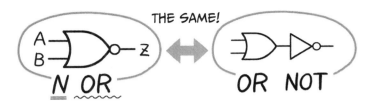

THE SAME!

N OR ⟷ OR NOT

The NOR gate is an OR gate wired to a NOT gate. The NOR gate's output is therefore the output of an OR gate run through a NOT (negation) gate. It's sometimes written as the equation $Z = \overline{A+B}$.

XOR GATE (EXCLUSIVE LOGIC UNION GATE)

SYMBOL	TRUTH TABLE			VENN DIAGRAM
	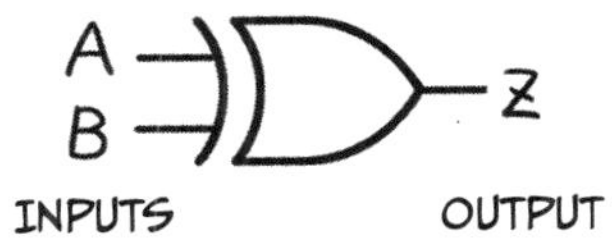 A	B	Z	
A → , B → OUTPUT Z, INPUTS	0	0	0	$Z = A \oplus B$
	0	1	1	
	1	0	1	
	1	1	0	

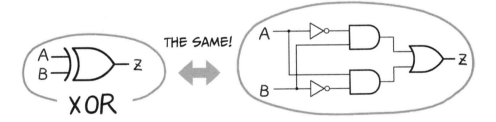

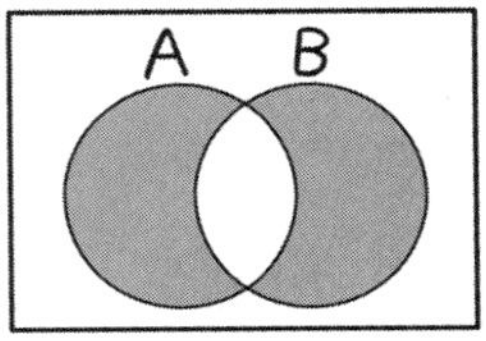

THE SAME!

XOR ⟷

The XOR gate outputs 1 only when the inputs A and B are different. This gate is some-times written as the equation $Z = A \oplus B$.

The XOR gate's function is shown in the schematic above, where you see a combination of AND, OR, and NOT gates. The X in XOR stands for *exclusive*.

Oho! You were right. These gates really are just combinations of the three basic gates.

DE MORGAN'S LAWS

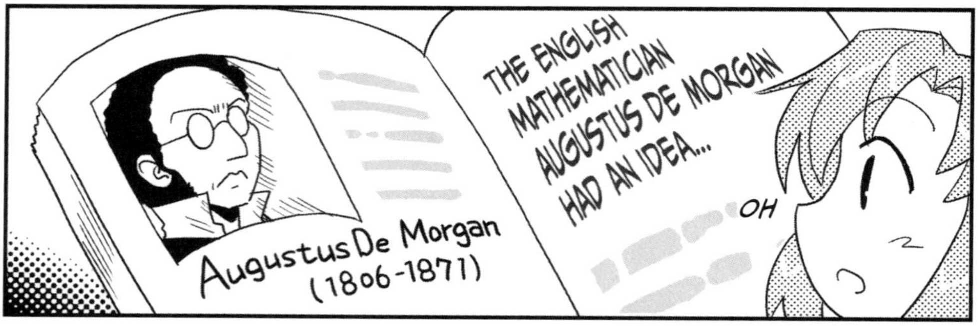
Augustus De Morgan
(1806-1871)
THE ENGLISH MATHEMATICIAN AUGUSTUS DE MORGAN HAD AN IDEA...
OH

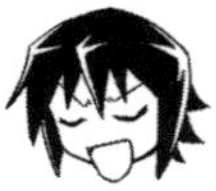

This might be kind of off topic, but don't you feel a certain fascination whenever you hear the word *theorem* or *law*? It's so charming and cool, I can't help but feel my heart throb wistfully every time. . . . Well, let me tell you about an important theorem: De Morgan's indispensable laws for logic operations. Here it is!

DE MORGAN'S THEOREM

$$\overline{A \cdot B} = \overline{A} + \overline{B}$$

$$\overline{A + B} = \overline{A} \cdot \overline{B}$$

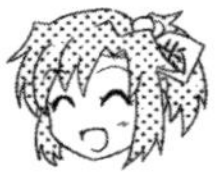

Aah, I might have eaten a little too much today. But fast food can be really good sometimes, don't you think?

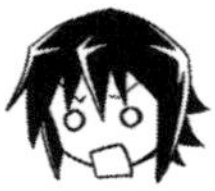

Stop ignoring me! Well, I suppose formulas like this can look complicated at first glance. . . . Let's start with the important part. This law basically just says a NAND gate is the same as using an OR gate on each input's complement, and a NOR gate is the same as using an AND gate on each input's complement. Does that make it clearer?

Yeah! I can see that the left and right sides have big differences in how they use · (AND) and + (OR). So according to De Morgan's law you can swap AND for OR operators and vice versa by using complements.

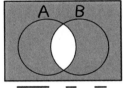 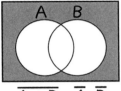

$$\overline{A \cdot B} = \overline{A} + \overline{B} \qquad \overline{A + B} = \overline{A} \cdot \overline{B}$$

 That's it! It also means that we can use De Morgan's laws to show our circuits in different ways. Using this technique, it's easy to simplify schematics when necessary. Here are some conversions using De Morgan's laws.

BOTH OF THESE ARE NAND GATES!

BOTH OF THESE ARE NOR GATES!

 But they're completely different! Is there really no problem even though the left and right side look nothing alike?

 Yeah, the expressions might be different, but their functions are the same. Since logic gates (digital gates) only work with 1s and 0s, everything stays logically the same even if you switch out all the gates. We're just leveraging that particular feature of the math.

 I see. . . . Then you won't mind if I just rewrite all of them? This is a law I like!

Circuits That Perform Arithmetic

THE ADDITION CIRCUIT

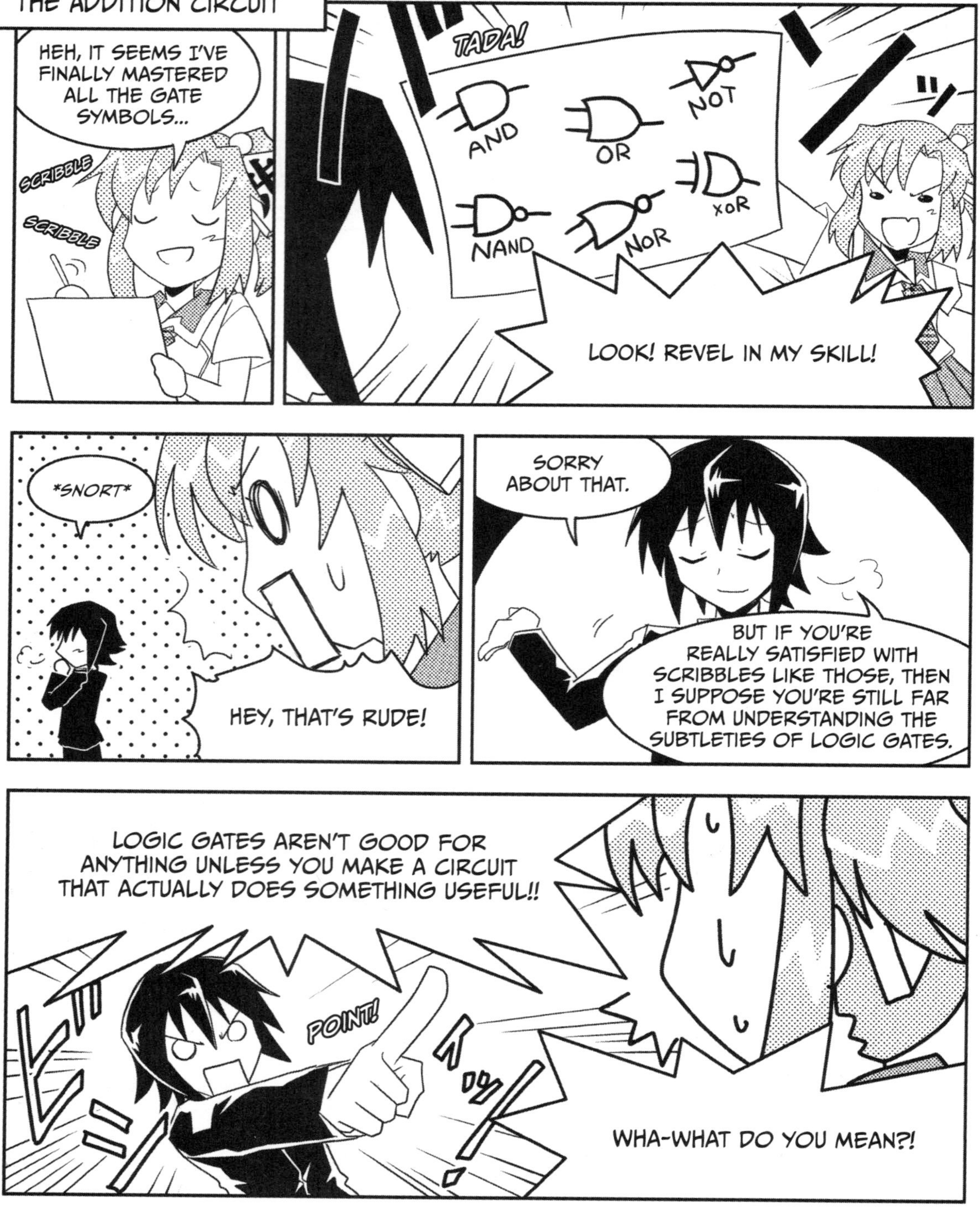

HEH, IT SEEMS I'VE FINALLY MASTERED ALL THE GATE SYMBOLS...
SCRIBBLE
SCRIBBLE
TADA!
AND
OR
NOT
NAND
NOR
XOR
LOOK! REVEL IN MY SKILL!
SNORT
HEY, THAT'S RUDE!
SORRY ABOUT THAT.
BUT IF YOU'RE REALLY SATISFIED WITH SCRIBBLES LIKE THOSE, THEN I SUPPOSE YOU'RE STILL FAR FROM UNDERSTANDING THE SUBTLETIES OF LOGIC GATES.
LOGIC GATES AREN'T GOOD FOR ANYTHING UNLESS YOU MAKE A CIRCUIT THAT ACTUALLY DOES SOMETHING USEFUL!!
POINT!
WHA-WHAT DO YOU MEAN?!

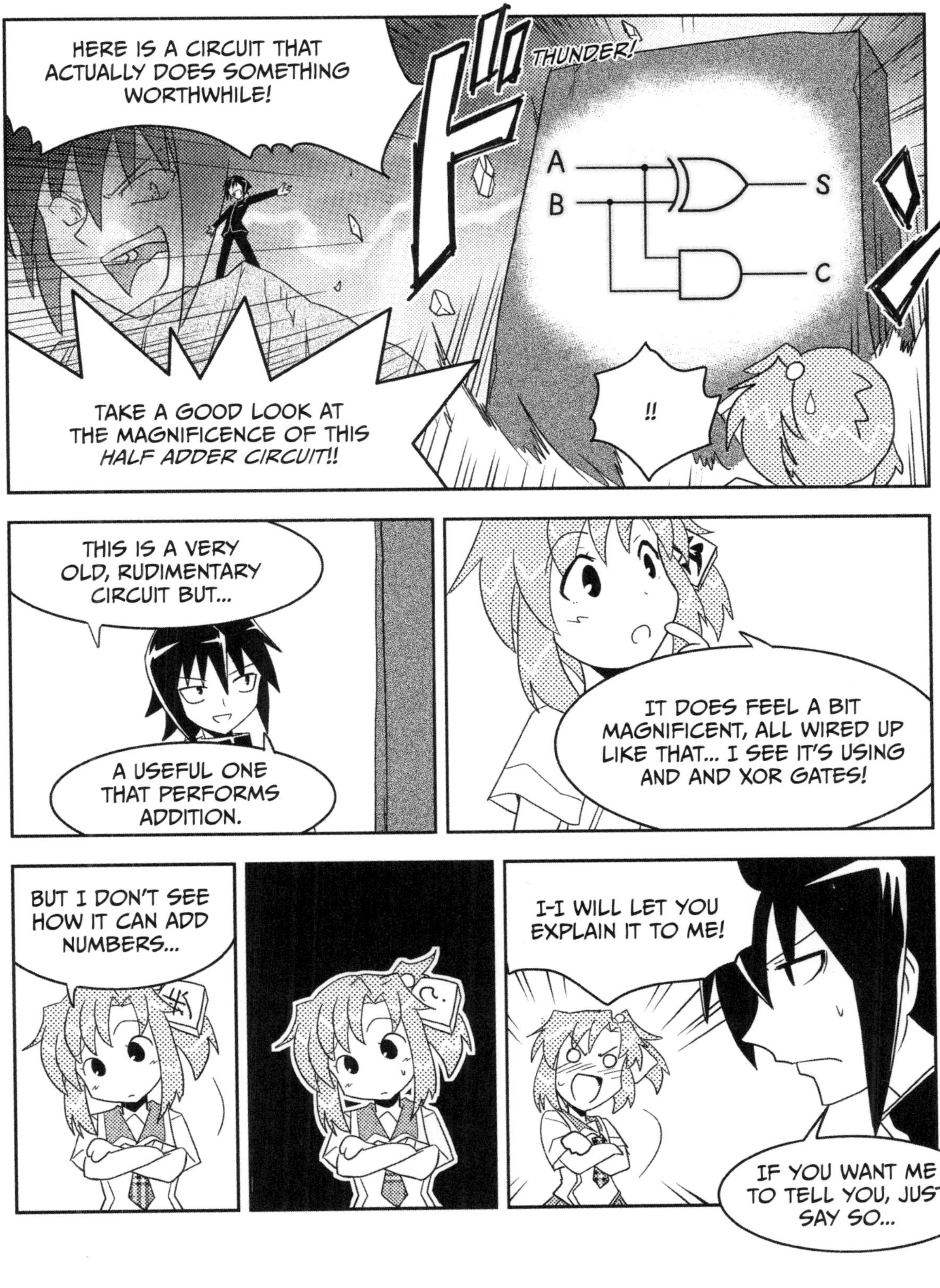
HERE IS A CIRCUIT THAT ACTUALLY DOES SOMETHING WORTHWHILE!
THUNDER!
A
B
S
C
TAKE A GOOD LOOK AT THE MAGNIFICENCE OF THIS *HALF ADDER CIRCUIT*!!
!!
THIS IS A VERY OLD, RUDIMENTARY CIRCUIT BUT...
A USEFUL ONE THAT PERFORMS ADDITION.
IT DOES FEEL A BIT MAGNIFICENT, ALL WIRED UP LIKE THAT... I SEE IT'S USING AND AND XOR GATES!
BUT I DON'T SEE HOW IT CAN ADD NUMBERS...
I-I WILL LET YOU EXPLAIN IT TO ME!
IF YOU WANT ME TO TELL YOU, JUST SAY SO...

THE HALF ADDER

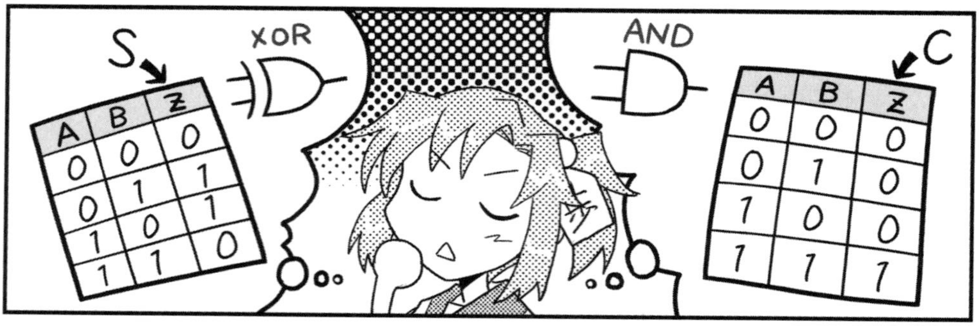
S
XOR
A B Z
0 0 0
0 1 1
1 0 1
1 1 0
AND
C
A B Z
0 0 0
0 1 0
1 0 0
1 1 1

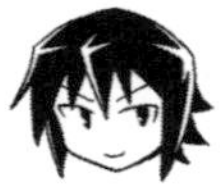

Let me explain what the *half adder* I showed you is all about (though I suspect you won't need that much explanation at this point). First off, do you remember single-bit addition?

0 + 0 = 0, 0 + 1 = 1, 1 + 0 = 1, 1 + 1 = 10

If we bundle all of these together, it kind of starts to look like a truth table, doesn't it? Let's treat the two bits as inputs A and B, and let's standardize our output to two digits. So, an output of 1 looks like 01.

A		B		OUTPUT	
0	+	0	=	00	
0	+	1	=	01	
1	+	0	=	01	
1	+	1	=	10	(THE DIGIT IS CARRIED.)

↑ THE LOWER DIGIT

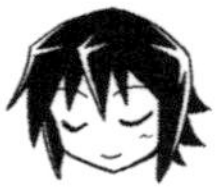

Well then, do you notice anything? Pay special attention to the gray area.

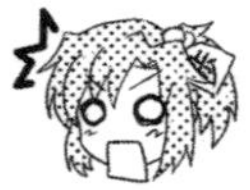

Wh—what? Could it be . . . ? The lower digit output... it looks just like an XOR gate's truth table (see page 59)! XOR produces an output of 1 only if the inputs are different, right?

That's correct. This time, look only at the upper output digit.

$$
\begin{array}{ccc}
A & B & \text{OUTPUT} \\
0+0 & = & 0\,0 \\
0+1 & = & 0\,1 \\
1+0 & = & 0\,1 \\
1+1 & = & 1\,0 \quad \text{(THE DIGIT IS CARRIED.)}
\end{array}
$$

↑
THE UPPER DIGIT

Hmm, that looks just like the truth table for an AND gate (see page 55)! An AND gate's output is 1 only when both inputs are 1. . . .

That must mean that by combining an XOR and an AND gate, we can get two outputs (one for the upper digit and one for the lower digit) and perform single-bit addition!

As soon as you get that part, it seems really easy, right? The lower digit comes from output S, and the upper digit comes from output C. In this case, S stands for *sum*, and C for *carry*.

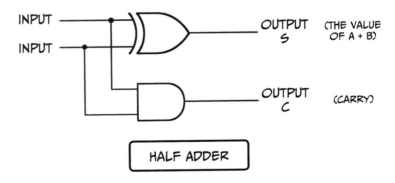

HALF ADDER

This is how we can get two outputs from two inputs with the same half adder circuit. And this is also how we can add two bits together!

THE FULL ADDER AND RIPPLE CARRY ADDER

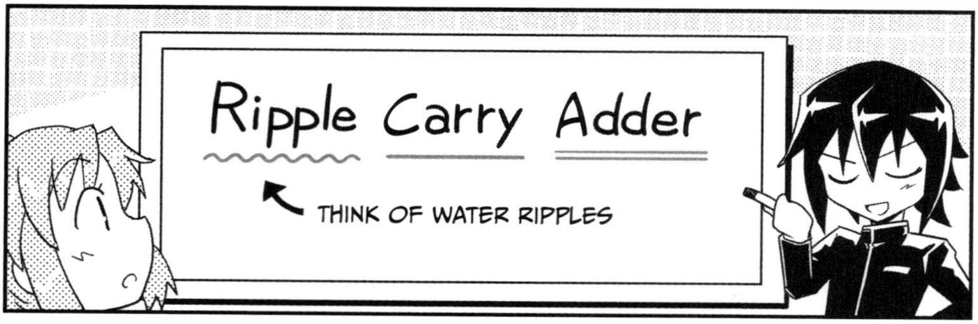

Ripple Carry Adder
THINK OF WATER RIPPLES

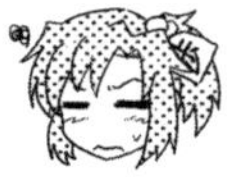

After learning how the half adder works, it seems really simple! Hmm . . . but, there's still something that bothers me about it.

In that circuit, there's an output for the carry, but there's no input for the carry from the previous digit. That means you can only ever add two single digits, right? That doesn't seem very useful. In fact, only being able to add two single digits seems pretty useless!

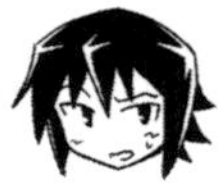

Heh, an acute observation, for sure. It's true that the half adder cannot deal with carries from previous digits and can therefore only ever add two single bits. That's why half adders are just that: "half an adder." It's no use putting it down for something it can't help.

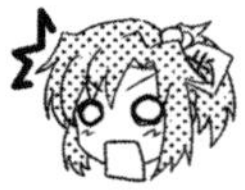

I'm not dissing anyone! Why am I the bad guy all of a sudden?!

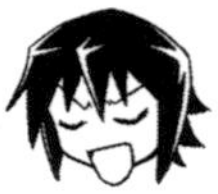

Don't underestimate the half adder though! By using two half adders, you can make a *full adder*. In addition to having the inputs A and B, you can use an additional input for the carry in this circuit.

Take a look at this next schematic. We call this circuit with three inputs and two outputs a *full adder*. We'll put each half adder into its own box to make the diagram a bit easier to understand.

THREE INPUTS
A
B
Cin
S
HALF ADDER
Cout
S
HALF ADDER
Cout
S
Cout

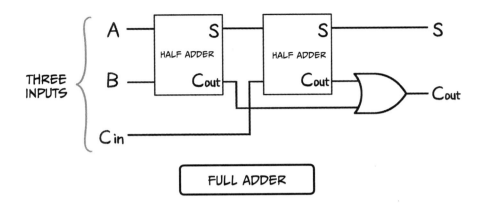

FULL ADDER

You were right—it's using two half adders! Two halves really make a whole. I guess C_{in} is the *carry input* and C_{out} is the *carry output* then.

That's right. And by connecting one half adder and several full adders, we can add any number of bits! We call a circuit like this a *ripple carry adder*.

In this example, we're using four adders, so we can add four digits. We've also put the individual adders into their own boxes. During subtraction, we would deal with the inverse carry instead (borrow).

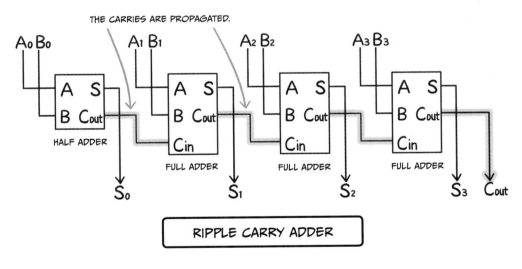

THE CARRIES ARE PROPAGATED.
A0 B0
A1 B1
A2 B2
A3 B3
A S
B Cout
HALF ADDER
A S
B Cout
Cin
FULL ADDER
A S
B Cout
Cin
FULL ADDER
A S
B Cout
Cin
FULL ADDER
S0
S1
S2
S3
Cout

RIPPLE CARRY ADDER

Uh-huh. So each adder's carry output goes into the next adder's carry input. This is how the carry flows so that we're able to do the calculation properly.

THE CARRY LOOK-AHEAD ADDER

But even then . . . that ripple carry adder kind of makes me feel like there's something familiar with how it moves the carry after each step in the calculation. It's really similar to how we humans do calculations with pen and paper by moving the carry from each lower place value to the next higher place value.

Yeah. But that's actually a big problem—it takes a lot of time to keep moving the carry from one calculation to the next.

In ripple carry adders, the more digits there are, the slower the calculation speed will be because of the larger *propagation delay*.

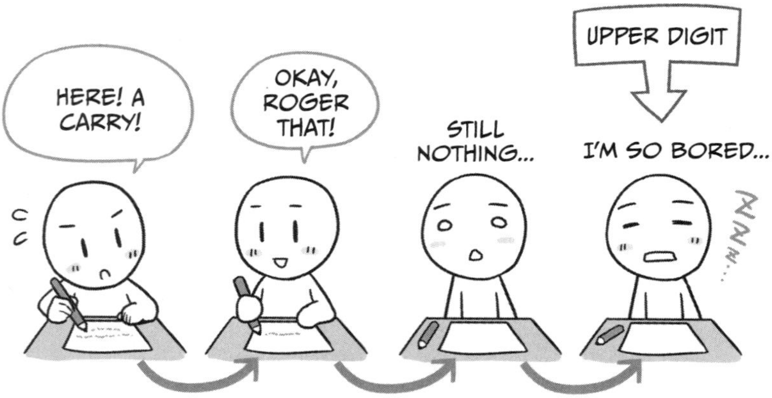
HERE! A CARRY!
OKAY, ROGER THAT!
STILL NOTHING...
UPPER DIGIT
I'M SO BORED...

PROPAGATION DELAY IN A RIPPLE CARRY ADDER

Yeah, that seems a bit slow. . . . Addition and subtraction are pretty common, too, so I suppose they're not something you want to be doing slowly. Hmm. So what do we do about it?!

Heh heh heh. To fix this problem, someone came up with what is known as a *carry look-ahead adder*.

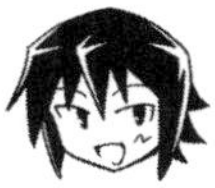

The carry look-ahead adder basically delegates the carry calculations to a completely different circuit that serves its results to each digit's adder. Using this method, the upper digits can do their calculations right away, without having to wait!

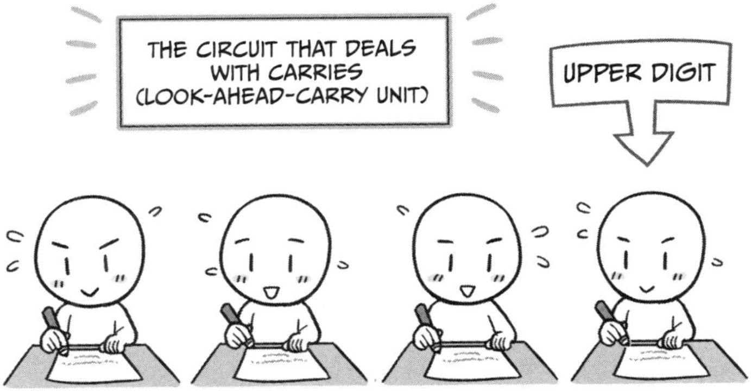
THE CIRCUIT THAT DEALS WITH CARRIES (LOOK-AHEAD-CARRY UNIT)
UPPER DIGIT

THEY DON'T HAVE TO WAIT FOR THE CARRY!

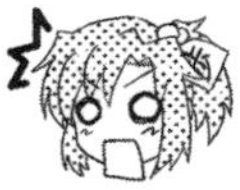

Eeeh, is that even possible? So does that mean there's some other dedicated circuit that decides whether or not there's a carry?

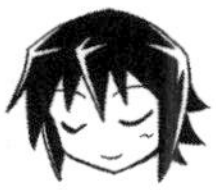

Yeah. It determines whether there is a carry in either direction during addition and subtraction. The downside is that the circuit is a lot bigger, but calculation times are drastically reduced.

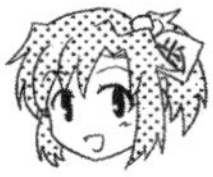

Hmm. So it's reducing calculation times with all kinds of smart tricks then. When we first talked about making a circuit for addition, I was imagining something pretty small, but the final product is quite impressive.

Circuits That Remember

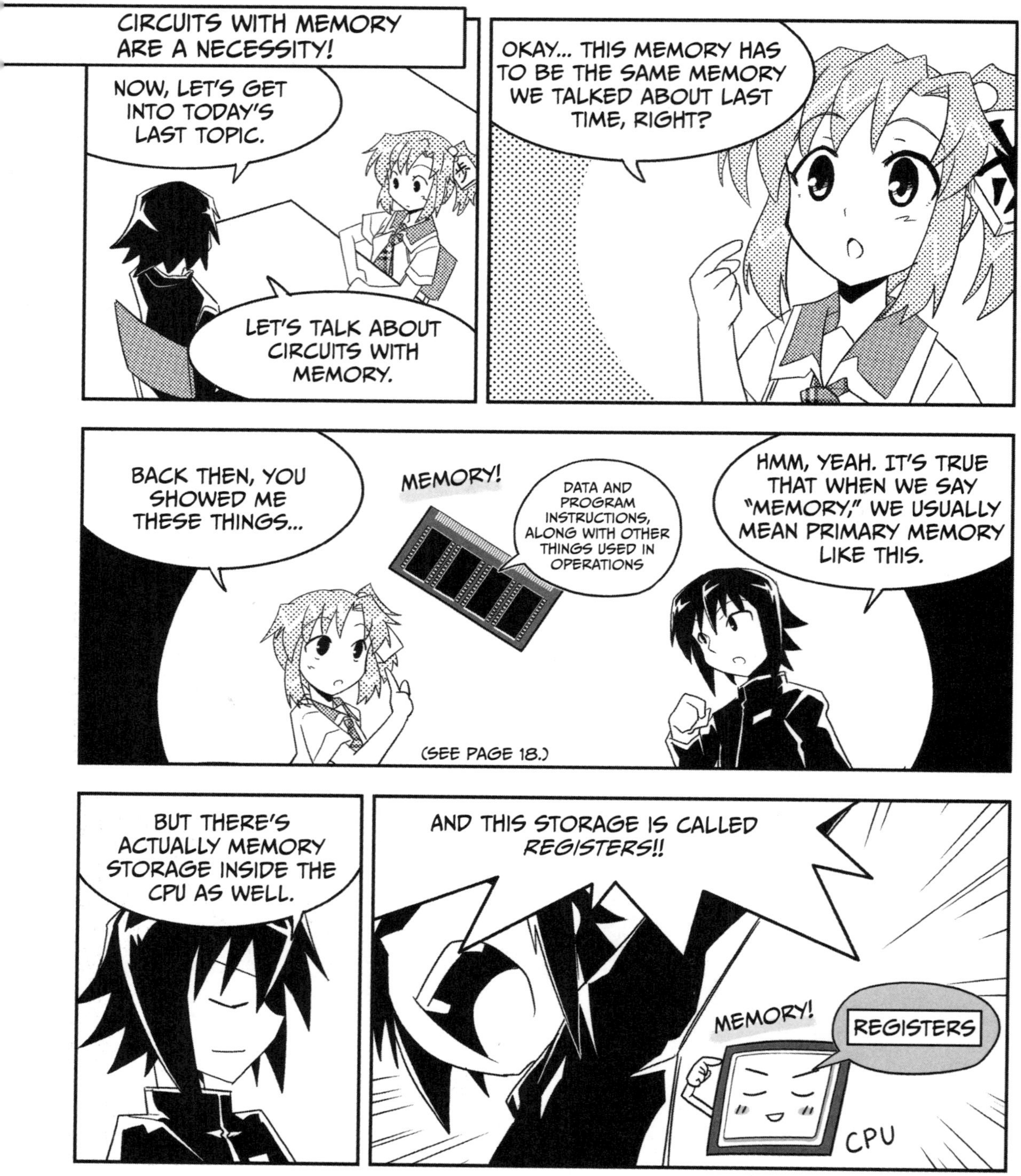

CIRCUITS WITH MEMORY ARE A NECESSITY!
NOW, LET'S GET INTO TODAY'S LAST TOPIC.
LET'S TALK ABOUT CIRCUITS WITH MEMORY.
OKAY... THIS MEMORY HAS TO BE THE SAME MEMORY WE TALKED ABOUT LAST TIME, RIGHT?
BACK THEN, YOU SHOWED ME THESE THINGS...
MEMORY!
DATA AND PROGRAM INSTRUCTIONS, ALONG WITH OTHER THINGS USED IN OPERATIONS
HMM, YEAH. IT'S TRUE THAT WHEN WE SAY "MEMORY," WE USUALLY MEAN PRIMARY MEMORY LIKE THIS.
(SEE PAGE 18.)
BUT THERE'S ACTUALLY MEMORY STORAGE INSIDE THE CPU AS WELL.
AND THIS STORAGE IS CALLED *REGISTERS*!!
MEMORY!
REGISTERS
CPU

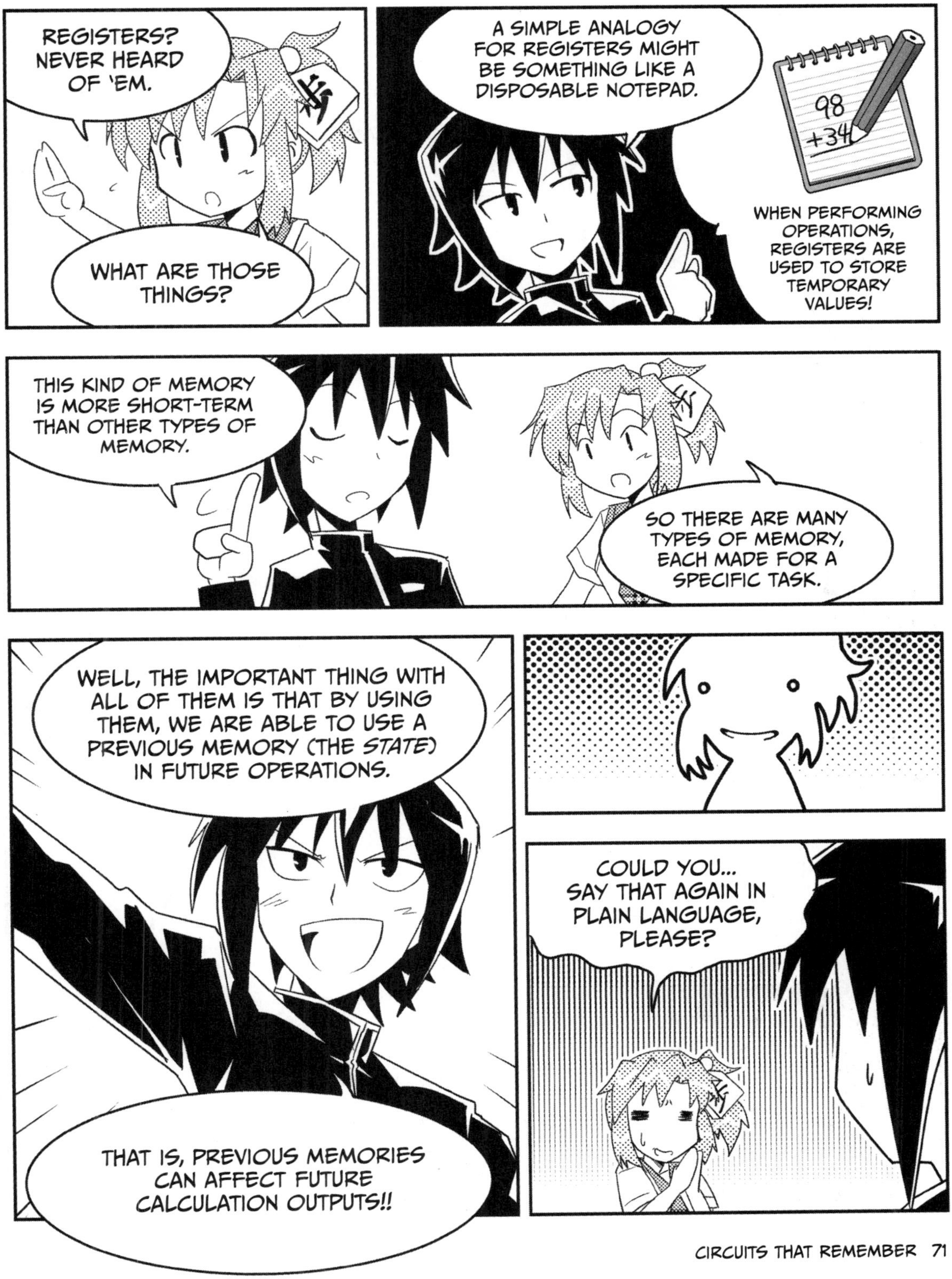
REGISTERS? NEVER HEARD OF 'EM.
WHAT ARE THOSE THINGS?
A SIMPLE ANALOGY FOR REGISTERS MIGHT BE SOMETHING LIKE A DISPOSABLE NOTEPAD.
98
+34
WHEN PERFORMING OPERATIONS, REGISTERS ARE USED TO STORE TEMPORARY VALUES!
THIS KIND OF MEMORY IS MORE SHORT-TERM THAN OTHER TYPES OF MEMORY.
SO THERE ARE MANY TYPES OF MEMORY, EACH MADE FOR A SPECIFIC TASK.
WELL, THE IMPORTANT THING WITH ALL OF THEM IS THAT BY USING THEM, WE ARE ABLE TO USE A PREVIOUS MEMORY (THE *STATE*) IN FUTURE OPERATIONS.
THAT IS, PREVIOUS MEMORIES CAN AFFECT FUTURE CALCULATION OUTPUTS!!
COULD YOU... SAY THAT AGAIN IN PLAIN LANGUAGE, PLEASE?

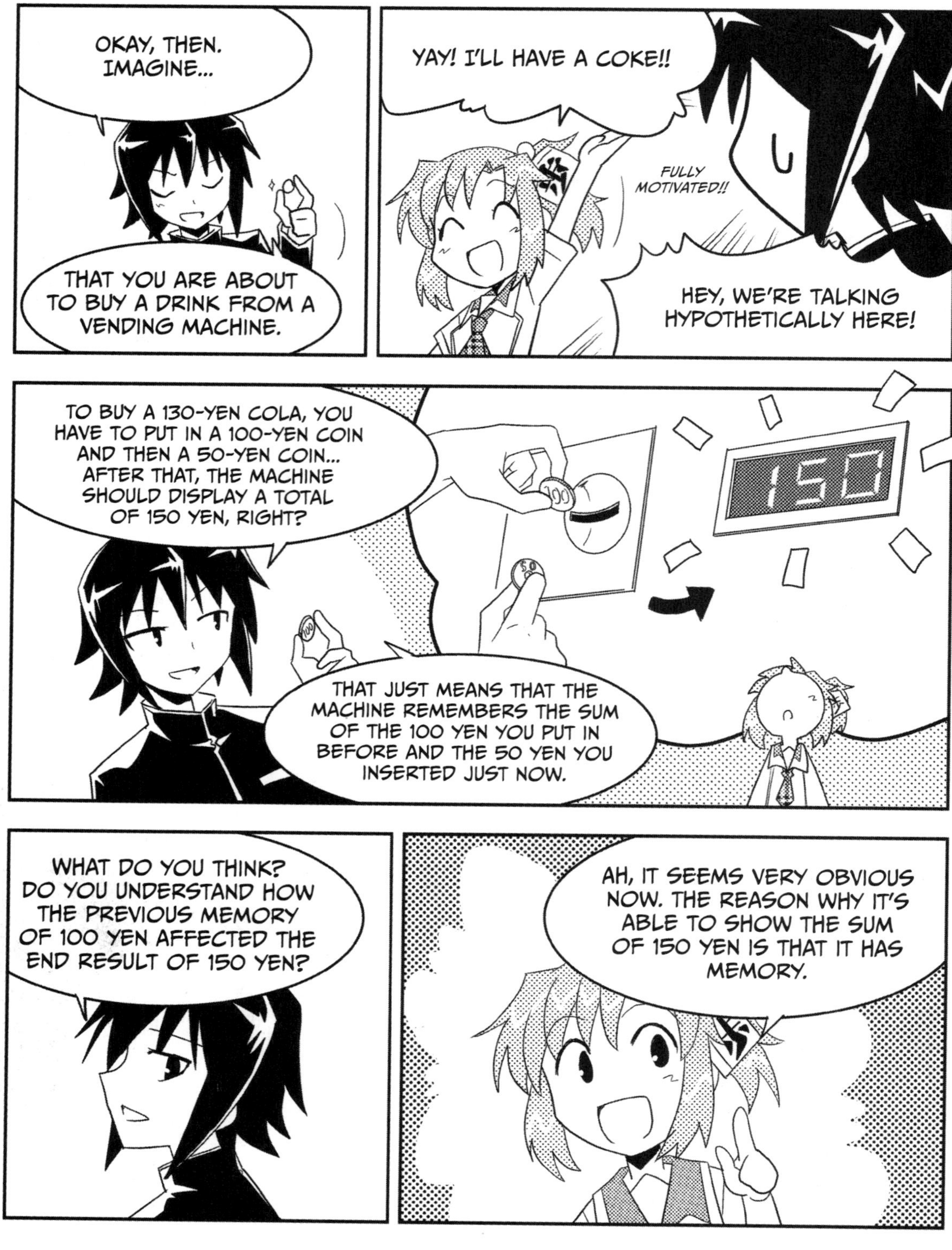
OKAY, THEN. IMAGINE...
THAT YOU ARE ABOUT TO BUY A DRINK FROM A VENDING MACHINE.
YAY! I'LL HAVE A COKE!!
FULLY MOTIVATED!!
HEY, WE'RE TALKING HYPOTHETICALLY HERE!
TO BUY A 130-YEN COLA, YOU HAVE TO PUT IN A 100-YEN COIN AND THEN A 50-YEN COIN... AFTER THAT, THE MACHINE SHOULD DISPLAY A TOTAL OF 150 YEN, RIGHT?
150
THAT JUST MEANS THAT THE MACHINE REMEMBERS THE SUM OF THE 100 YEN YOU PUT IN BEFORE AND THE 50 YEN YOU INSERTED JUST NOW.
WHAT DO YOU THINK? DO YOU UNDERSTAND HOW THE PREVIOUS MEMORY OF 100 YEN AFFECTED THE END RESULT OF 150 YEN?
AH, IT SEEMS VERY OBVIOUS NOW. THE REASON WHY IT'S ABLE TO SHOW THE SUM OF 150 YEN IS THAT IT HAS MEMORY.

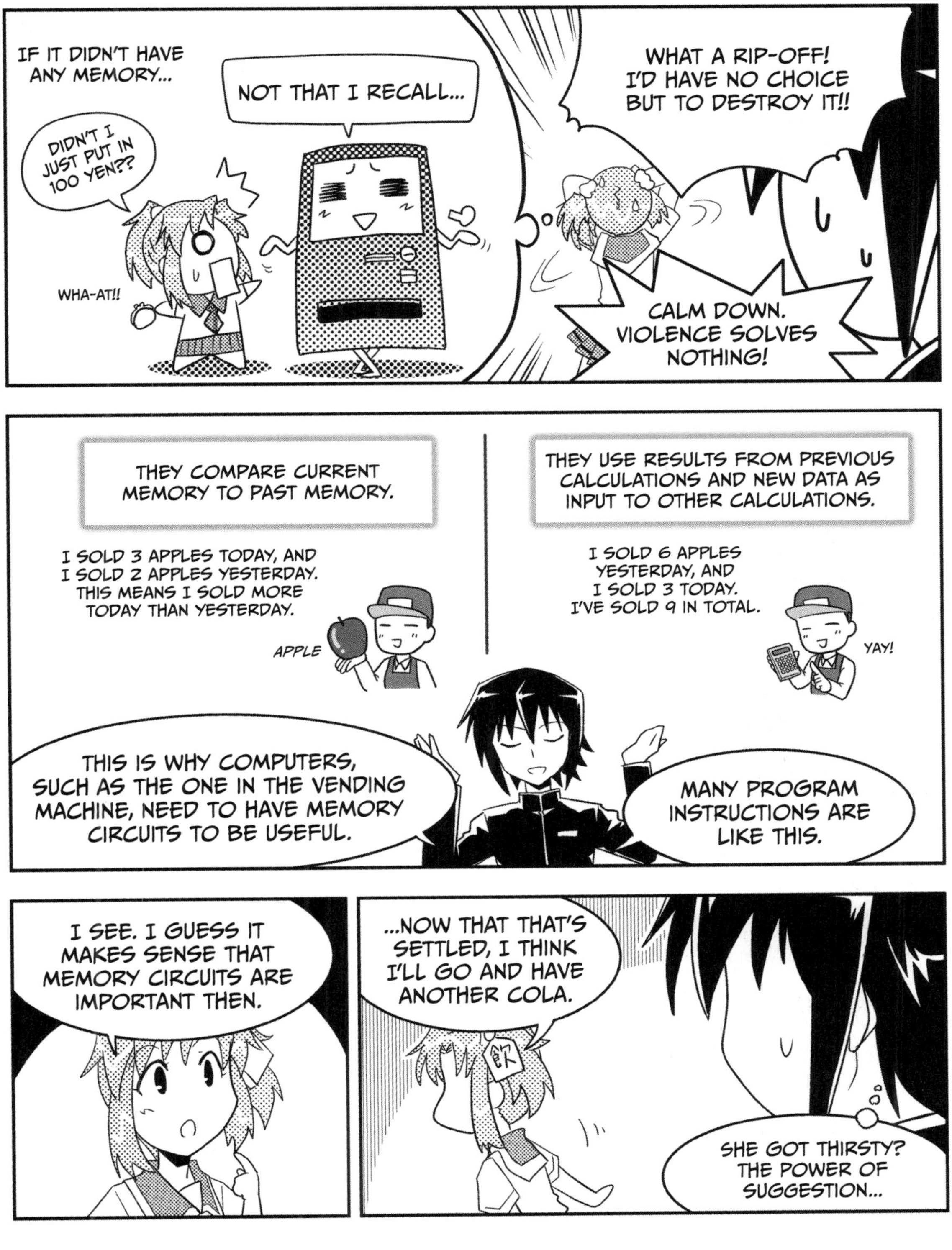
IF IT DIDN'T HAVE ANY MEMORY...
DIDN'T I JUST PUT IN 100 YEN??
WHA-AT!!
NOT THAT I RECALL...
WHAT A RIP-OFF! I'D HAVE NO CHOICE BUT TO DESTROY IT!!
CALM DOWN. VIOLENCE SOLVES NOTHING!
THEY COMPARE CURRENT MEMORY TO PAST MEMORY.
I SOLD 3 APPLES TODAY, AND I SOLD 2 APPLES YESTERDAY. THIS MEANS I SOLD MORE TODAY THAN YESTERDAY.
APPLE
THEY USE RESULTS FROM PREVIOUS CALCULATIONS AND NEW DATA AS INPUT TO OTHER CALCULATIONS.
I SOLD 6 APPLES YESTERDAY, AND I SOLD 3 TODAY. I'VE SOLD 9 IN TOTAL.
YAY!
THIS IS WHY COMPUTERS, SUCH AS THE ONE IN THE VENDING MACHINE, NEED TO HAVE MEMORY CIRCUITS TO BE USEFUL.
MANY PROGRAM INSTRUCTIONS ARE LIKE THIS.
I SEE. I GUESS IT MAKES SENSE THAT MEMORY CIRCUITS ARE IMPORTANT THEN.
...NOW THAT THAT'S SETTLED, I THINK I'LL GO AND HAVE ANOTHER COLA.
SHE GOT THIRSTY? THE POWER OF SUGGESTION...

FLIP-FLOP: THE BASICS OF MEMORY CIRCUITS

Ngh. I can't even imagine a circuit that has memory. Even human memory is really complicated, you know. . . .

Yeah. You have to think really simply. Computers can only use 1s and 0s, right? That means that to a computer, *memory* means somehow storing the states of 1s and 0s.

I've already explained that these 1s and 0s actually correspond to different voltage levels (low and high) (see page 37). This means that to save a 1, we would have to create something that can retain that state over a longer period of time, as in the graph below. We call storing data like this *latching*.

STATE REMAINS 1
(H) 1
(L) 0
TIME
SO THIS IS A LATCH THEN!

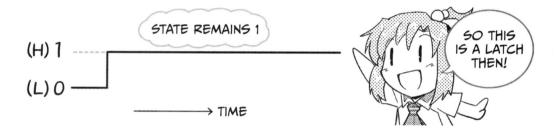

I see. But it's probably not very useful if it just stays in that state forever. What if I want it to go back to 0 later on or I want to overwrite the memory with something else? Wouldn't it make sense to be able to store whatever I want, whenever I want?

Yeah, that's right! For example, if you turn on a room's light switch, it would stay on until someone turns it off again, and then it would stay off until someone turns it on again. It would be great if we could create some kind of *trigger condition* to freely swap the 1 and 0 states, just as we do with the light switch.

That is, we would like to be able to store 1s and 0s indefinitely while still being able to flip each bit individually whenever we want. This is exactly what memory circuits do!

Um, that sounds a bit selfish, doesn't it? I want to store 1s and 0s, but I also want to be able to flip them at will.

It is selfish, but *flip-flop* circuits are a basic component of any memory circuit.

Flip-flop . . . that's a cute name, but how are they useful?

They're super useful!! They grant us the ability to change states. First, take a look at the picture below. To make it easier to understand, I've put the flip-flop in its own box. Using one of these, we can store one bit of data.

IMPORTANT!
Q
$\bar{Q}$
INPUTS
OUTPUTS

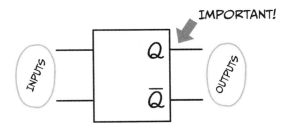

The reason why there are no concrete symbols for the inputs is that they change depending on the type of flip-flop we use.

Okay. There are inputs. . . . And two outputs Q and $\bar{Q}$ . . .

Yes. Pay special attention to the Q output! This is the output that will stay either 1 or 0. Q will always be the inverse of $\bar{Q}$. So, if Q is 1, then $\bar{Q}$ will be 0. $\bar{Q}$ can be very useful to have when designing a circuit, but we're going to ignore it for now.

Uh-huh. Then how does it work? Tell me what's inside that box!

All in good time. First off, there are several types of flip-flops. Both the function and circuit depend on the type. Out of these types, I'll teach you about RS flip-flops, D flip-flops, and T flip-flops.

THE RS FLIP-FLOP

 Okay, I guess *RS flip-flops* come first. So the box has two input signals, R and S. Rice . . . sushi . . . rice and sushi?!

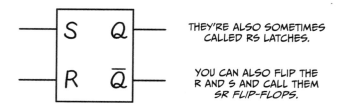

THEY'RE ALSO SOMETIMES CALLED RS LATCHES.

YOU CAN ALSO FLIP THE R AND S AND CALL THEM SR FLIP-FLOPS.

 Um, no. *R* means *reset* and *S* means *set*. The reset and set inputs are the two main features of this type of circuit.

I might be jumping to the main point too quickly here, but setting S to 1 will set Q to 1 and setting R to 1 will reset Q to 0. Once Q has changed state, removing the input signal won't change it back. It will keep that state until the countersignal (S for R and vice versa) is sent. As soon as that happens it will, of course, flip the saved state back.

 Hmm, so that means that it remembers which of the two got set to 1 last? If S got set to 1 most recently, then the latch remembers 1, and if R was the last 1, it remembers 0! Is that it?

 Yeah. It might seem a bit complicated here, but the circuit looks like the figure on the next page. In accordance with De Morgan's laws (see page 60), it can be created using either NAND gates or NOR gates.

 Whoa. It looks a bit weird. . . . There are two NAND gates (or NOR gates), but they're all tangled up in figure eights.

 Yep! The two circuits are interconnected, with the output of one acting as one of the inputs of the other.

$\overline{S}$
$\overline{R}$
Q
$\overline{Q}$
$\overline{S}$
$\overline{R}$
Q
$\overline{Q}$

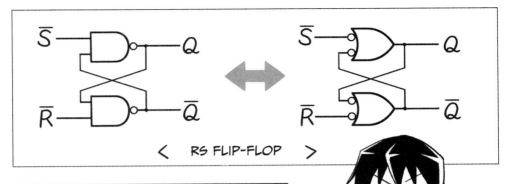

< RS FLIP-FLOP >

INPUTS		OUTPUTS		FUNCTION
$\overline{S}$	$\overline{R}$	Q	$\overline{Q}$	
1	1	DOES NOT CHANGE		RETAINS ITS CURRENT OUTPUT
0	1	1	0	SET
1	0	0	1	RESET
0	0	1	1	NOT ALLOWED

NOTE THAT S AND R HAVE NEGATION SYMBOLS! THIS IS CALLED *ACTIVE-LOW*, AND IT MEANS THEY ARE ACTIVATED WHEN THE INPUT VOLTAGE IS LOW (0) INSTEAD OF HIGH (1).

It's thanks to this figure eight that the circuit is able to retain either a 1 or a 0. We call this a *latch*. You could say this figure eight is the most important characteristic of a memory circuit!

Hmm, even so, it's pretty complex. If I look back and forth between the schematic and the truth table, I get the feeling I kind of get it, but still. . . .

Let's see, the part of the truth table that says "does not change" means that output Q either stays a 1 or a 0 indefinitely, right? But what does the "not allowed" on the bottom mean? What's not allowed?!

Ah, yeah. That just means that you are not allowed to trigger both set and reset at the same time. Remember that since the circuit is active-low, this means that both inputs can't be 0 at the same time. If you were to set both to 0, this would make both Q and $\overline{Q}$ output 1 until you changed one of them back—but the outputs are always supposed to be either 0 and 1, or 1 and 0. It's not allowed to invalidate the rules we set for this logic circuit.

Oh, I see. So just follow the traffic, er, circuit rules, right?

THE D FLIP-FLOP AND THE CLOCK

 Let's see. The next one is the *D flip-flop*. The inputs are D and . . . what's this triangle next to the C?! It looks like that piece of cloth Japanese ghosts wear on their headbands!!

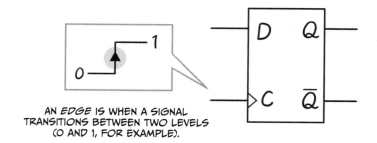

AN *EDGE* IS WHEN A SIGNAL
TRANSITIONS BETWEEN TWO LEVELS
(0 AND 1, FOR EXAMPLE).

 That observation is pretty far removed from the computer world. But I suppose it's a bit cryptic and warrants an explanation. First off, it's easiest to think of the *D* as standing for *data*. That triangle is the symbol for a rising edge, and the *C* stands for *clock*.

 Um . . . Rising edge?? And the clock—is that just a normal clock?

 That's right! Computers need some kind of fixed-interval digital signal to synchronize all the operational states in their circuits. That's what the clock does!

Just like a normal clock measuring time, it flips between high and low voltage (1 and 0) in fixed intervals. It has nothing to do with the circuit's input or output though—it's completely separate.

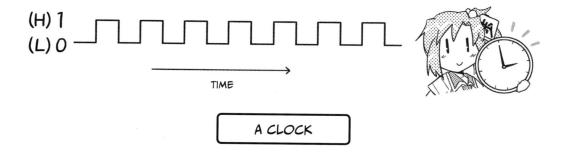

A CLOCK

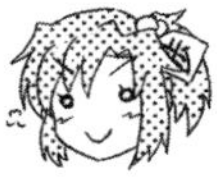

Hmm. It really reminds me of a clock . . . tick-tock, tick-tock. . . . Just like we plan our days with the help of clocks, I guess circuits need them, too.

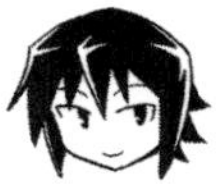

Yeah. When a circuit needs to take some action, the clock can sometimes act as its cue. Inside the clock, what is known as the rising edge acts as that *action signal*. Have a look!

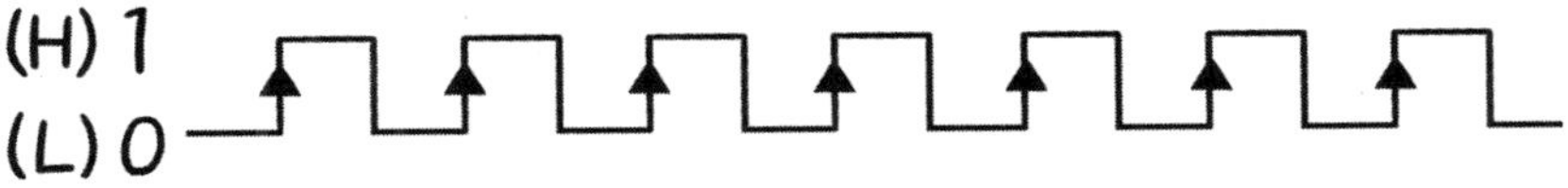

(H) 1
(L) 0

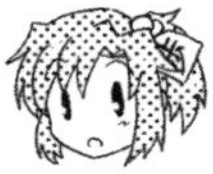

Ohh! Those arrows are at even intervals on the clock graph.

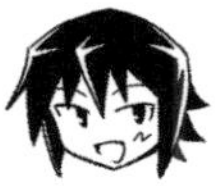

When the clock goes from low to high (0 to 1), we see a *rising edge*, and when it goes back from high to low (1 to 0), we see a *falling edge*.

RISING EDGE	FALLING EDGE
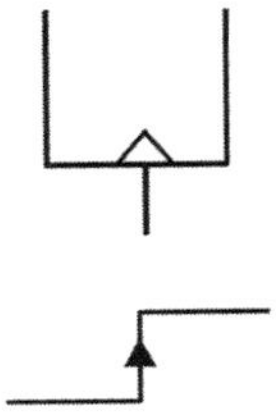	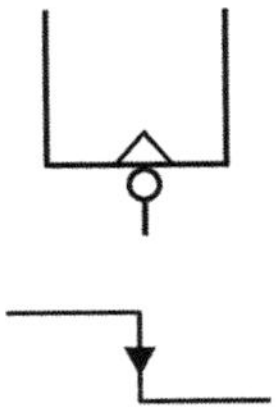
WHEN THE CLOCK GOES FROM LOW TO HIGH	WHEN THE CLOCK GOES FROM HIGH TO LOW

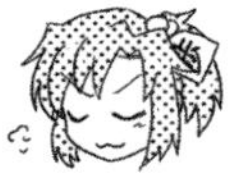

Oho, I think I get it. So the rising and falling edges are like ringing bells on the clock, right? When the bell rings, it acts as a signal to take action, like at the start and end of class, for example.

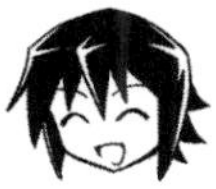

That's just it! That's a pretty good analogy coming from you.

Okay, let's get back to the problem. In a D flip-flop, every time a rising edge passes, the D input 1 or 0 is copied directly to the Q output.

It might be easier to understand by looking at the timing diagram below. A timing diagram is a good way to see how signals change their state over time.

D
H
L
H
CLK
(CLOCK)
COPY!
Q
H
L
H

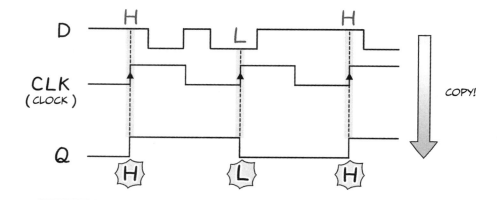

The important lesson here is that the D input can change as much as it wants, but Q won't change until a rising edge arrives!

Mmmh. It's a bit complicated, but I think I get it now that I've looked over the timing diagram. In any case, the main characteristic of the D flip-flop seems to be that it acts in sync with the clock's rising edges! Hmm, it seems like clocks are super important both to modern man and circuits.

THE T FLIP-FLOP AND COUNTERS

0
1
2
3
4
Q0
Q1
Q2
Q
T
Q̄

So the last one is the T flip-flop. Wait, it has only one input! Did you forget to draw the rest?

T
Q
Q̄

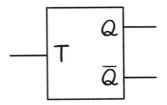

Fuhahaha! Like I would ever forget! The *T flip-flop* has only one input, as you can see, and is pretty simple. Whenever the input T changes from 0 to 1, or 1 to 0, the output stored in Q flips state. It looks something like this time chart.

0→1
0→1
0→1
INPUT T
OUTPUT Q
FLIP
FLIP
FLIP

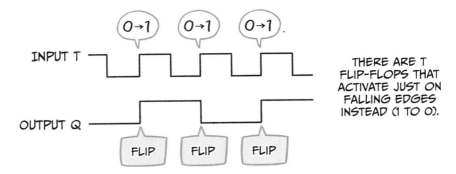

THERE ARE T FLIP-FLOPS THAT ACTIVATE JUST ON FALLING EDGES INSTEAD (1 TO 0).

Oh, this was super easy to understand! It's a memory circuit even though it has only one input.

By the way, flipping between 1 and 0 is called *toggling*. The *T* in T flip-flop actually stands for *toggle*! Also, by connecting several T flip-flops, as in the following schematic, you can make a circuit that can count—a *counter circuit*.

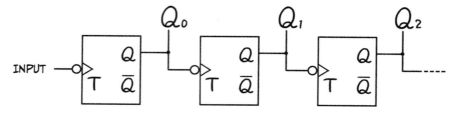

**SEVERAL T FLIP-FLOPS TOGGLED BY THE FALLING
EDGE OF AN INPUT SIGNAL CAN ACT AS A COUNTER.**

COUNTER CIRCUITS

The first flip-flop will toggle its output state every time the input on the far left changes from high to low. Consequently, the second flip-flop will toggle its output whenever the first flip-flop's output changes from high to low. All following outputs will keep toggling in this pattern. If the input signal is connected to a clock, then each flip-flop in the series will toggle every $2^{(n-1)}$ clock cycles if n is the flip-flop's position in the series. Put another way, the period of each flip-flop's output signal will be $2n$ of the original signal's period.

Counters that work this way are called *asynchronous counters*, since not all flip-flops are connected to the same clock but, instead, each flip-flop's clock after the first is the output signal of the flip-flop that came before. In contrast, there is a circuit commonly found in CPUs called a *synchronous counter*. As the name here implies, all flip-flops in this type of counter trigger on the signal from the same clock, meaning they all toggle at the same time, in parallel. It's worth mentioning that I've simplified these descriptions to make them easier to understand.

Umm, but why do we say that the circuit can count?

Looking at the time chart, do you see that each output signal has half as many toggles as its input signal? This means that the period of the output signals is twice as long as the period of the input signals. I've put all three of the flip-flops in the schematic above into this time chart so you can see all of their individual outputs next to each other when they are connected.

If you look at each column in this graph individually, you should see that the digits from Q_2, Q_1, and Q_0 form binary numbers! Isn't it cool that every time we have a falling edge on the input of the first T flip-flop, this binary number increases by 1? It's counting!

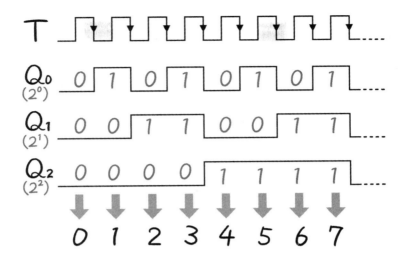

$$T \quad \text{(clock signal)}$$

$$Q_0 \; (2^0) \quad 0 \;\; 1 \;\; 0 \;\; 1 \;\; 0 \;\; 1 \;\; 0 \;\; 1 \quad \ldots$$

$$Q_1 \; (2^1) \quad 0 \;\; 0 \;\; 1 \;\; 1 \;\; 0 \;\; 0 \;\; 1 \;\; 1 \quad \ldots$$

$$Q_2 \; (2^2) \quad 0 \;\; 0 \;\; 0 \;\; 0 \;\; 1 \;\; 1 \;\; 1 \;\; 1 \quad \ldots$$

$$0 \quad 1 \quad 2 \quad 3 \quad 4 \quad 5 \quad 6 \quad 7$$

Wow, you're right! Q_2 corresponds to the 2^2 digit, Q_1 to 2^1, and Q_0 to 2^0, right?

If you look at Q_2, Q_1, and Q_0 in order, the first column forms 000 (the number 0), the second one 001 (1), the third 010 (2), and the fourth 011 (3) in binary. So using this technique, you can actually make the circuit count! That's a really smart design.

Yeah. In this example, we used three flip-flops, so that lets us express 2^3 (8) numbers, meaning we can count from zero to seven.

You can actually make counters from other types of flip-flops, like D flip-flops, for example. Using some other tricks, you can also make circuits that count down, if you want.

Oh, that seems like it could be really useful for a lot of things.

Yeah, well that's it for flip-flops. Just don't forget what I said at the start: flip-flops are the foundation of any memory circuit!

This means that both primary memory and CPU registers use flip-flops at their core. And flip-flops are also the basis of any counter circuit, just like what we just talked about.

Haha, so they're the base for a lot of different devices, basically. And even though they have a cute name, they're super useful circuits we can't do without!

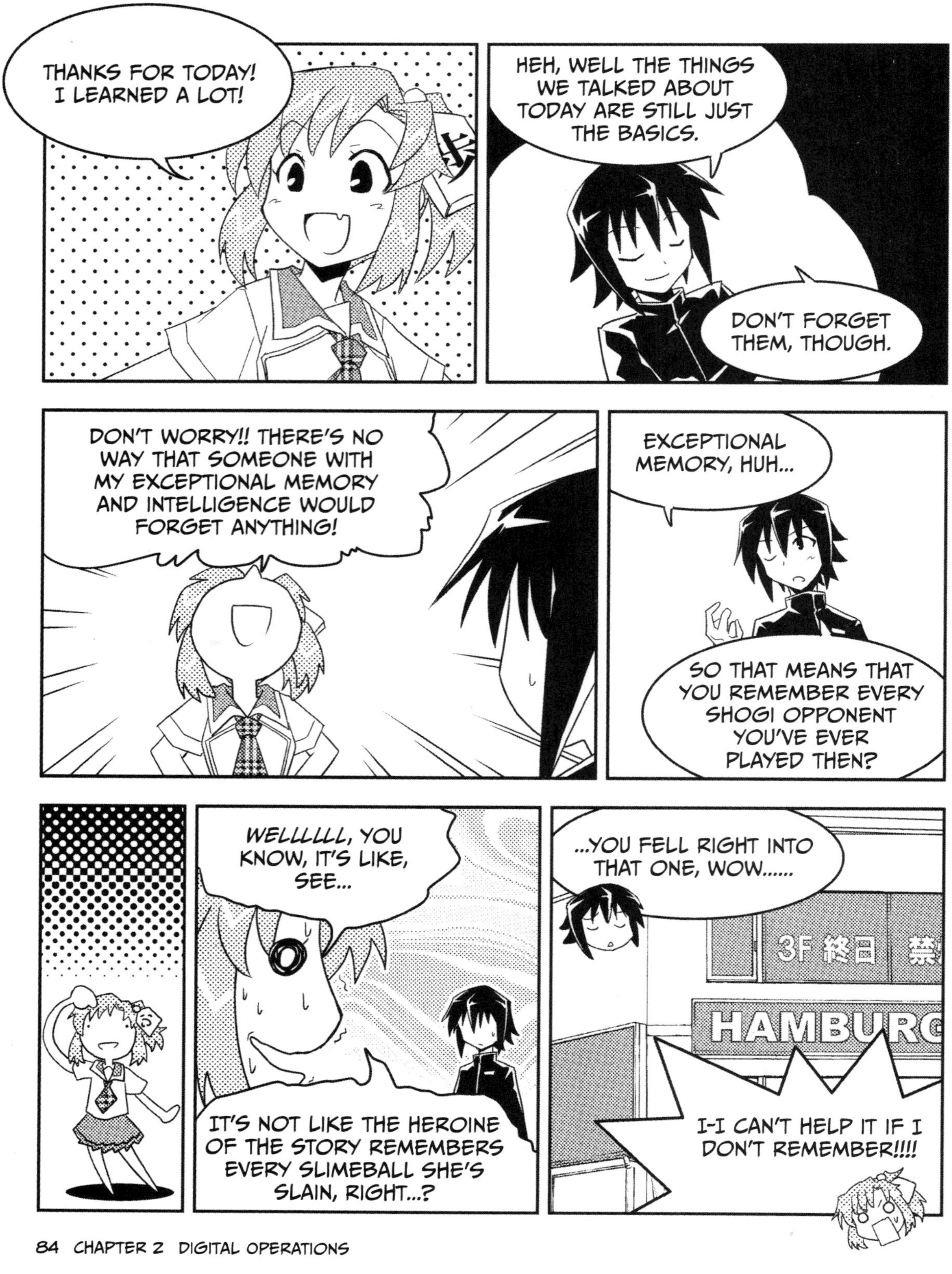
THANKS FOR TODAY! I LEARNED A LOT!
HEH, WELL THE THINGS WE TALKED ABOUT TODAY ARE STILL JUST THE BASICS.
DON'T FORGET THEM, THOUGH.
DON'T WORRY!! THERE'S NO WAY THAT SOMEONE WITH MY EXCEPTIONAL MEMORY AND INTELLIGENCE WOULD FORGET ANYTHING!
EXCEPTIONAL MEMORY, HUH...
SO THAT MEANS THAT YOU REMEMBER EVERY SHOGI OPPONENT YOU'VE EVER PLAYED THEN?
WELLLLLL, YOU KNOW, IT'S LIKE, SEE...
IT'S NOT LIKE THE HEROINE OF THE STORY REMEMBERS EVERY SLIMEBALL SHE'S SLAIN, RIGHT...?
...YOU FELL RIGHT INTO THAT ONE, WOW......
3F 終日
HAMBURG
I-I CAN'T HELP IT IF I DON'T REMEMBER!!!!

MODERN CIRCUIT DESIGN: CAD AND FPGA

Multipurpose integrated circuit design is surprisingly similar to software development these days. It's usually accomplished using a *hardware description language (HDL)* to define the operation of a circuit.

In the past, circuits were drawn using logical circuit symbols, much like the ones we have shown in this book, but these symbols are now used mostly for very simple circuits. The development of *computer-aided design (CAD) programs* allows people to design complicated circuits with relative ease.

But, it's important to learn the basics. It can be useful to know these symbols if you're trying to figure out how data flows through a digital circuit or when you're trying to understand a particular feature of some schematic.

At the dawn of CPU development, it was common to create reference circuits consisting of many AND, OR, and NOT gates. These were then used when iterating, prototyping, and evaluating new generations of CPUs and other ICs.

By doing this, it was possible to test each function of the advanced circuit individually and even hardwire the circuits together to try to work out problems in the design if some error was detected.

Nowadays, reference circuits like these are rarely used in development. Instead much more flexible *field-programmable gate array (FPGA) circuits* are preferred.

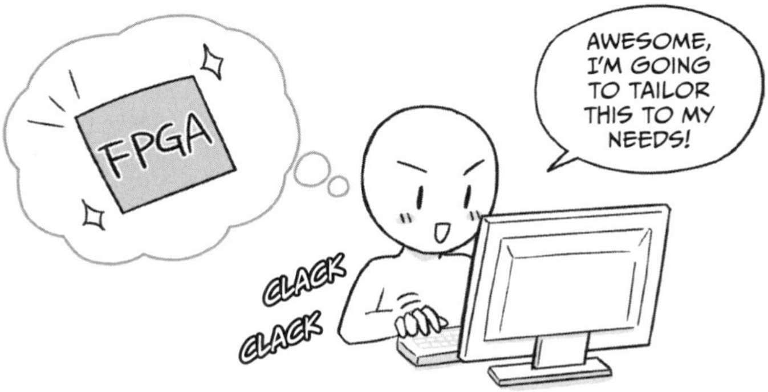
FPGA
AWESOME, I'M GOING TO TAILOR THIS TO MY NEEDS!
CLACK
CLACK

FPGAs CAN, JUST AS THE NAME SUGGESTS, BE REPROGRAMMED "IN THE FIELD" TO CHANGE THE FUNCTION OF THE IC COMPLETELY. THEY ARE INDISPENSABLE TO CIRCUIT DESIGNERS.

FPGAs consist of a series of logic blocks that can be wired together in different ways depending on the programming. Some of these blocks contain lookup tables to map the 4–6 bits of input to output in a format that's similar to a truth table. The number of lookup tables in an FPGA can range anywhere from a few hundred to more than several million, depending on the FPGA model.

And of course, it's possible to reprogram all of the tables whenever needed. In this way, the same FPGA circuit can be used to perform the functions of many different types of ICs. You can simulate the function of a CPU using an FPGA if you want to, but it's a lot cheaper and easier to mass-produce a dedicated circuit instead. Even so, since the price of FPGAs is dropping and development costs for new ICs are high, if the life span or projected sales of a particular IC are not high enough, it might be more cost-effective to simply use an FPGA.

3

CPU ARCHITECTURE

AYUMI

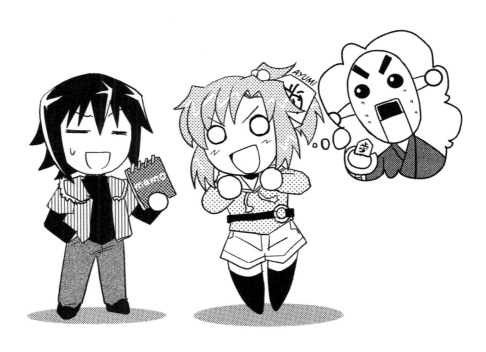

All About Memory and the CPU

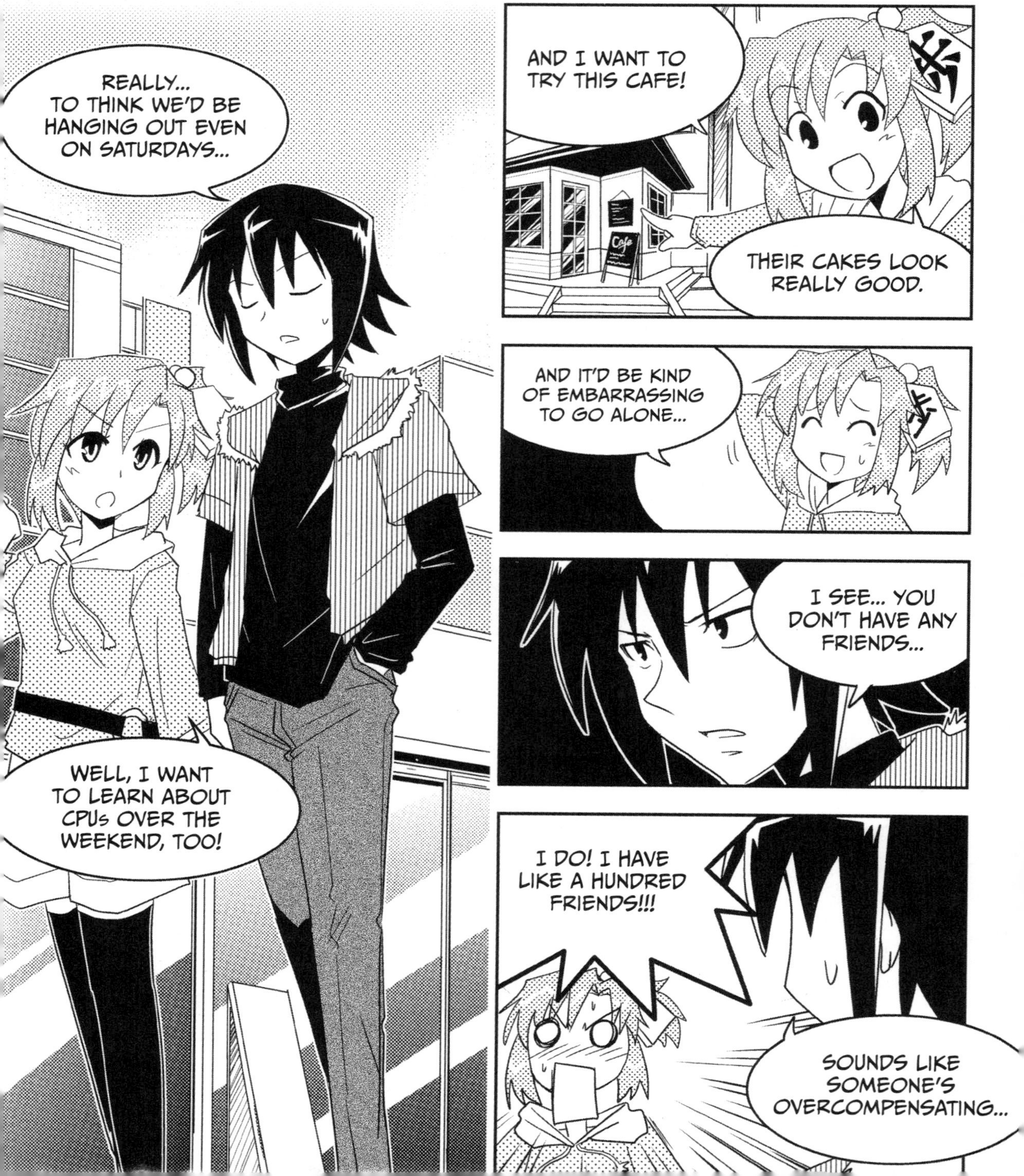
REALLY... TO THINK WE'D BE HANGING OUT EVEN ON SATURDAYS...
WELL, I WANT TO LEARN ABOUT CPUs OVER THE WEEKEND, TOO!
AND I WANT TO TRY THIS CAFE!
THEIR CAKES LOOK REALLY GOOD.
Cafe
AND IT'D BE KIND OF EMBARRASSING TO GO ALONE...
I SEE... YOU DON'T HAVE ANY FRIENDS...
I DO! I HAVE LIKE A HUNDRED FRIENDS!!!
SOUNDS LIKE SOMEONE'S OVERCOMPENSATING...

MEMORY HAS ASSIGNED ADDRESSES

WELL THEN...

DO YOU KNOW WHAT ADDRESSES ARE?

OF COURSE I DO! LIKE I WOULDN'T KNOW WHERE MY FRIENDS LIVE!!

LIE

UH, I WASN'T TALKING ABOUT MAILING ADDRESSES.

YOU SEE, LOCATIONS IN MEMORY...

...ARE CALLED ADDRESSES.

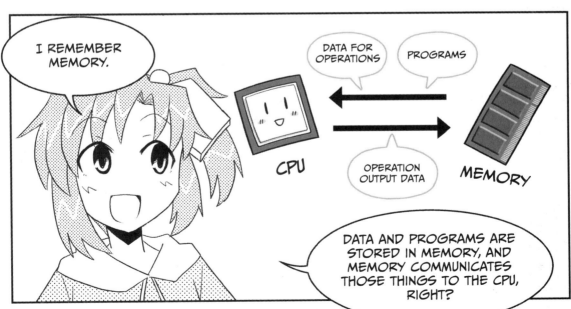

I REMEMBER MEMORY.

DATA FOR OPERATIONS

PROGRAMS

CPU

OPERATION OUTPUT DATA

MEMORY

DATA AND PROGRAMS ARE STORED IN MEMORY, AND MEMORY COMMUNICATES THOSE THINGS TO THE CPU, RIGHT?

THAT'S RIGHT.

PROGRAMS AND DATA ARE SAVED TO MEMORY IN AN ORGANIZED WAY.

EVERYTHING IS ASSIGNED A UNIQUE ADDRESS DEPENDING ON WHERE IT IS STORED.

《 INSIDE MEMORY 》

ADDRESS	TYPE
0	INSTRUCTION
1	INSTRUCTION
2	INSTRUCTION
3	INSTRUCTION
4	INSTRUCTION
⋮	⋮
30	DATA
31	DATA
32	DATA
33	DATA
⋮	⋮

PROGRAMS

DATA FOR USE IN OPERATIONS

YOU'RE RIGHT!! EVERYTHING HAS A UNIQUE ADDRESS AND IS NEATLY SORTED IN ORDER.

YOU SHOULD ALSO REMEMBER THAT THE CPU...

HAS FULL CONTROL OVER THIS *ADDRESS SPACE*, WHICH CAN ALSO BE CALLED *MEMORY SPACE*.

ADDRESS	TYPE
0	INSTRUCTION
1	INSTRUCTION
2	INSTRUCTION
3	INSTRUCTION
4	INSTRUCTION
⋮	⋮
30	DATA
31	DATA
32	DATA
33	DATA
⋮	⋮

ADDRESS SPACE (MEMORY SPACE)

UH-HUH. SO THE CPU CONTROLS THE MEMORY SPACE...

AND IF IT CAN READ AND WRITE WHEREVER IT WANTS...

DOESN'T THAT MAKE THE CPU LOOK KIND OF LIKE A BAD GUY?

CPU

HEH HEH HEH...

I CLAIM DOMINION OVER THIS MEMORY...

ADDRESS SPACE (MEMORY SPACE)

ADDRESS	TYPE
0	INSTRUCTION
1	INSTRUCTION
2	INSTRUCTION
3	INSTRUCTION
4	INSTRUCTION
⋮	⋮
30	DATA
31	DATA
32	DATA
33	DATA
⋮	⋮

YOU HAVE A PRETTY DARK IMAGINATION.

BUT WHY DO DATA NEED ADDRESSES?

HOW IS ASSIGNING THEM NUMBERS USEFUL?

HEH... DON'T YOU SEE?

ADDRESSES MAKE IT POSSIBLE TO FIND DATA JUST BY POINTING TO THE CORRECT NUMBER.

ACTUALLY, THIS IS HOW THE CPU ACCESSES ALL DATA AND PROGRAMS (OR STORES THEM, FOR THAT MATTER)...

BY POINTING TO AN ADDRESS!

NUMBER 83, PLEASE!

OKAY!

CPU

ADDRESS POINTER

MEMORY

OH, IT JUST SENDS THE NUMBER ALONG!

I GUESS USING NUMBERS IS PRETTY PRACTICAL AND EASY TO UNDERSTAND.

BUT IT SEEMS SO MECHANICAL AND COLD... DEVOID OF HUMANITY...

WELL, IT IS A MACHINE, YOU KNOW.

DATA PASSES THROUGH THE BUS

WELL SINCE WE ALREADY TALKED ABOUT ADDRESSES, LET'S ALSO TALK A BIT ABOUT THE *BUS*.

THE BUS...?

YEAH, IT ACTUALLY COMES FROM THE WORD *OMNIBUS*.

BUT THE KIND OF BUS WE'RE TALKING ABOUT IS A PATH THAT TRANSMITS DATA INSIDE A COMPUTER.

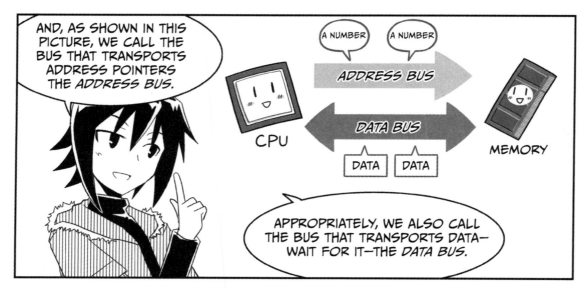

AND, AS SHOWN IN THIS PICTURE, WE CALL THE BUS THAT TRANSPORTS ADDRESS POINTERS THE *ADDRESS BUS*.

A NUMBER

A NUMBER

ADDRESS BUS

CPU

DATA BUS

DATA

DATA

MEMORY

APPROPRIATELY, WE ALSO CALL THE BUS THAT TRANSPORTS DATA— WAIT FOR IT—THE *DATA BUS*.

I SEE. SO THEY'RE KIND OF LIKE TWO ROUTES WITH COMPLETELY DIFFERENT PURPOSES.

YEAH, AND THERE ARE ALSO EXTERNAL BUSES AND THE INTERNAL DATA BUS.

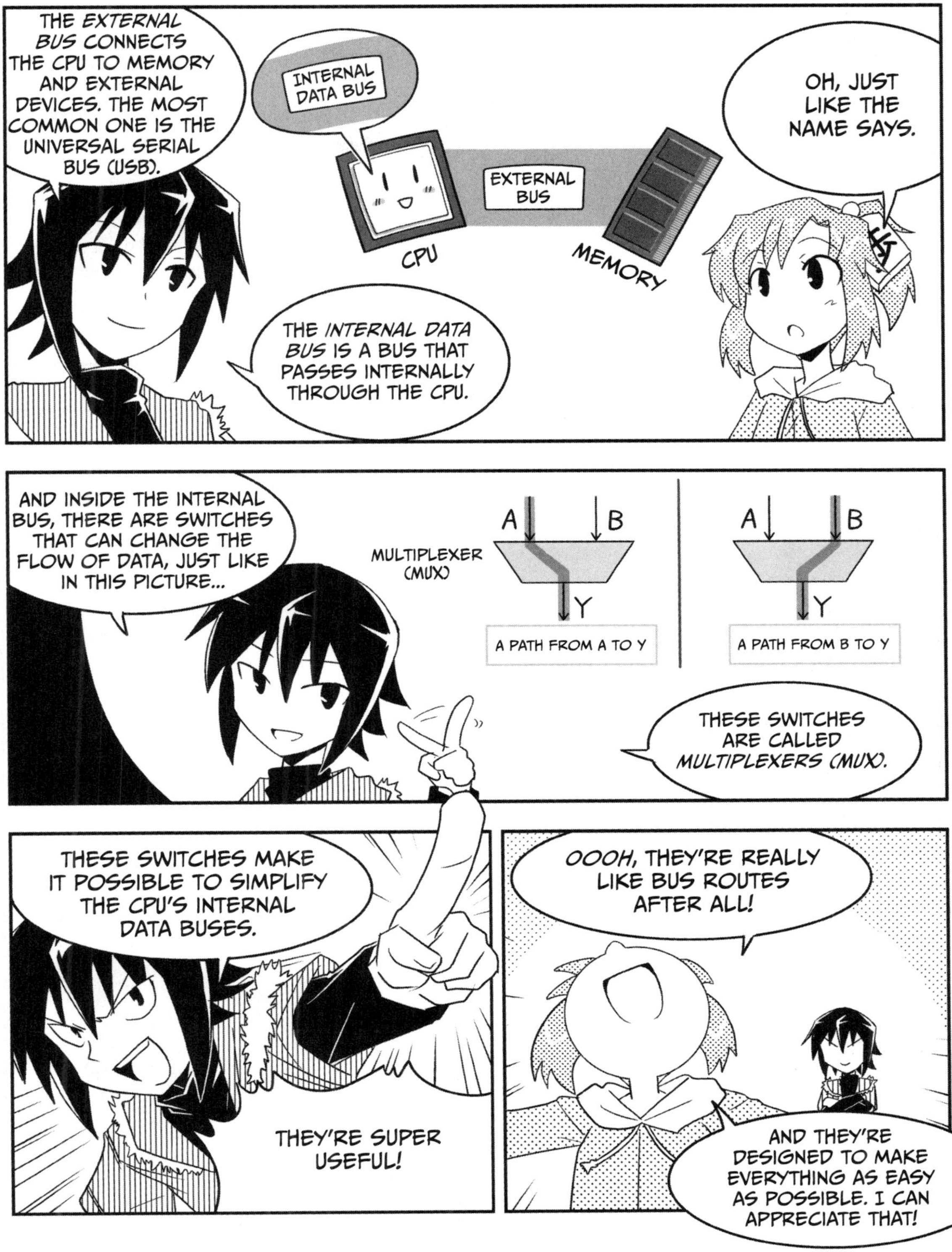

THE *EXTERNAL BUS* CONNECTS THE CPU TO MEMORY AND EXTERNAL DEVICES. THE MOST COMMON ONE IS THE UNIVERSAL SERIAL BUS (USB).
INTERNAL DATA BUS
EXTERNAL BUS
CPU
MEMORY
OH, JUST LIKE THE NAME SAYS.
THE *INTERNAL DATA BUS* IS A BUS THAT PASSES INTERNALLY THROUGH THE CPU.
AND INSIDE THE INTERNAL BUS, THERE ARE SWITCHES THAT CAN CHANGE THE FLOW OF DATA, JUST LIKE IN THIS PICTURE...
MULTIPLEXER (MUX)
A
B
Y
A PATH FROM A TO Y
A
B
Y
A PATH FROM B TO Y
THESE SWITCHES ARE CALLED *MULTIPLEXERS (MUX)*.
THESE SWITCHES MAKE IT POSSIBLE TO SIMPLIFY THE CPU'S INTERNAL DATA BUSES.
THEY'RE SUPER USEFUL!
OOOH, THEY'RE REALLY LIKE BUS ROUTES AFTER ALL!
AND THEY'RE DESIGNED TO MAKE EVERYTHING AS EASY AS POSSIBLE. I CAN APPRECIATE THAT!

BUS WIDTH AND BITS

WITH 4 BITS...
0000 0100 1000 1100
0001 0101 1001 1101
0010 0110 1010 1110
0011 0111 1011 1111
2^4 = 16 WIDE

Let's talk a bit more about buses. I said that buses are for transporting data, but to be more exact, they're actually *bundled signal pathways*.

Ah, signal pathways, I remember those from before. They're lines that transmit 1s and 0s, right?

That's right! And, the number of pathways determines how many values those pathways can represent. For example, if you have four pathways, and each can be a 0 or a 1, then those pathways can be used to send or receive a four-digit (four-bit) binary number.

FOUR SIGNAL PATHWAYS
1 (2^0) ONES
0 (2^1) TWOS
0 (2^2) FOURS
1 (2^8) EIGHTS
1001
4 BITS

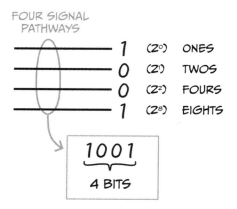

Uh-huh. So that means that the number of pathways equals the number of bits. With four pathways, we can send and receive 16 (2^4) different numbers from 0000 (0 in decimal) to 1111 (15 in decimal).

Hah! I think I might have figured out something important! Doesn't that mean that the more signal pathways you have, the better? If you can express larger numbers, that also has to mean you can process more data.

Heh heh heh, good guess. You're correct! We call the number of signal pathways (or bits) the *bus width*. A wider bus width gives the CPU faster processing capabilities.

For example, the ALU in the following diagram can process four-bit operations. This means that the data bus serving this ALU also has to be four bits wide.

1000
0010
4-BIT INPUTS
ALU
4-BIT OUTPUT
1010

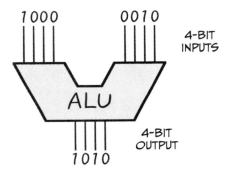

We chose 4 bits to make the diagram simpler, but most modern ALUs work with 64 bits. It makes sense to use a bus with a bus width that matches the ALU's data width, which means buses end up being 64 bits wide more often than not. In general, the 64-bit CPUs that you hear so much about have 64-bit ALUs and 64-bit data buses.

64-BIT CPU
64-BIT DATA WIDTH ALUs
64-BIT BUS WIDTH
64

It's worthwhile to point out that the data bus doesn't necessarily have to have the same width as the working bit length of the CPU. For example, in 1982, you could find 16-bit CPUs with 16-bit ALUs using an 8-bit wide data bus. This simply meant that you had to send data over the bus two times before the CPU could start doing any work.

Haha! So that just means that the CPU's performance is determined in part by the width of the data bus. And the wider the data bus, the better the CPU's performance!

You should try to remember these things about data bus width.

By looking at the width of the external bus between the CPU and memory, you can see how many bits can be sent between these two systems at once. By looking at the width of the internal data bus, you can see how many bits can be processed at the same time in a single operation.

 Okay! So data bus width is super important. Gotcha!

 That's it for now about data buses. Let's talk a bit about the address bus. By looking at the address bus width, you can see how large your system memory is. We call this the *address space size*.

 The address space size . . . ? Does that mean how many addresses there are? Then if the address bus has a width of 4 bits, wouldn't that give us 2^4, so a total of 16 different addresses?

 Yeah. On the other hand, if we have an address bus width of 32 bits, that would give us 2^{32}, or 4,294,967,296, different addresses. We can say that the size of our address space for 32 bits is roughly 4.3 gigabytes.

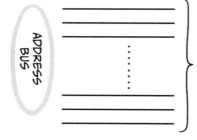

FOR AN ADDRESS BUS WIDTH OF 32 BITS, WE HAVE 2^{32}, OR ROUGHLY 4.3GB, DIFFERENT ADDRESSES.

And the size of the address bus directly relates to memory capacity (see "Memory Capacity and Bus Width" below).

 Hmm, so address bus width is also really important. Does that mean it should be as large as possible?

 Is that greed or naive honesty I detect? Well I suppose it's true that the bigger the buses, the better.

MEMORY CAPACITY AND BUS WIDTH

Let's think a bit about the relationship between memory capacity and bus width by looking at a simple example. As shown in the diagram, one byte corresponds to one address. One byte is eight bits. A *byte* is a unit commonly used to describe the size of data.

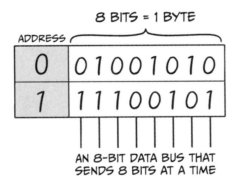

8 BITS = 1 BYTE

ADDRESS

| 0 | 0 1 0 0 1 0 1 0 |
| 1 | 1 1 1 0 0 1 0 1 |

AN 8-BIT DATA BUS THAT SENDS 8 BITS AT A TIME

If instead our address space (address bus width) was 12 bits, then we would have 2^{12}, or 4,096 addresses. Each address fills 1 byte, so that means our memory capacity is 4,096 bytes, or roughly 4 kilobytes (KB).

R/W SIGNALS AND I/O SIGNALS

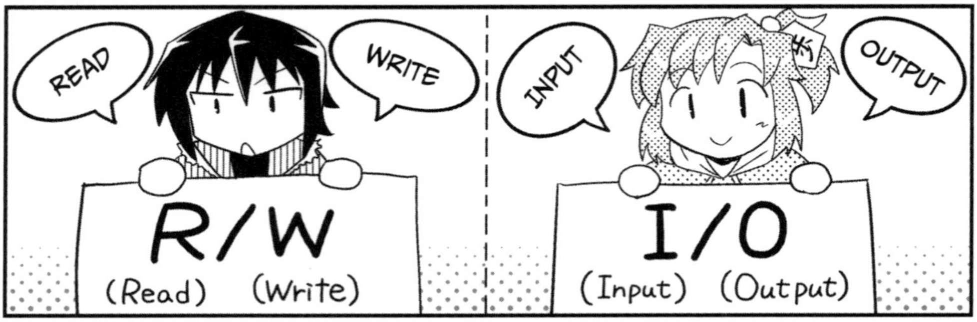
READ
WRITE
R/W
(Read) (Write)
INPUT
OUTPUT
I/O
(Input) (Output)

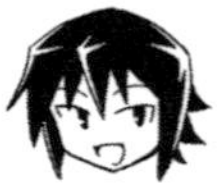

Next up, I'll explain a bit about *control signals*. Do you happen to know what *R/W* stands for?

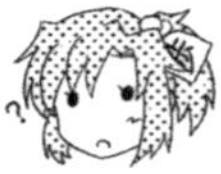

Red and white . . . is it something related to festivities . . . ? Santa?

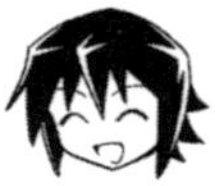

Ah. Well, it sure seems festive inside that head of yours. It actually stands for two really important terms related to the CPU—*read* and *write*.

Read means to extract data that has previously been stored somewhere. *Write* means to save data to some place. We also sometimes use the words *load* and *store* instead.

WHAT IS THE DIFFERENCE BETWEEN READ/WRITE AND LOAD/STORE?

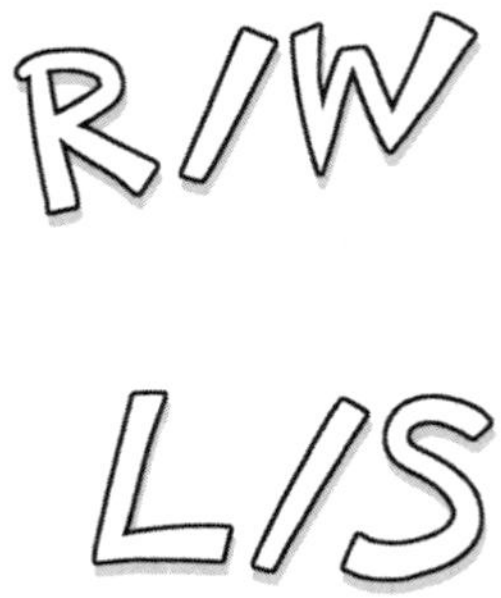
R/W
L/S

Read/write is the term we use when speaking from the hardware perspective, and *load/store* is the term we use when speaking from the software perspective.

R/W is an electrical operation in the memory, and the memory doesn't care where the data is going or where we want to save something.

In contrast, a load operation reads some particular data to store it in a register. Conversely, a store operation grabs some register data and writes it to memory. So these operations deal with data flow.

Ah, in that case, I think I kind of get it. The CPU deals with memory and data, right? It reads data to use for operations and then writes the result of those operations to memory.

Yes! It seems you're really getting the hang of it. So the CPU issues read and write instructions to the memory—instructions such as "*Fetch* some data" or "*Save* some data." We call these *R/W instruction signals*.

We've talked about the address bus and data buses, but there is one more really important bus—the *control bus*! And it's this bus that is conveying these control signals from the CPU.

83
ADDRESS BUS
Read
CONTROL BUS
CPU
DATA BUS
MEMORY

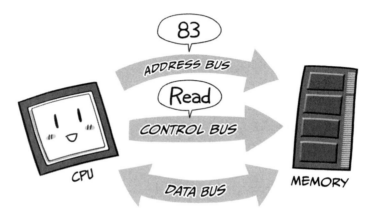

Hmm. So if, for example, I wanted the data in number 83, I would send 83 on the address bus and read on the control bus, like in the picture! And the data I wanted would then arrive on the data bus.

Yeah, that's it. You seem to be getting it now, so let's move on to the next topic. Have you heard of I/O before?

Maybe . . . ice cream and oreos? Hee!

Ah, you're just choosing words at random now, huh? *I/O* stands for *input/output*.

Input is data traveling from the outside world into the computer. Conversely, output is data traveling from the computer to the outside world.

 Yeah, I know. The keyboard and mouse are two input devices, and the monitor and printer are two output devices, right? Input and output!

 Yeah. To control external devices like this, we use I/O control signals. You should also remember the term *I/O port*. Just as the word *port* suggests, ports are the gateway we use when communicating data to external devices.

The CPU is connected to external devices like keyboards* through these I/O ports! Have a look at the image below.

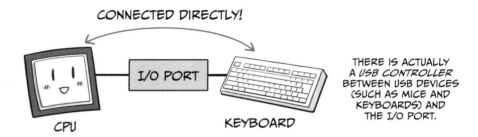

CONNECTED DIRECTLY!

I/O PORT

CPU

KEYBOARD

THERE IS ACTUALLY A *USB CONTROLLER* BETWEEN USB DEVICES (SUCH AS MICE AND KEYBOARDS) AND THE I/O PORT.

 Port . . . Yeah, it really feels like there are unknown seas at the end of the map! But these ports don't connect to other lands; they just connect to other devices.

 Yeah. And additionally, we have an address port and a data port between the CPU and memory, which in turn connect to the address bus and data bus, respectively.**

* Other external devices, such as the display, are not necessarily in direct communication with the CPU, however.

** The address port, data port, R/W control, and I/O control are shown in the helpful CPU overview diagram on page 106.

INSTRUCTIONS ARE MADE OF OPERANDS AND OPCODES

BY THE WAY, I HAVE ONE QUESTION...

WHEN YOU FIRST SHOWED ME MEMORY, THERE WERE THESE INSTRUCTIONS.

THESE

0	INSTRUCTIONS
1	INSTRUCTIONS
2	INSTRUCTIONS

WHAT ARE THEY? THEY SEEM AWFULLY FULL OF THEMSELVES.

IT'S BEEN BOTHERING ME FOR AGES! HURRY UP AND TELL ME ALREADY!!

SHE SAYS WHILE GIVING ME INSTRUCTIONS, ALL HIGH AND MIGHTY!!

UHH, YEAH... INSTRUCTIONS ARE PARTS OF PROGRAMS WRITTEN BY HUMANS THAT THE CPU EXECUTES.

| INSTRUCTION |
| INSTRUCTION |
| INSTRUCTION |

PROGRAM

YOU COULD SAY THAT PROGRAMS ARE CHAINS OF INSTRUCTIONS.

OH, SO IT'S KINDA LIKE HOW CAKE RECIPES SAY: "BREAK SOME EGGS."

"MIX THE EGGS WITH SUGAR." PROGRAMS ARE A CHAIN OF INSTRUCTIONS LIKE THAT?

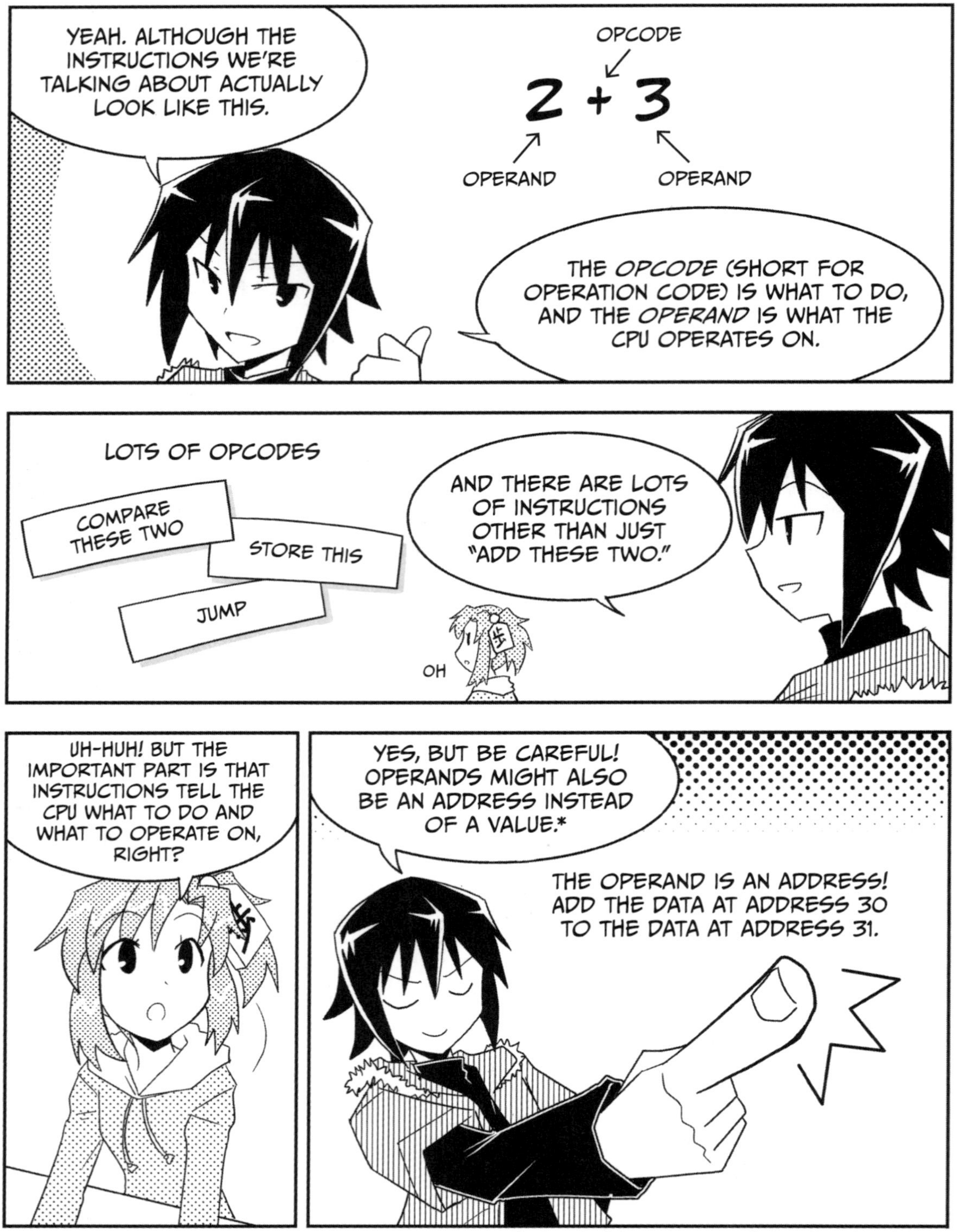
YEAH. ALTHOUGH THE INSTRUCTIONS WE'RE TALKING ABOUT ACTUALLY LOOK LIKE THIS.
OPCODE
2 + 3
OPERAND
OPERAND
THE *OPCODE* (SHORT FOR OPERATION CODE) IS WHAT TO DO, AND THE *OPERAND* IS WHAT THE CPU OPERATES ON.
LOTS OF OPCODES
COMPARE THESE TWO
STORE THIS
JUMP
AND THERE ARE LOTS OF INSTRUCTIONS OTHER THAN JUST "ADD THESE TWO."
OH
UH-HUH! BUT THE IMPORTANT PART IS THAT INSTRUCTIONS TELL THE CPU WHAT TO DO AND WHAT TO OPERATE ON, RIGHT?
YES, BUT BE CAREFUL! OPERANDS MIGHT ALSO BE AN ADDRESS INSTEAD OF A VALUE.*
THE OPERAND IS AN ADDRESS! ADD THE DATA AT ADDRESS 30 TO THE DATA AT ADDRESS 31.

* THE ACCUMULATORS AND REGISTERS WE'RE GOING TO TALK ABOUT NEXT CAN ALSO BE OPERANDS.

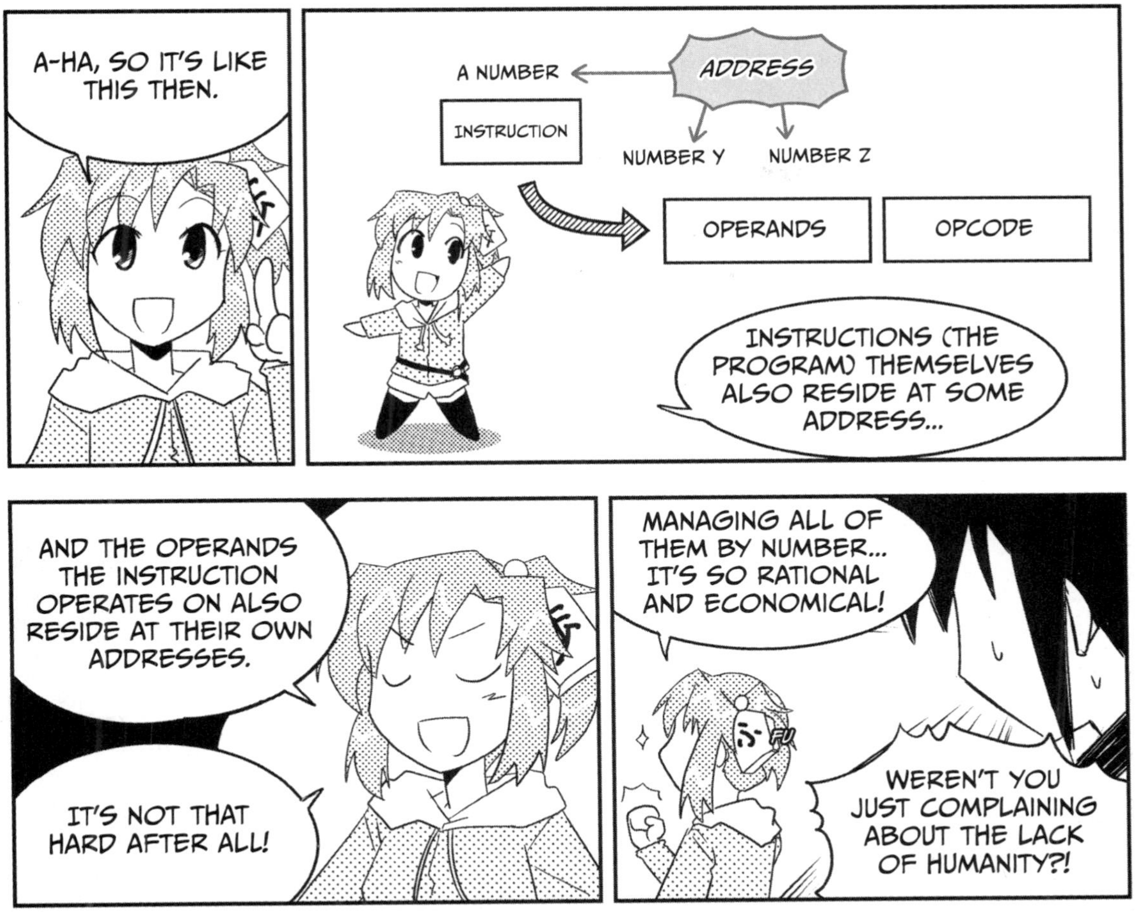
A-HA, SO IT'S LIKE THIS THEN.
A NUMBER
ADDRESS
INSTRUCTION
NUMBER Y
NUMBER Z
OPERANDS
OPCODE
INSTRUCTIONS (THE PROGRAM) THEMSELVES ALSO RESIDE AT SOME ADDRESS...
AND THE OPERANDS THE INSTRUCTION OPERATES ON ALSO RESIDE AT THEIR OWN ADDRESSES.
IT'S NOT THAT HARD AFTER ALL!
MANAGING ALL OF THEM BY NUMBER... IT'S SO RATIONAL AND ECONOMICAL!
FU
WEREN'T YOU JUST COMPLAINING ABOUT THE LACK OF HUMANITY?!

ACCUMULATORS AND OTHER REGISTERS ARE USED IN OPERATIONS

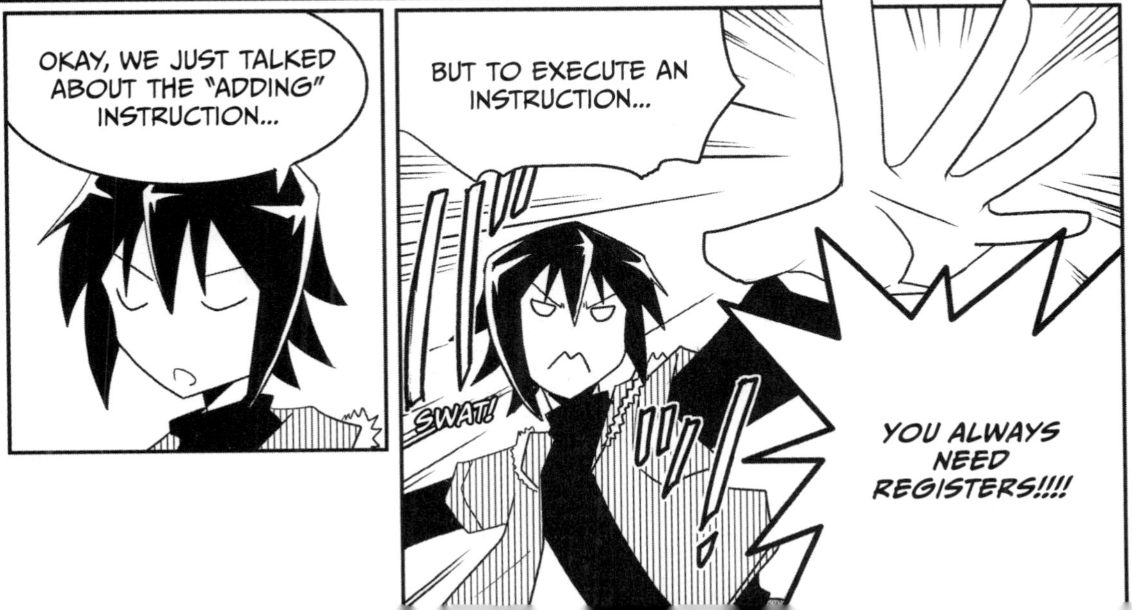
OKAY, WE JUST TALKED ABOUT THE "ADDING" INSTRUCTION...
BUT TO EXECUTE AN INSTRUCTION...
SWAT!
YOU ALWAYS NEED REGISTERS!!!!

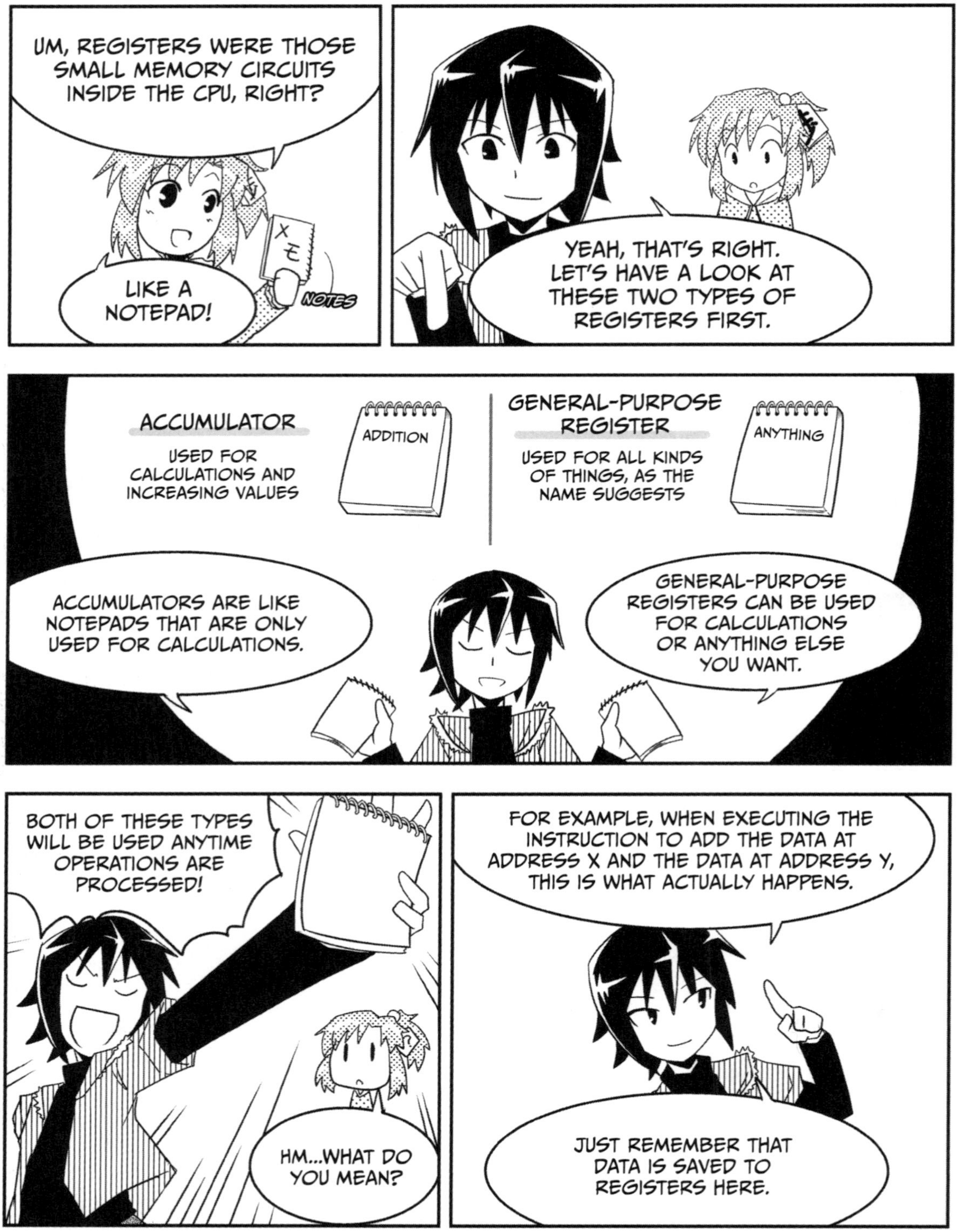
UM, REGISTERS WERE THOSE SMALL MEMORY CIRCUITS INSIDE THE CPU, RIGHT?
メモ
LIKE A NOTEPAD!
NOTES
YEAH, THAT'S RIGHT. LET'S HAVE A LOOK AT THESE TWO TYPES OF REGISTERS FIRST.
ACCUMULATOR
USED FOR CALCULATIONS AND INCREASING VALUES
ADDITION
GENERAL-PURPOSE REGISTER
USED FOR ALL KINDS OF THINGS, AS THE NAME SUGGESTS
ANYTHING
ACCUMULATORS ARE LIKE NOTEPADS THAT ARE ONLY USED FOR CALCULATIONS.
GENERAL-PURPOSE REGISTERS CAN BE USED FOR CALCULATIONS OR ANYTHING ELSE YOU WANT.
BOTH OF THESE TYPES WILL BE USED ANYTIME OPERATIONS ARE PROCESSED!
HM...WHAT DO YOU MEAN?
FOR EXAMPLE, WHEN EXECUTING THE INSTRUCTION TO ADD THE DATA AT ADDRESS X AND THE DATA AT ADDRESS Y, THIS IS WHAT ACTUALLY HAPPENS.
JUST REMEMBER THAT DATA IS SAVED TO REGISTERS HERE.

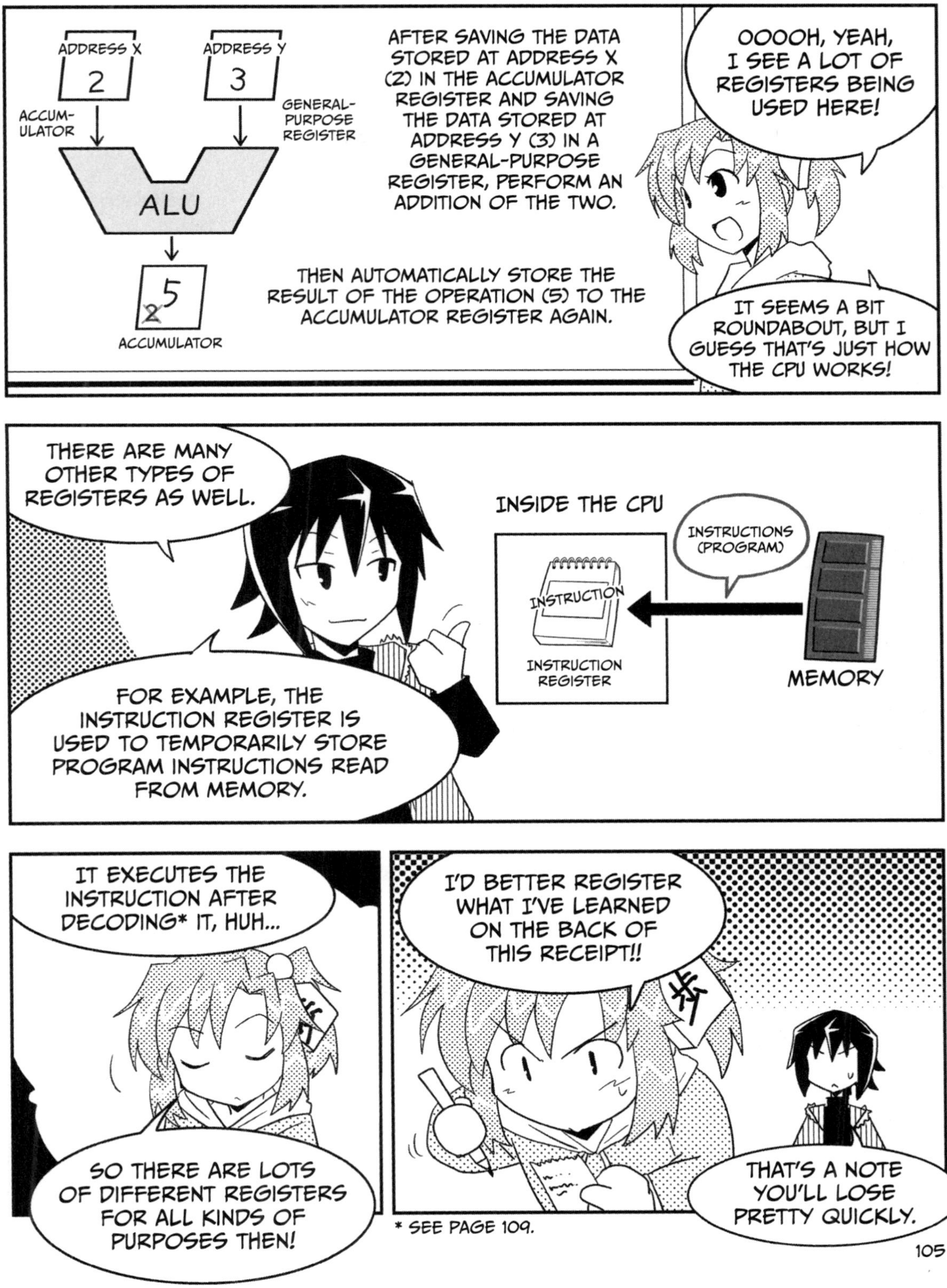
ADDRESS X
2
ADDRESS Y
3
ACCUM-ULATOR
GENERAL-PURPOSE REGISTER
ALU
5
ACCUMULATOR
AFTER SAVING THE DATA STORED AT ADDRESS X (2) IN THE ACCUMULATOR REGISTER AND SAVING THE DATA STORED AT ADDRESS Y (3) IN A GENERAL-PURPOSE REGISTER, PERFORM AN ADDITION OF THE TWO.
THEN AUTOMATICALLY STORE THE RESULT OF THE OPERATION (5) TO THE ACCUMULATOR REGISTER AGAIN.
OOOOH, YEAH, I SEE A LOT OF REGISTERS BEING USED HERE!
IT SEEMS A BIT ROUNDABOUT, BUT I GUESS THAT'S JUST HOW THE CPU WORKS!
THERE ARE MANY OTHER TYPES OF REGISTERS AS WELL.
INSIDE THE CPU
INSTRUCTION
INSTRUCTION REGISTER
INSTRUCTIONS (PROGRAM)
MEMORY
FOR EXAMPLE, THE INSTRUCTION REGISTER IS USED TO TEMPORARILY STORE PROGRAM INSTRUCTIONS READ FROM MEMORY.
IT EXECUTES THE INSTRUCTION AFTER DECODING* IT, HUH...
SO THERE ARE LOTS OF DIFFERENT REGISTERS FOR ALL KINDS OF PURPOSES THEN!
I'D BETTER REGISTER WHAT I'VE LEARNED ON THE BACK OF THIS RECEIPT!!
THAT'S A NOTE YOU'LL LOSE PRETTY QUICKLY.

* SEE PAGE 109.

CPU Instruction Processing

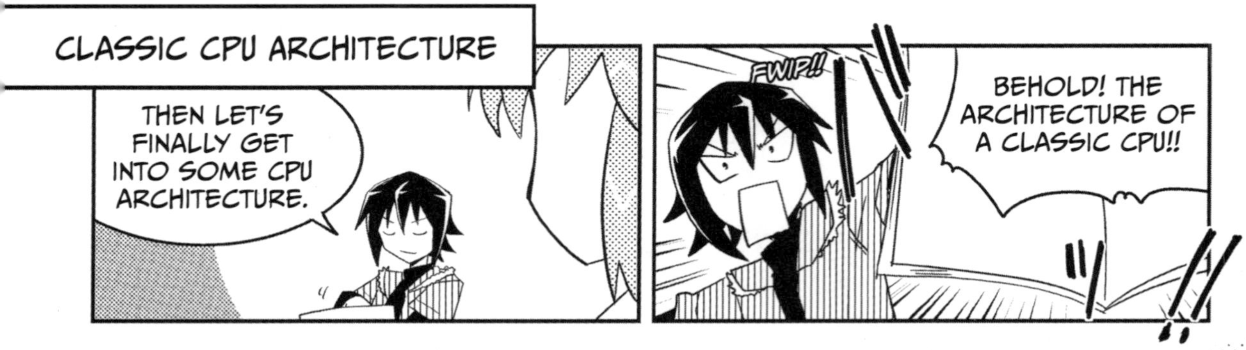
CLASSIC CPU ARCHITECTURE
THEN LET'S FINALLY GET INTO SOME CPU ARCHITECTURE.
FWIP!!
BEHOLD! THE ARCHITECTURE OF A CLASSIC CPU!!

《OVERVIEW OF A CLASSIC CPU》

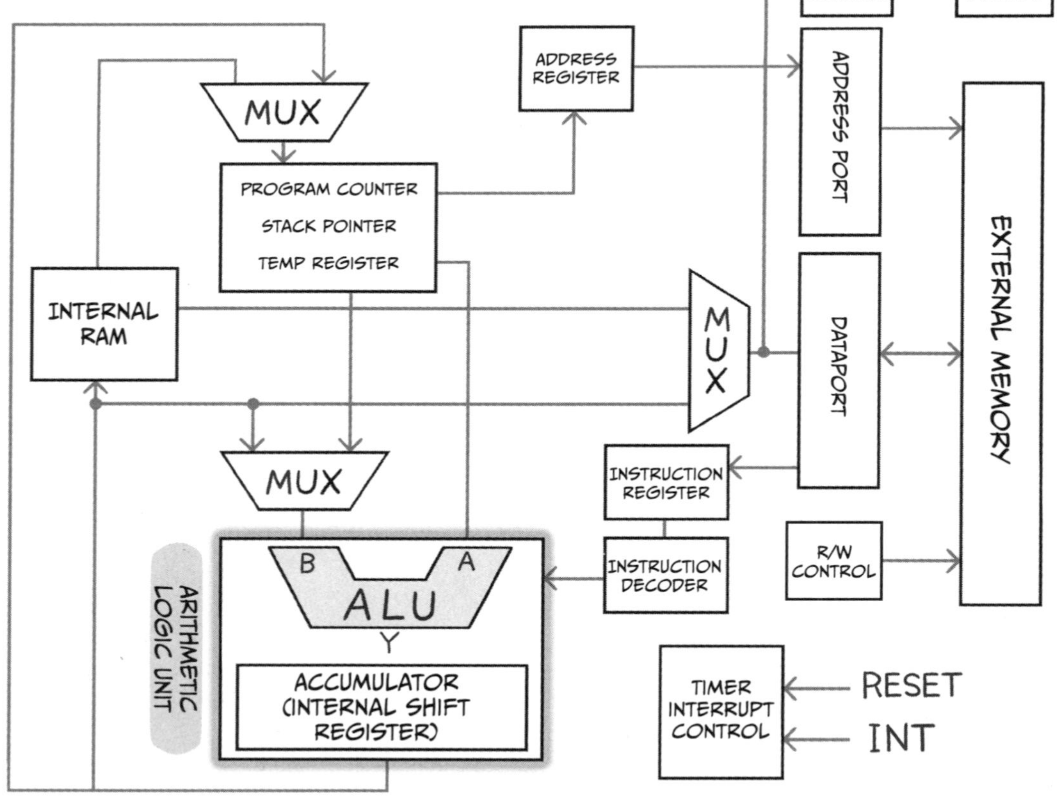
I/O CONTROL
EXTERNAL DEVICES
ADDRESS REGISTER
MUX
ADDRESS PORT
PROGRAM COUNTER
STACK POINTER
TEMP REGISTER
EXTERNAL MEMORY
INTERNAL RAM
MUX
DATAPORT
MUX
INSTRUCTION REGISTER
ARITHMETIC LOGIC UNIT
B
A
ALU
Y
ACCUMULATOR (INTERNAL SHIFT REGISTER)
INSTRUCTION DECODER
R/W CONTROL
TIMER INTERRUPT CONTROL
RESET
INT

* ALL BUSES ARE SIMPLIFIED IN THIS DIAGRAM AND ARE DRAWN ONLY AS SINGLE LINES.

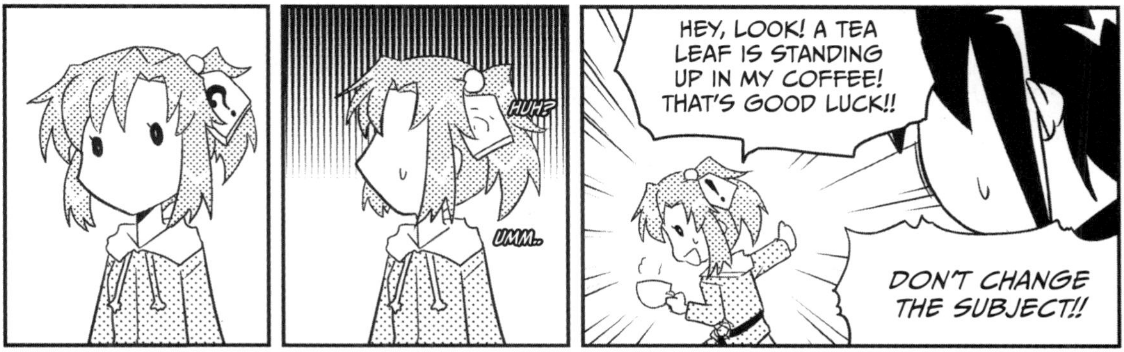
HUH?
UMM..
HEY, LOOK! A TEA LEAF IS STANDING UP IN MY COFFEE! THAT'S GOOD LUCK!!
DON'T CHANGE THE SUBJECT!!

THE INSTRUCTION CYCLE

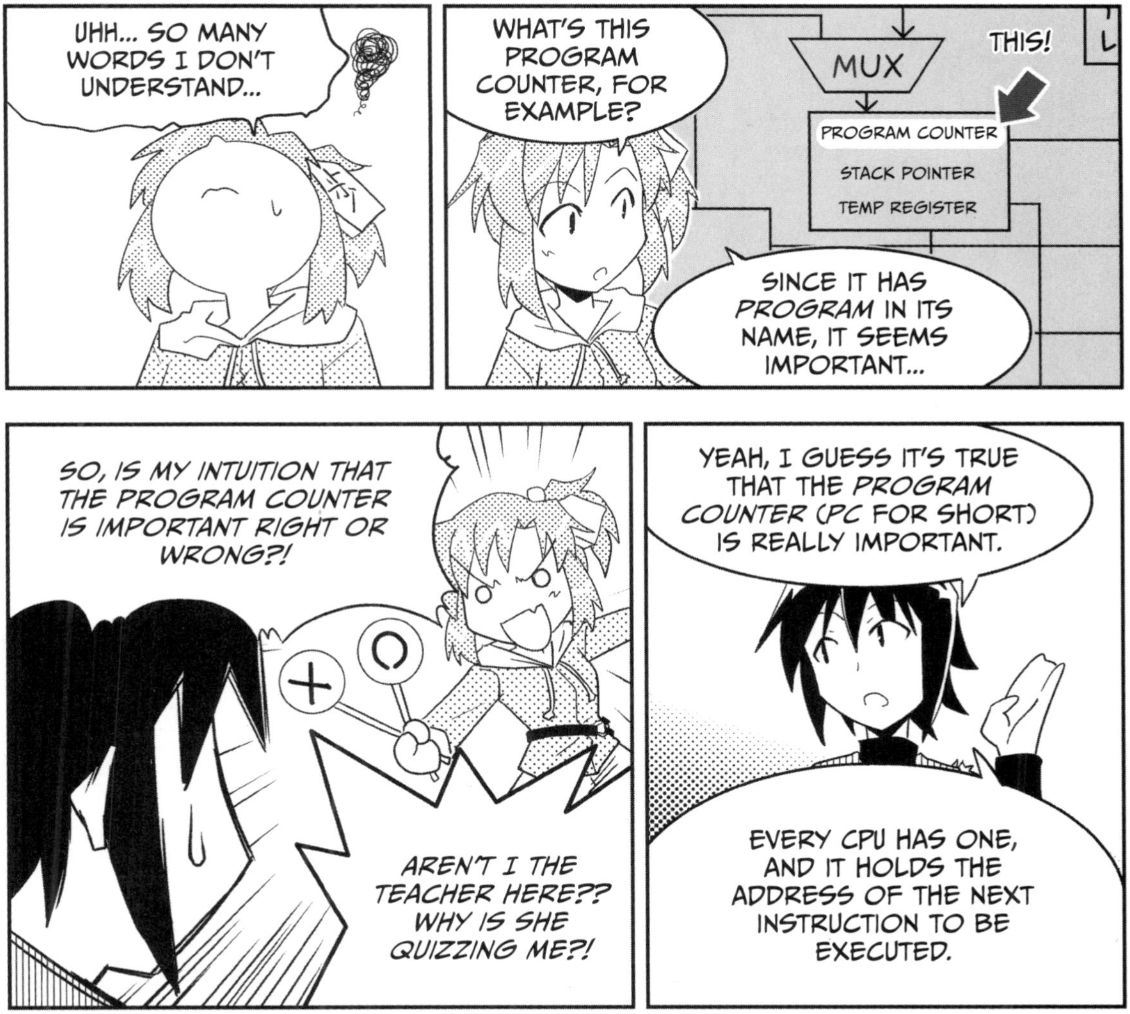
UHH... SO MANY WORDS I DON'T UNDERSTAND...
WHAT'S THIS PROGRAM COUNTER, FOR EXAMPLE?
MUX
THIS!
PROGRAM COUNTER
STACK POINTER
TEMP REGISTER
SINCE IT HAS *PROGRAM* IN ITS NAME, IT SEEMS IMPORTANT...
SO, IS MY INTUITION THAT THE PROGRAM COUNTER IS IMPORTANT RIGHT OR WRONG?!
AREN'T I THE TEACHER HERE?? WHY IS SHE QUIZZING ME?!
YEAH, I GUESS IT'S TRUE THAT THE *PROGRAM COUNTER* (PC FOR SHORT) IS REALLY IMPORTANT.
EVERY CPU HAS ONE, AND IT HOLDS THE ADDRESS OF THE NEXT INSTRUCTION TO BE EXECUTED.

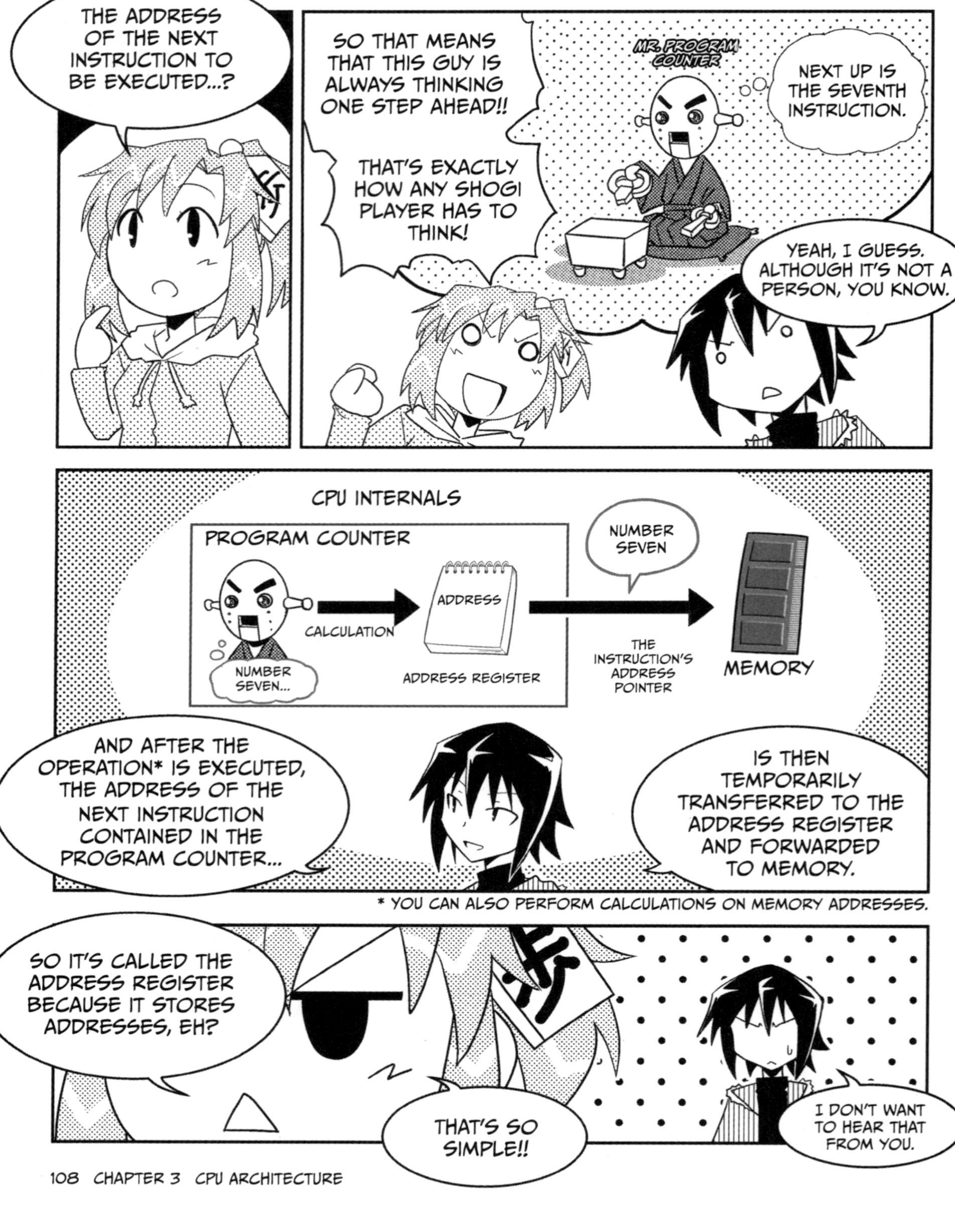

THE ADDRESS OF THE NEXT INSTRUCTION TO BE EXECUTED...?
SO THAT MEANS THAT THIS GUY IS ALWAYS THINKING ONE STEP AHEAD!!
THAT'S EXACTLY HOW ANY SHOGI PLAYER HAS TO THINK!
MR. PROGRAM COUNTER
NEXT UP IS THE SEVENTH INSTRUCTION.
YEAH, I GUESS. ALTHOUGH IT'S NOT A PERSON, YOU KNOW.
CPU INTERNALS
PROGRAM COUNTER
NUMBER SEVEN...
CALCULATION
ADDRESS
ADDRESS REGISTER
NUMBER SEVEN
THE INSTRUCTION'S ADDRESS POINTER
MEMORY
AND AFTER THE OPERATION* IS EXECUTED, THE ADDRESS OF THE NEXT INSTRUCTION CONTAINED IN THE PROGRAM COUNTER...
IS THEN TEMPORARILY TRANSFERRED TO THE ADDRESS REGISTER AND FORWARDED TO MEMORY.
* YOU CAN ALSO PERFORM CALCULATIONS ON MEMORY ADDRESSES.
SO IT'S CALLED THE ADDRESS REGISTER BECAUSE IT STORES ADDRESSES, EH?
THAT'S SO SIMPLE!!
I DON'T WANT TO HEAR THAT FROM YOU.

LET'S MOVE ON.

THE MEMORY THEN SENDS THE INSTRUCTION LOCATED AT THAT ADDRESS BACK TO THE CPU.

CPU INTERNALS

INSTRUCTION DECODER

INSTRUCTION

INSTRUCTION (PROGRAM)

DECODING!

INSTRUCTION REGISTER

MEMORY

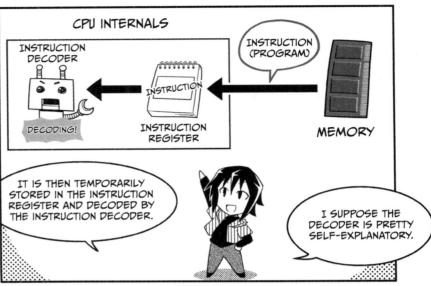

IT IS THEN TEMPORARILY STORED IN THE INSTRUCTION REGISTER AND DECODED BY THE INSTRUCTION DECODER.

I SUPPOSE THE DECODER IS PRETTY SELF-EXPLANATORY.

BUT WHY IS DECODING NECESSARY AT ALL? CAN'T THE CPU JUST USE WHAT WAS SENT FROM MEMORY RIGHT AWAY?

NO.

INSTRUCTIONS MUST BE DECODED BECAUSE THE INSTRUCTION CODE STORED IN MEMORY IS NOT THE SAME AS THE MACHINE CODE THE CPU UNDERSTANDS.

INSTRUCTION DECODER

THE INSTRUCTION RETRIEVED FROM MEMORY NEEDS TO BE BROKEN DOWN BEFORE IT CAN BE USED IN AN OPERATION. THE DECODER TRANSLATES FROM INSTRUCTION-LEVEL LANGUAGE TO HARDWARE-FRIENDLY MACHINE CODE FORMAT.

OH WOW, IT SEEMS A LOT OF DIFFERENT PROCESSES ARE NECESSARY...

THE INSTRUCTION DECODER PUTS THE INSTRUCTIONS READ FROM MEMORY INTO A FORM THAT CAN BE USED IN OPERATION EXECUTION.

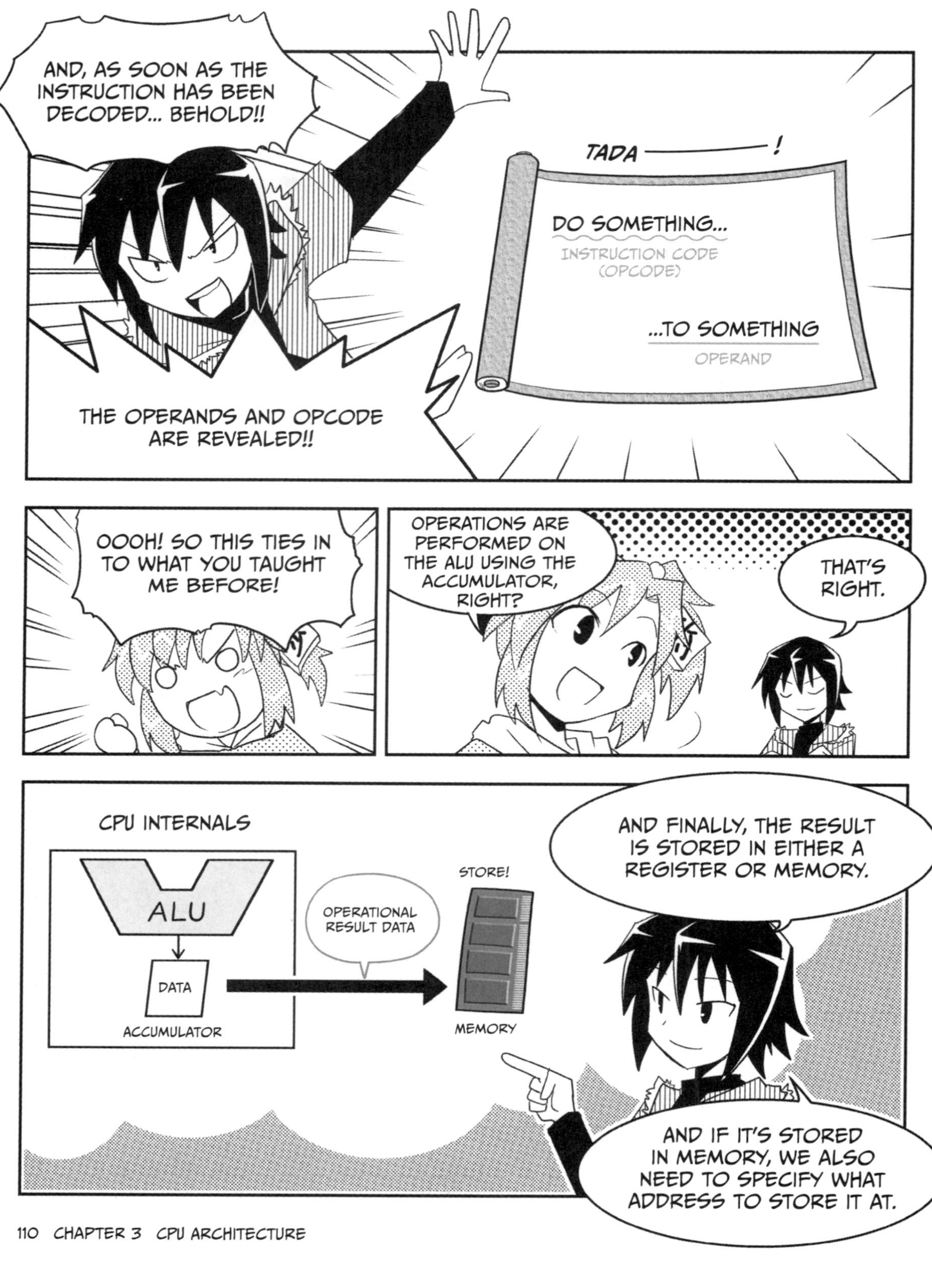
AND, AS SOON AS THE INSTRUCTION HAS BEEN DECODED... BEHOLD!!
TADA ——————!
DO SOMETHING...
INSTRUCTION CODE (OPCODE)
...TO SOMETHING
OPERAND
THE OPERANDS AND OPCODE ARE REVEALED!!
OOOH! SO THIS TIES IN TO WHAT YOU TAUGHT ME BEFORE!
OPERATIONS ARE PERFORMED ON THE ALU USING THE ACCUMULATOR, RIGHT?
THAT'S RIGHT.
CPU INTERNALS
ALU
DATA
ACCUMULATOR
OPERATIONAL RESULT DATA
STORE!
MEMORY
AND FINALLY, THE RESULT IS STORED IN EITHER A REGISTER OR MEMORY.
AND IF IT'S STORED IN MEMORY, WE ALSO NEED TO SPECIFY WHAT ADDRESS TO STORE IT AT.

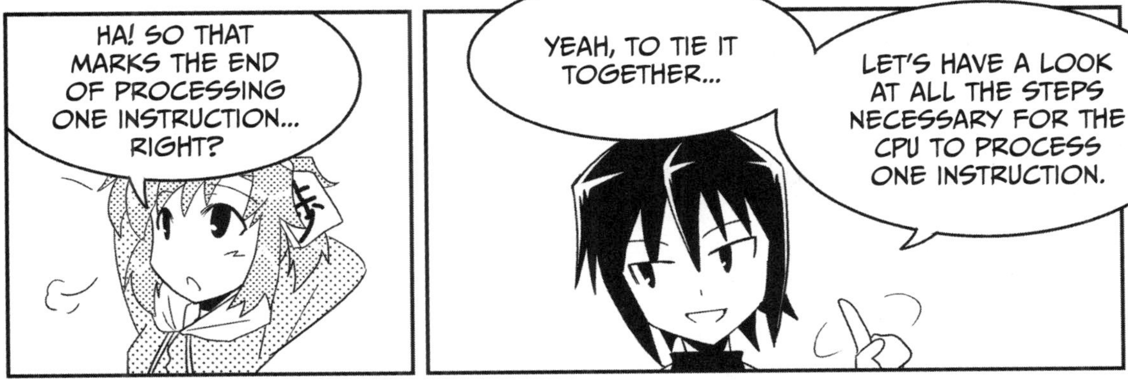
HA! SO THAT MARKS THE END OF PROCESSING ONE INSTRUCTION... RIGHT?
YEAH, TO TIE IT TOGETHER...
LET'S HAVE A LOOK AT ALL THE STEPS NECESSARY FOR THE CPU TO PROCESS ONE INSTRUCTION.

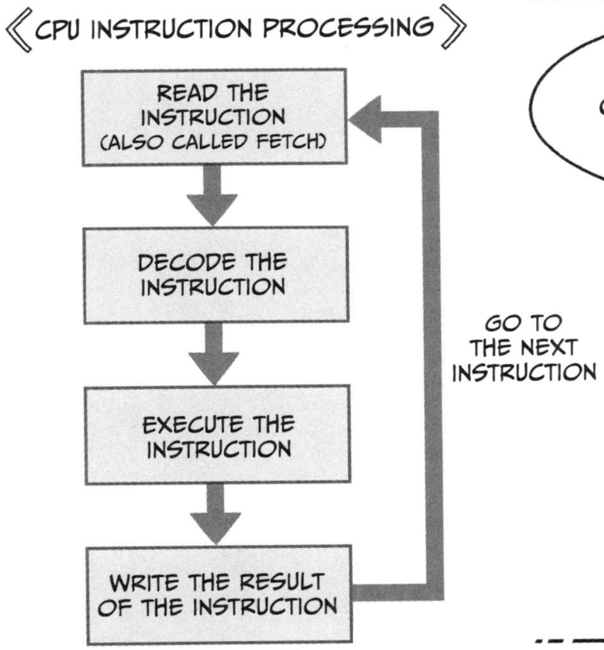
《CPU INSTRUCTION PROCESSING》
READ THE INSTRUCTION (ALSO CALLED FETCH)
DECODE THE INSTRUCTION
EXECUTE THE INSTRUCTION
WRITE THE RESULT OF THE INSTRUCTION
GO TO THE NEXT INSTRUCTION

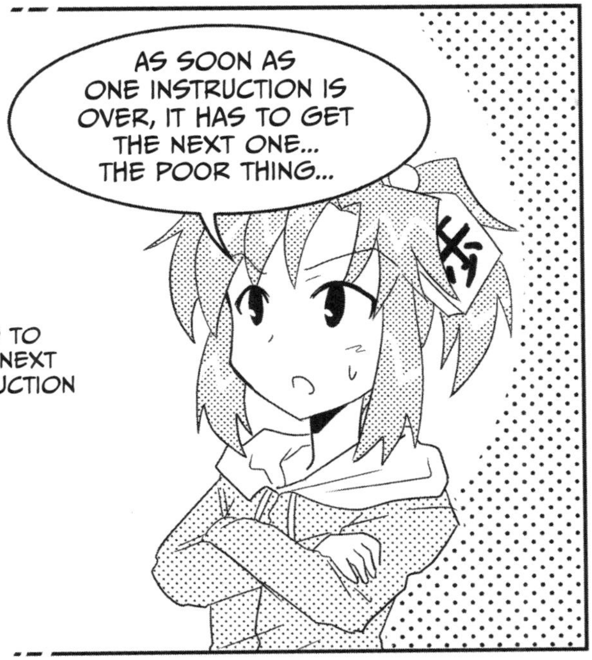
AS SOON AS ONE INSTRUCTION IS OVER, IT HAS TO GET THE NEXT ONE... THE POOR THING...

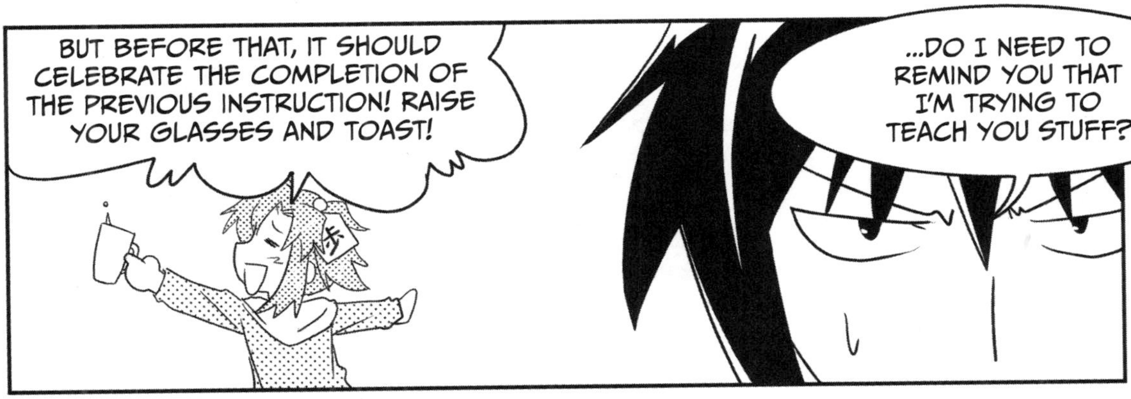
BUT BEFORE THAT, IT SHOULD CELEBRATE THE COMPLETION OF THE PREVIOUS INSTRUCTION! RAISE YOUR GLASSES AND TOAST!
...DO I NEED TO REMIND YOU THAT I'M TRYING TO TEACH YOU STUFF?

THE INSTRUCTION WE PROCESS CHANGES DEPENDING ON THE PROGRAM COUNTER

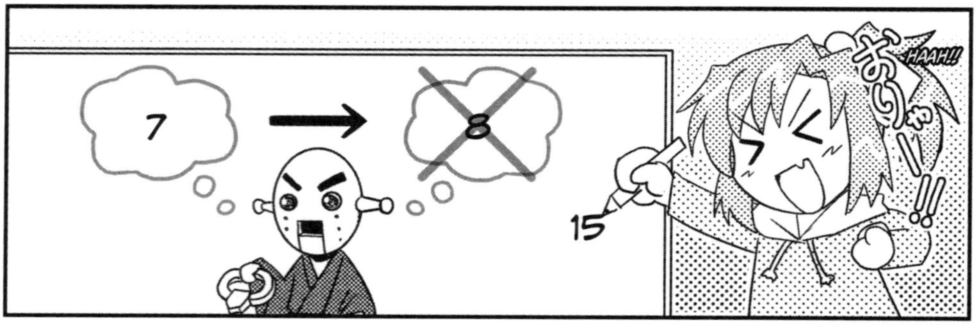
7
8
15
HAAH!!

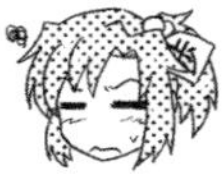

Hmm, about that CPU overview diagram from before, though (see page 106). . . . There are still a lot of words there I don't know. It all feels a bit hazy now.

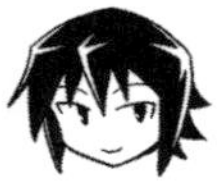

Well, there's no rush. Take another look after the next lesson. But for now, let's look at the program counter (PC).

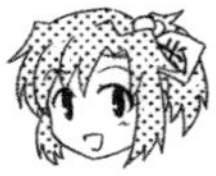

Ooh, that guy who's always one step ahea— no, I mean the guy who remembers the address to the next instruction! That reminds me, didn't we talk about counters before? The circuits that count?

After the seventh instruction is done, we go to the eighth, and then the ninth, and so on. . . . Is that how the saved address keeps changing?

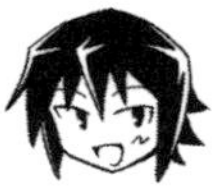

Basically, yes. And by the way, the instruction register gets saved at the same time as the counter changes, like in the image below.

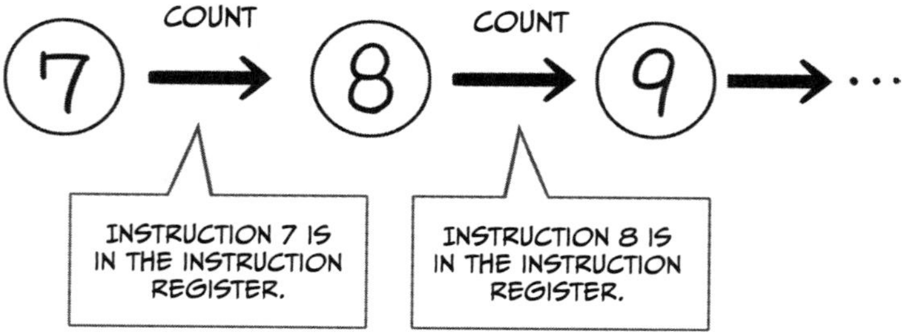
COUNT
COUNT
7
8
9
. . .
INSTRUCTION 7 IS IN THE INSTRUCTION REGISTER.
INSTRUCTION 8 IS IN THE INSTRUCTION REGISTER.

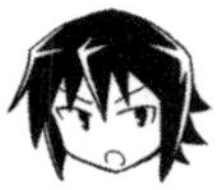

But be careful! Instruction number eight doesn't necessarily follow instruction number seven here.

The program counter stores the address of the instruction to be executed next. After 7, it might jump to number 15 or return to number 3.

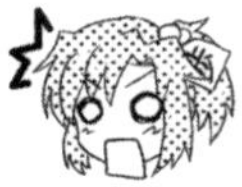

Eeeeeh, why?! Why would the address return and jump around like that?

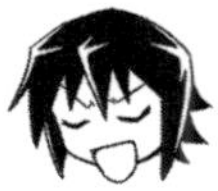

Hah! This is important, so pay attention. The reason it can jump around like this is that a program might contain conditionals such as *branches* and *loops*!

When the program encounters one of these conditionals, the address of the instruction to be executed next might *jump*. It might be easier to understand this by looking at a diagram.

EXECUTION
CONDITION
BRANCH!
EXECUTION
EXECUTION
EXECUTION
RETURN!
CONDITION
EXECUTION

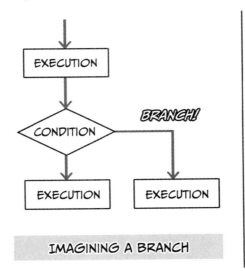

IMAGINING A BRANCH

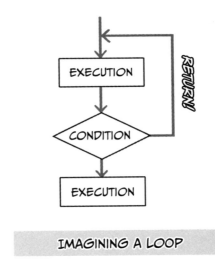

IMAGINING A LOOP

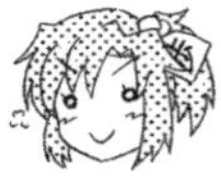

Ah! It's like the ATM example we talked about a while back! It decided that the balance was insufficient, so the outcome changed. And the ATM might throw you back to the main screen if your PIN code is wrong.

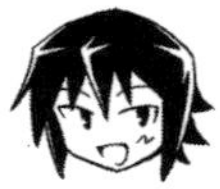

Yeah, the ATM is a great example! And to accomplish these branches and loops, we only have to rewrite the address inside the program counter to the address we want to jump to.

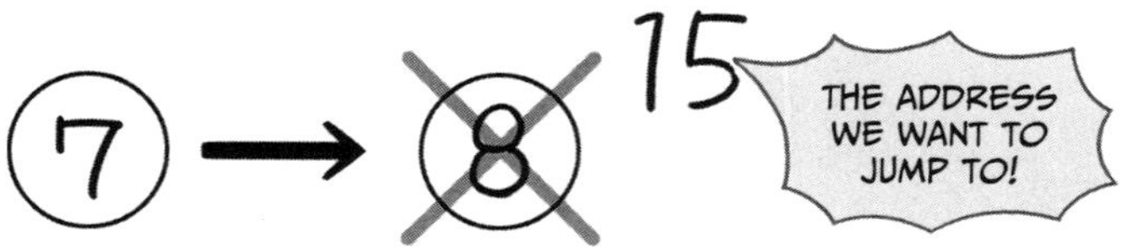
7
8
15
THE ADDRESS WE WANT TO JUMP TO!

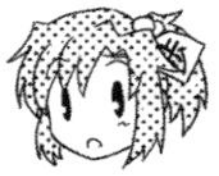

I see. So by rewriting the address in the program counter, we can change which instruction to execute! This way, the program is able to proceed appropriately.

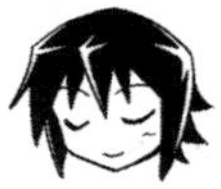

It's also good to know that the bit width of the program counter (the bit width of the addresses in the PC) is the same as both the address bus bit and the address space bit width. If you think calmly about that for a bit, you should realize that they have to have the same bit width.

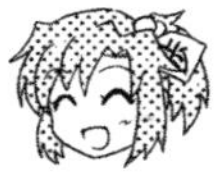

I see. It seems obvious, but it feels really nice to see the relationship between the different things we've talked about so far!

By the way, the program counter only knows what the next step is, right? Shogi players have to read reeeally far into the future, so maybe the program counter and shogi players are slightly different after all!

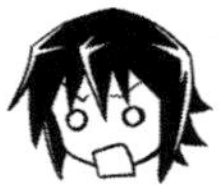

Slightly? You're joking, right?!

VIRTUAL MEMORY

Most computer programmers don't have to care about the CPU address bit length of the programs they write for any modern operating system (such as Windows). It is the operating system that decides how it will actually interact with the physical memory, and it exposes this through something called *virtual memory*. The hardware that maps this virtual memory to its physical counterparts is known as the *memory management unit (MMU)*.

All Kinds of Memory Devices

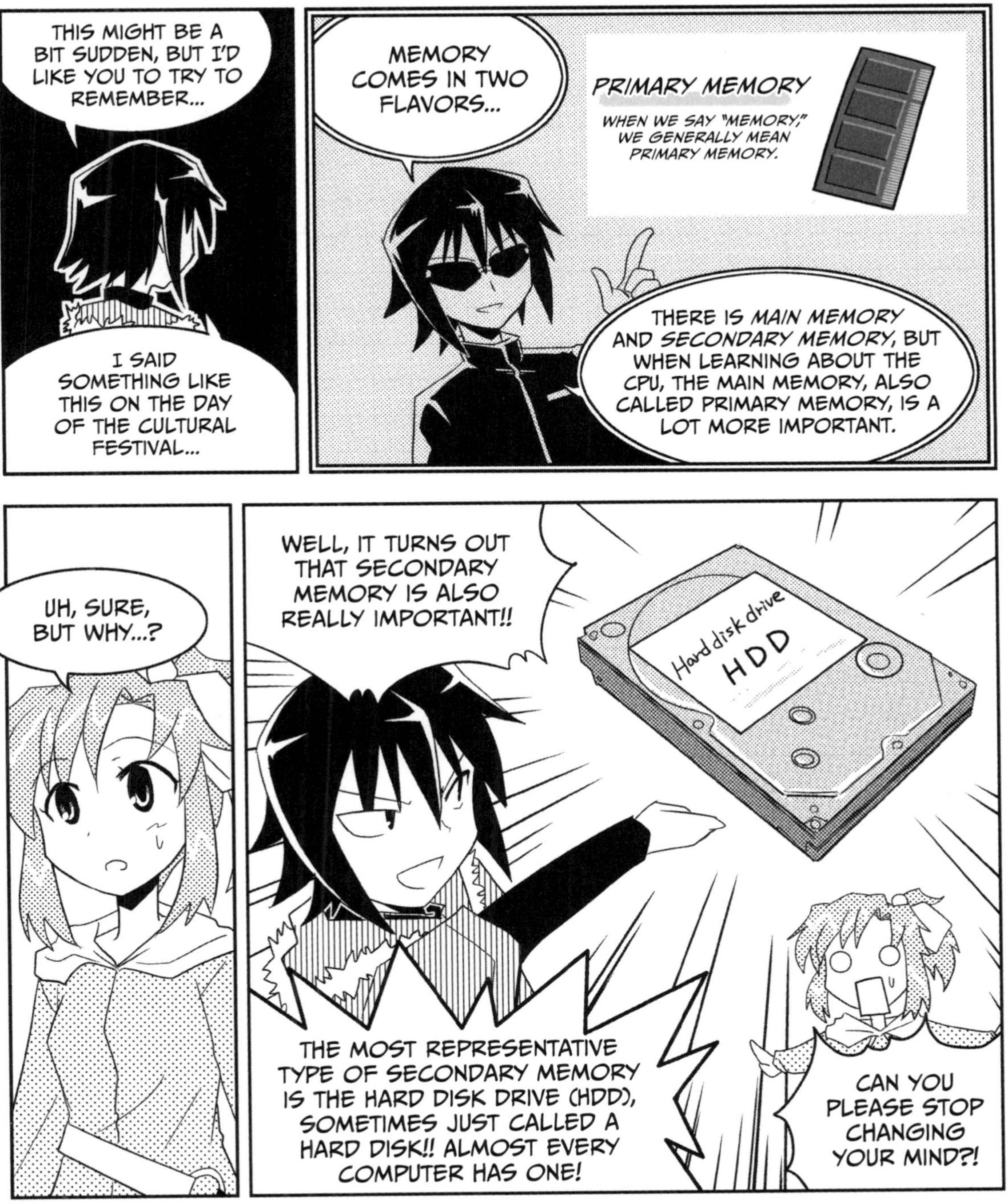

THIS MIGHT BE A BIT SUDDEN, BUT I'D LIKE YOU TO TRY TO REMEMBER...
I SAID SOMETHING LIKE THIS ON THE DAY OF THE CULTURAL FESTIVAL...
MEMORY COMES IN TWO FLAVORS...
PRIMARY MEMORY
WHEN WE SAY "MEMORY," WE GENERALLY MEAN PRIMARY MEMORY.
THERE IS MAIN MEMORY AND SECONDARY MEMORY, BUT WHEN LEARNING ABOUT THE CPU, THE MAIN MEMORY, ALSO CALLED PRIMARY MEMORY, IS A LOT MORE IMPORTANT.
UH, SURE, BUT WHY...?
WELL, IT TURNS OUT THAT SECONDARY MEMORY IS ALSO REALLY IMPORTANT!!
Hard disk drive
HDD
THE MOST REPRESENTATIVE TYPE OF SECONDARY MEMORY IS THE HARD DISK DRIVE (HDD), SOMETIMES JUST CALLED A HARD DISK!! ALMOST EVERY COMPUTER HAS ONE!
CAN YOU PLEASE STOP CHANGING YOUR MIND?!

A COMPARISON BETWEEN HDD AND MEMORY

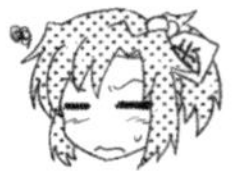

Umm, I'm shocked by this new information. So what does this small box-looking thingy . . . this hard drive (secondary memory) . . . do?

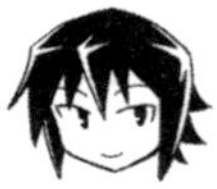

The easiest way to answer that is to compare it to primary memory. Let's start with the first big difference! When you turn your computer off, everything in primary memory disappears! But any data stored on your hard drive does not.

This is why the operating system running your computer (for example Windows), all your programs, and any data you might have created or downloaded (text, video, and so on) are stored on your hard drive.

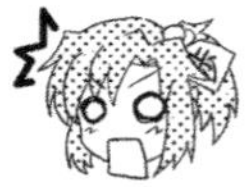

Eeeeeee!! That's amazing!! But didn't you say that all data and programs used for operations are stored in primary memory?

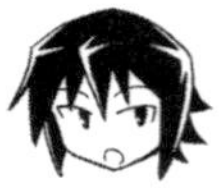

Yeah. Actually, when you turn on your computer's power, certain parts of the data in your hard drive are copied to primary memory. Anyway, when you turn your computer off, all your data is safely stored on your hard drive. Take a look below.

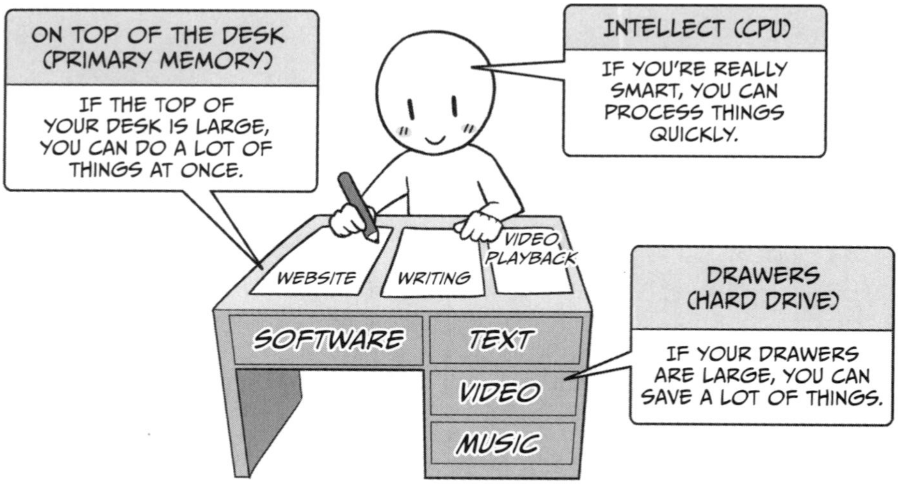
ON TOP OF THE DESK (PRIMARY MEMORY)
IF THE TOP OF YOUR DESK IS LARGE, YOU CAN DO A LOT OF THINGS AT ONCE.
INTELLECT (CPU)
IF YOU'RE REALLY SMART, YOU CAN PROCESS THINGS QUICKLY.
WEBSITE
WRITING
VIDEO PLAYBACK
SOFTWARE
TEXT
VIDEO
MUSIC
DRAWERS (HARD DRIVE)
IF YOUR DRAWERS ARE LARGE, YOU CAN SAVE A LOT OF THINGS.

Let's imagine how the CPU, memory, and hard drive interact. We could say your memory is like the top of your desk and your hard drive is like the drawers of that desk. You should be able to understand their roles better by using this analogy.

Oooh, they're really different! If primary memory is large, it becomes easier to process large amounts of data at once! And if the hard drive is large, you can save and store a lot of data.

Now, let's talk about the second difference between the two. The CPU can read directly from primary memory but not from the hard drive!

The CPU sends control signals to something called the hard disk interface located in a piece of memory called the *I/O space*. It is this hard disk interface that then controls the hard drive itself.

HDD INTERFACE
I/O
CONTROL SIGNAL
I/O SPACE
MANAGED
CPU
HDD
THE CPU CANNOT ACCESS MEMORY ADDRESSES ON THE HARD DRIVE DIRECTLY!

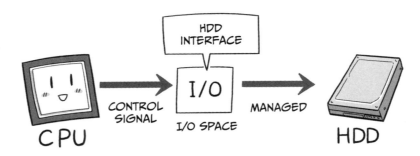

This might seem counterintuitive since we manipulate the data on the hard drive all the time when using our computers. But really it works like in the picture above.

That is, your CPU only works directly with the address space, which your hard drive is not part of!!

Aha. The only things that can interact with the CPU directly are the primary memory and I/O devices. So that's why you placed so much emphasis on the importance of primary memory. . . .

Then let's talk about the third and final difference: hard drives are a lot slower than primary memory!

There are lots of different types of memory inside any computer, but by comparing each of their relative storage sizes and speeds, you end up with something like this pyramid.

CPU
FAST
PROCESSING SPEED
SLOW
REG-
ISTERS
INSIDE
THE CPU
CACHE
MEMORY*
PRIMARY MEMORY
DISK CACHE*
HARD DRIVE (SECONDARY MEMORY)
MEMORY STORAGE SIZE
* CACHE MEMORY IS
USED TO TEMPORARILY
STORE FREQUENTLY
USED DATA. THIS MAKES
IT EASIER TO QUICKLY
ACCESS DATA YOU
MIGHT WANT.

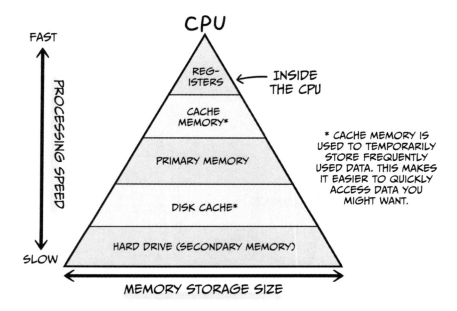

Huh?! So memory close to the CPU is fast but small. As you get further away from the CPU, it gradually grows larger but slower!

That's it. So, for example, registers have fast processing speeds but small memory sizes. A good comparison might be a small, handy notepad.

Yeah. Anyway, I think I understand the difference between primary memory and hard drives now. Even though they're both memory devices, their uses are completely different.

But that's why we can play to their strengths, when appropriate.

An interesting example is that today's computers, especially laptops, have started using solid state drives (SSDs) instead of mechanical hard disk drives (HDDs). SSDs store all data using semiconductor memory technology. This makes SSDs much faster and more resistant to shaking and other types of blunt force than mechanical disks.

RAM SPACE, ROM SPACE, AND I/O SPACE

RAM SPACE
ROM SPACE
JUST A LITTLE BIT...
I/O SPACE

Okay, let's talk a bit about address space (memory space) again. Do you remember what I taught you before?

Yeah, no problem! It's the dark space ruled by the CPU's iron fist. . . . No, I mean . . . it's the space directly managed by the CPU, right?

ADDRESS SPACE
(MEMORY SPACE)

TYPE	ADDRESS
0	INSTRUCTION
1	INSTRUCTION
2	INSTRUCTION
3	INSTRUCTION
4	INSTRUCTION
⋮	⋮
30	DATA
31	DATA
32	DATA
33	DATA
⋮	⋮

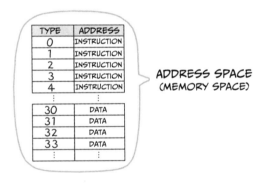

Indeed. But to be more exact, *address space* comprises all the memory space *outside* of the CPU that is controlled by the CPU.

Hmm? All the memory space outside of the CPU? That seems a bit convoluted. Are there other types of memory in there other than primary memory?

Yes. This is important. The address space is actually divided into two parts: *RAM* (memory you can read from and write to) and *ROM* (memory you can only read from). We say that we have RAM space and ROM space inside our memory space.

RAM

YOU CAN BOTH READ FROM AND WRITE TO IT. THE DATA DISAPPEARS IF YOU TURN OFF THE POWER.

EXAMPLE: PRIMARY MEMORY

ROM

YOU CAN ONLY READ FROM IT. THE DATA IS SAVED EVEN IF YOU TURN OFF THE POWER.

EXAMPLE: BIOS-ROM

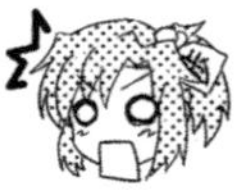

Huh? What's this about rams and roms?! Okay, so RAM is our old friend the primary memory, right? We can read from and write to it, and its data disappears if you turn off the power. . . .

But what about ROM? So the data is intact even if you turn off the power and you can only read from it, and this is somehow part of the memory space? Umm, what is it, though?!

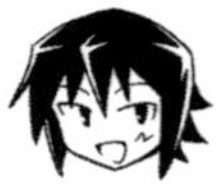

Yeah. We haven't really talked about it yet, but there is ROM on something called the motherboard inside the computer. This is where you can find the program the CPU runs when you start your computer. This program that runs before any others is called the *BIOS*.

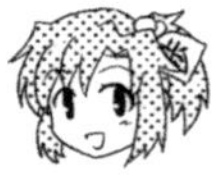

I see. So if it couldn't run this program, the computer would just be a very expensive box? That's why the BIOS is put into a special part of read-only memory—so it won't be forgotten!

WHAT IS THE BIOS?

The *BIOS (Basic Input/Output System)* is a program found in ROM that the computer runs when you first turn it on. The BIOS checks that all the devices in your computer are in working order after you turn on the power. It also launches your operating system from your hard disk.

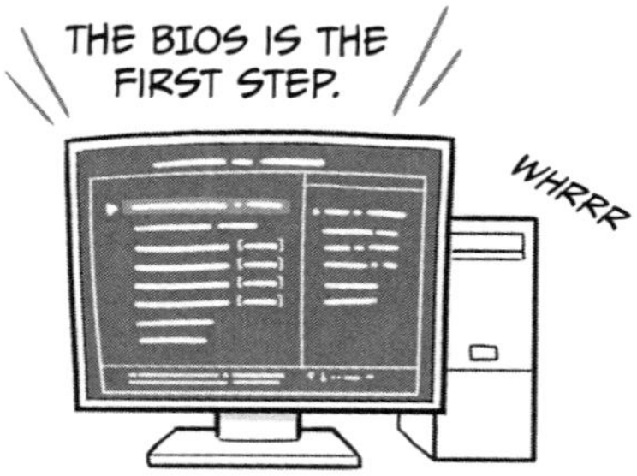
THE BIOS IS THE FIRST STEP.
WHRRR

In addition to the RAM space and ROM space, there is also a very tiny space called the *I/O space*.

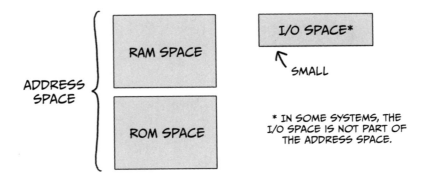

ADDRESS SPACE

RAM SPACE

ROM SPACE

I/O SPACE*

↖ SMALL

* IN SOME SYSTEMS, THE I/O SPACE IS NOT PART OF THE ADDRESS SPACE.

I think I remember hearing you mention I/O earlier today. Ice cream and oreos . . . no . . . input/output, right?

Yeah. The I/O ports live inside this I/O space. As I explained before, the CPU uses these I/O ports to talk to external devices directly (such as keyboards and mice). This is why your computer responds when you press a key on the keyboard.

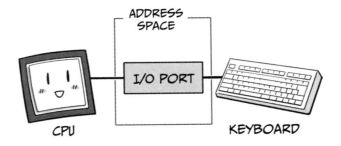

ADDRESS SPACE

I/O PORT

CPU

KEYBOARD

Hoho! Go CPU! So that means that since external devices use the address space managed by the CPU, they are also managed by the CPU, right? In any case, I think I get that there are different types of spaces inside the address space!

What Are Interrupts?

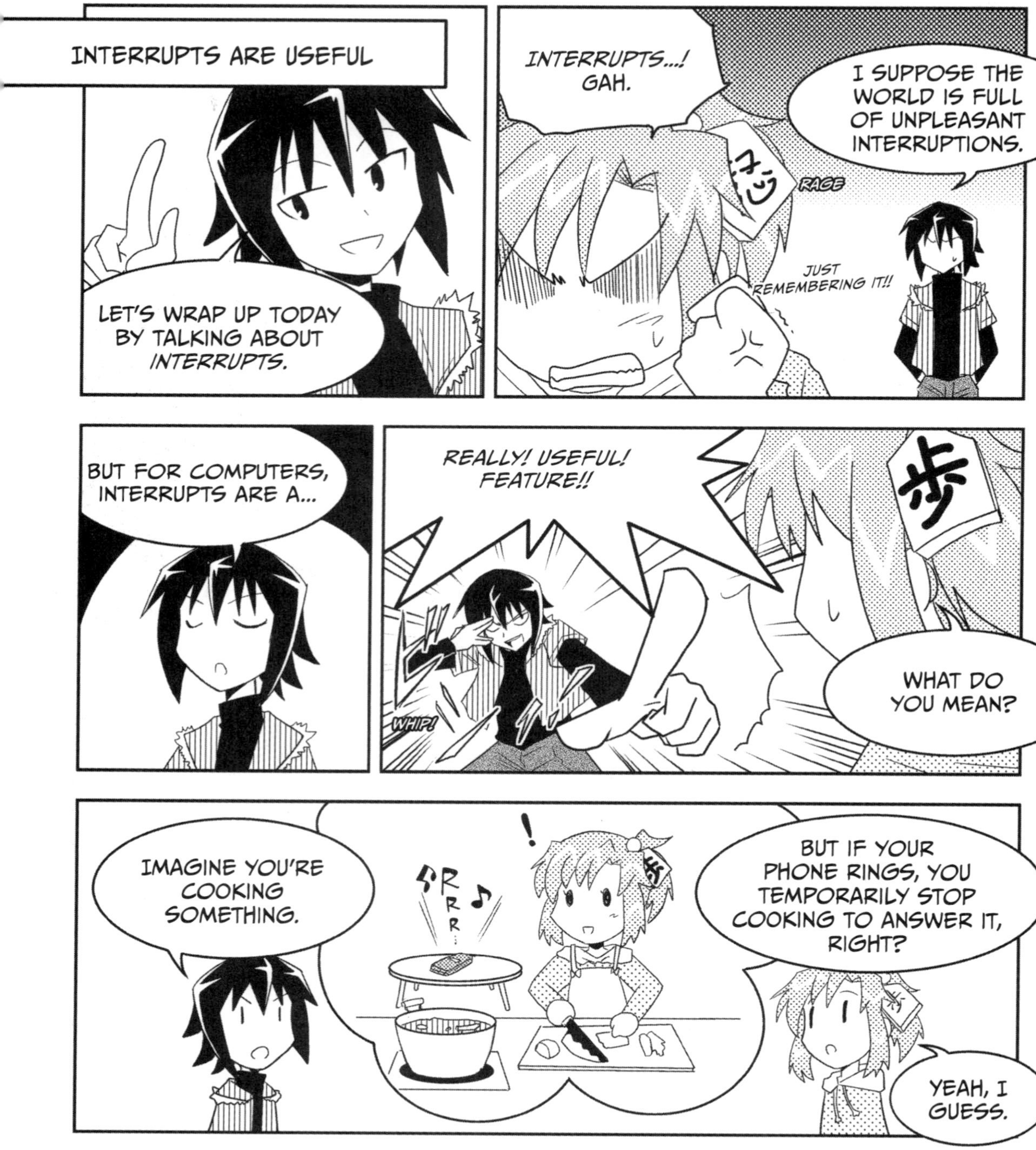
INTERRUPTS ARE USEFUL
LET'S WRAP UP TODAY BY TALKING ABOUT INTERRUPTS.
INTERRUPTS...! GAH.
RAGE
JUST REMEMBERING IT!!
I SUPPOSE THE WORLD IS FULL OF UNPLEASANT INTERRUPTIONS.
BUT FOR COMPUTERS, INTERRUPTS ARE A...
REALLY! USEFUL! FEATURE!!
WHIP!
WHAT DO YOU MEAN?
IMAGINE YOU'RE COOKING SOMETHING.
RRR...
BUT IF YOUR PHONE RINGS, YOU TEMPORARILY STOP COOKING TO ANSWER IT, RIGHT?
YEAH, I GUESS.

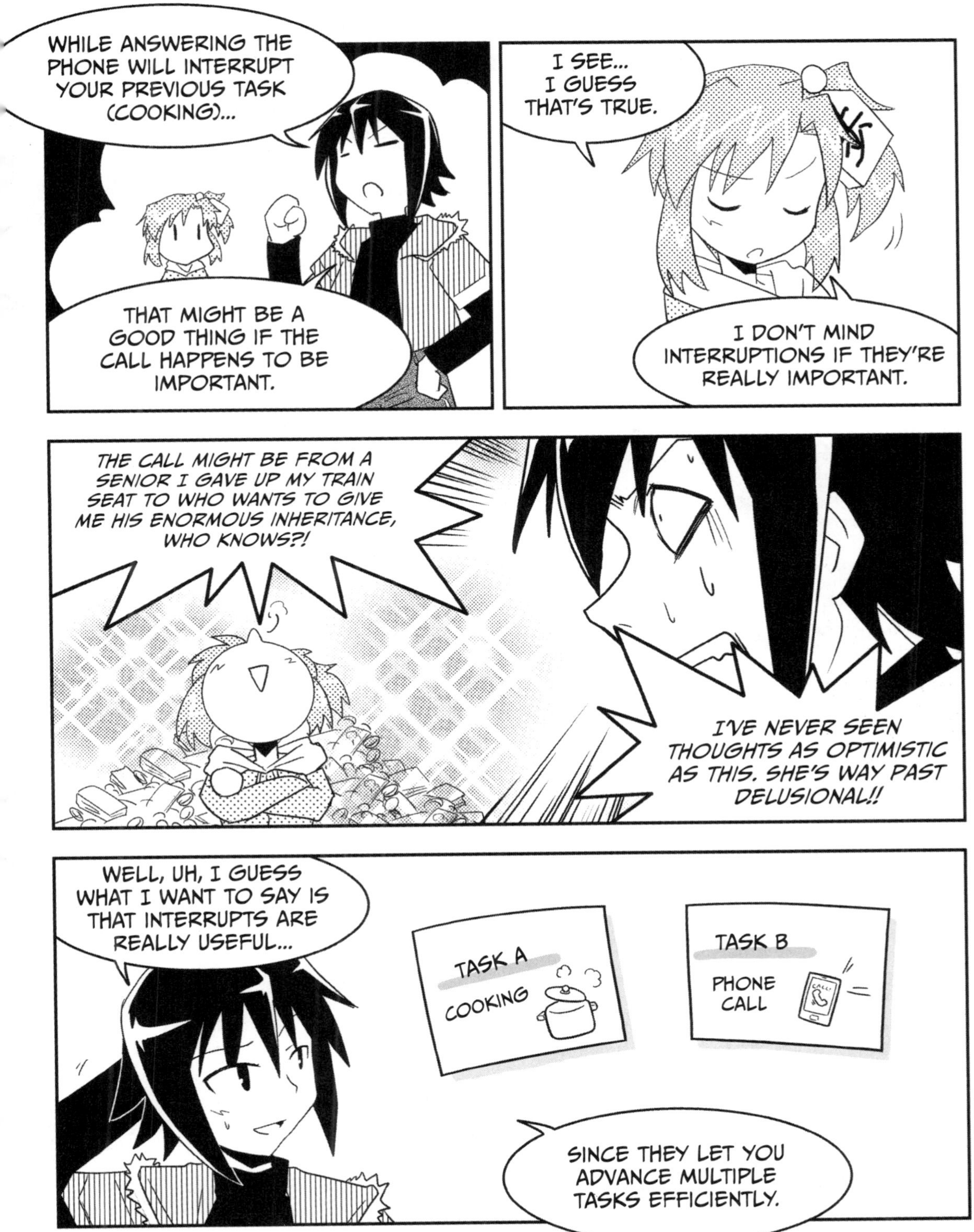
WHILE ANSWERING THE PHONE WILL INTERRUPT YOUR PREVIOUS TASK (COOKING)...
THAT MIGHT BE A GOOD THING IF THE CALL HAPPENS TO BE IMPORTANT.
I SEE... I GUESS THAT'S TRUE.
I DON'T MIND INTERRUPTIONS IF THEY'RE REALLY IMPORTANT.
THE CALL MIGHT BE FROM A SENIOR I GAVE UP MY TRAIN SEAT TO WHO WANTS TO GIVE ME HIS ENORMOUS INHERITANCE, WHO KNOWS?!
I'VE NEVER SEEN THOUGHTS AS OPTIMISTIC AS THIS. SHE'S WAY PAST DELUSIONAL!!
WELL, UH, I GUESS WHAT I WANT TO SAY IS THAT INTERRUPTS ARE REALLY USEFUL...
TASK A
COOKING
TASK B
PHONE CALL
SINCE THEY LET YOU ADVANCE MULTIPLE TASKS EFFICIENTLY.

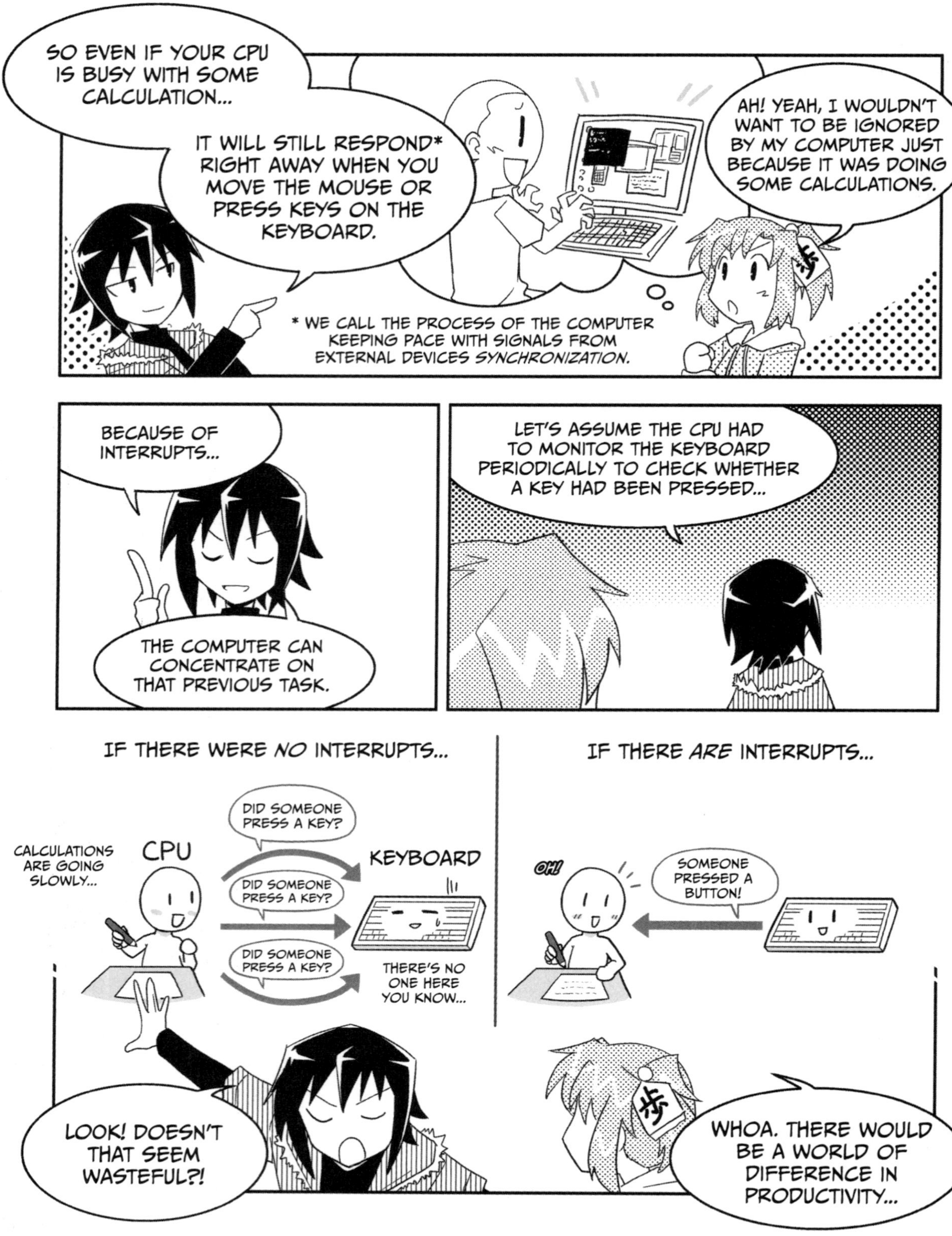
SO EVEN IF YOUR CPU IS BUSY WITH SOME CALCULATION...
IT WILL STILL RESPOND* RIGHT AWAY WHEN YOU MOVE THE MOUSE OR PRESS KEYS ON THE KEYBOARD.
AH! YEAH, I WOULDN'T WANT TO BE IGNORED BY MY COMPUTER JUST BECAUSE IT WAS DOING SOME CALCULATIONS.
* WE CALL THE PROCESS OF THE COMPUTER KEEPING PACE WITH SIGNALS FROM EXTERNAL DEVICES *SYNCHRONIZATION*.
BECAUSE OF INTERRUPTS...
THE COMPUTER CAN CONCENTRATE ON THAT PREVIOUS TASK.
LET'S ASSUME THE CPU HAD TO MONITOR THE KEYBOARD PERIODICALLY TO CHECK WHETHER A KEY HAD BEEN PRESSED...
IF THERE WERE *NO* INTERRUPTS...
CALCULATIONS ARE GOING SLOWLY...
CPU
DID SOMEONE PRESS A KEY?
DID SOMEONE PRESS A KEY?
DID SOMEONE PRESS A KEY?
KEYBOARD
THERE'S NO ONE HERE YOU KNOW...
IF THERE *ARE* INTERRUPTS...
OH!
SOMEONE PRESSED A BUTTON!
LOOK! DOESN'T THAT SEEM WASTEFUL?!
WHOA. THERE WOULD BE A WORLD OF DIFFERENCE IN PRODUCTIVITY...

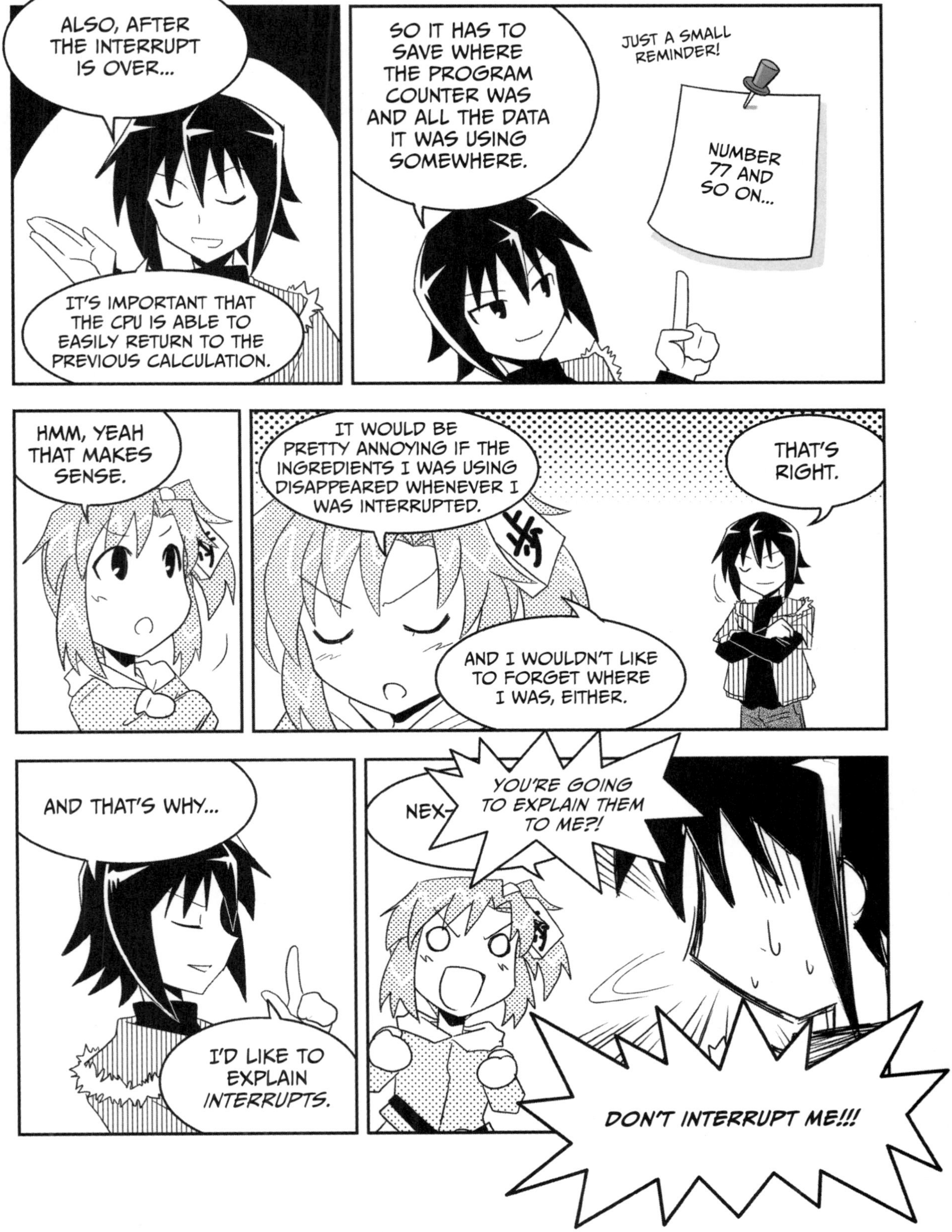
ALSO, AFTER THE INTERRUPT IS OVER...
IT'S IMPORTANT THAT THE CPU IS ABLE TO EASILY RETURN TO THE PREVIOUS CALCULATION.
SO IT HAS TO SAVE WHERE THE PROGRAM COUNTER WAS AND ALL THE DATA IT WAS USING SOMEWHERE.
JUST A SMALL REMINDER!
NUMBER 77 AND SO ON...
HMM, YEAH THAT MAKES SENSE.
IT WOULD BE PRETTY ANNOYING IF THE INGREDIENTS I WAS USING DISAPPEARED WHENEVER I WAS INTERRUPTED.
AND I WOULDN'T LIKE TO FORGET WHERE I WAS, EITHER.
THAT'S RIGHT.
AND THAT'S WHY...
I'D LIKE TO EXPLAIN *INTERRUPTS*.
NEX-
YOU'RE GOING TO EXPLAIN THEM TO ME?!
DON'T INTERRUPT ME!!!

THE STACK AND THE STACK POINTER

Okay, let's get right into it. As I said, to be able to return to the task it was doing before the interrupt, the computer needs to take some memos before it starts a new task.

It uses something called the *stack*—a part of main memory reserved for bookkeeping—to do this. The way it does this is pretty interesting—take a look.

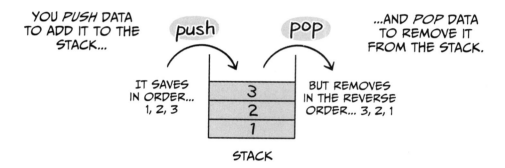

YOU *PUSH* DATA TO ADD IT TO THE STACK...

push   pop

...AND *POP* DATA TO REMOVE IT FROM THE STACK.

IT SAVES IN ORDER... 1, 2, 3

| 3 |
| 2 |
| 1 |

BUT REMOVES IN THE REVERSE ORDER... 3, 2, 1

STACK

Ooh, that's a funny way to remember things! It's kind of like a stack of books that you can keep piling up, but if you want to take one out, you always have to take one from the top. You can't just take data from anywhere.

That's exactly right. And a special register holds something called the *stack pointer* (*SP* for short) that points to the last stack address we worked with.

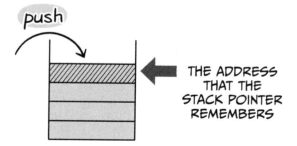

push

THE ADDRESS THAT THE STACK POINTER REMEMBERS

I see. While the program counter keeps track of the address for the next instruction, the stack pointer keeps track of the last address on the stack.

When using stacks, it's important to use the stack pointer correctly. Because . . .

With just one interrupt, everything is fine. But if you keep adding interrupts one after another, the stack will keep growing and eventually bad stuff will happen. . . .

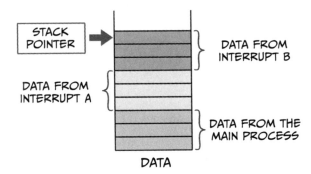

STACK POINTER
DATA FROM INTERRUPT B
DATA FROM INTERRUPT A
DATA FROM THE MAIN PROCESS
DATA

The data that is saved during an interrupt consists of the accumulator, status registers, and the program counter.

Whoaaa! I'm not sure I'm getting what's happening there.

Bugs or even just frequent interrupts that the stack has no coping mechanisms for can result in the stack pointer losing control over the program's execution.

This usually means that the person or people who wrote the software didn't properly understand the implications of using a stack...

Ah! Have you ever made one of your programs go out of control like this?

When working with the CPU, interrupts can be really efficient. But if you don't know how to work with the stack, you're bound to make a program that runs into problems like this. And that's all I have to say about that!!

So you were also like that once, right? You didn't know how to work with the stack and something happened right? I'm right, aren't I?!

Fuhahahah! I'm just talking hypothetically!

INTERRUPT PRIORITY

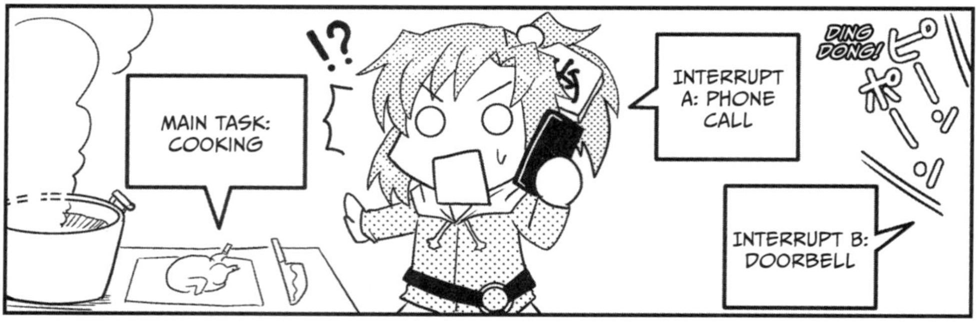
MAIN TASK: COOKING
INTERRUPT A: PHONE CALL
DING DONG!
INTERRUPT B: DOORBELL

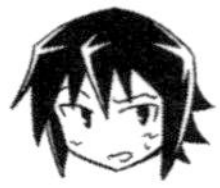

Ahem. Let's try to refocus and talk a bit about *interrupt priority.*

Let's once again assume that you were interrupted with a phone call while cooking. Now let's assume that you also hear the doorbell while on the phone. What would you do?

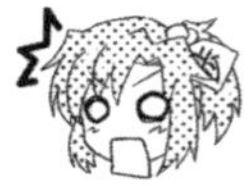

Eeeeh!? That's just bad timing! I don't think I could deal with that. I'd rather people would stop interrupting me all the time. . . .

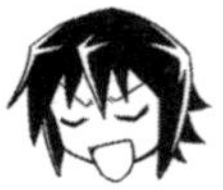

Heh heh heh. Yeah, I thought so. This is when *interrupt masks* are really useful! By using an interrupt mask, you can avoid being interrupted at all. You know, like how you can hide your face behind a mask.

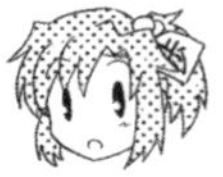

Yeah, wearing a mask can stop all kinds of things!

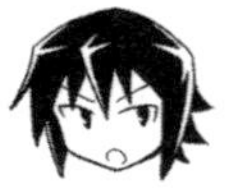

But you can't let your guard down. You can still be forcefully interrupted by some things, even if you're using a mask. We call these *resets*!

Resets are the interrupts with the absolute highest priority. They are special interrupts that are not affected by masks.

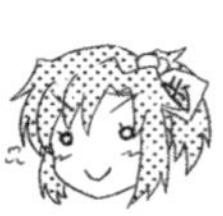

Resets! The word does have a kind of "don't argue with me" air about it. Just like when you press the reset button on your game console, it returns to its initial state, right? It really gives me this "let's start over" vibe.

Yeah, that's right. And whether it's your computer or your console, both of them start at their initial state when you turn on the power, right? That's because when you turn on the power, the first thing the system does is issue a reset.

Resets return programs to their initial state. Put another way, they return all the circuits to their initial state. Completely. This is why when we want the computer to wake up nicely—that is, when we want it to start in a functional state—we have to issue a reset.

Oooh, it felt a bit scary when you said it was forceful, but I guess a bit of force is necessary.

There are also some interrupts of the highest priority that the CPU will not mask even though these interrupts might not be resets.

We call these interrupt signals that go through masks *non-maskable interrupts (NMI)*. They can have many uses depending on the system architecture, and they're really convenient in some cases.

It seems interrupts have all sorts of uses.

There are also *timer interrupts* that issue an interrupt when they reach zero after counting down using a decrementing counter. (Think 3, 2, 1, interrupt now!) Using these, it's possible to execute programs at regularly timed intervals.

Ah! That timer interrupt gave me an idea! There is a program that runs every day at 7 AM that sounds a bell when I'm executing my sleep task. It's issuing an interrupt right when I'm snoozing away peacefully!!

Ah. That's just your alarm clock.

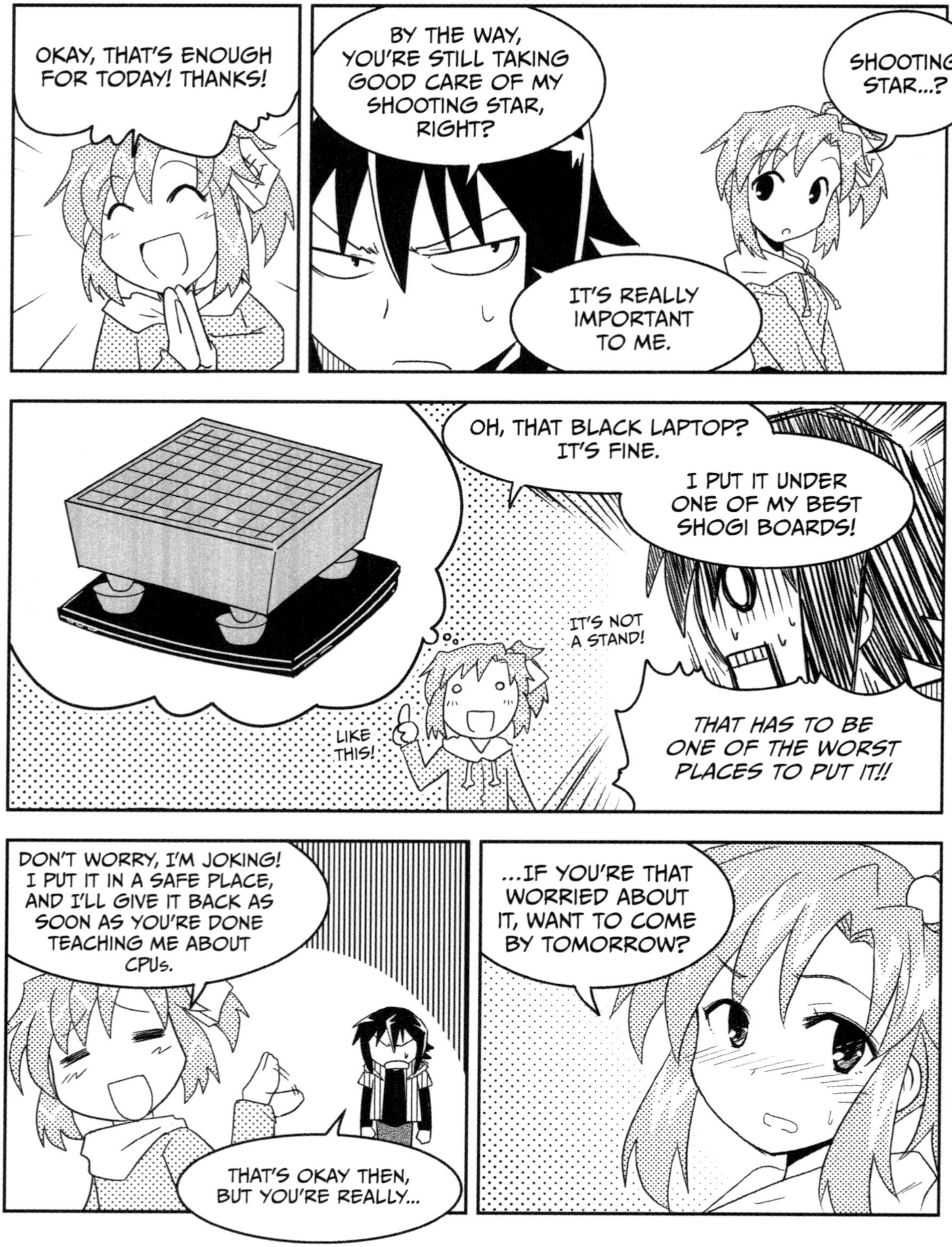
OKAY, THAT'S ENOUGH FOR TODAY! THANKS!
BY THE WAY, YOU'RE STILL TAKING GOOD CARE OF MY SHOOTING STAR, RIGHT?
SHOOTING STAR...?
IT'S REALLY IMPORTANT TO ME.
OH, THAT BLACK LAPTOP? IT'S FINE.
I PUT IT UNDER ONE OF MY BEST SHOGI BOARDS!
IT'S NOT A STAND!
LIKE THIS!
THAT HAS TO BE ONE OF THE WORST PLACES TO PUT IT!!
DON'T WORRY, I'M JOKING! I PUT IT IN A SAFE PLACE, AND I'LL GIVE IT BACK AS SOON AS YOU'RE DONE TEACHING ME ABOUT CPUs.
THAT'S OKAY THEN, BUT YOU'RE REALLY...
...IF YOU'RE THAT WORRIED ABOUT IT, WANT TO COME BY TOMORROW?

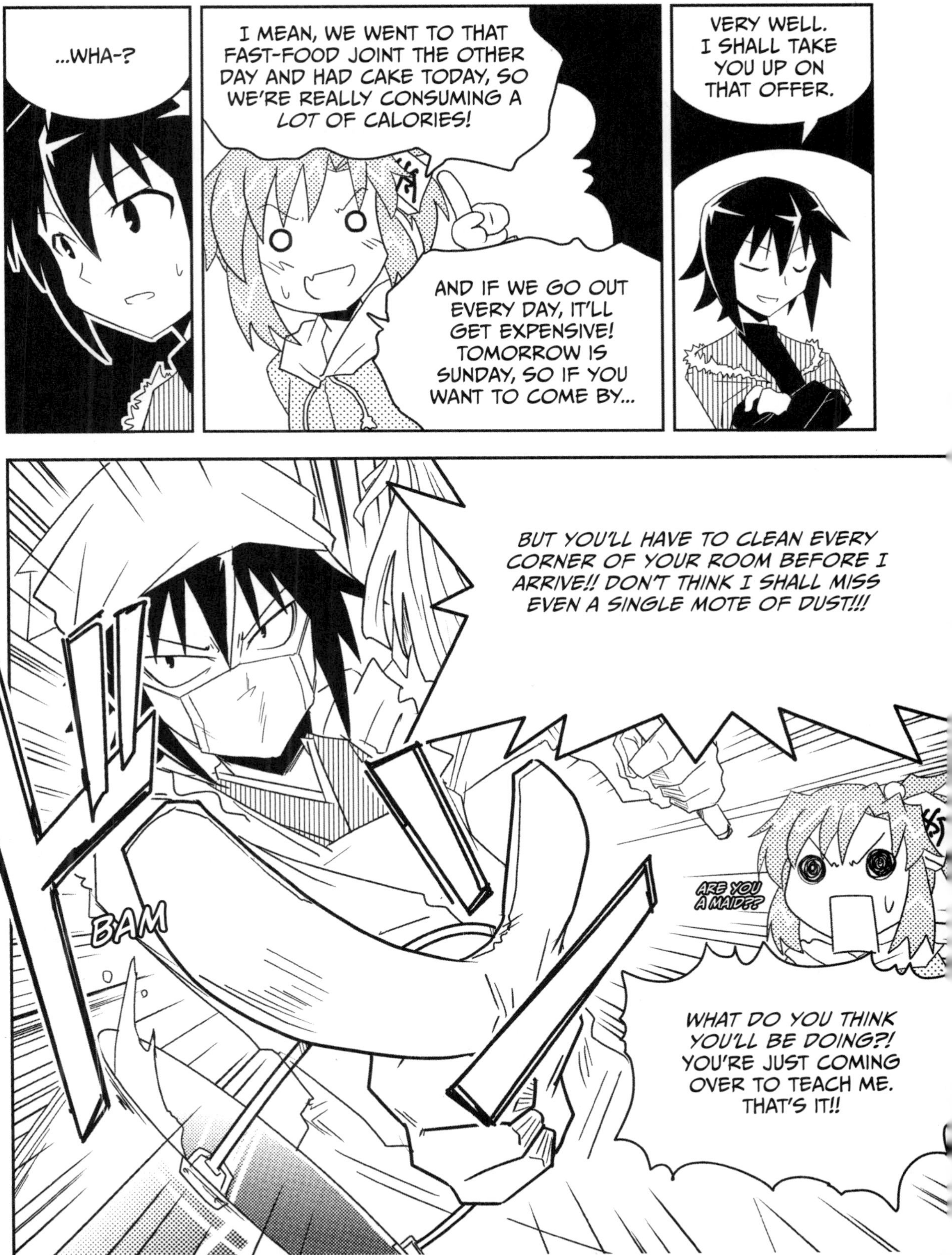
...WHA-?
I MEAN, WE WENT TO THAT FAST-FOOD JOINT THE OTHER DAY AND HAD CAKE TODAY, SO WE'RE REALLY CONSUMING A LOT OF CALORIES!
AND IF WE GO OUT EVERY DAY, IT'LL GET EXPENSIVE! TOMORROW IS SUNDAY, SO IF YOU WANT TO COME BY...
VERY WELL. I SHALL TAKE YOU UP ON THAT OFFER.
BUT YOU'LL HAVE TO CLEAN EVERY CORNER OF YOUR ROOM BEFORE I ARRIVE!! DON'T THINK I SHALL MISS EVEN A SINGLE MOTE OF DUST!!!
BAM
ARE YOU A MAID??
WHAT DO YOU THINK YOU'LL BE DOING?! YOU'RE JUST COMING OVER TO TEACH ME. THAT'S IT!!

MEMORY CLASSIFICATIONS

ROM stands for read-only memory and is a type of memory that will not lose its data even if the power is turned off. As the name implies, you can only read from ROM. You can't write to it.

In contrast, with RAM, which stands for random access memory, you can read from or write to any address in any order. You might think that ROM and RAM are opposites, but that isn't necessarily the case.

MEMORY
RWM
CAN READ AND WRITE
ROM
CAN ONLY READ
RAM
CAN BE ACCESSED RANDOMLY
SAM
CAN ONLY BE ACCESSED SEQUENTIALLY

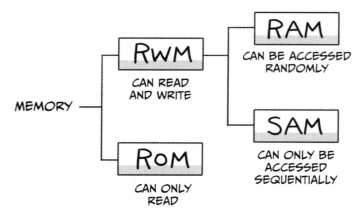

As you can see in the image above, the opposite of RAM is actually *SAM (sequential access memory)*, which was an older type of memory commonly found on magnetic tapes and drums. As the name suggests, it could only read memory addresses in order. In addition, the opposite of ROM is the now defunct *RWM (read-write memory)*.

Memory that retains its data even when the power is turned off and allows this data to be accessed again when the power comes back on is called *non-volatile memory*. Memory that loses its data when the power is turned off is called *volatile memory*.

These terms are no longer commonly used, however, and have largely been replaced by RAM (instead of volatile memory) and ROM (instead of non-volatile memory).

I/O PORTS AND THE GPU

If there were no connection between input/output devices and the CPU's registers or ALU, the CPU would be unable to accept external input. External input doesn't only come in the form of character input from the keyboard; it can be a mouse click or any electrical signal. If we didn't have some output, such as LEDs that light up when an operation is complete or some other signal, it would be very hard for us to interact with any computer. In the same way we need feedback, the internal data bus needs *input and output ports (I/O ports)* to communicate with external devices such as memory and so on.

The most commonly used output device is the computer display. This is an example of a device that is not connected directly to the CPU. The display is instead connected to a special IC called the *GPU (graphics processing unit)*, which generates and outputs images on demand. When the CPU needs to use the GPU, it has a special I/O port dedicated to GPU communication.

DIRECTLY CONNECTED!
CPU
I/O PORT
KEYBOARD
EXCLUSIVE I/O PORT
GPU
NO DIRECT CONNECTION
DISPLAY

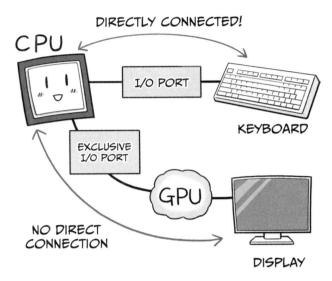

Smaller systems sometimes don't have a GPU but are still attached to a color LCD (liquid crystal display). In these cases, the CPU communicates by sending any necessary data through an I/O port to an LCD controller. This LCD controller and its driver then output the image data to the display.

CLOCK FREQUENCY AND DEGREES OF ACCURACY

Of course, you need electricity for the CPU to work. But you also need a clock frequency. A *clock* is a signal that alternates between high and low voltage at regular intervals. The *clock frequency* is how many times this signal alternates in one second.

The clock is like the heartbeat of the CPU. It is essential for updating the CPU's internal circuits, such as the latching of the data inside the ALU and the block* advancing the program counter.

Clock frequency is measured in Hz (hertz), which is a measure of how many times the clock cycles in one second. So, a clock running at 40 MHz would be cycling 40 million times per second.

This *clock speed* is also a measure of the performance of the CPU. Everything that the CPU does, like instruction decoding and ALU operations, it does in synchronization with the clock. The CPU can execute one action per clock cycle, so the higher the clock frequency, the higher the clock speed and the faster the execution speed of the CPU.

* *Block* is a term used to denote the group of things needed to realize some function.

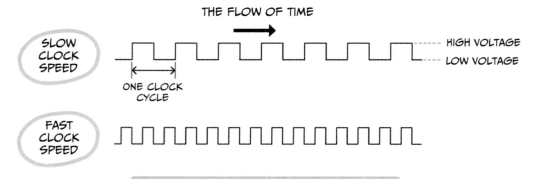

THE FLOW OF TIME

SLOW CLOCK SPEED

HIGH VOLTAGE

LOW VOLTAGE

ONE CLOCK CYCLE

FAST CLOCK SPEED

WE GET A HIGHER NUMBER OF CLOCK CYCLES OVER THE SAME AMOUNT OF TIME!

The degree to which the clock speed matches the clock frequency is called the *degree of accuracy*. When using computers for communication applications, connecting two devices with clock frequencies that do not match can cause timing problems.

CLOCK GENERATORS

We call circuits that generate clock signals *clock generators*. Most CPUs have internal clock generators, but it is also possible to connect externally generated clock signals to a CPU. The different components inside the CPU that make up the clock generator—including the crystal oscillator, capacitors, and resistors—all contribute to the accuracy of a clock signal's frequency. Some situations don't require high accuracy, but if a CPU must be synchronized with other devices to exchange data, for example, then the accuracy of the clock signal's frequency is a high priority.

WHAT ARE CRYSTAL OSCILLATORS?

Crystal oscillators are made from small artificial crystal shards that have been cut incredibly thin. If you attach two electrodes to a shard and apply a voltage, the crystal warps. By fluctuating the direction of the voltage, it is possible to create vibrations that give rise to a stable frequency. Consequently, you can generate oscillations at very precise time intervals.

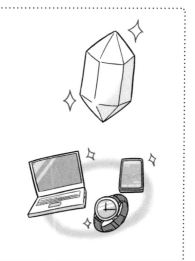

Crystal oscillators are used in many kinds of devices in which precise time intervals need to be measured, such as computers, phones, and watches. The quartz in a quartz watch is actually a crystal oscillator.

By connecting clock generators to crystal oscillators and *condensers* (electronic components that store and release electrical charge), it's possible to create an alternating signal.

To achieve a high degree of accuracy, you can use an external clock signal instead of the clock signal from the CPU's internal clock generator. External oscillators usually provide higher quality clock signals than internal clock generators.

TIMER INTERRUPTS

By using the decrementing counter inside CPUs, we can initiate interrupts whenever the timer reaches zero. We call this a *timer interrupt*.

MASTER CLOCK
LOWERS THE FREQUENCY
PRESCALER (FREQUENCY DIVIDER)
TIMER BASIS CLOCK
A COUNTDOWN 3, 2, 1, 0
DECREASING TIMER
TIMER INTERRUPT
LATCH SIGNAL
SELECT REGISTER
INITIAL VALUE REGISTER
MULTIPLICATION FACTOR
AMOUNT TO COUNT FROM

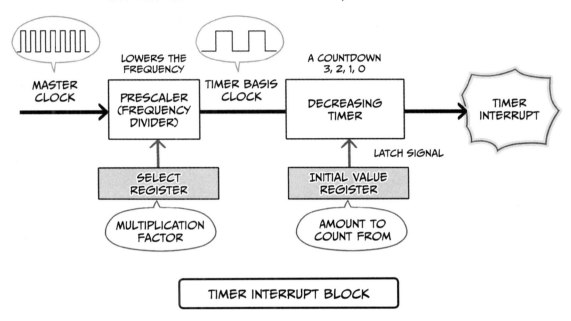

TIMER INTERRUPT BLOCK

It is also possible to use the CPU's base clock (or master clock) with a *frequency divider.** Dividing the CPU's base clock with a frequency divider allows you to increase the time required for a countdown timer to count to zero. Indeed, you can change the amount of time required for the timer to count down to zero from several seconds to several hundred seconds.

It is then possible to execute some program at given intervals by setting the initial value of the countdown timer to some value (for example, 100). To change the interrupt frequency, all you need to do is tell the CPU to rewrite the register where the "value to count down from" is stored. Changing this value from 100 to 50, for example, would double the interrupt frequency.

You can set a countdown timer to run even while other programs are running, and it will issue an interrupt when it has counted down to zero. There are many uses for this. For example, you can turn a light on and off at fixed intervals. Timer interrupts are more effective than other methods for doing this because they save valuable CPU time.

* *Frequency dividers* change the period by lowering the frequency.

HOW TO USE TIMER INTERRUPTS

To use a timer interrupt, you must first configure it by writing a value into its control register. The value written to this register determines the clock source, whether the clock frequency is to be divided before counting and by how much, and other timer behavior.

Next, we write the initial value into the counter and set the timer to start on the reset signal. After it has started, the timer will interrupt the CPU every time it counts down to zero.

We then rig the timer to start on the reset signal (see the next page) and to cancel if commanded by the CPU to do so. After it has started, an *interrupt signal* will be sent from the timer block to the CPU control circuit every (master clock cycle) × (multiplication factor) × (value to count from) units of time.

Finally, let's examine the timer interrupt component present in classic CPU architectures, which can be seen in the image below. *INT* here is the signal that the CPU uses to send instructions to the timer interrupt block. *RESET* (timer reset) is the signal used to start the timer.

TIMER INTERRUPT CONTROL
RESET
INT

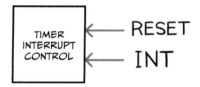

If you were to leave the reset input in an active state, the timer would stop and never start. If you then were to clear the timer reset, it would start counting down again and eventually issue an interrupt. After this, it would count down from the set value on every cycle of the multiplied master clock frequency, issuing an interrupt signal when it reached zero.

When it reached zero, it would once again latch to the value stored in the "value to count from" register and start over. By doing this over and over again, the component is able to produce interrupts at fixed intervals indefinitely.

RESET SIGNALS

To *reset* means to set programs and internal circuits to their initial state. The program counter is set to zero, and temporary operational data is cleared. A reset signal is issued every time you start your computer. This is extremely important as it makes sure that any programs you run after the start-up process work correctly.

Let's take a closer look at the reset process. The reset signal is raised by setting an active state after a low voltage state. After you turn on the power, the voltage will fluctuate a bit before finally settling down at a stable level. If the CPU were active during this period, all kinds of problems would result. This is why the reset signal is constantly active during this period, making the CPU unable to process anything. In other words, we protect the CPU by maintaining the reset state until the voltage has stabilized. Then, when the voltage has stabilized, we release the reset signal by raising the voltage.

STABLE
POWER VOLTAGE
VOLTAGE
RESET INPUT
THE VOLTAGE IS UNSTABLE, SO WE KEEP THE RESET ACTIVE.
IT HAS STABILIZED, SO WE CAN RELEASE THE RESET.

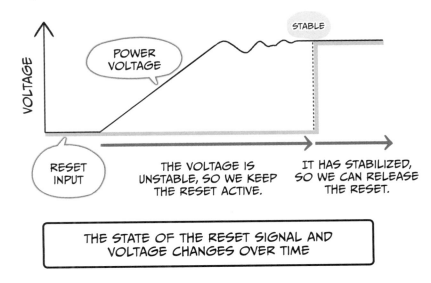

THE STATE OF THE RESET SIGNAL AND VOLTAGE CHANGES OVER TIME

If, for example, the CPU were to start acting in an unexpected manner, it is possible to initiate a forced reset by lowering the voltage below the necessary level (and therefore enabling the reset) and setting all programs and circuits to their initial state. Resets are an essential function needed to ensure that the computer will work as we expect it to.

CPU PERFORMANCE IS MEASURED IN FLOPS

CPU performance is determined by the CPU clock speed and its operation execution speed. The clock speed tells us how often the logic circuits in the ALU can perform calculations. And the *operation execution speed* tells us how quickly the CPU can perform calculations one after another.

Older CPU ALU blocks worked only with integer arithmetic. Back then, the CPU's performance was measured by how many instructions it could handle in one second, or its *MIPS (million instructions per second)* value, rather than by how quickly it could perform calculation operations. As its name suggests, MIPS indicated how many millions of instructions the CPU could handle in one second.

These older CPUs were, of course, also able to work with floating-point values, but modern CPUs have specialized integrated hardware for just this purpose. This is why in more recent years the preferred measure of performance has become how many floating-point operations the CPU can handle in one second, or *MFLOPS (million floating-point operations per second)*. Once again, as its name suggests, this value indicates how many millions of floating-point operations with 15 significant digits the CPU can handle in one second.

We sometimes use units other than MFLOPS, such as *GFLOPS (gigaFLOPS)* and *TFLOPS (teraFLOPS)*. One GFLOPS is the processing of a billion floating-point operations with 15 significant digits in one second. One TFLOPS is the ability to process a whopping trillion floating-point operations with 15 significant digits in one second.

YOU CAN SEE THE PERFORMANCE OF A CPU BY LOOKING AT ITS FLOPS VALUE!

KYAA~~~~!

I'M SO EMBARRASSED...

OPERATIONS

Types of Operations

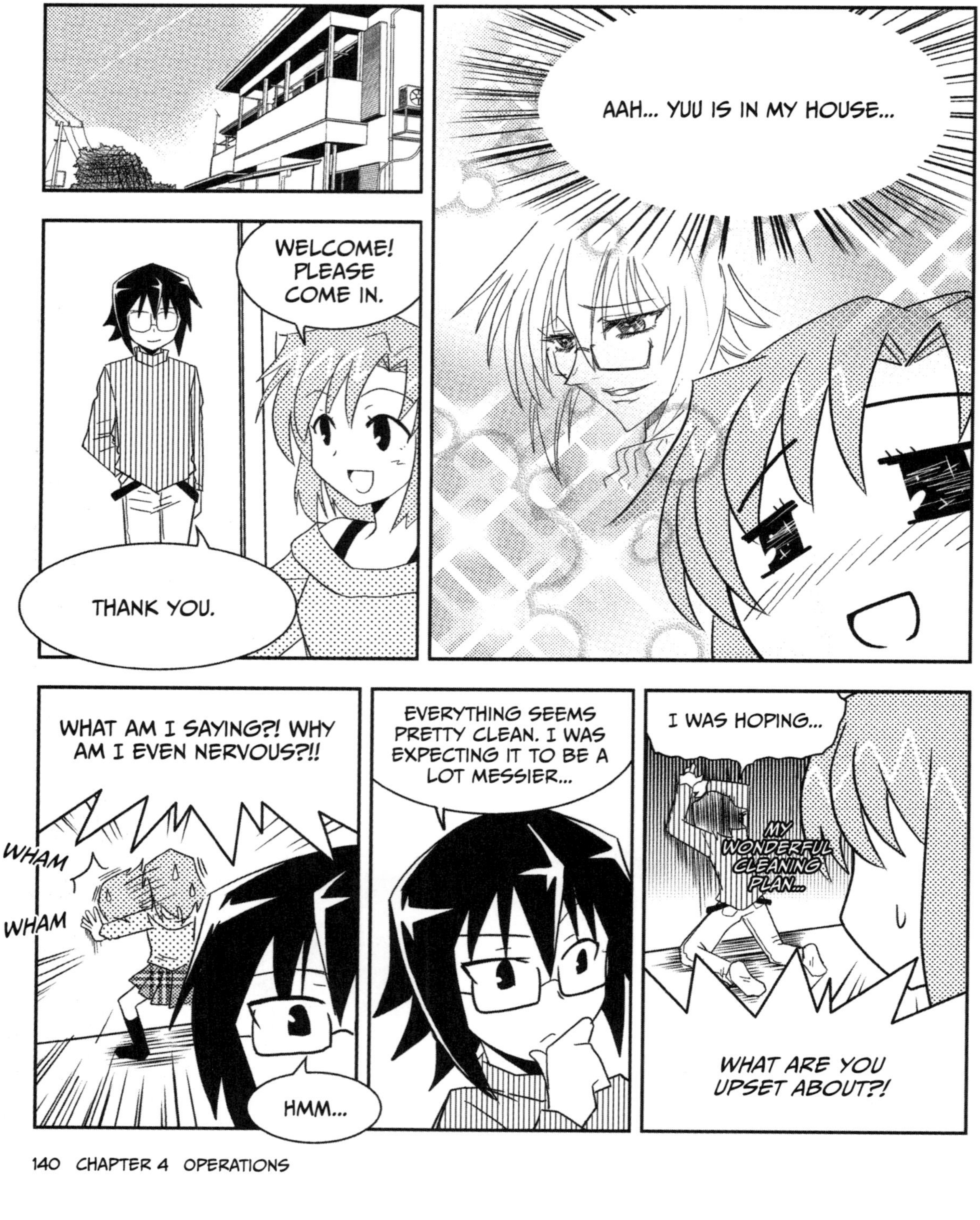
WELCOME! PLEASE COME IN.
THANK YOU.
AAH... YUU IS IN MY HOUSE...
WHAT AM I SAYING?! WHY AM I EVEN NERVOUS?!!
WHAM
WHAM
EVERYTHING SEEMS PRETTY CLEAN. I WAS EXPECTING IT TO BE A LOT MESSIER...
HMM...
I WAS HOPING...
MY WONDERFUL CLEANING PLAN...
WHAT ARE YOU UPSET ABOUT?!

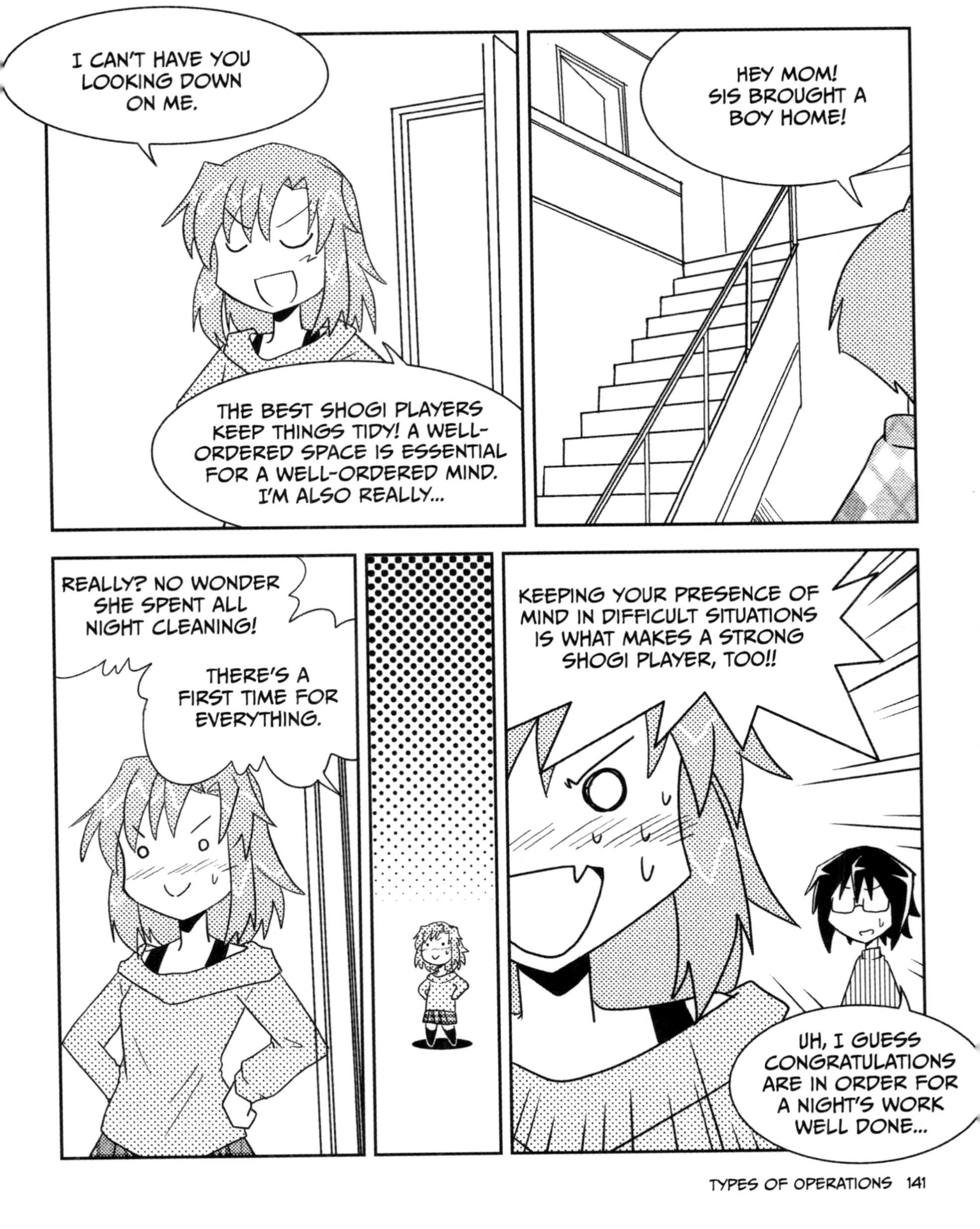
I CAN'T HAVE YOU LOOKING DOWN ON ME.
THE BEST SHOGI PLAYERS KEEP THINGS TIDY! A WELL-ORDERED SPACE IS ESSENTIAL FOR A WELL-ORDERED MIND. I'M ALSO REALLY...
HEY MOM! SIS BROUGHT A BOY HOME!
REALLY? NO WONDER SHE SPENT ALL NIGHT CLEANING!
THERE'S A FIRST TIME FOR EVERYTHING.
KEEPING YOUR PRESENCE OF MIND IN DIFFICULT SITUATIONS IS WHAT MAKES A STRONG SHOGI PLAYER, TOO!!
UH, I GUESS CONGRATULATIONS ARE IN ORDER FOR A NIGHT'S WORK WELL DONE...

THERE ARE MANY TYPES OF INSTRUCTIONS

OKAY, TODAY WE'RE GOING TO TALK ABOUT *INSTRUCTIONS*.

OH, I REMEMBER WE TALKED ABOUT INSTRUCTIONS BEFORE. THESE ONES, RIGHT?

DO SOMETHING...

INSTRUCTION CODE (OPCODE)

...TO SOMETHING

OPERAND

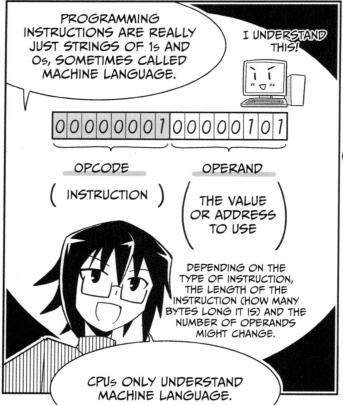

PROGRAMMING INSTRUCTIONS ARE REALLY JUST STRINGS OF 1s AND 0s, SOMETIMES CALLED *MACHINE LANGUAGE*.

I UNDERSTAND THIS!

| 0 | 0 | 0 | 0 | 0 | 0 | 0 | 1 | 0 | 0 | 0 | 0 | 0 | 1 | 0 | 1 |

OPCODE

(INSTRUCTION)

OPERAND

THE VALUE OR ADDRESS TO USE

DEPENDING ON THE TYPE OF INSTRUCTION, THE LENGTH OF THE INSTRUCTION (HOW MANY BYTES LONG IT IS) AND THE NUMBER OF OPERANDS MIGHT CHANGE.

CPUs ONLY UNDERSTAND MACHINE LANGUAGE.

TYPES OF OPCODES

COMPARE

STORE

JUMP

UH-HUH...

SO THERE ARE LOTS OF DIFFERENT KINDS OF INSTRUCTIONS, RIGHT?

THAT'S RIGHT! I'VE CATEGORIZED DIFFERENT TYPES OF INSTRUCTIONS HERE IN THIS TABLE.

INSTRUCTION TYPES	
INSTRUCTIONS THAT DEAL WITH CALCULATIONS	INSTRUCTIONS THAT DON'T DEAL WITH CALCULATIONS
1. Arithmetic instructions	1. Data transfer instructions
2. Logic instructions	2. Input and output instructions
3. Bit shift instructions	3. Branching instructions
	4. Conditionals (comparison instructions and so on)

I'LL BE GOING THROUGH THESE IN ORDER TODAY.

WOW, THERE ARE THAT MANY...?

WELL, YOU'VE ALREADY LEARNED A LOT, SO I WOULDN'T BE THAT WORRIED.

IF YOU UNDERSTAND THESE INSTRUCTIONS, THEN YOU'LL KNOW WHAT IS HAPPENING INSIDE THE CPU.

I SEE...

THEN GIVE ME A DETAILED EXPLANATION OF ALL THESE INSTRUCTIONS IN UNDER THREE SECONDS!!

DON'T GIVE ME IMPOSSIBLE INSTRUCTIONS LIKE THAT!!!

INSTRUCTIONS FOR ARITHMETIC AND LOGIC OPERATIONS

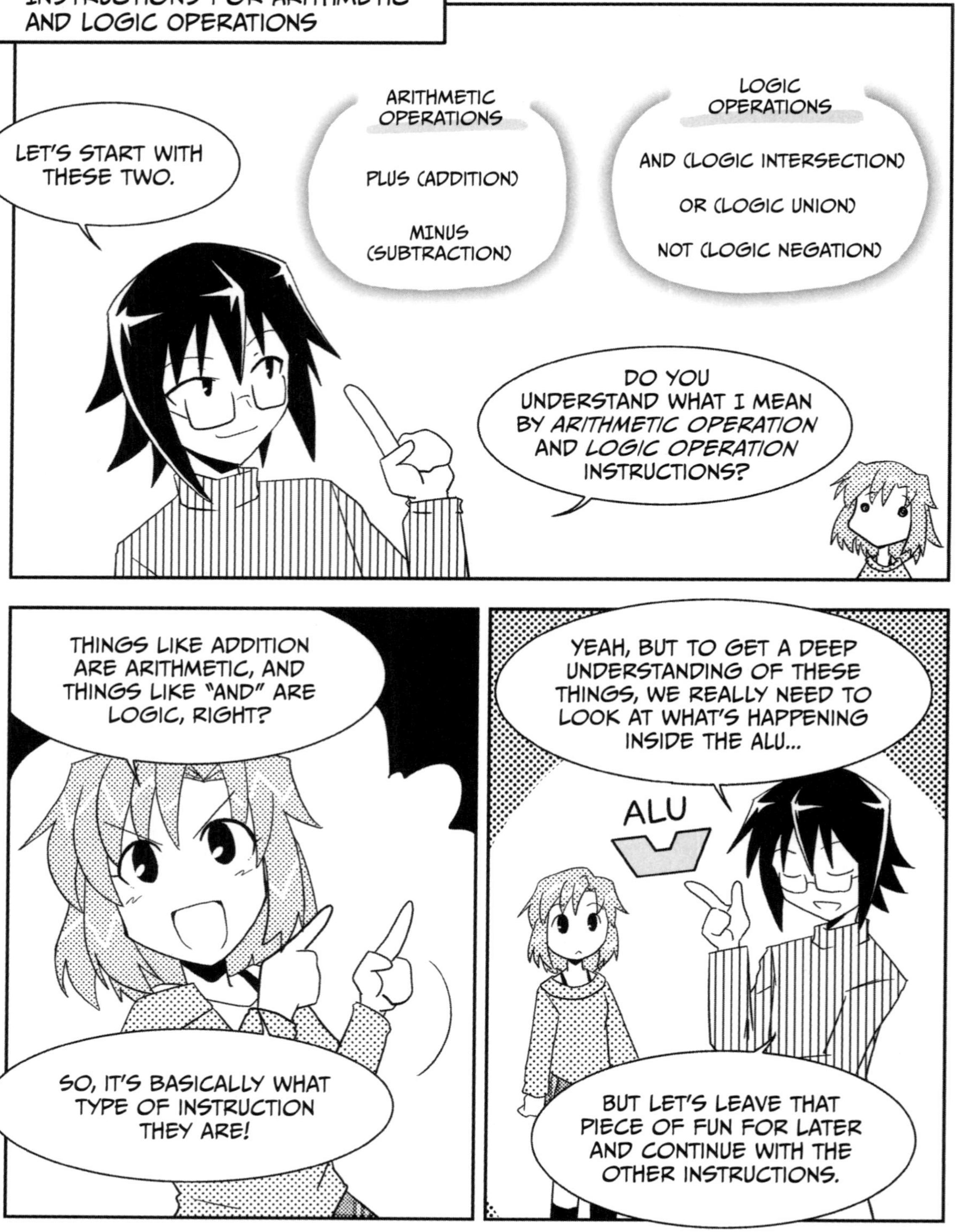

LET'S START WITH THESE TWO.
ARITHMETIC OPERATIONS
PLUS (ADDITION)
MINUS (SUBTRACTION)
LOGIC OPERATIONS
AND (LOGIC INTERSECTION)
OR (LOGIC UNION)
NOT (LOGIC NEGATION)
DO YOU UNDERSTAND WHAT I MEAN BY *ARITHMETIC OPERATION* AND *LOGIC OPERATION* INSTRUCTIONS?
THINGS LIKE ADDITION ARE ARITHMETIC, AND THINGS LIKE "AND" ARE LOGIC, RIGHT?
SO, IT'S BASICALLY WHAT TYPE OF INSTRUCTION THEY ARE!
YEAH, BUT TO GET A DEEP UNDERSTANDING OF THESE THINGS, WE REALLY NEED TO LOOK AT WHAT'S HAPPENING INSIDE THE ALU...
ALU
BUT LET'S LEAVE THAT PIECE OF FUN FOR LATER AND CONTINUE WITH THE OTHER INSTRUCTIONS.

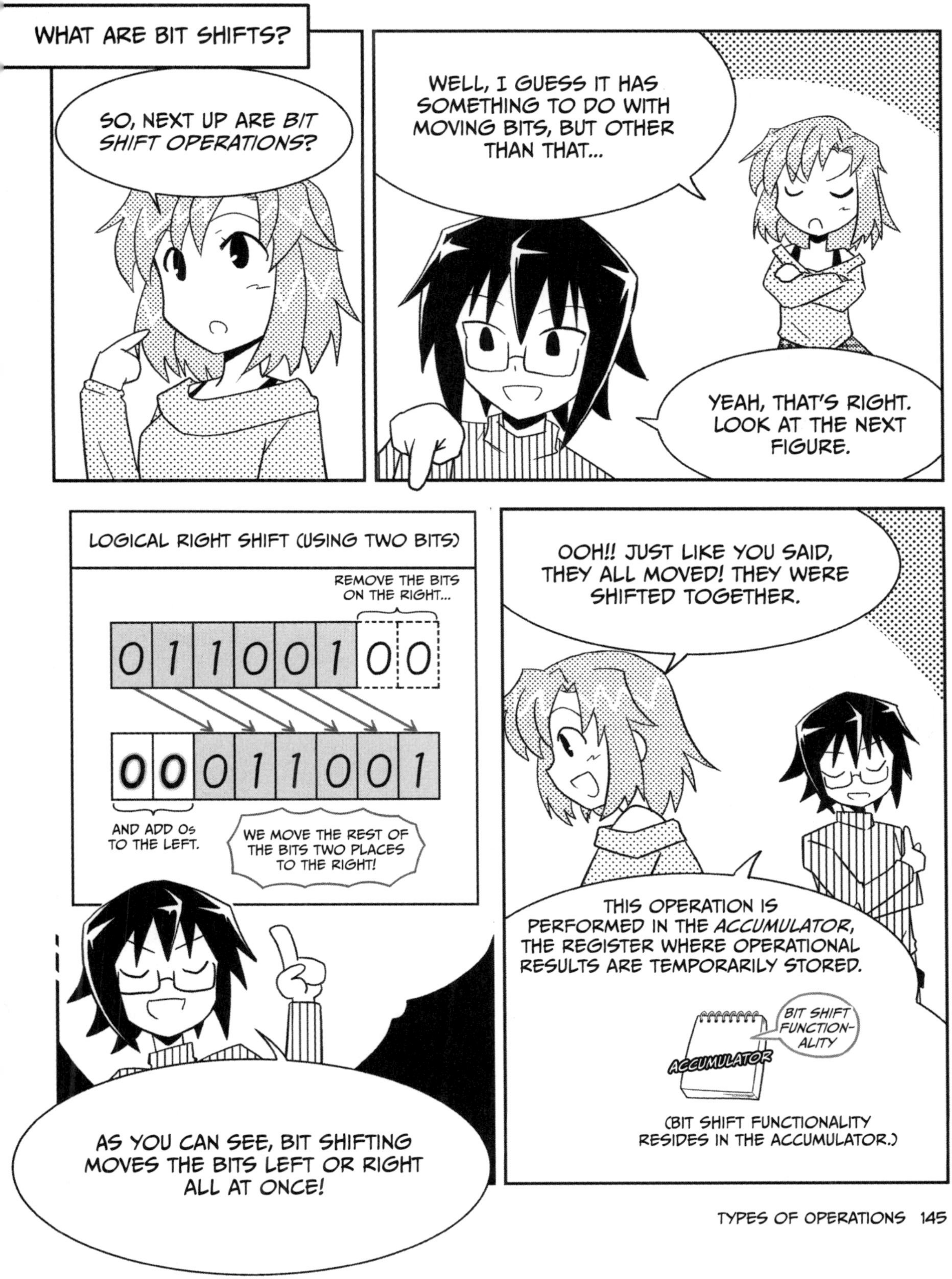
WHAT ARE BIT SHIFTS?
SO, NEXT UP ARE *BIT SHIFT OPERATIONS*?
WELL, I GUESS IT HAS SOMETHING TO DO WITH MOVING BITS, BUT OTHER THAN THAT...
YEAH, THAT'S RIGHT. LOOK AT THE NEXT FIGURE.
LOGICAL RIGHT SHIFT (USING TWO BITS)
REMOVE THE BITS ON THE RIGHT...
0 1 1 0 0 1 0 0
0 0 0 1 1 0 0 1
AND ADD 0s TO THE LEFT.
WE MOVE THE REST OF THE BITS TWO PLACES TO THE RIGHT!
AS YOU CAN SEE, BIT SHIFTING MOVES THE BITS LEFT OR RIGHT ALL AT ONCE!
OOH!! JUST LIKE YOU SAID, THEY ALL MOVED! THEY WERE SHIFTED TOGETHER.
THIS OPERATION IS PERFORMED IN THE *ACCUMULATOR*, THE REGISTER WHERE OPERATIONAL RESULTS ARE TEMPORARILY STORED.
ACCUMULATOR
BIT SHIFT FUNCTION-ALITY
(BIT SHIFT FUNCTIONALITY RESIDES IN THE ACCUMULATOR.)

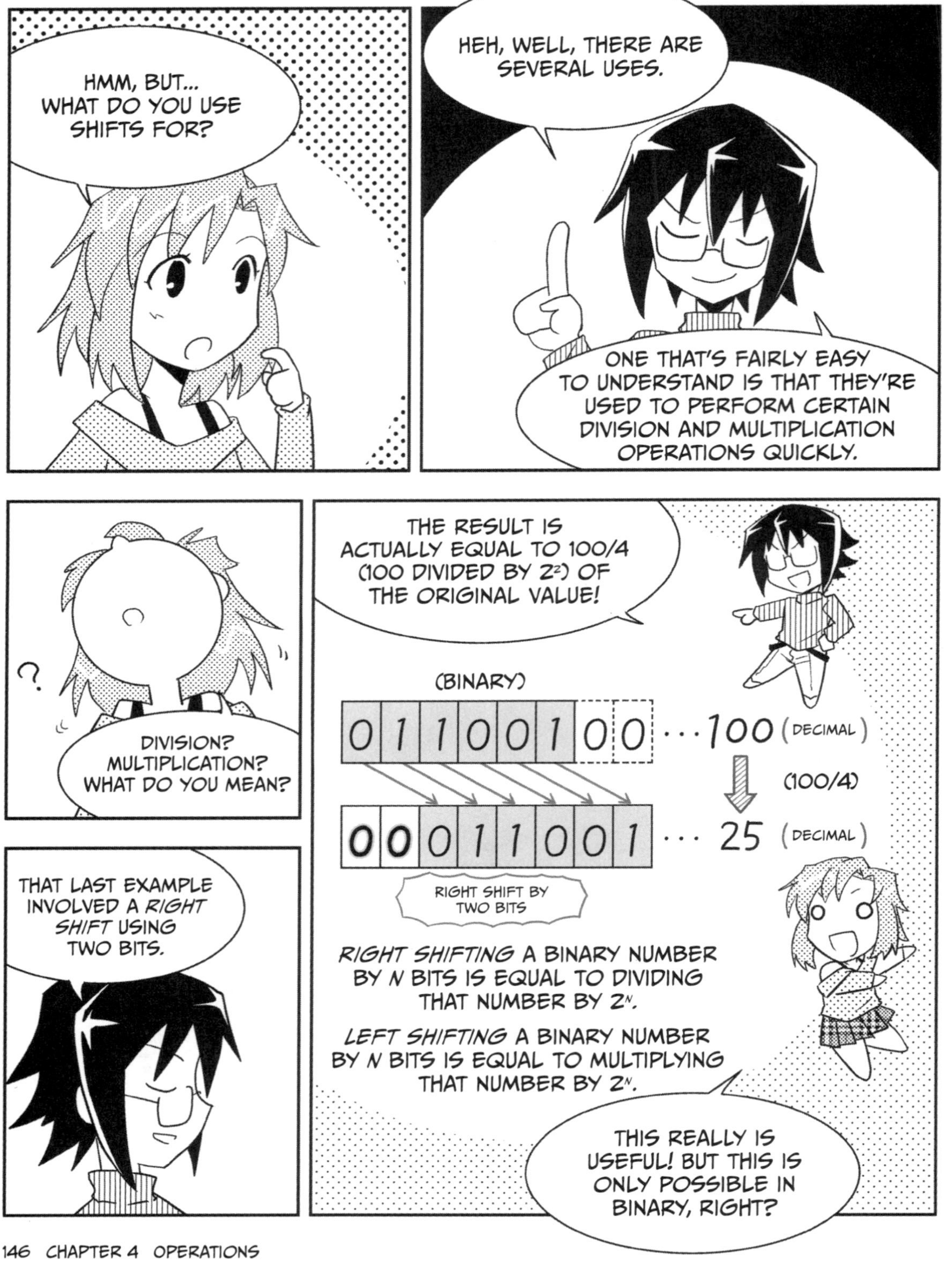
HMM, BUT... WHAT DO YOU USE SHIFTS FOR?
HEH, WELL, THERE ARE SEVERAL USES.
ONE THAT'S FAIRLY EASY TO UNDERSTAND IS THAT THEY'RE USED TO PERFORM CERTAIN DIVISION AND MULTIPLICATION OPERATIONS QUICKLY.
?
DIVISION? MULTIPLICATION? WHAT DO YOU MEAN?
THAT LAST EXAMPLE INVOLVED A *RIGHT SHIFT* USING TWO BITS.
THE RESULT IS ACTUALLY EQUAL TO 100/4 (100 DIVIDED BY 2^2) OF THE ORIGINAL VALUE!
(BINARY)
0 1 1 0 0 1 0 0 ···100 (DECIMAL)
(100/4)
0 0 0 1 1 0 0 1 ··· 25 (DECIMAL)
RIGHT SHIFT BY TWO BITS
RIGHT SHIFTING A BINARY NUMBER BY *N* BITS IS EQUAL TO DIVIDING THAT NUMBER BY 2^N.
LEFT SHIFTING A BINARY NUMBER BY *N* BITS IS EQUAL TO MULTIPLYING THAT NUMBER BY 2^N.
THIS REALLY IS USEFUL! BUT THIS IS ONLY POSSIBLE IN BINARY, RIGHT?

THE SIGN BIT LETS US EXPRESS NEGATIVE BINARY NUMBERS

Before I explain bit shifts more, I want to talk briefly about *sign bits*.

Sign bits . . . ? What are those?

In a binary number, the sign bit is the bit to the far left, and it tells us if the number is positive or negative. If the left digit is 0, the number is positive, and if it's 1, the number is negative.

Look at the image below. The most significant bit, which is the leftmost bit, is the sign bit. The sign bit, along with the rest of the bits, determines what numerical value is being represented.

SIGN BIT
(0 MEANS POSITIVE,
AND 1 MEANS NEGATIVE)
NUMBER
SIGN BIT
EXAMPLES
011 (REPRESENTS +3)
101 (REPRESENTS -3)

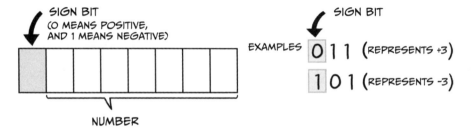

Uhh . . . I can see how 011 would make +3 just by thinking in simple binary. But why does 101 equal –3? That doesn't make any sense.

Remember complements? When expressing negative numbers in binary, we use the *two's complement*.

011
① FLIP ALL THE BITS!
100
② ADD 1.
101

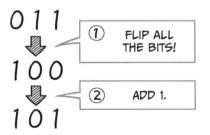

Oh, now I see it! So to express the negative value of 3 (011), we get 101. With the important part being the *sign bit to the far left*.

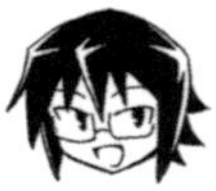

Yes. Using three bits without a bit sign, we could express eight different numbers from 0 to 7, but using three bits including one sign bit, the range changes to -4 to 3. We still get eight numbers though, as shown in the table below.

NUMBER	TWO'S COMPLEMENT
3	0 1 1
2	0 1 0
1	0 0 1
0	0 0 0
-1	1 1 1
-2	1 1 0
-3	1 0 1
-4	1 0 0

SIGN BIT

SIGNED THREE-BIT NUMBERS

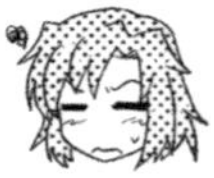

Doesn't that mean that if I have some binary number—say 101—I could interpret that number as -3 if I assumed it was signed or as 5 if I assumed it was not signed?

They look the same, but the expressed values are completely different. . . . That's just confusing, don't you think?! What were they thinking??

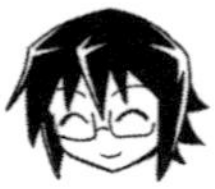

Ah, it's true that humans wouldn't be able to tell the difference. Computers, however, have dedicated systems that keep track of this.* So don't worry about it!

* Programs have a flag that changes depending on the calculation's result to track changes to the sign. If the program monitors this flag, it's possible to tell whether any unforeseen changes occur to the sign of a number. Not all CPUs support this feature, though, and if the CPU doesn't, it's up to the program to keep track of the sign bit.

LOGICAL SHIFTS AND ARITHMETIC SHIFTS

SHOULD WE FILL IN THE BLANKS WITH 1s OR 0s?
1
1
0
0

Now let's return to bit shifts. There are two types, *logical shifts* and *arithmetic shifts*. Essentially, the difference is whether we are using the sign bit we talked about before.

SHIFT OPERATION
LOGICAL SHIFT
(NO SIGN BIT)
ARITHMETIC SHIFT
(HAS SIGN BIT)

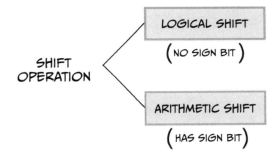

Oho! So logical shifts don't have sign bits, but the arithmetic shifts do. I see where this is going.

The outcome of a logic operation is always either true or false, right? That means that concepts like sign bits or negative numbers wouldn't exist. But since arithmetic operations deal with adding and subtracting numbers, those concepts would be necessary.

Mm, yes! That is an astute observation—you are correct.

Logical shifts are very simple, and we've already talked about them. Arithmetic shifts, on the other hand, are a bit tricky.

Look at the next figure. When performing arithmetic shifts, we fill in the blank spaces with 1s if the sign bit is 1 and with 0s if the sign bit is 0. You have to pay attention to the sign bit, essentially.

ARITHMETIC RIGHT SHIFT
LOST
SIGN BIT
0 1 1 0 0 1 0 0
POSITIVE VALUE
WHEN SHIFTING ONE BIT TO THE RIGHT
0 0 1 1 0 0 1 0
FILL IN WITH 0
LOST
SIGN BIT
1 1 0 1 0 1 0 0
NEGATIVE VALUE
WHEN SHIFTING TWO BITS TO THE RIGHT
1 1 1 1 0 1 0 1
FILL IN WITH 1s

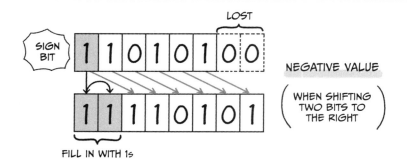

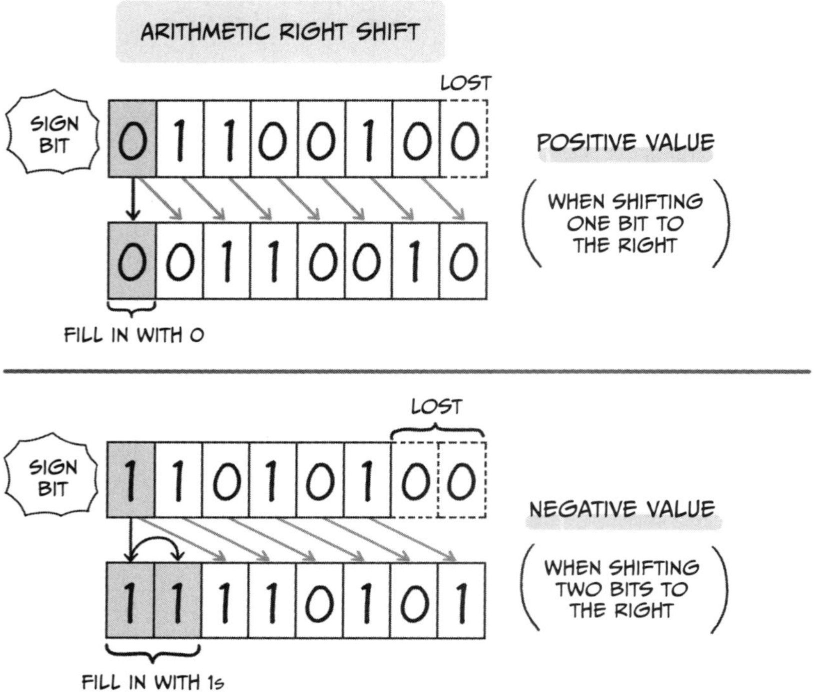

Ohh! With logical shifts, you could just fill the blank spaces with 0s without a second thought, but with arithmetic shifts, you have to keep the sign bit in mind.

There is another really important thing, though. Please look at the next image. We shift a positive number (the sign bit is 0) to the left and . . . whoa! A 1 from the number value bits might end up becoming the most significant bit.

Oh my . . . that can't be good. It would look like the number turned negative all of a sudden (since the sign bit is 1).

Yeah. While the operation was only supposed to multiply the value 2^N, it ended up flipping the sign bit instead. We call this *overflow*, just like how water can overflow from a cup if you pour too much in. When this happens, it means that the calculation result used more digits than it was allowed and therefore "overflowed."

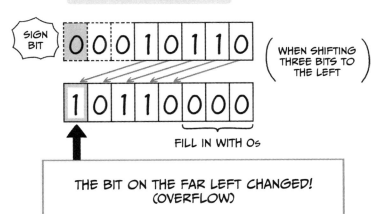

ARITHMETIC LEFT SHIFT

TAKE NOTE! NOT ALL CPUs ARE GUARANTEED TO HAVE THIS FEATURE.

SIGN BIT

0 0 0 1 0 1 1 0

(WHEN SHIFTING THREE BITS TO THE LEFT)

1 0 1 1 0 0 0 0

FILL IN WITH 0s

THE BIT ON THE FAR LEFT CHANGED!
(OVERFLOW)

 A serious state of affairs, for sure! I guess this is an error? It's not like you can pretend it didn't happen . . . and you couldn't continue the calculation like this.

 Mhm. When overflow occurs, the *overflow flag (overflow bit)* of the status register is set. It makes sure to remember that an overflow occurred as a result of a calculation.

 Hah! So another register is in charge of taking notes about any grave errors that might occur in the accumulator register. This way they won't be missed!

OVERFLOW AND UNDERFLOW

Calculations using floating-point numbers (as opposed to the integer operations we've been talking about) can both overflow and underflow if the algorithm (the method of calculation) used produces a result that falls outside of the acceptable range of values.

For example, if the result of some calculation is a value that is so close to zero that it cannot accurately be expressed using the available bits (think 0.00000000000 . . . 1), it would generate an underflow.

CIRCULAR SHIFTS (ROTATING SHIFTS)

Before we move on to the next subject, I would like to talk a bit about *circular shifts (rotating shifts)*, which are important in cryptography.

The easiest way to think about it is as if the edges of the bit sequence in the accumulator were glued together into a wheel that can rotate freely.

LEFT EDGE
(MOST SIGNIFICANT BIT)
RIGHT EDGE
(LEAST SIGNIFICANT BIT)
0110010001100101
ROTATES!

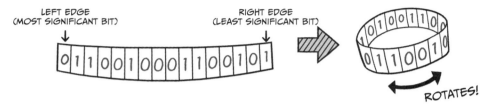

Oh. It's like we stuck the two edges of the tape together. *Spinnn!*

Applying circular shifts has the following effect. Remember that the left edge (most significant bit) and the right edge (least significant bit) are connected.

CIRCULAR SHIFT
THE BITS AT THE LEFT EDGE...
01100100
(WHEN SHIFTING FOUR BITS TO THE LEFT)
01000110
...APPEAR ON THE RIGHT!
01100100
THE BITS AT THE RIGHT EDGE...
(WHEN SHIFTING THREE BITS TO THE RIGHT)
...APPEAR ON THE LEFT!
10001100

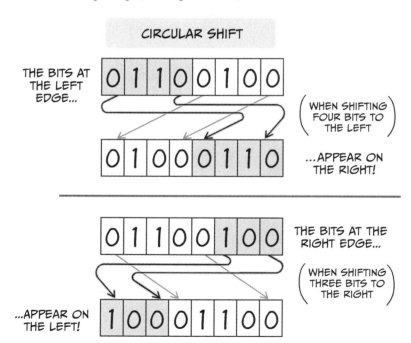

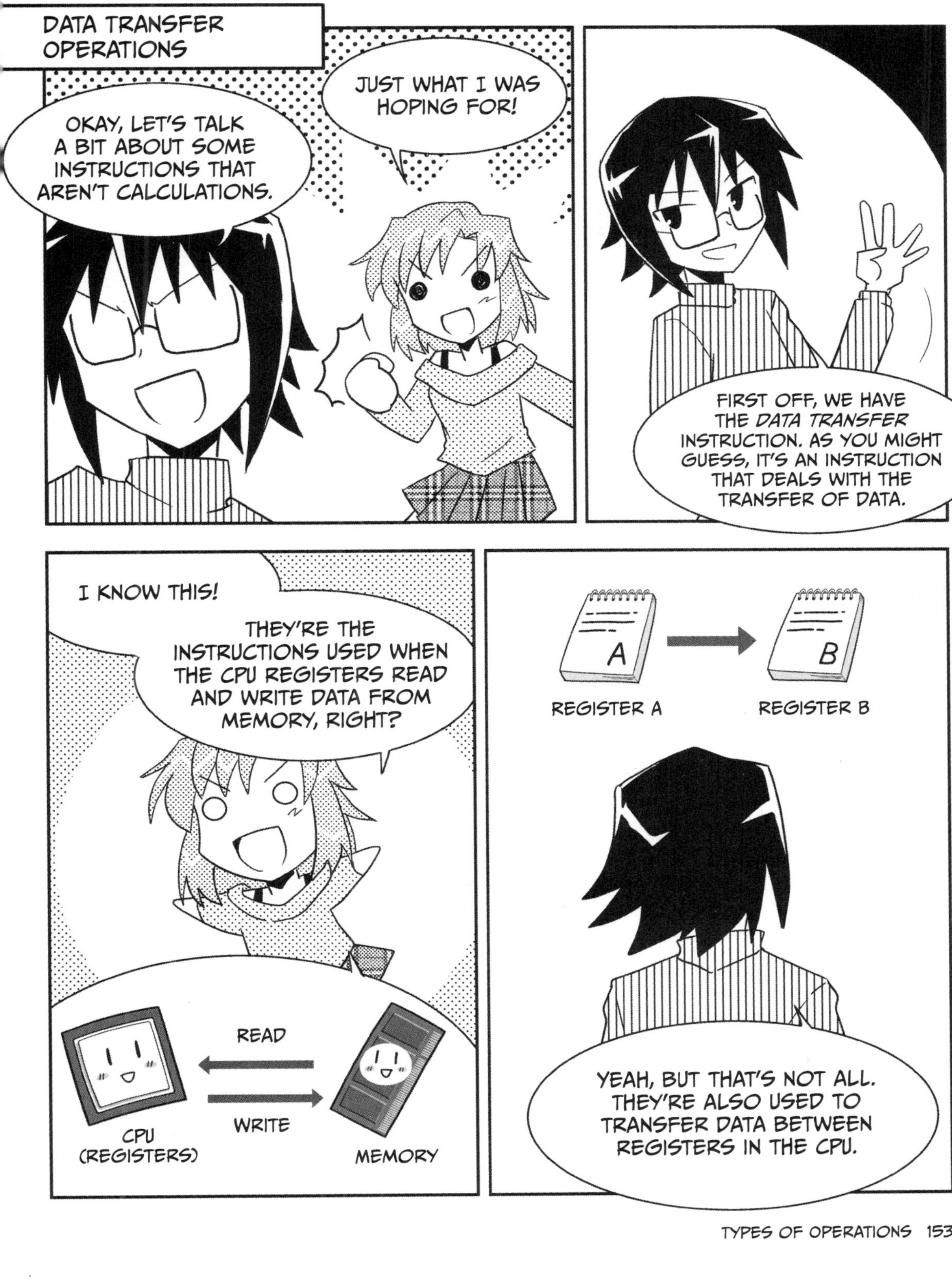
DATA TRANSFER OPERATIONS
OKAY, LET'S TALK A BIT ABOUT SOME INSTRUCTIONS THAT AREN'T CALCULATIONS.
JUST WHAT I WAS HOPING FOR!
FIRST OFF, WE HAVE THE *DATA TRANSFER* INSTRUCTION. AS YOU MIGHT GUESS, IT'S AN INSTRUCTION THAT DEALS WITH THE TRANSFER OF DATA.
I KNOW THIS!
THEY'RE THE INSTRUCTIONS USED WHEN THE CPU REGISTERS READ AND WRITE DATA FROM MEMORY, RIGHT?
READ
WRITE
CPU (REGISTERS)
MEMORY
A
B
REGISTER A
REGISTER B
YEAH, BUT THAT'S NOT ALL. THEY'RE ALSO USED TO TRANSFER DATA BETWEEN REGISTERS IN THE CPU.

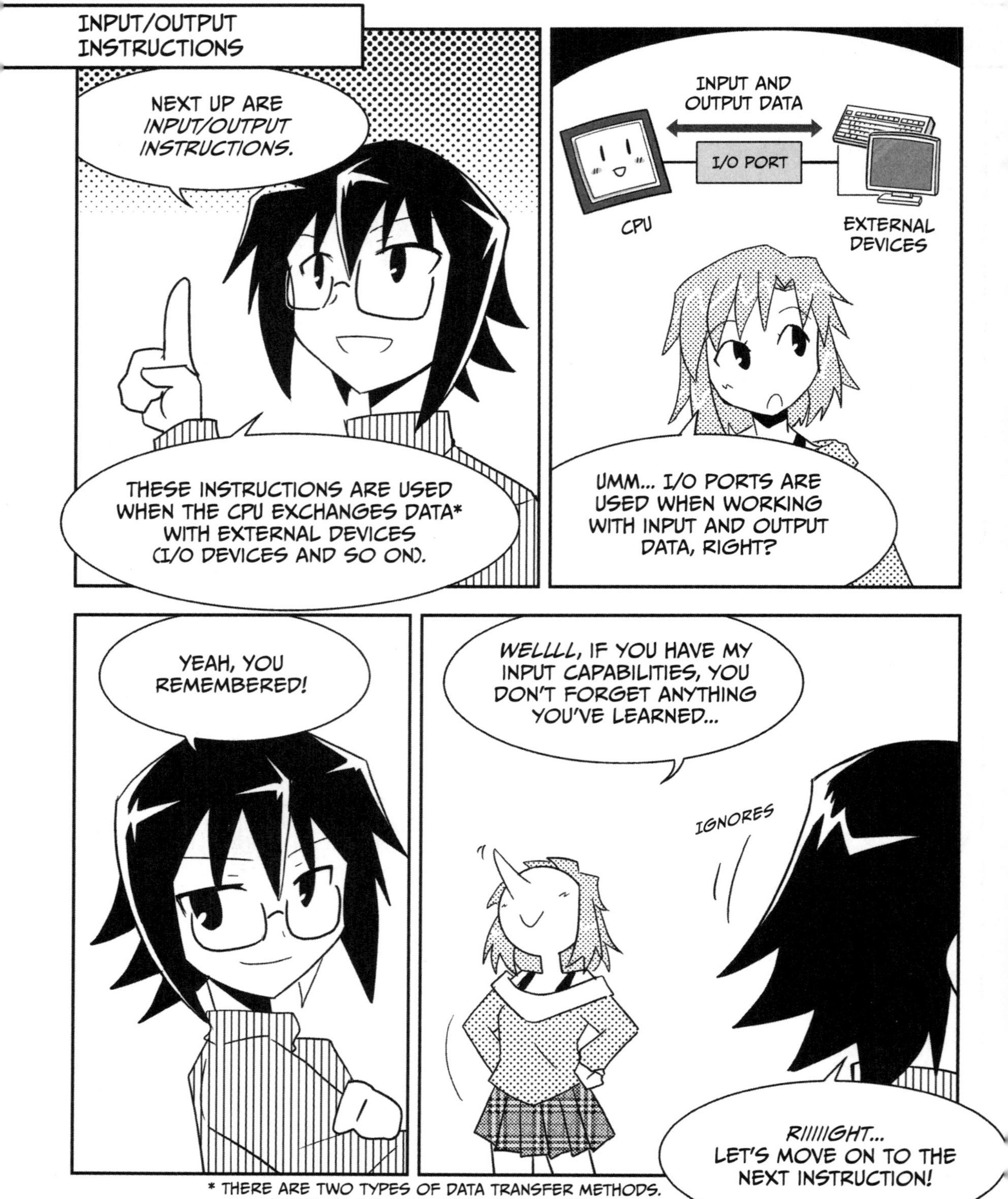
INPUT/OUTPUT INSTRUCTIONS
NEXT UP ARE *INPUT/OUTPUT INSTRUCTIONS.*
THESE INSTRUCTIONS ARE USED WHEN THE CPU EXCHANGES DATA* WITH EXTERNAL DEVICES (I/O DEVICES AND SO ON).
INPUT AND OUTPUT DATA
I/O PORT
CPU
EXTERNAL DEVICES
UMM... I/O PORTS ARE USED WHEN WORKING WITH INPUT AND OUTPUT DATA, RIGHT?
YEAH, YOU REMEMBERED!
WELLLL, IF YOU HAVE MY INPUT CAPABILITIES, YOU DON'T FORGET ANYTHING YOU'VE LEARNED...
IGNORES
RIIIIIGHT... LET'S MOVE ON TO THE NEXT INSTRUCTION!

* THERE ARE TWO TYPES OF DATA TRANSFER METHODS. SEE PAGE 185 FOR MORE INFORMATION.

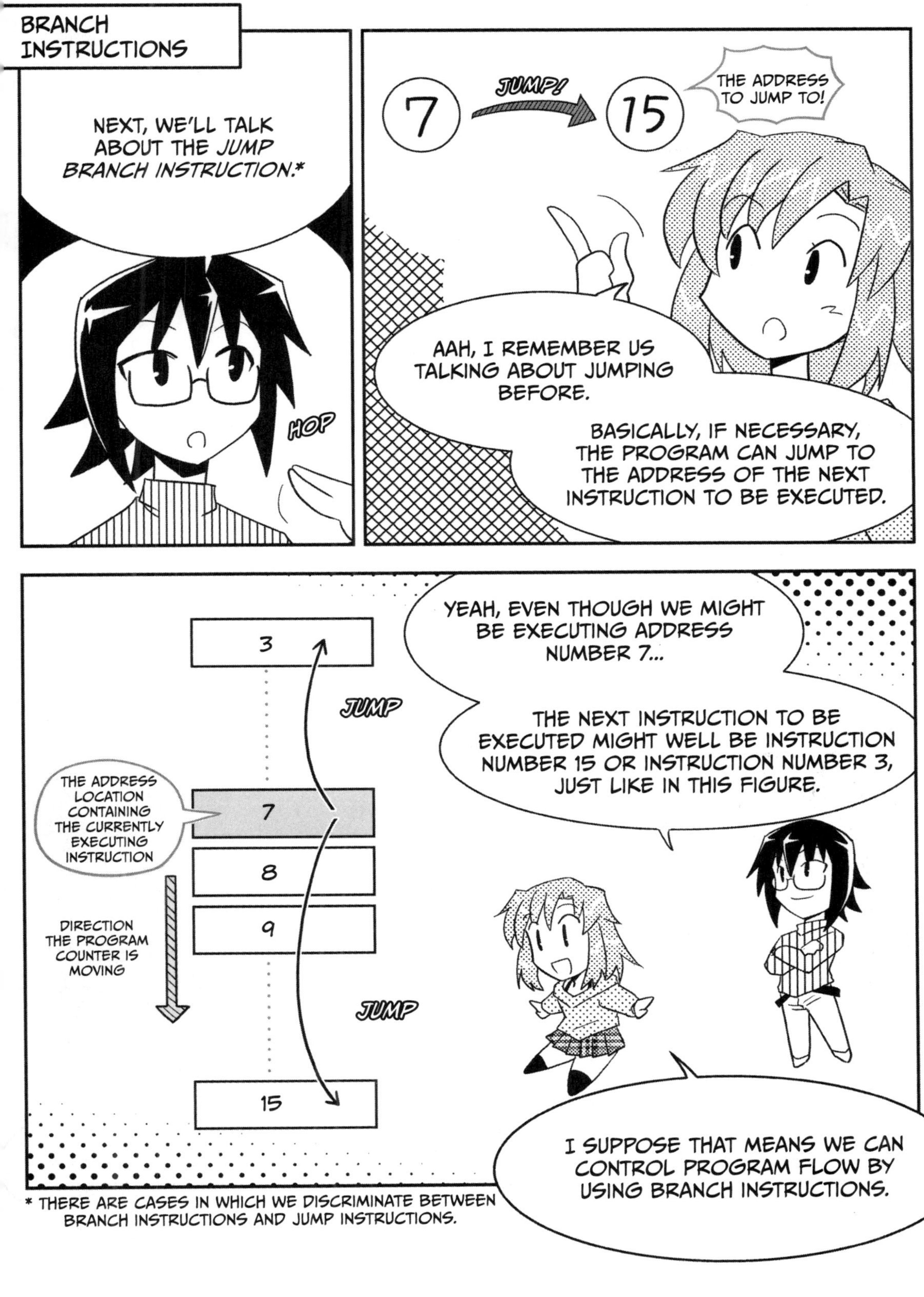
BRANCH INSTRUCTIONS
NEXT, WE'LL TALK ABOUT THE *JUMP BRANCH INSTRUCTION.**
HOP
7
JUMP!
15
THE ADDRESS TO JUMP TO!
AAH, I REMEMBER US TALKING ABOUT JUMPING BEFORE.
BASICALLY, IF NECESSARY, THE PROGRAM CAN JUMP TO THE ADDRESS OF THE NEXT INSTRUCTION TO BE EXECUTED.
3
JUMP
THE ADDRESS LOCATION CONTAINING THE CURRENTLY EXECUTING INSTRUCTION
7
8
9
DIRECTION THE PROGRAM COUNTER IS MOVING
JUMP
15
YEAH, EVEN THOUGH WE MIGHT BE EXECUTING ADDRESS NUMBER 7...
THE NEXT INSTRUCTION TO BE EXECUTED MIGHT WELL BE INSTRUCTION NUMBER 15 OR INSTRUCTION NUMBER 3, JUST LIKE IN THIS FIGURE.
I SUPPOSE THAT MEANS WE CAN CONTROL PROGRAM FLOW BY USING BRANCH INSTRUCTIONS.

* THERE ARE CASES IN WHICH WE DISCRIMINATE BETWEEN BRANCH INSTRUCTIONS AND JUMP INSTRUCTIONS.

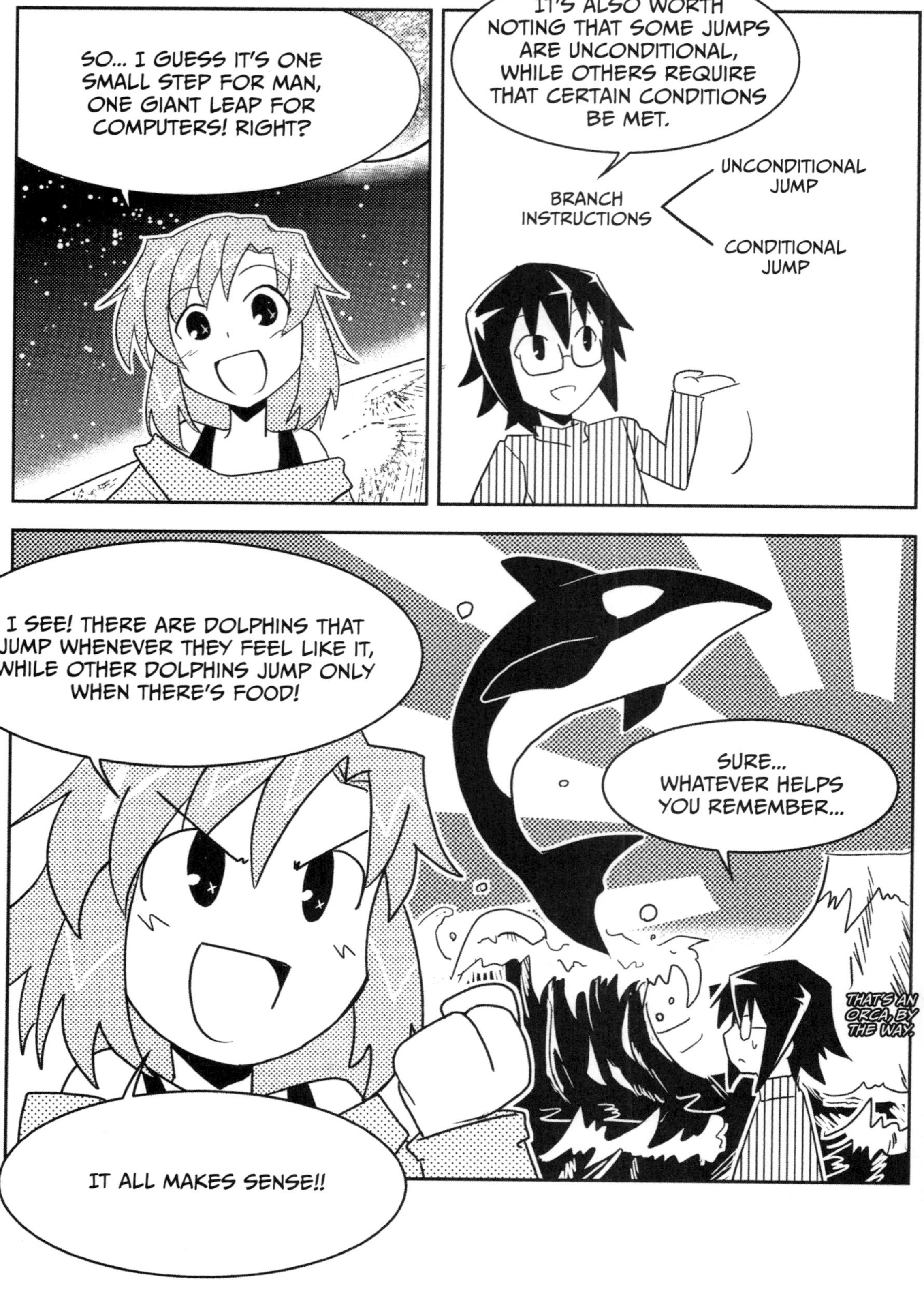
SO... I GUESS IT'S ONE SMALL STEP FOR MAN, ONE GIANT LEAP FOR COMPUTERS! RIGHT?
IT'S ALSO WORTH NOTING THAT SOME JUMPS ARE UNCONDITIONAL, WHILE OTHERS REQUIRE THAT CERTAIN CONDITIONS BE MET.
BRANCH INSTRUCTIONS
UNCONDITIONAL JUMP
CONDITIONAL JUMP
I SEE! THERE ARE DOLPHINS THAT JUMP WHENEVER THEY FEEL LIKE IT, WHILE OTHER DOLPHINS JUMP ONLY WHEN THERE'S FOOD!
SURE... WHATEVER HELPS YOU REMEMBER...
THAT'S AN ORCA, BY THE WAY.
IT ALL MAKES SENSE!!

BRANCH INSTRUCTIONS, JUMP INSTRUCTIONS, AND SKIP INSTRUCTIONS

When it comes to branch instructions, there is unfortunately no standard terminology. Depending on the CPU maker, the instructions might be known as branches, jumps, or even skips. But lately, it's become popular to differentiate among them in the following way.

BRANCH
ADDRESS CONTAINING THE CURRENTLY EXECUTING INSTRUCTION
SKIP
DIRECTION THE PROGRAM COUNTER IS MOVING
BRANCH
JUMP
JUMP

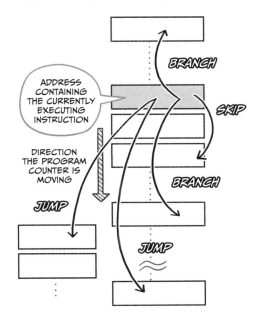

THE DIFFERENCES AMONG THE THREE

1. *Branch instructions* branch to addresses not far from the execution site.
2. *Jump instructions* jump to addresses farther away from the execution site than branch instructions do.
3. *Skip instructions* can either skip or not skip the next instruction to be executed.

Ohh! So they're different in terms of the distance moved. Pretty cool.

There are also other program control instructions, such as STOP and SLEEP instructions.

DIFFERENT CPUs USE DIFFERENT TERMINOLOGY

If you look at the mnemonic tables of CPUs from companies like Intel (the i8080) and Zilog (the Z80) at the dawn of the 8-bit CPU, you can't even find the word *branch* mentioned. If you instead look at the single-chip 16-bit TMS9900 CPUs made by Texas Instruments (TI) in 1974, *jump* was used for short branch operations, while *branch* was used solely for branch operations concerning registers. Then, the ATMega series CPUs made by Atmel, which are part of the Arduino micro-controllers, use *jump* for changing the current execution address unconditionally, but they also have skips and branch instructions that relate to the currently executing address.

CONDITION EVALUATION AND STATUS FLAGS

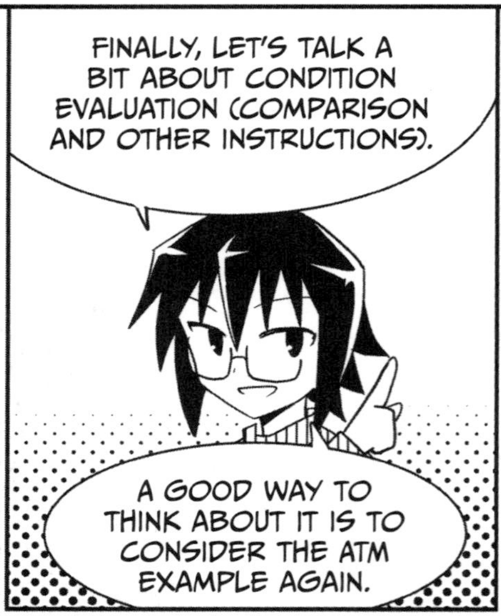
FINALLY, LET'S TALK A BIT ABOUT CONDITION EVALUATION (COMPARISON AND OTHER INSTRUCTIONS).
A GOOD WAY TO THINK ABOUT IT IS TO CONSIDER THE ATM EXAMPLE AGAIN.

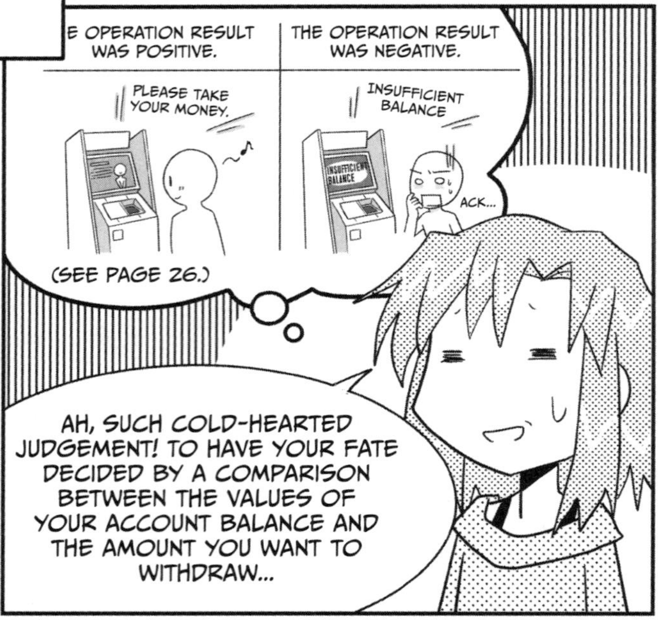
E OPERATION RESULT WAS POSITIVE.
THE OPERATION RESULT WAS NEGATIVE.
PLEASE TAKE YOUR MONEY.
INSUFFICIENT BALANCE
INSUFFICIENT BALANCE
ACK...
(SEE PAGE 26.)
AH, SUCH COLD-HEARTED JUDGEMENT! TO HAVE YOUR FATE DECIDED BY A COMPARISON BETWEEN THE VALUES OF YOUR ACCOUNT BALANCE AND THE AMOUNT YOU WANT TO WITHDRAW...

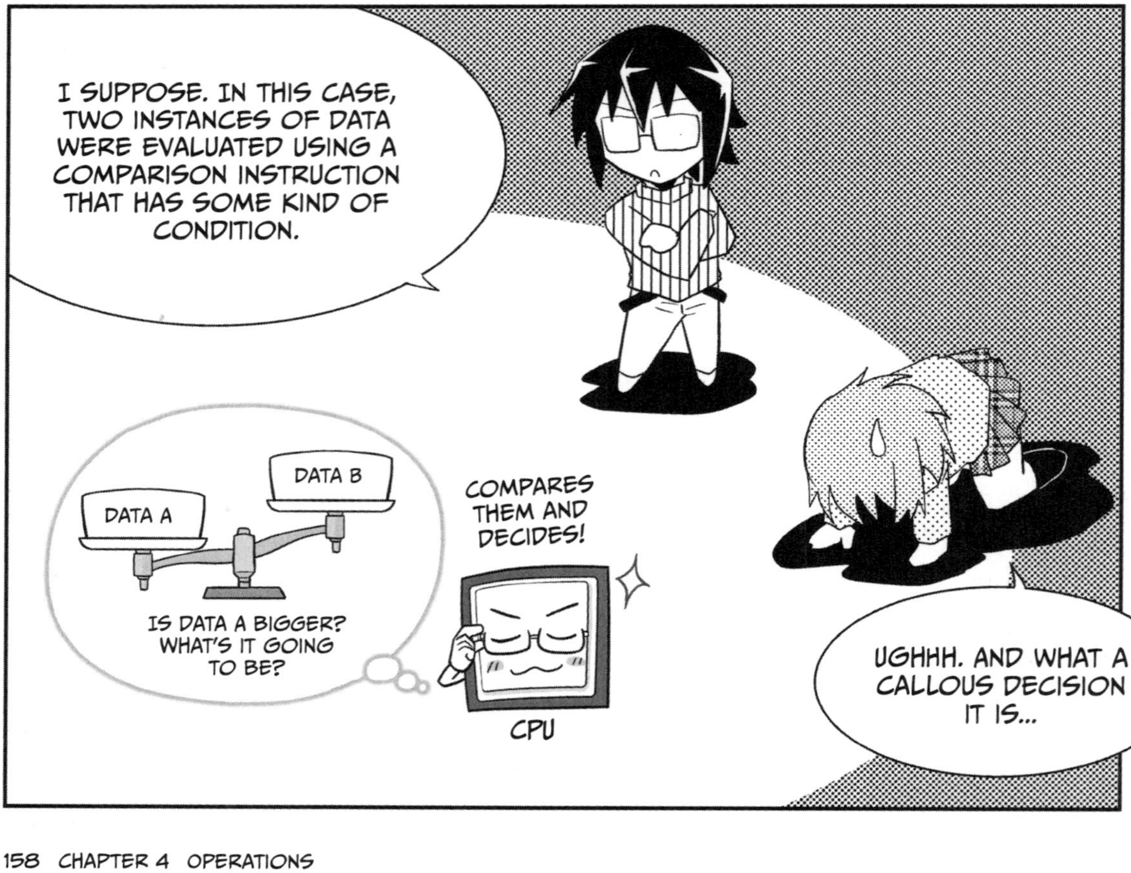
I SUPPOSE. IN THIS CASE, TWO INSTANCES OF DATA WERE EVALUATED USING A COMPARISON INSTRUCTION THAT HAS SOME KIND OF CONDITION.
DATA A
DATA B
IS DATA A BIGGER? WHAT'S IT GOING TO BE?
COMPARES THEM AND DECIDES!
CPU
UGHHH. AND WHAT A CALLOUS DECISION IT IS...

NOW, I WANT YOU TO PAY ATTENTION TO...

THE *STATUS FLAG** THAT IS USED WHEN EVALUATING WHETHER A CONDITION IS MET.

* ALSO CALLED A *STATUS BIT*

EXAMPLE: $5 - 3 = 2$

COMMAND INPUT SUBSTRACTION →

STATUS OUTPUT → POSITIVE VALUE

STATUS FLAG... DIDN'T WE TALK ABOUT STATUS OUTPUT BEFORE? WASN'T THAT SOME VALUE THAT INDICATED THE STATE OF SOME OPERATIONAL RESULT, LIKE WHETHER IT WAS POSITIVE AND STUFF LIKE THAT?

YEAH. THE PURPOSE OF THE STATUS FLAG IS TO RECORD INFORMATION LIKE THAT.

IT SIGNALS THE RESULT OF A CALCULATION USING EITHER A ZERO OR A ONE.

THE FLAG IS UP!	THE FLAG IS NOT UP...
SET (1)	RESET (0)
THE RESULT OF THE CALCULATION IS NEGATIVE!	THE RESULT OF THE CALCULATION IS POSITIVE!

HMM. SO A FLAG IS SET WHENEVER A CONDITION IS EVALUATED TO BE NEGATIVE?

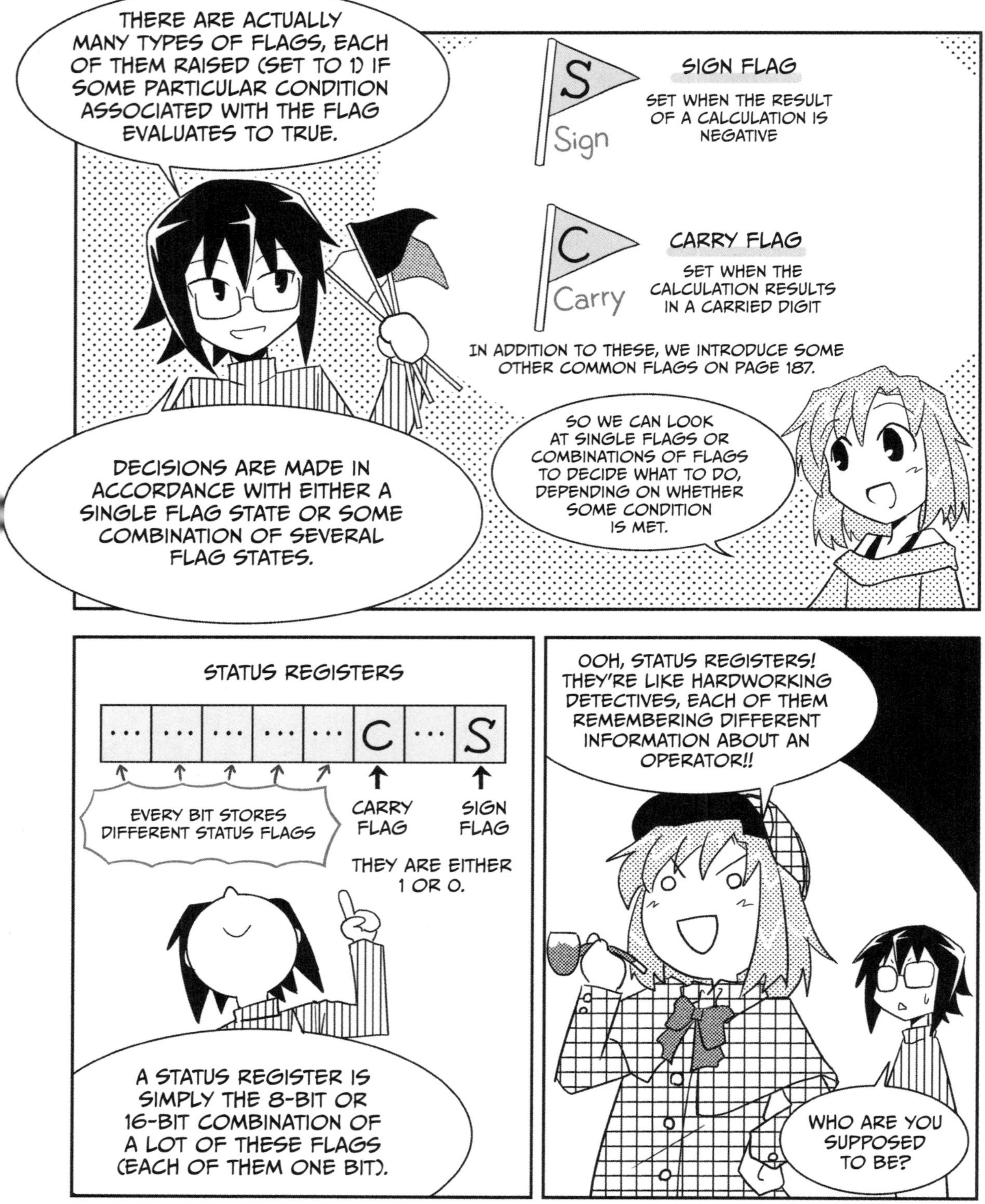
THERE ARE ACTUALLY MANY TYPES OF FLAGS, EACH OF THEM RAISED (SET TO 1) IF SOME PARTICULAR CONDITION ASSOCIATED WITH THE FLAG EVALUATES TO TRUE.
S
Sign
SIGN FLAG
SET WHEN THE RESULT OF A CALCULATION IS NEGATIVE
C
Carry
CARRY FLAG
SET WHEN THE CALCULATION RESULTS IN A CARRIED DIGIT
IN ADDITION TO THESE, WE INTRODUCE SOME OTHER COMMON FLAGS ON PAGE 187.
DECISIONS ARE MADE IN ACCORDANCE WITH EITHER A SINGLE FLAG STATE OR SOME COMBINATION OF SEVERAL FLAG STATES.
SO WE CAN LOOK AT SINGLE FLAGS OR COMBINATIONS OF FLAGS TO DECIDE WHAT TO DO, DEPENDING ON WHETHER SOME CONDITION IS MET.
STATUS REGISTERS
... ... C ... S
EVERY BIT STORES DIFFERENT STATUS FLAGS
CARRY FLAG
SIGN FLAG
THEY ARE EITHER 1 OR 0.
A STATUS REGISTER IS SIMPLY THE 8-BIT OR 16-BIT COMBINATION OF A LOT OF THESE FLAGS (EACH OF THEM ONE BIT).
OOH, STATUS REGISTERS! THEY'RE LIKE HARDWORKING DETECTIVES, EACH OF THEM REMEMBERING DIFFERENT INFORMATION ABOUT AN OPERATOR!!
WHO ARE YOU SUPPOSED TO BE?

PUTTING BRANCHES AND CONDITION EVALUATION TOGETHER

Okay, we've learned about branch instructions and condition evaluation, but we can get some truly useful instructions by putting the two together.

One example is the *jump on minus* instruction. It simply states that the program should jump to some address if the value in the accumulator is negative.

CONDITION
WHEN NEGATIVE...
BRANCH (JUMP)
JUMP TO SOME ADDRESS

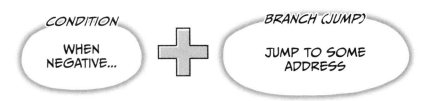

So basically, jump to this address if these conditions are all met!

Or, put another way, the program is able to change its execution depending on some condition.

Yeah, we can also make other combinations of instructions like *conditional jumps*, *conditional skips*, and *conditional branches*. Thanks to these, we can do some really useful things.

SOME THINGS WE CAN DO USING CONDITIONAL JUMPS AND OTHER INSTRUCTIONS

1. We can run a different program depending on some condition.
2. We can decide not to run a program (skipping it) depending on some condition.
3. We can set and reset bits on output ports depending on some condition.

For example, we could control a lamp by setting or resetting some I/O port value to turn the lamp on and off.

Whoa! This seems absolutely essential not only for computers but also for any electrical application really!

Operand Types

HOW MANY OPERANDS DO WE HAVE?

IT SEEMS YOU UNDERSTAND THE DIFFERENT INSTRUCTIONS WE'VE TALKED ABOUT.

SO LET'S MOVE ON TO LEARNING ABOUT OPERANDS NEXT!!

OPERANDS... OPER-OPERATION? AS IN SURGERY?

I'LL JUST PRETEND I DIDN'T SEE THAT COSPLAY, OKAY...?

SAYS THE ONE WHO WAS COSPLAYING AS A DETECTIVE JUST A MINUTE AGO!!

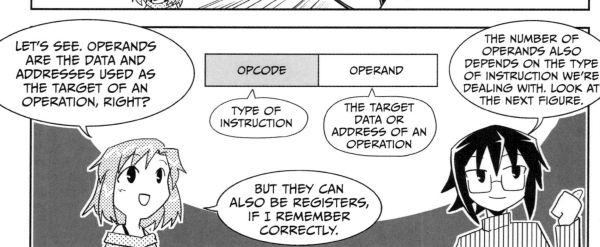

LET'S SEE. OPERANDS ARE THE DATA AND ADDRESSES USED AS THE TARGET OF AN OPERATION, RIGHT?

OPCODE	OPERAND
TYPE OF INSTRUCTION	THE TARGET DATA OR ADDRESS OF AN OPERATION

THE NUMBER OF OPERANDS ALSO DEPENDS ON THE TYPE OF INSTRUCTION WE'RE DEALING WITH. LOOK AT THE NEXT FIGURE.

BUT THEY CAN ALSO BE REGISTERS, IF I REMEMBER CORRECTLY.

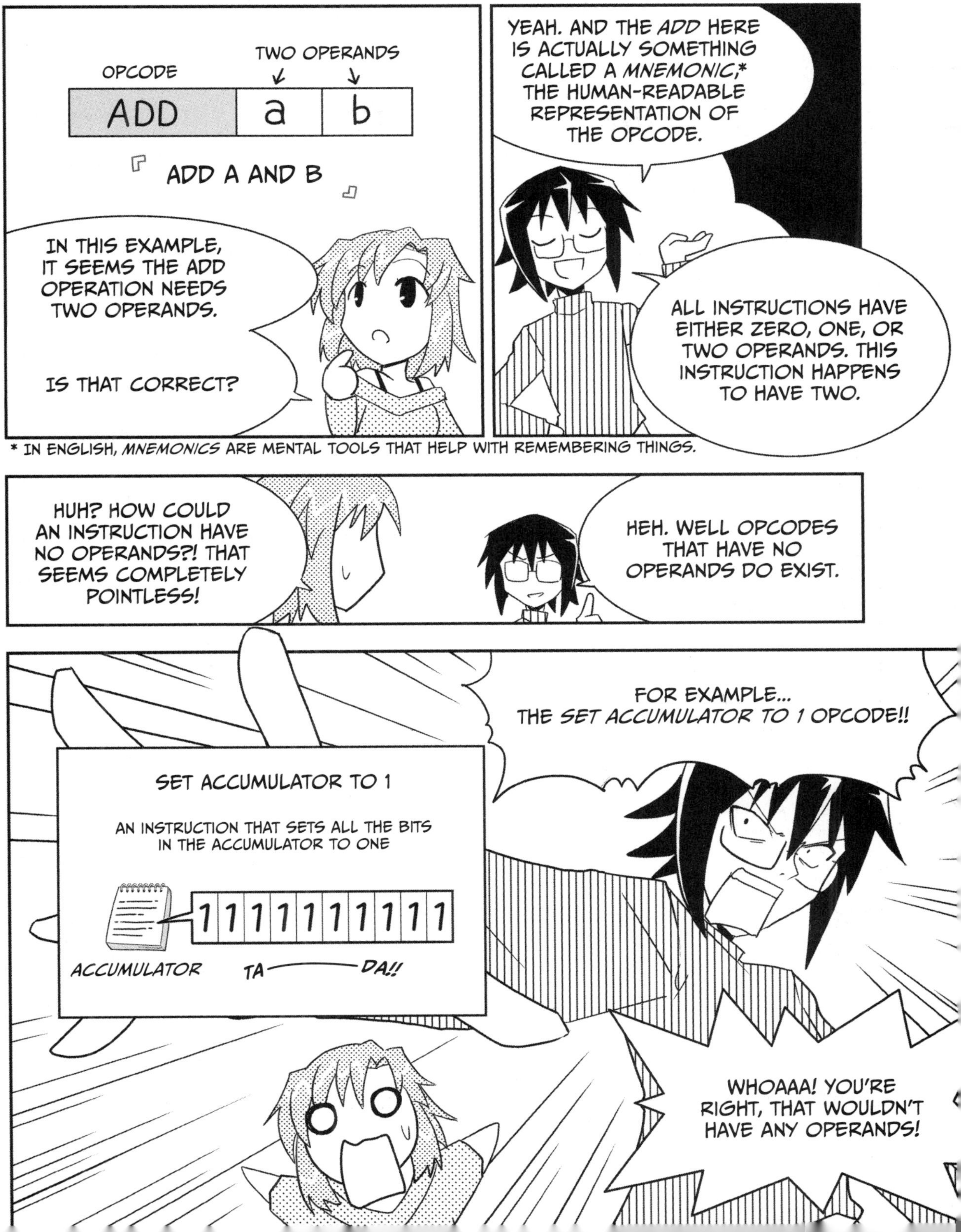
TWO OPERANDS
OPCODE
ADD a b
ADD A AND B
IN THIS EXAMPLE, IT SEEMS THE ADD OPERATION NEEDS TWO OPERANDS.
IS THAT CORRECT?
YEAH. AND THE *ADD* HERE IS ACTUALLY SOMETHING CALLED A *MNEMONIC*,* THE HUMAN-READABLE REPRESENTATION OF THE OPCODE.
ALL INSTRUCTIONS HAVE EITHER ZERO, ONE, OR TWO OPERANDS. THIS INSTRUCTION HAPPENS TO HAVE TWO.
* IN ENGLISH, *MNEMONICS* ARE MENTAL TOOLS THAT HELP WITH REMEMBERING THINGS.
HUH? HOW COULD AN INSTRUCTION HAVE NO OPERANDS?! THAT SEEMS COMPLETELY POINTLESS!
HEH. WELL OPCODES THAT HAVE NO OPERANDS DO EXIST.
FOR EXAMPLE... THE *SET ACCUMULATOR TO 1* OPCODE!!
SET ACCUMULATOR TO 1
AN INSTRUCTION THAT SETS ALL THE BITS IN THE ACCUMULATOR TO ONE
1 1 1 1 1 1 1 1 1 1
ACCUMULATOR
TA——DA!!
WHOAAA! YOU'RE RIGHT, THAT WOULDN'T HAVE ANY OPERANDS!

A LOT OF OPERATIONS WITH ZERO OR ONE OPERANDS SIMPLY WORK ON WHAT'S IN THE ACCUMULATOR REGISTER AT THAT TIME.

I SEE! THE ACCUMULATOR IS A POPULAR GUY!

ALSO, FOR TWO-OPERAND OPERATIONS WHERE BOTH OPERANDS ARE ADDRESSES...

WE CALL THE FIRST OPERAND THE *SOURCE OPERAND* AND THE SECOND THE *DESTINATION OPERAND*.

SO THEIR ROLES ARE DECIDED ALREADY.

SOURCE OPERAND	DESTINATION OPERAND

OPCODE	FIRST	SECOND

AS YOU CAN TELL FROM THE NAMES, OPERATIONS LIKE THIS USE THE DATA IN THE SOURCE OPERAND TO AFFECT DATA IN THE DESTINATION OPERAND.

OPERANDS TAKE MANY FORMS

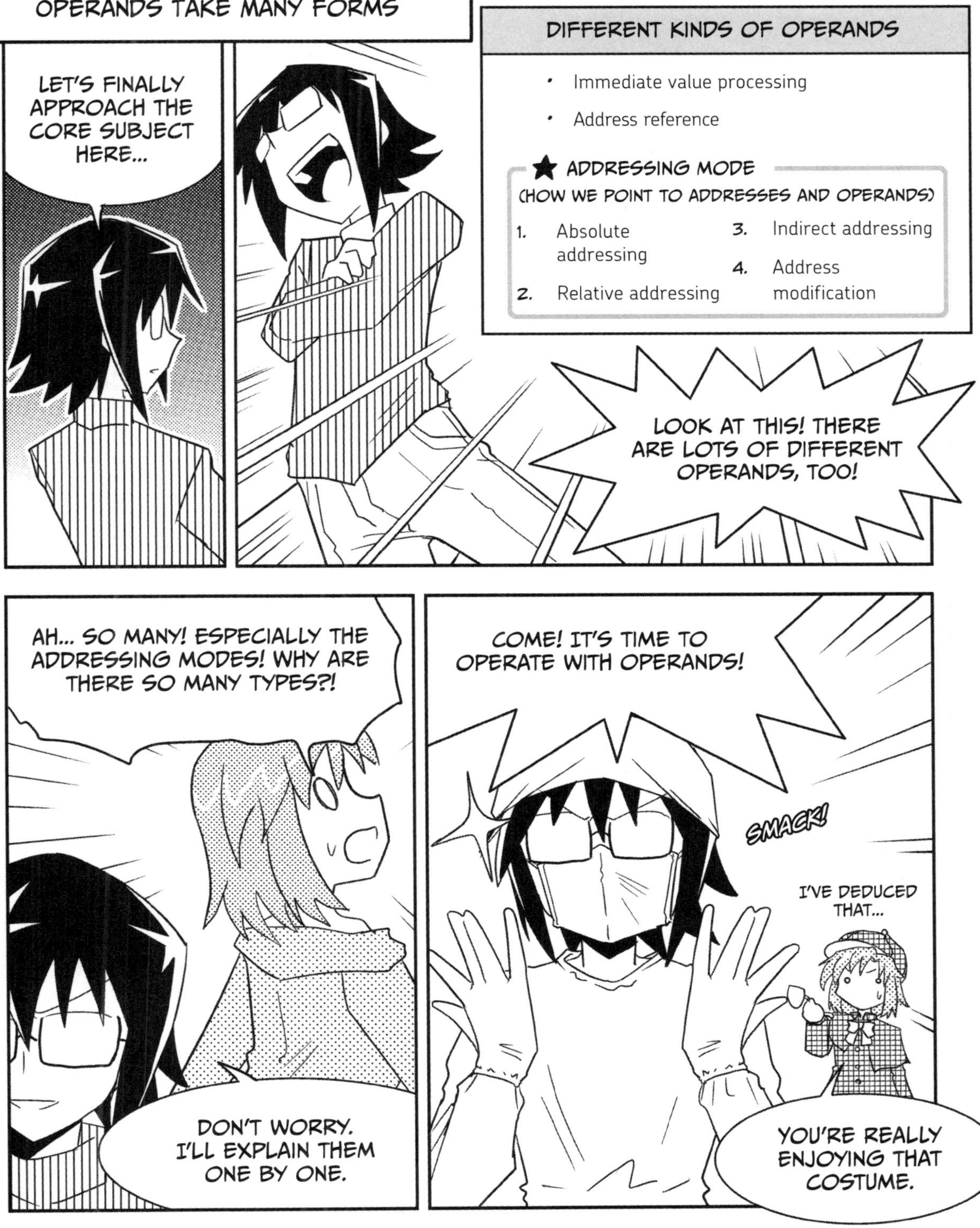
LET'S FINALLY APPROACH THE CORE SUBJECT HERE...
DIFFERENT KINDS OF OPERANDS
• Immediate value processing
• Address reference
★ ADDRESSING MODE
(HOW WE POINT TO ADDRESSES AND OPERANDS)
1. Absolute addressing
2. Relative addressing
3. Indirect addressing
4. Address modification
LOOK AT THIS! THERE ARE LOTS OF DIFFERENT OPERANDS, TOO!
AH... SO MANY! ESPECIALLY THE ADDRESSING MODES! WHY ARE THERE SO MANY TYPES?!
DON'T WORRY. I'LL EXPLAIN THEM ONE BY ONE.
COME! IT'S TIME TO OPERATE WITH OPERANDS!
SMACK!
I'VE DEDUCED THAT...
YOU'RE REALLY ENJOYING THAT COSTUME.

IMMEDIATE VALUE PROCESSING

IMMEDIATE NOODLES
Add2
IMMEDIATE OPERAND
JUST AS IT IS RIGHT NOW!

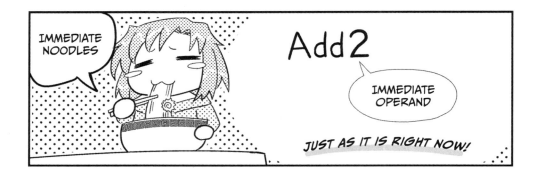

Let's start with *immediate values.*

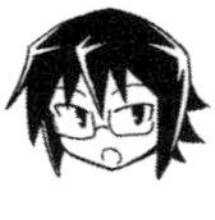

The word *immediate* here means that the value will be used right away, just as it is. In other words, the operand itself is a value.

Add 2
MNEMONIC "ADD"
IMMEDIATE VALUE OPERAND

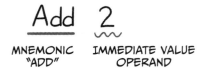

You're right! So I guess this would mean, "Add two to the value in the accumulator."

A Shift L 2
ARITHMETIC
SHIFT
LEFT
IMMEDIATE VALUE OPERAND

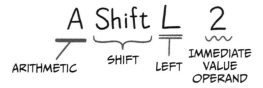

And this example shows a two-bit arithmetic left shift. Immediate value operands can be used with many different operations—for example, arithmetic operations, shift operations, and logic operations.

In the end, it's just a concrete value though, right? I learned about immediate values immediately!

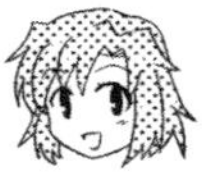

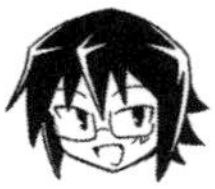

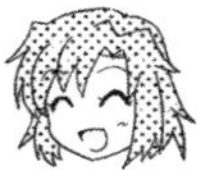

ADDRESS REFERENCES

I guess *address references* have to be operands that are addresses, like address number 1 or number 2. . . .

Yeah. Either internal* or external memory addresses, to be exact. The operation will grab the data on the address in question and use it.

Hmm, so for example, I could instruct the CPU to get the data on address 1 and address 2, add them, and store the result on address 3—right?

Yeah, in that case, it would turn out like this.

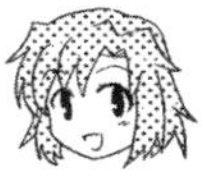

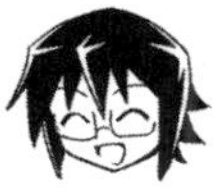

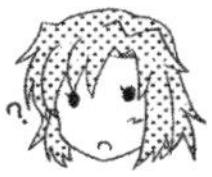

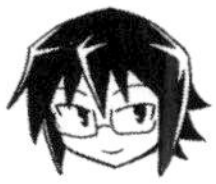

LDA ADDRESS 1	Read the data on address 1 and store it in the accumulator.
ADD ADDRESS 2	Add the data on address 2 to the accumulator.
STA ADDRESS 3	Store the value in the accumulator to address 3.

ACCUMULATOR
READOUT
MEMORY
ADD
STORE
1
2
3
CPU

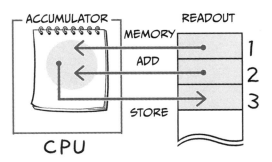

Oh! So is it important that calculations are always done in the accumulator then?

That's right. The accumulator even has its own mnemonic: *A*. The mnemonic *LDA* means *LoaD to Accumulator*, while *STA* means *STore Accumulator*.

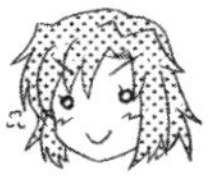

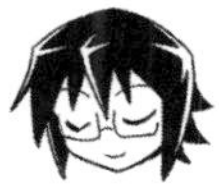

* If you look at the architectural diagram on page 106, you can see that classic CPUs had internal RAM. These were also referenced using memory addresses.

WHAT ARE ADDRESSING MODES?

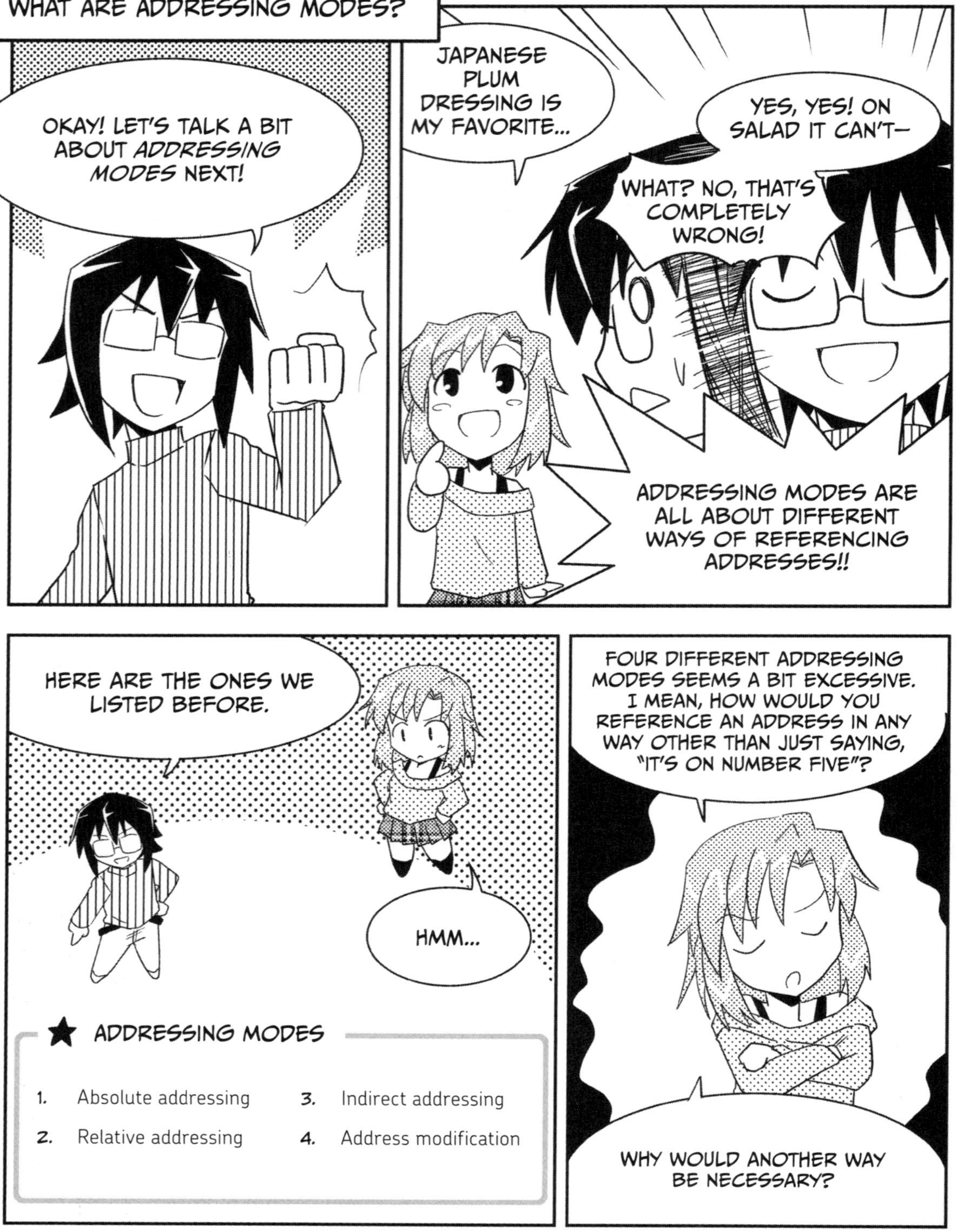
OKAY! LET'S TALK A BIT ABOUT *ADDRESSING MODES* NEXT!
JAPANESE PLUM DRESSING IS MY FAVORITE...
YES, YES! ON SALAD IT CAN'T—
WHAT? NO, THAT'S COMPLETELY WRONG!
ADDRESSING MODES ARE ALL ABOUT DIFFERENT WAYS OF REFERENCING ADDRESSES!!
HERE ARE THE ONES WE LISTED BEFORE.
HMM...
★ ADDRESSING MODES
1. Absolute addressing
2. Relative addressing
3. Indirect addressing
4. Address modification
FOUR DIFFERENT ADDRESSING MODES SEEMS A BIT EXCESSIVE. I MEAN, HOW WOULD YOU REFERENCE AN ADDRESS IN ANY WAY OTHER THAN JUST SAYING, "IT'S ON NUMBER FIVE"?
WHY WOULD ANOTHER WAY BE NECESSARY?

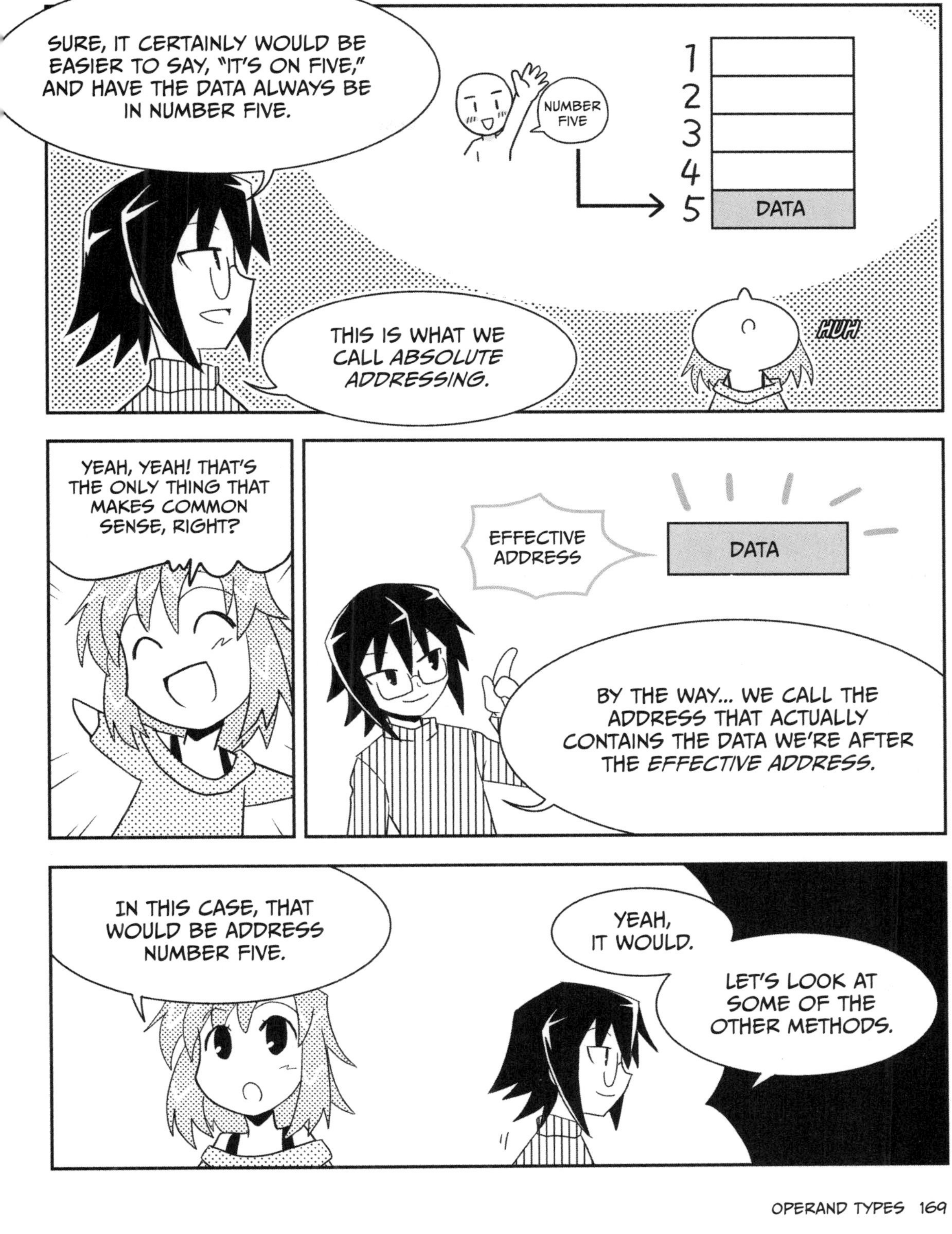
SURE, IT CERTAINLY WOULD BE EASIER TO SAY, "IT'S ON FIVE," AND HAVE THE DATA ALWAYS BE IN NUMBER FIVE.
NUMBER FIVE
1
2
3
4
5
DATA
THIS IS WHAT WE CALL *ABSOLUTE ADDRESSING.*
HUH
YEAH, YEAH! THAT'S THE ONLY THING THAT MAKES COMMON SENSE, RIGHT?
EFFECTIVE ADDRESS
DATA
BY THE WAY... WE CALL THE ADDRESS THAT ACTUALLY CONTAINS THE DATA WE'RE AFTER THE *EFFECTIVE ADDRESS.*
IN THIS CASE, THAT WOULD BE ADDRESS NUMBER FIVE.
YEAH, IT WOULD.
LET'S LOOK AT SOME OF THE OTHER METHODS.

LET'S SAY WE POINTED OUT NUMBER TWO, AND WHEN WE OPENED IT...

NUMBER TWO

A REFERENCE TO NUMBER FIVE (ADDRESS NUMBER FIVE).

1
2
3
4
5 DATA

WE FOUND OUR DATA WAS AT NUMBER FIVE!

THIS IS WHAT WE WOULD CALL *INDIRECT ADDRESSING.*

WHAAAT? WHY WOULD YOU EVER DO SOMETHING SO UNNECESSARILY COMPLICATED...

HA! IT'S LIKE FINDING A LONG-LOST WILL OR SEARCHING FOR HIDDEN TREASURE! ONLY THE ONES WHO ARE TENACIOUS ENOUGH TO MAKE IT TO THE END CAN GET THE PRIZE.

CALM DOWN.

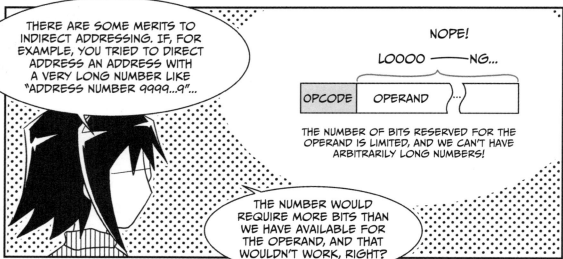

THERE ARE SOME MERITS TO INDIRECT ADDRESSING. IF, FOR EXAMPLE, YOU TRIED TO DIRECT ADDRESS AN ADDRESS WITH A VERY LONG NUMBER LIKE "ADDRESS NUMBER 9999...9"...

NOPE!

LOOOO ——— NG...

OPCODE OPERAND ...

THE NUMBER OF BITS RESERVED FOR THE OPERAND IS LIMITED, AND WE CAN'T HAVE ARBITRARILY LONG NUMBERS!

THE NUMBER WOULD REQUIRE MORE BITS THAN WE HAVE AVAILABLE FOR THE OPERAND, AND THAT WOULDN'T WORK, RIGHT?

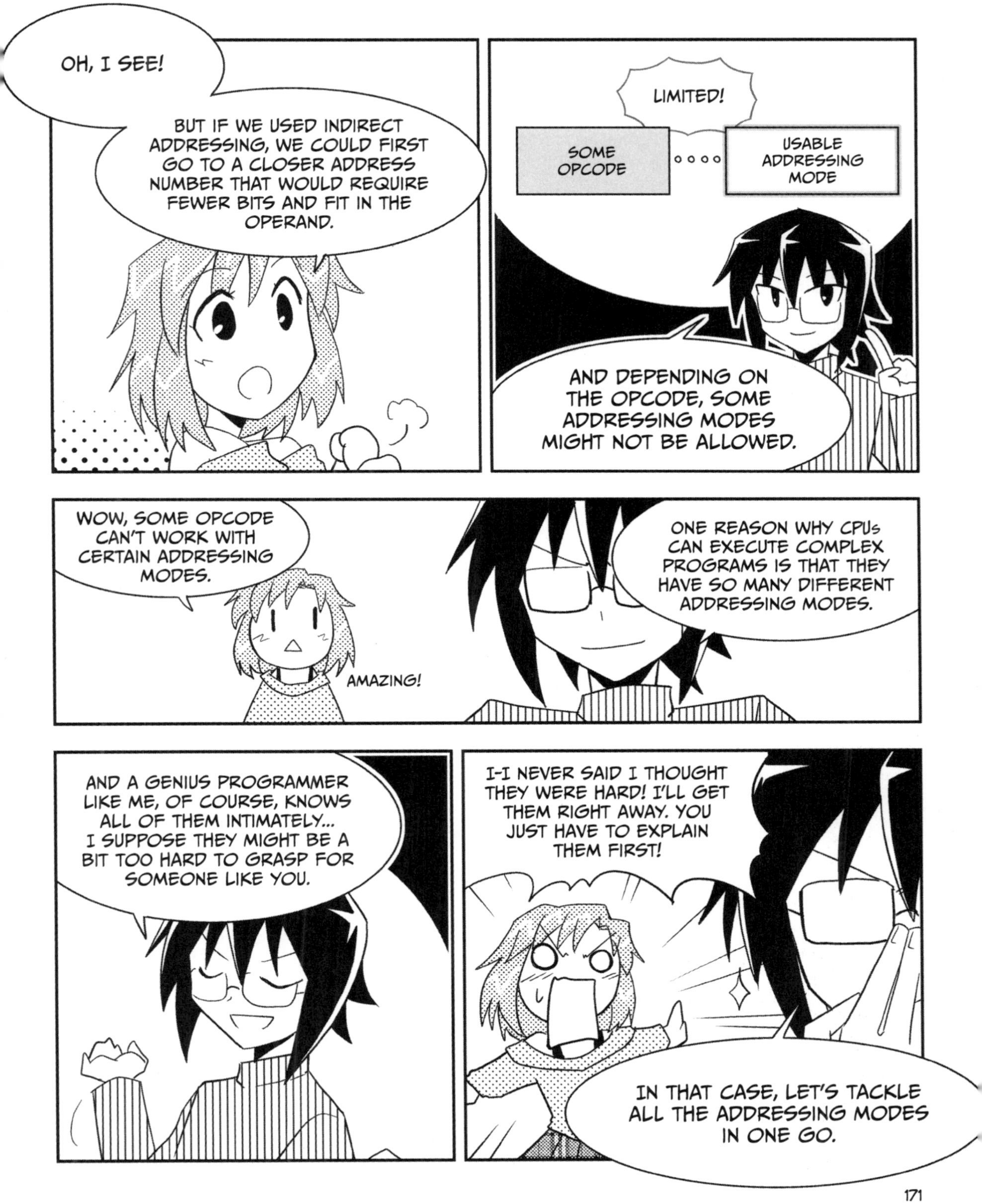
OH, I SEE!
BUT IF WE USED INDIRECT ADDRESSING, WE COULD FIRST GO TO A CLOSER ADDRESS NUMBER THAT WOULD REQUIRE FEWER BITS AND FIT IN THE OPERAND.
LIMITED!
SOME OPCODE
USABLE ADDRESSING MODE
AND DEPENDING ON THE OPCODE, SOME ADDRESSING MODES MIGHT NOT BE ALLOWED.
WOW, SOME OPCODE CAN'T WORK WITH CERTAIN ADDRESSING MODES.
AMAZING!
ONE REASON WHY CPUs CAN EXECUTE COMPLEX PROGRAMS IS THAT THEY HAVE SO MANY DIFFERENT ADDRESSING MODES.
AND A GENIUS PROGRAMMER LIKE ME, OF COURSE, KNOWS ALL OF THEM INTIMATELY... I SUPPOSE THEY MIGHT BE A BIT TOO HARD TO GRASP FOR SOMEONE LIKE YOU.
I-I NEVER SAID I THOUGHT THEY WERE HARD! I'LL GET THEM RIGHT AWAY. YOU JUST HAVE TO EXPLAIN THEM FIRST!
IN THAT CASE, LET'S TACKLE ALL THE ADDRESSING MODES IN ONE GO.

ADDRESSING MODE OVERVIEW

Modern CPUs can address memory in several different ways, which we call addressing modes.

ABSOLUTE ADDRESSING

Absolute addressing is when the operand's value is used as the effective address (the address where the operation's target data is located). It is also sometimes called *direct addressing*.

INSTRUCTION
OPERAND
20
ADDRESS
MEMORY
0
10
20
DATA

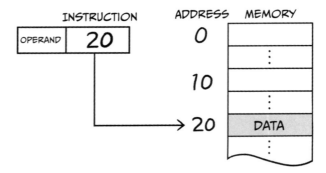

Depending on the CPU, there are cases where the size of the opcode makes it so the CPU can't address the entire address space. It's possible to lengthen the operand size if need be, however. In 16-bit CPUs, it's common practice to store the opcode and the operand in 16 bits (2 bytes), but if the operand is lengthened, the instruction could end up being 4 bytes, or even 8.

HMMM...

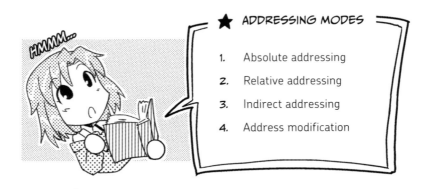

★ ADDRESSING MODES

1. Absolute addressing
2. Relative addressing
3. Indirect addressing
4. Address modification

RELATIVE ADDRESSING

Relative addressing is when the effective address is the result of the sum of the operand value and the program counter.

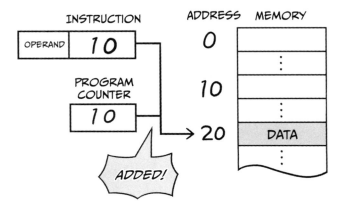

INSTRUCTION
OPERAND
10
PROGRAM COUNTER
10
ADDED!
ADDRESS
MEMORY
0
10
20
DATA

Relative addressing is most commonly used for jump instructions. Since the distance to the address we want to point out is limited by the range expressed by the two's complement of the number of bits available in the operand, relative addressing is best used for conditional branching instructions in the program and is not recommended for any larger jumps in the address space.

The base value for an operation that uses relative addresses is the current value of the program counter, or PC. As soon as the PC has read an opcode, it immediately starts pointing to the next opcode to be processed.

Also, besides using the program counter as the base value for the relative address, we can use the address in a register instead. We call addresses like these *xx-register relative addresses*.

INDIRECT ADDRESSING

Indirect addressing is used when the operand contains the address to some register and that register, in turn, contains the effective address for our target data.

INSTRUCTION
OPERAND
10
REGISTER
10
20
20
DATA

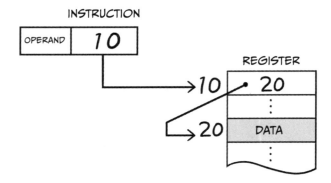

The best way to think about indirect addresses (and the address modification mode coming up next) is their close relationship with arrays in the programming language C. When working with arrays, you generally use the effective address as a starting point and add or subtract some offset values to or from it, ending up with a new address in the end. This process is what we call address modification.

IT WAS A BIT DIFFICULT, BUT I THINK I GOT EVERYTHING!
I SUPPOSE AFTER THIS, I'M ALSO AN ADDRESS MASTER! OR *ADMAS* FOR SHORT!
address master
WHY WOULD YOU SHORTEN THAT?!

ADDRESS MODIFICATION

Address modification is the process of using the value stored in a modification register to modify a number or address. We get the effective address by adding the value in the modification register to a base value, which may be stored in another register or in the program counter or even in an immediate value.

OPERAND
INSTRUCTION
MODIFICATION REGISTER
COMES WITH THE OPTION TO MODIFY THE VALUE IN THE OPERAND
MODIFICATION REGISTER
40
BASE REGISTER
100
ADDED!
INDIRECTLY REFERENCED ADDRESS
ADDRESS
100
120
20
140
40
DATA
ONLY ADD THE VALUE IN THE MODIFICATION REGISTER!
BASE
+
MODIFI-CATION

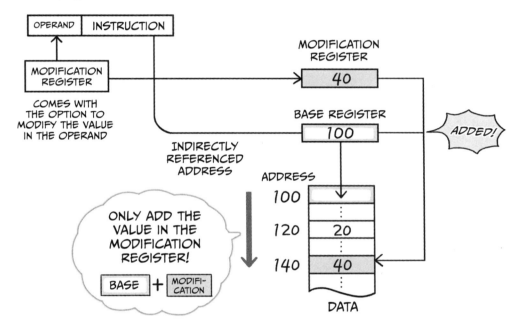

One of the most commonly used modification registers is the *index register*. We usually call the register containing the value we want to use as a base the *base register*. Most CPUs create the effective address in this case by simply adding the value in the base register and the value in the modification register (the index register, for example) together.

By using address modification in this way, you can achieve very practical effects. For example, you could extract some particular data from a set by specifying the offset in the index register and the start of the data set in a base register.

The Structure of Operations in the ALU

WE'VE FINALLY ARRIVED AT TODAY'S HIGH POINT! IT'S THE THING YOU'VE BEEN WAITING FOR...

LET'S GO INTO FUN-TIME MODE!!

...HUH? I WASN'T WAITING FOR ANYTHING.

SO COLD!

REMEMBER, TO UNDERSTAND ARITHMETIC OPERATION INSTRUCTIONS AND LOGIC OPERATION INSTRUCTIONS, YOU HAVE TO...

ARITHMETIC LOGIC UNIT

ALU

AAH! RIGHT, WE WERE TALKING ABOUT THE ALU!

YEP! I'M GOING TO USE THIS 4-BIT ALU IC AS AN EXAMPLE. ITS NAME IS 74S181.*

A 74S181, MADE BY TEXAS INSTRUMENTS

BUT IT'S SOMETIMES CALLED A *BIT SLICE.*

* THE TI MICROCONTROLLER WE TALKED ABOUT ON PAGE 157 USED FOUR OF THESE 74S181 CIRCUITS. THEY WERE USED IN MANY HIGH-SPEED CALCULATION COMPUTERS—FOR EXAMPLE, IN AIRCRAFT SIMULATORS AND THE LIKE. THE 74S181 CIRCUIT WAS EVENTUALLY SIMPLIFIED INTO THE 74S381 CIRCUIT.

HMM...? SO EVEN ONE OF THESE ICs IS CAPABLE OF BOTH ARITHMETIC OPERATIONS AND LOGIC OPERATIONS? THAT'S PRETTY IMPRESSIVE!

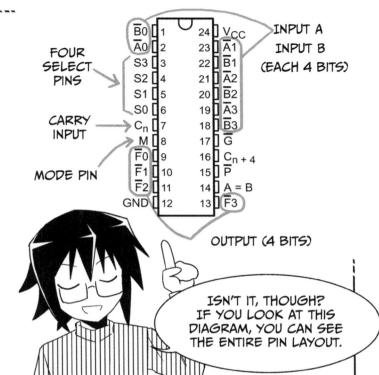

INPUT A
INPUT B
(EACH 4 BITS)

FOUR SELECT PINS

CARRY INPUT

MODE PIN

$\overline{B0}$	1	24	V_{CC}
$\overline{A0}$	2	23	$\overline{A1}$
S3	3	22	$\overline{B1}$
S2	4	21	$\overline{A2}$
S1	5	20	$\overline{B2}$
S0	6	19	$\overline{A3}$
C_n	7	18	$\overline{B3}$
M	8	17	$\overline{G}$
$\overline{F0}$	9	16	C_{n+4}
$\overline{F1}$	10	15	$\overline{P}$
$\overline{F2}$	11	14	A = B
GND	12	13	$\overline{F3}$

OUTPUT (4 BITS)

ISN'T IT, THOUGH? IF YOU LOOK AT THIS DIAGRAM, YOU CAN SEE THE ENTIRE PIN LAYOUT.

YOU CHOOSE ARITHMETIC OR LOGIC OPERATIONS USING THE *MODE PIN*, AND YOU USE THE *SELECT PINS* TO DETERMINE WHICH OPERATION TO DO.

I SEE. SO, FOR EXAMPLE, IF I HOOKED UP THE IC TO AN AIR CONDITIONER, THE *MODE PIN* WOULD LET ME CHOOSE IF I WANTED HOT OR COLD AIR.

EXCELLENT! LET'S FINISH UP TODAY'S LESSON BY HAVING A LOOK AT THE *ARCHITECTURE* (CIRCUIT DIAGRAM) AND THE *FUNCTION TABLE* OF THE 74S181 IC.

BASIC CIRCUIT ARCHITECTURE OF THE 74S181

REFERENCED FROM A TEXAS INSTRUMENTS DATA SHEET (PARTIALLY REVISED)

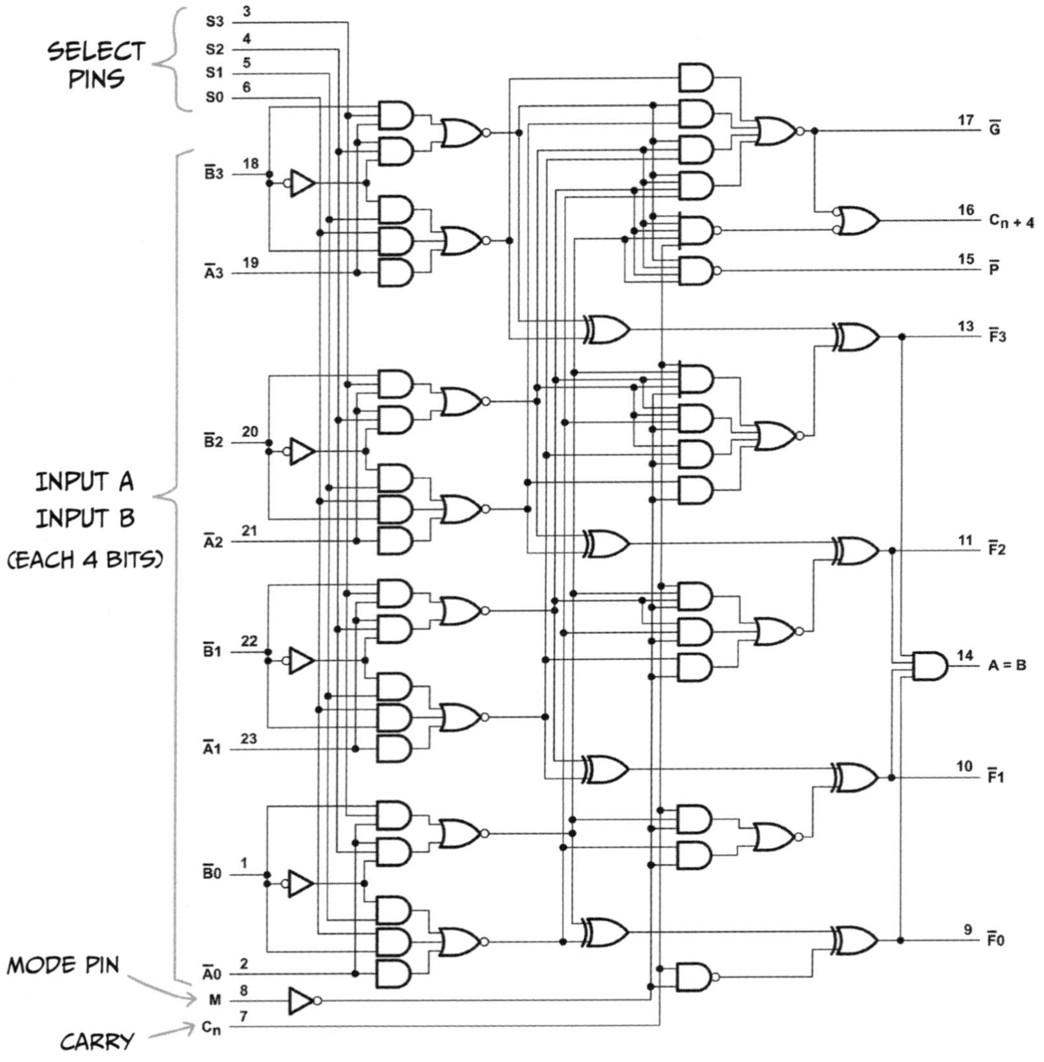

SELECT PINS
S3 3
S2 4
S1 5
S0 6
INPUT A
INPUT B
(EACH 4 BITS)
B̄3 18
Ā3 19
B̄2 20
Ā2 21
B̄1 22
Ā1 23
B̄0 1
Ā0 2
MODE PIN
M 8
CARRY
Cn 7
17 Ḡ
16 Cn + 4
15 P̄
13 F̄3
11 F̄2
14 A = B
10 F̄1
9 F̄0

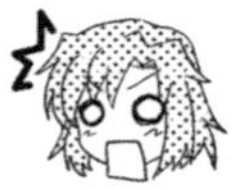

Whaa! It's really complicated, but I can see the four-bit inputs A and B clearly. I also see the select pins S0 through S3 and the mode pin M.

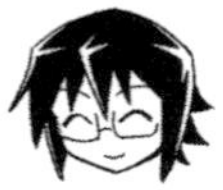

Yeah, that's right. The carry is also there, denoted by *Cn*.

74S181 FUNCTION TABLE

SELECTION				ACTIVE-HIGH DATA		
				M = H LOGIC OPERATIONS	M = L; ARITHMETIC OPERATIONS	
S3	S2	S1	S0		C_n = H (no carry)	C_n = L (with carry)
L	L	L	L	$F = \overline{A}$	F = A	F = A PLUS 1
L	L	L	H	$F = \overline{A + B}$	F = A + B	F = (A + B) PLUS 1
L	L	H	L	$F = \overline{A}B$	$F = A + \overline{B}$	$F = (A + \overline{B})$ PLUS 1
L	L	H	H	F = 0	F = MINUS 1 (2'S COMPL)	F = ZERO
L	H	L	L	$F = \overline{AB}$	F = A PLUS $A\overline{B}$	F = A PLUS $A\overline{B}$ PLUS 1
L	H	L	H	$F = \overline{B}$	F = (A + B) PLUS $A\overline{B}$	F = (A + B) PLUS $A\overline{B}$ PLUS 1
L	H	H	L	$F = A \oplus B$	F = A MINUS B MINUS 1	F = A MINUS B
L	H	H	H	$F = A\overline{B}$	$F = A\overline{B}$ MINUS 1	$F = A\overline{B}$
H	L	L	L	$F = \overline{A} + B$	F = A PLUS AB	F = A PLUS AB PLUS 1
H	L	L	H	$F = \overline{A \oplus B}$	F = A PLUS B	F = A PLUS B PLUS 1
H	L	H	L	F = B	$F = (A + \overline{B})$ PLUS AB	$F = (A + \overline{B})$ PLUS AB PLUS 1
H	L	H	H	F = AB	F = AB MINUS 1	F = AB
H	H	L	L	F = 1	F = A PLUS A*	F = A PLUS A PLUS 1
H	H	L	H	$F = A + \overline{B}$	F = (A + B) PLUS A	F = (A + B) PLUS A PLUS 1
H	H	H	L	F = A + B	$F = (A + \overline{B})$ PLUS A	$F = (A + \overline{B})$ PLUS A PLUS 1
H	H	H	H	F = A	F = A MINUS 1	F = A

* Each bit is shifted to the more significant position.

For more information on the symbols used in these formulas, please see pages 55–59. PLUS and MINUS are exactly what they seem. The symbols +, –, and ⊕ are symbols used in Boolean algebra (logical algebra).

There are also some redundant or unnecessary operations in the diagram, as you might see.

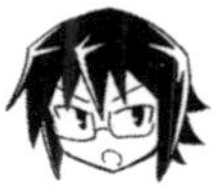

The most important parts of the 74S181 function table are marked with gray.

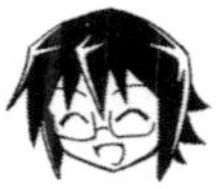

First off, *M* is the mode pin, *H* stands for high, and *L* stands for low. When M = H, we are using logic operations. If M = L, arithmetic operations are being used instead.

Arithmetic operations then further differ depending on whether we have a carry or not. If C_n = H, that means we do not have a carry, and if C_n = L, we do have a carry.

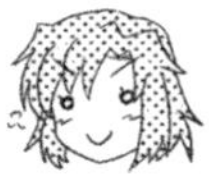

And *S* is the four select pins, right? Depending on the combination, we have 16 (2^4) different operations to choose from!

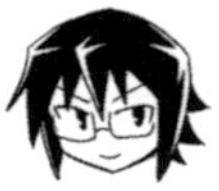

Now let's take a closer look at the opcodes in the function table. For convenience, let's assign a number to each of the opcodes: 0–15, or 16 in total. Of course these numbers may not be the same for other CPUs.

I'll explain the ones with gray backgrounds in detail.

	Arithmetic Operations	
	No Carry	**With Carry**
0	$F = A$	$F = A$ PLUS 1
1	$F = A + B$	$F = (A + B)$ PLUS 1
2	$F = A + \overline{B}$	$F = (A + \overline{B})$ PLUS 1
3	F = MINUS 1 (2'S COMPL)	F = ZERO
4	$F = A$ PLUS $A\overline{B}$	$F = A$ PLUS $A\overline{B}$ PLUS 1
5	$F = (A + B)$ PLUS $A\overline{B}$	$F = (A + B)$ PLUS $A\overline{B}$ PLUS 1
6	$F = A$ MINUS B MINUS 1	$F = A$ MINUS B
7	$F = A\overline{B}$ MINUS 1	$F = A\overline{B}$
8	$F = A$ PLUS AB	$F = A$ PLUS AB PLUS 1
9	$F = A$ PLUS B	$F = A$ PLUS B PLUS 1
10	$F = (A + \overline{B})$ PLUS AB	$F = (A + \overline{B})$ PLUS AB PLUS 1
11	$F = AB$ MINUS 1	$F = AB$
12	$F = A$ PLUS A	$F = A$ PLUS A PLUS 1
13	$F = (A + B)$ PLUS A	$F = (A + B)$ PLUS A PLUS 1
14	$F = (A + \overline{B})$ PLUS A	$F = (A + \overline{B})$ PLUS A PLUS 1
15	$F = A$ MINUS 1	$F = A$

Logic Operations	
0	$F = \overline{A}$
1	$F = \overline{A + B}$
2	$F = \overline{A}B$
3	$F = 0$
4	$F = \overline{AB}$
5	$F = \overline{B}$
6	$F = A \oplus B$
7	$F = A\overline{B}$
8	$F = \overline{A} + B$
9	$F = \overline{A \oplus B}$
10	$F = B$
11	$F = AB$
12	$F = 1$
13	$F = A + \overline{B}$
14	$F = A + B$
15	$F = A$

IMPORTANT ARITHMETIC OPERATION INSTRUCTIONS

OPCODE 6

No carry: The calculation result F is the difference between A and B minus 1.
With carry: The calculation result F is the difference between A and B.

OPCODE 9

No carry: The calculation result F is the sum of A and B.
With carry: The calculation result F is the sum of A and B plus 1.

IMPORTANT LOGIC OPERATION INSTRUCTIONS

OPCODE 1: NOR (A, B)

The operational result F is the negated output of the OR between the A and B bits. That is, it is the NOR of the bits in A and B.

OPCODE 3: ZERO

The operational result F is 0, regardless of the input.

OPCODE 4: NAND (A, B)

The operational result F is the negated output of the AND between the A and B bits. That is, it is the NAND of the bits in A and B.

OPCODE 5: NOT (B)

The operational result F is the NOT of input B. That is, every 0 bit in B is flipped to a 1, and every 1 bit in B is flipped to a 0.

OPCODE 6: EXOR (A, B)

The operational result F is the EXOR of the bits in A and B.

OPCODE 9: EXNOR (A, B)

The operational result F is the negated output of the EXOR of the bits in A and B.

OPCODE 10: B

The operational result F is simply B.

OPCODE 11: AND (A, B)

The operational result F is the AND of the bits in A and B.

OPCODE 12: ONES

The operational result F is all 1s, regardless of the input.

OPCODE 14: OR (A, B)

The operational result F is the OR of the bits in A and B.

OPCODE 15: A

The operational result F is simply A.

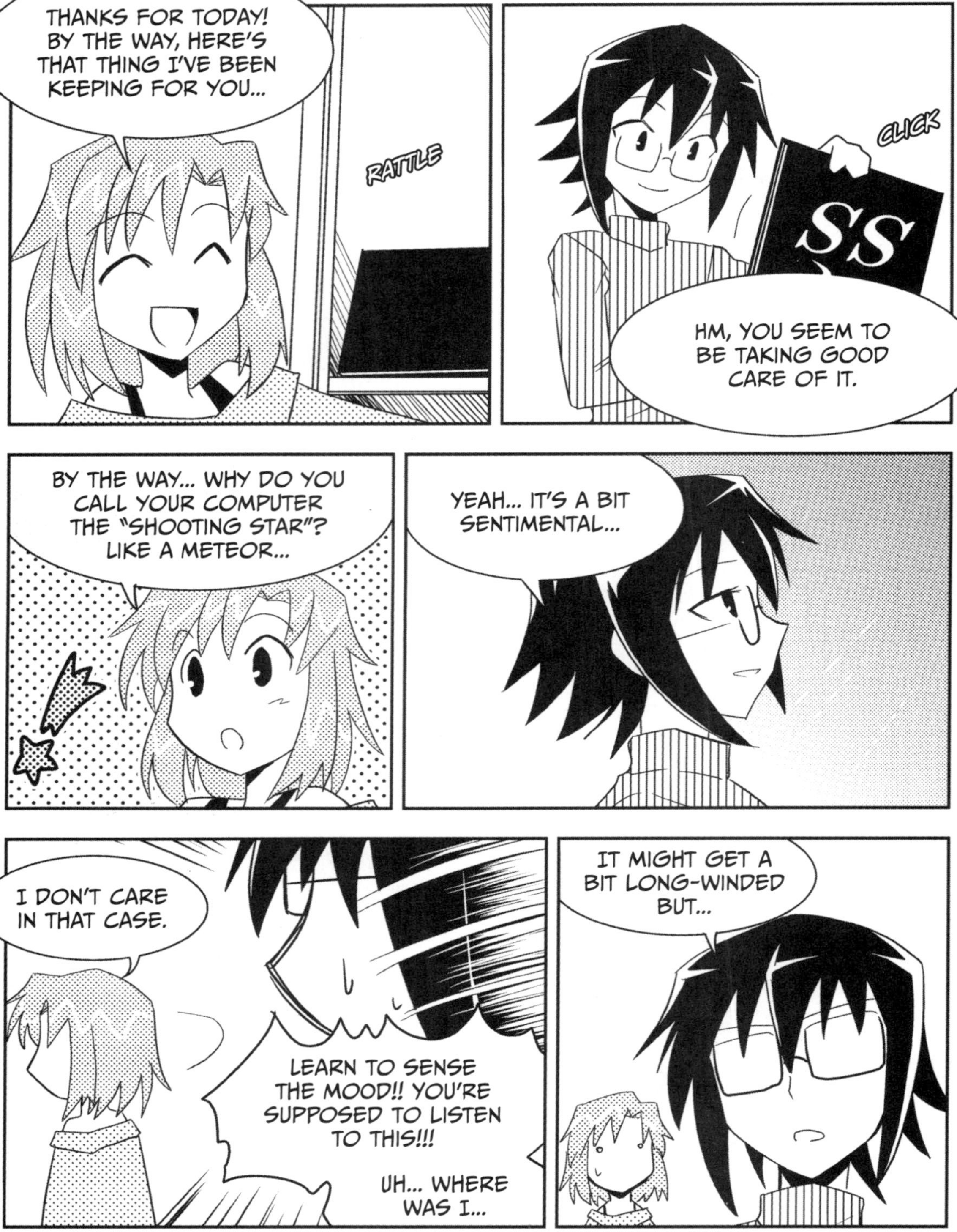
THANKS FOR TODAY! BY THE WAY, HERE'S THAT THING I'VE BEEN KEEPING FOR YOU...
RATTLE
CLICK
SS
HM, YOU SEEM TO BE TAKING GOOD CARE OF IT.
BY THE WAY... WHY DO YOU CALL YOUR COMPUTER THE "SHOOTING STAR"? LIKE A METEOR...
YEAH... IT'S A BIT SENTIMENTAL...
I DON'T CARE IN THAT CASE.
LEARN TO SENSE THE MOOD!! YOU'RE SUPPOSED TO LISTEN TO THIS!!!
UH... WHERE WAS I...
IT MIGHT GET A BIT LONG-WINDED BUT...

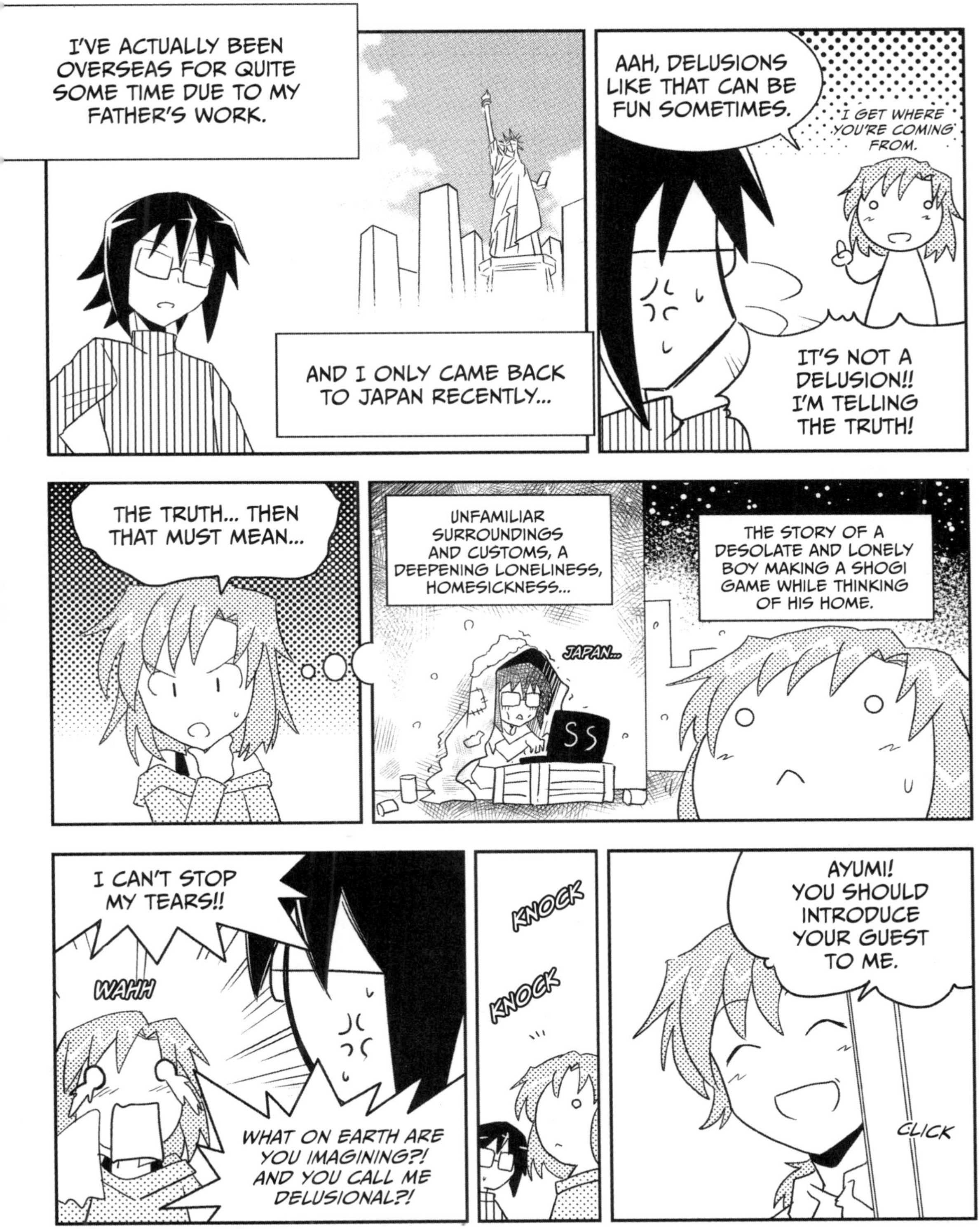
I'VE ACTUALLY BEEN OVERSEAS FOR QUITE SOME TIME DUE TO MY FATHER'S WORK.
AND I ONLY CAME BACK TO JAPAN RECENTLY...
AAH, DELUSIONS LIKE THAT CAN BE FUN SOMETIMES.
I GET WHERE YOU'RE COMING FROM.
IT'S NOT A DELUSION!! I'M TELLING THE TRUTH!
THE TRUTH... THEN THAT MUST MEAN...
UNFAMILIAR SURROUNDINGS AND CUSTOMS, A DEEPENING LONELINESS, HOMESICKNESS...
JAPAN...
THE STORY OF A DESOLATE AND LONELY BOY MAKING A SHOGI GAME WHILE THINKING OF HIS HOME.
I CAN'T STOP MY TEARS!!
WAHH
WHAT ON EARTH ARE YOU IMAGINING?! AND YOU CALL ME DELUSIONAL?!
KNOCK
KNOCK
AYUMI! YOU SHOULD INTRODUCE YOUR GUEST TO ME.
CLICK

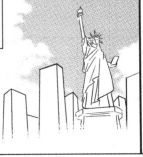

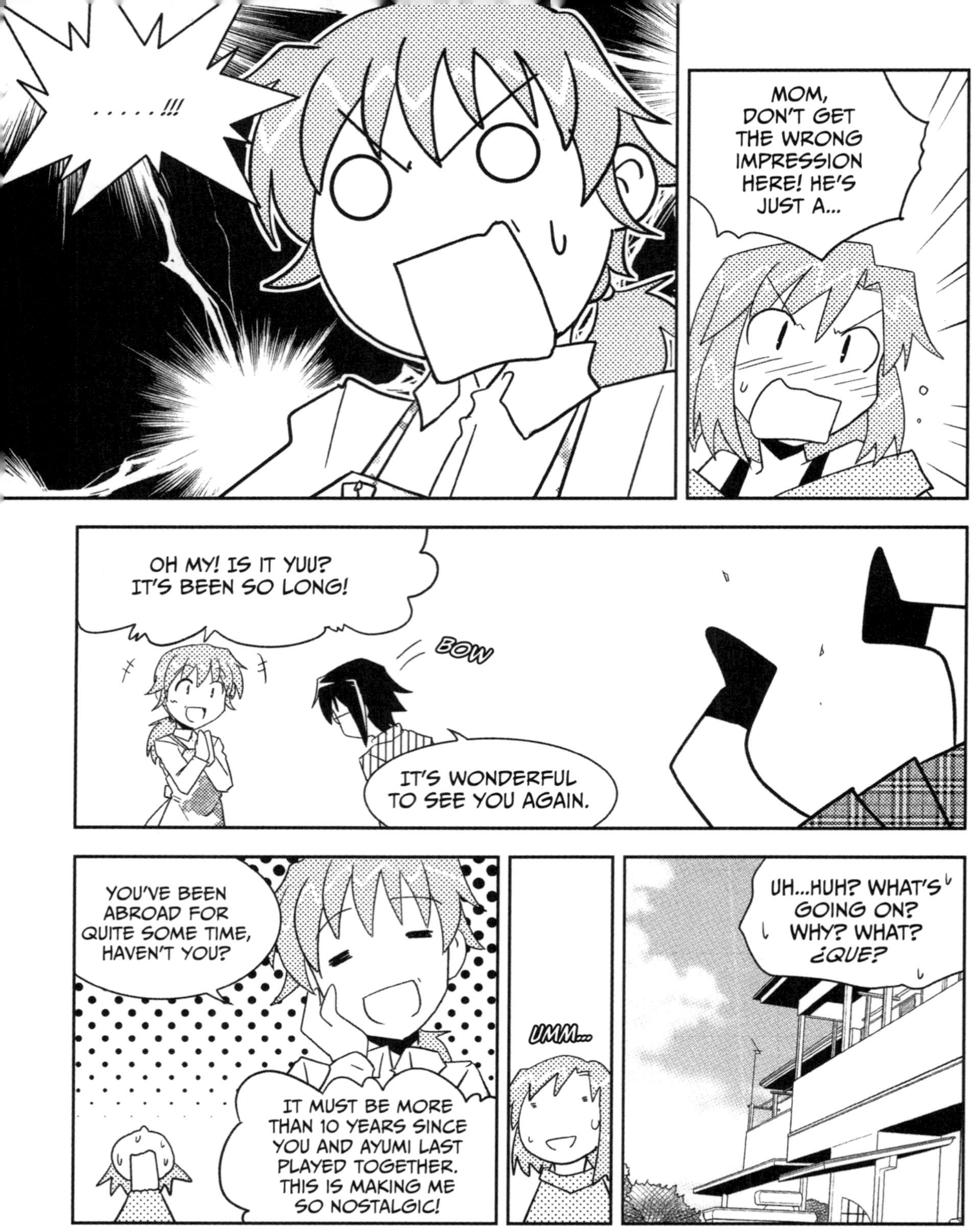
......!!!
MOM, DON'T GET THE WRONG IMPRESSION HERE! HE'S JUST A...
OH MY! IS IT YUU? IT'S BEEN SO LONG!
BOW
IT'S WONDERFUL TO SEE YOU AGAIN.
YOU'VE BEEN ABROAD FOR QUITE SOME TIME, HAVEN'T YOU?
IT MUST BE MORE THAN 10 YEARS SINCE YOU AND AYUMI LAST PLAYED TOGETHER. THIS IS MAKING ME SO NOSTALGIC!
UMM...
UH...HUH? WHAT'S GOING ON? WHY? WHAT? ¿QUE?

SERIAL TRANSMISSION AND PARALLEL TRANSMISSION

There are two types of digital data transmission: *serial transmission* and *parallel transmission.*

ONE BIT AT A TIME
SENDER
→0→1→1→0→
RECEIVER
SERIAL TRANSMISSION

SIMULTANEOUSLY!
SENDER
→ 0
→ 1
→ 1
→ 0
RECEIVER
PARALLEL TRANSMISSION

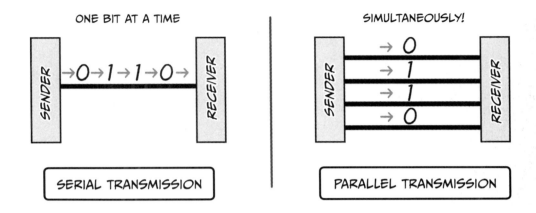

Systems that use serial transmission send data one bit at a time; systems that use parallel transmission send several bits at a time. An interesting thing to note is that *USB* (as in USB memory or USB connectors) is short for Universal Serial Bus, which, as you might have guessed, uses serial transmission.

SHIFT REGISTERS AND PARALLEL-SERIAL CONVERSION

One of the components often used in logic circuits is a *shift register*. This type of register can perform shift operations and nothing else. An example is the accumulator within the ALU.

The most common use for shift registers is to parallel shift several bits of data (for example, 8 bits) to the right in one clock cycle. The rightmost bits are then converted and sent as serial data.

There is some discussion about whether this serial transmission function should be seen as part of CPU functionality or as part of I/O. Overall, it's easier to think of it as the means by which the CPU communicates with devices other than the memory, all bundled together as "I/O devices," and as distinct from things not directly operated by the CPU block.

AN OVERVIEW OF SOME BASIC REGISTERS

Registers are useful in many contexts, and they are essential to the CPU. Here are some basic registers and their functionalities.

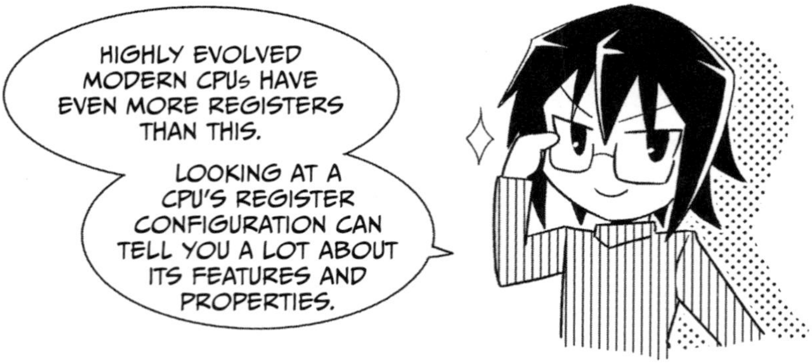
HIGHLY EVOLVED MODERN CPUs HAVE EVEN MORE REGISTERS THAN THIS.
LOOKING AT A CPU'S REGISTER CONFIGURATION CAN TELL YOU A LOT ABOUT ITS FEATURES AND PROPERTIES.

ACCUMULATOR

This register stores calculation results from the ALU. It's designed in such a way as to be ready for the next calculation as soon as the previous one is done. It's called the accumulator in part because it's generally used when incrementing values and counting sequentially, but also since it's often used as the input for a follow-up sum right after another calculation has finished.

INSTRUCTION REGISTER & INSTRUCTION DECODER

These registers store and decode the program instructions. This decoding process determines not only which operation to execute but also the operands on which to operate.

STATUS REGISTER

The status register is a collection of flags that take the value 1 or 0 as a result of calculations and operations. These flags can determine the order of program execution and how the CPU interacts with I/O devices. Since flags are only 1 bit each, it is very common to lump them together in 8-bit or even 16-bit registers. There are many different kinds of flags, and you can read more about them starting on page 187.

MODIFICATION REGISTERS (BASE REGISTERS, INDEX REGISTERS)

These registers serve as the starting point in certain addressing modes. The base register serves as a basis for address calculations. In relative addressing, adding an offset to the base register yields an effective address.

Index registers hold fixed values that modify operand immediate values in special circumstances to form the effective address. For example, you would add the offset found in the index register to a data array's base address to find a specific value in the array.

TEMP REGISTER (TEMPORARY REGISTER)

Temp registers are used to save temporary data during the many tasks undertaken by the CPU. Depending on the CPU, some blocks of the circuit might have several temp registers available. You can see a temp register labeled in the diagram of classic CPU architecture on page 106.

PROGRAM COUNTER (PC)

The program counter holds the address to the next instruction to be executed. All CPUs have this register.

STACK POINTER

Necessary when working with a stack, this register holds the last used stack address.

AN OVERVIEW OF SOME BASIC STATUS FLAGS

When the CPU calculates a result, status flags (status bits) might be set or reset. The CPU makes decisions by evaluating the status flags, either just a single flag or a combination of several flags. As a result of these decisions, the program might take different branches or end up doing different calculations.

ZERO FLAG (Z-FLAG)

Indicates whether the accumulator (the result of a calculation) is zero. If the CPU doesn't have a dedicated module for doing comparisons, the Z-flag might also double as the flag that reports the outcome of a comparison test (the EQ-flag).

SIGN FLAG (S-FLAG) OR NEGATIVE FLAG (N-FLAG)

If the accumulator contains a number, this flag tells you whether the number is negative or positive.

CARRY FLAG (C-FLAG) OR OVERFLOW FLAG (OV-FLAG)

Indicates whether a carry or an overflow occurred in the latest arithmetic add operation. It is also set if a shift operation resulted in overflow. In the case of an arithmetic subtraction operation, it is not set if borrowing (the inverse of carrying) didn't occur.

BORROW FLAG

Indicates whether a borrow occurred during a subtraction. More often than not, a borrow is indicated by the carry flag not being set, but in some cases, the borrow flag might be used instead.

GT FLAG

This flag is set if the outcome of a comparison operation was "greater than." The GT flag's associated symbol is >.

LT FLAG

This flag is set if the outcome of a comparison operation was "less than." The LT flag's associated symbol is <.

ODD FLAG

Indicates whether the result of a calculation is an odd number.

INTERRUPT MASK

Set beforehand, the interrupt mask determines what types of interrupts will occur. Setting it to all 1s will disable interrupts.

INTERRUPT FLAG

Indicates whether an interrupt is in progress or not. This flag will be set even if interrupts have been disabled.

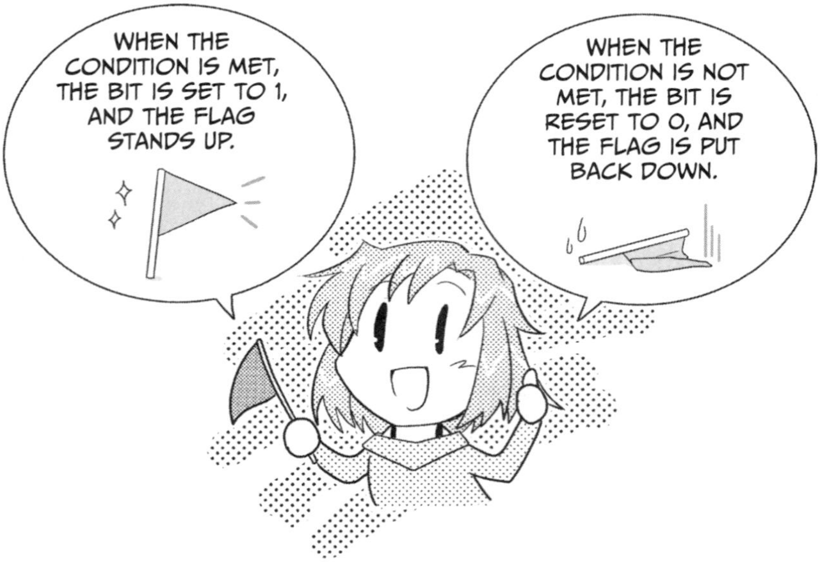
WHEN THE CONDITION IS MET, THE BIT IS SET TO 1, AND THE FLAG STANDS UP.
WHEN THE CONDITION IS NOT MET, THE BIT IS RESET TO 0, AND THE FLAG IS PUT BACK DOWN.

THE SLEEP INSTRUCTION

In addition to other control instructions, such as branches and jumps, there are instructions like STOP and SLEEP. The *SLEEP instruction* disables the program completely, putting it into a resting state temporarily until some input (such as an interrupt) occurs. This function exists on the system level as well.

By using the SLEEP instruction, the CPU is able to slow the period of the clock and thereby the program, leading to lower power consumption. To return the CPU to its normal state, some kind of button on the device usually has to be pressed to trigger an interrupt in the CPU itself, rousing the system and programs back to full speed.

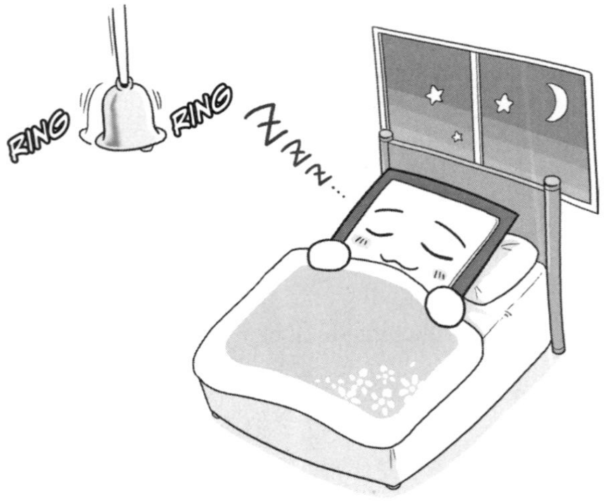
RING
RING
ZZZ...

5

PROGRAMS

PROCESSING
CONDITION
PROCESSING
PROCESSI
MONEY
HIGH CLASS?

Assembly and High-Level Languages

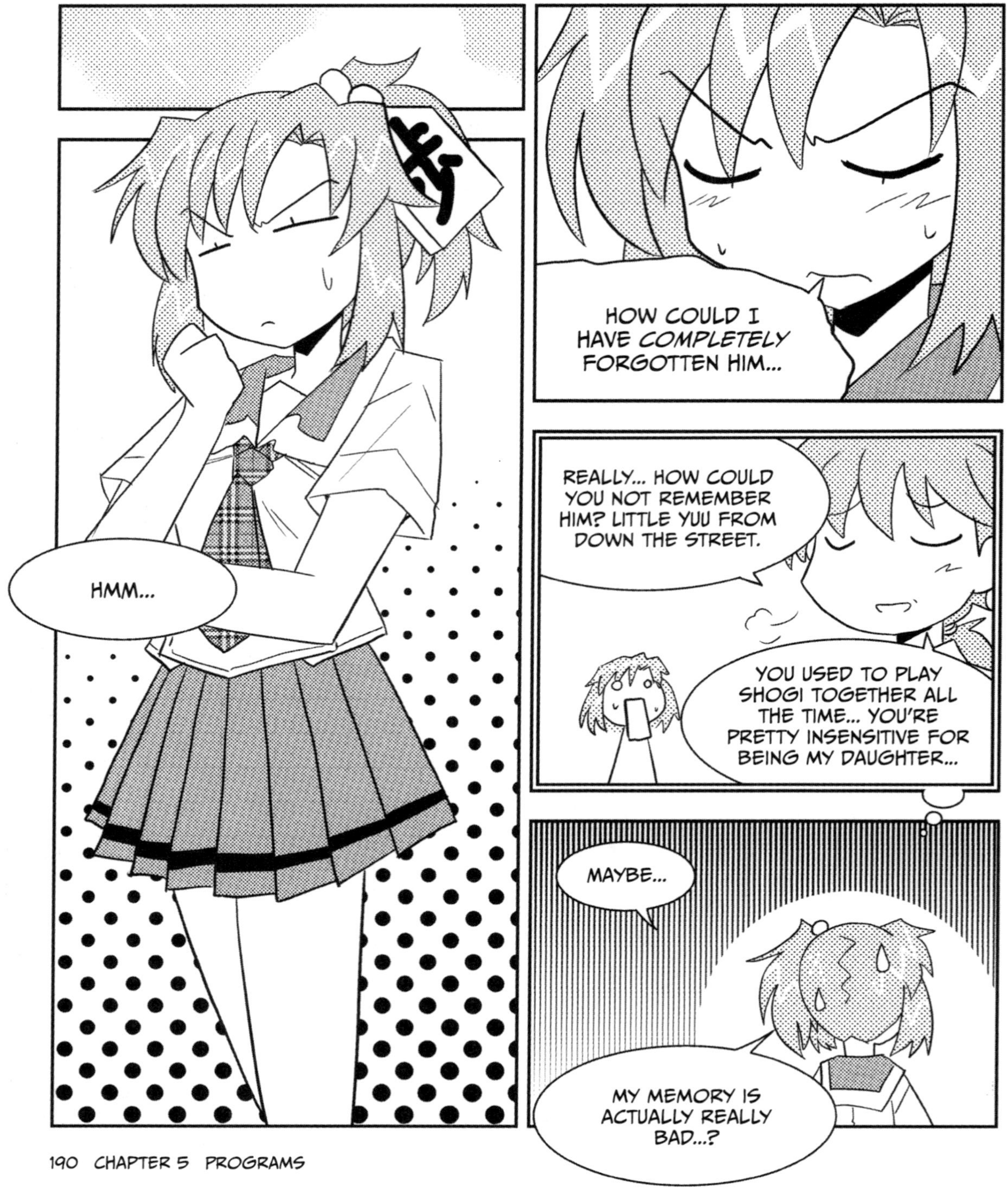
HMM...
HOW COULD I HAVE *COMPLETELY* FORGOTTEN HIM...
REALLY... HOW COULD YOU NOT REMEMBER HIM? LITTLE YUU FROM DOWN THE STREET.
YOU USED TO PLAY SHOGI TOGETHER ALL THE TIME... YOU'RE PRETTY INSENSITIVE FOR BEING MY DAUGHTER...
MAYBE...
MY MEMORY IS ACTUALLY REALLY BAD...?

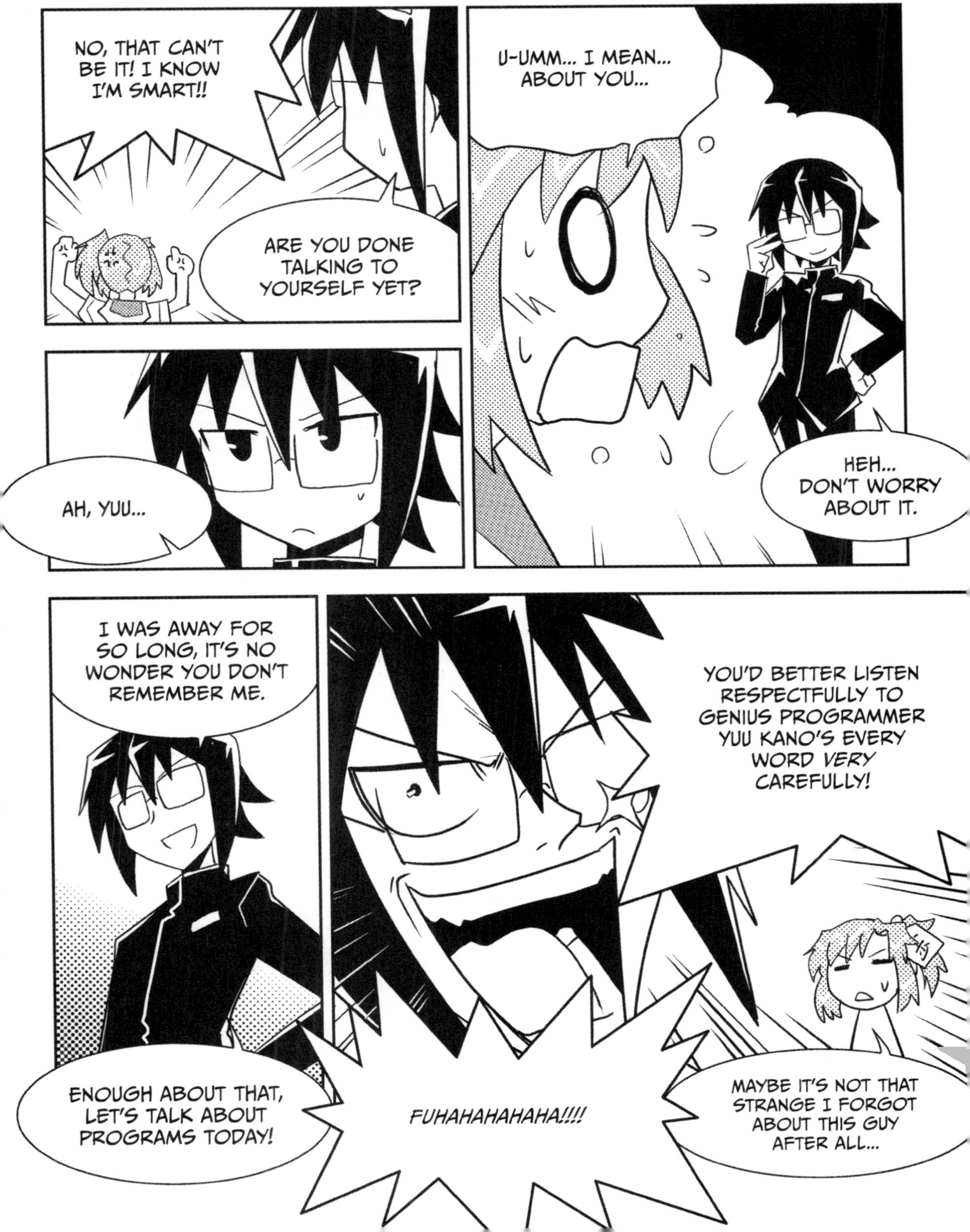
NO, THAT CAN'T BE IT! I KNOW I'M SMART!!
ARE YOU DONE TALKING TO YOURSELF YET?
U-UMM... I MEAN... ABOUT YOU...
HEH... DON'T WORRY ABOUT IT.
AH, YUU...
I WAS AWAY FOR SO LONG, IT'S NO WONDER YOU DON'T REMEMBER ME.
ENOUGH ABOUT THAT, LET'S TALK ABOUT PROGRAMS TODAY!
YOU'D BETTER LISTEN RESPECTFULLY TO GENIUS PROGRAMMER YUU KANO'S EVERY WORD *VERY* CAREFULLY!
FUHAHAHAHAHAHA!!!!
MAYBE IT'S NOT THAT STRANGE I FORGOT ABOUT THIS GUY AFTER ALL...

WHAT ARE ASSEMBLY LANGUAGES?

LIKE I SAID, TODAY WE'RE GOING TO LEARN ABOUT PROGRAMS...

BUT WE SHOULD SKIP STRAIGHT TO THE CONCLUSION BECAUSE YOU ACTUALLY ALREADY KNOW ABOUT THEM!!

WHAAA, SO MY MEMORY REALLY IS BAD AFTER ALL?!

DO YOU REMEMBER THAT WE LEARNED ABOUT THESE INSTRUCTIONS USING MNEMONICS?

LDA ADDRESS 1
READ THE DATA AT ADDRESS 1 AND STORE IT IN THE ACCUMULATOR

ADD ADDRESS 2
ADD THE CONTENT AT ADDRESS 2 TO THE ACCUMULATOR

STA ADDRESS 3
STORE THE CONTENT IN THE ACCUMULATOR TO ADDRESS 3

ANY COMBINATION OF THESE INSTRUCTIONS IS ALREADY A *PROGRAM* (OR RATHER, THE SOURCE CODE FOR ONE*).

AH! I REMEMBER THESE!

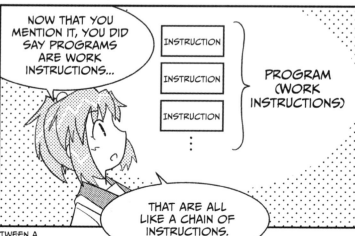

NOW THAT YOU MENTION IT, YOU DID SAY PROGRAMS ARE WORK INSTRUCTIONS...

INSTRUCTION

INSTRUCTION

INSTRUCTION

PROGRAM (WORK INSTRUCTIONS)

THAT ARE ALL LIKE A CHAIN OF INSTRUCTIONS.

* YOU CAN LEARN ABOUT THE DIFFERENCE BETWEEN A PROGRAM AND ITS SOURCE CODE ON PAGE 199.

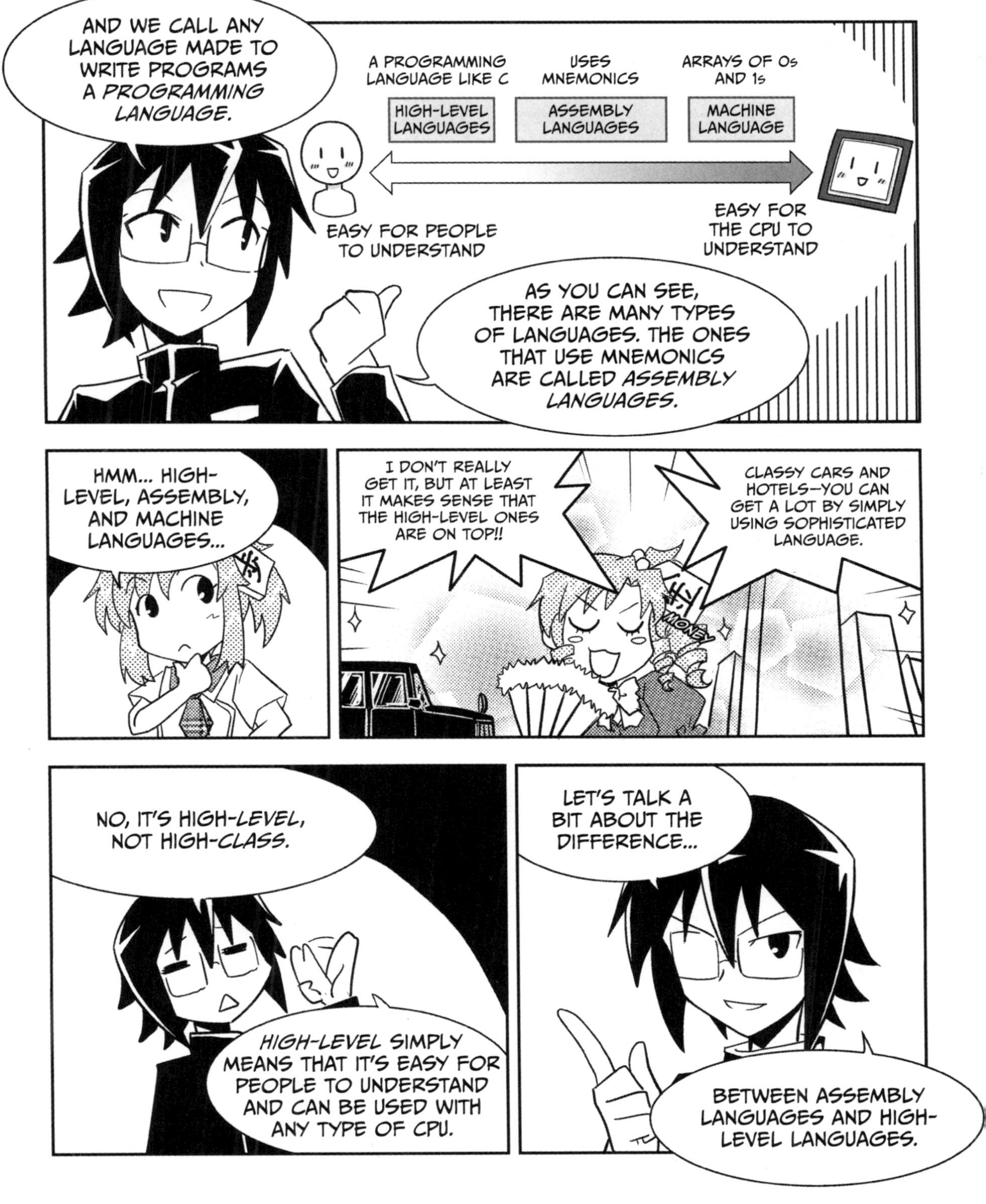
AND WE CALL ANY LANGUAGE MADE TO WRITE PROGRAMS A *PROGRAMMING LANGUAGE*.
A PROGRAMMING LANGUAGE LIKE C
USES MNEMONICS
ARRAYS OF 0s AND 1s
HIGH-LEVEL LANGUAGES
ASSEMBLY LANGUAGES
MACHINE LANGUAGE
EASY FOR PEOPLE TO UNDERSTAND
EASY FOR THE CPU TO UNDERSTAND
AS YOU CAN SEE, THERE ARE MANY TYPES OF LANGUAGES. THE ONES THAT USE MNEMONICS ARE CALLED *ASSEMBLY LANGUAGES*.
HMM... HIGH-LEVEL, ASSEMBLY, AND MACHINE LANGUAGES...
I DON'T REALLY GET IT, BUT AT LEAST IT MAKES SENSE THAT THE HIGH-LEVEL ONES ARE ON TOP!!
CLASSY CARS AND HOTELS—YOU CAN GET A LOT BY SIMPLY USING SOPHISTICATED LANGUAGE.
MONEY
NO, IT'S HIGH-*LEVEL*, NOT HIGH-*CLASS*.
HIGH-LEVEL SIMPLY MEANS THAT IT'S EASY FOR PEOPLE TO UNDERSTAND AND CAN BE USED WITH ANY TYPE OF CPU.
LET'S TALK A BIT ABOUT THE DIFFERENCE...
BETWEEN ASSEMBLY LANGUAGES AND HIGH-LEVEL LANGUAGES.

THE CHARACTERISTICS OF ASSEMBLY LANGUAGES AND HIGH-LEVEL LANGUAGES

こんにちは!
Ciao
Bonjour
DID YOU KNOW... HUMAN LANGUAGES ARE CALLED *NATURAL LANGUAGES*?
你好
Hello

Okay, let's talk a bit about the assembly languages that are easy for CPUs (machines) to understand and the high-level languages that are easy for people to understand.

A PROGRAMMING LANGUAGE LIKE C
HIGH-LEVEL LANGUAGES
USES MNEMONICS
ASSEMBLY LANGUAGES
ARRAYS OF 0s AND 1s
MACHINE LANGUAGE
EASY FOR PEOPLE TO UNDERSTAND
EASY FOR THE CPU TO UNDERSTAND

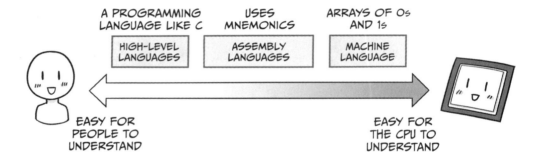

Umm. I don't think I really understand what you're saying. Because machine language is made up of arrays of 1s and 0s, I see how that would only be understandable to CPUs and not people.

But wouldn't assembly languages be pretty easy for people to understand because they use mnemonics . . . ? Instructions like ADD are just plain English. . . .

So how could high-level languages be even easier to understand than that?!

Heh, that's a valid question. It's true that assembly languages are rather easy to understand.

But that's because you already know how a CPU works and you've learned about registers (like the accumulator), addresses, and different kinds of instructions!

With a high-level language, you don't have to care about things like registers, addresses, and instructions if you don't want to. Some high-level languages don't even let you work with low-level concepts like that. For example, if you want to add two and three together in a high-level language, you can just write, "a = 2+3"!

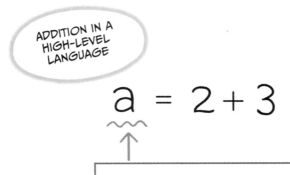

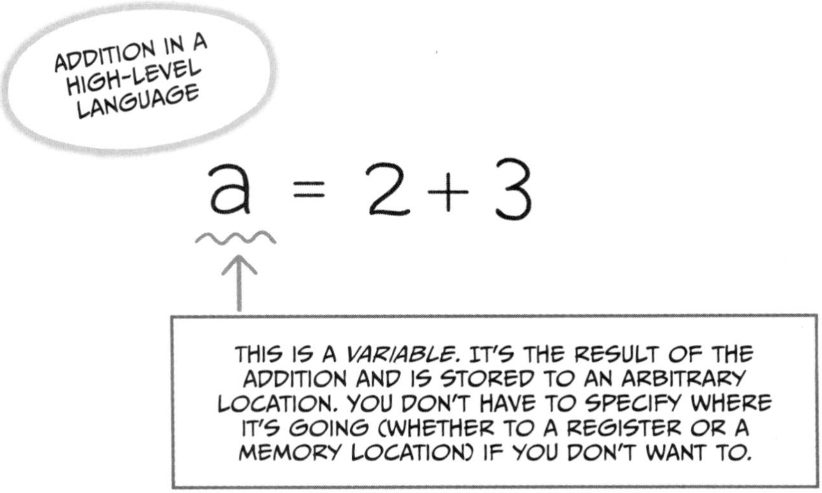

ADDITION IN A HIGH-LEVEL LANGUAGE

$$a = 2 + 3$$

THIS IS A *VARIABLE*. IT'S THE RESULT OF THE ADDITION AND IS STORED TO AN ARBITRARY LOCATION. YOU DON'T HAVE TO SPECIFY WHERE IT'S GOING (WHETHER TO A REGISTER OR A MEMORY LOCATION) IF YOU DON'T WANT TO.

Whaaa??! But that's completely different from everything we've learned so far!

So high-level languages are easy for people to understand. You're saying they let us write more intuitive instructions without having to care about how the CPU works! Is that right? If it is, that would be groundbreakingly useful, and it makes a lot of sense why it would appeal to people. It's really close to how we think.

Heh heh heh. It seems you understand the appeal of high-level languages then. High-level languages are used for all large-scale program development, essentially.

There are other advantages of high-level languages, as well. Let's look at those.

Programs written in high-level languages can be used on a variety of CPUs. In contrast, assembly language instructions (represented by mnemonics) that run on one CPU probably will not run on other CPUs. They are *CPU type dependent*. Mnemonics relate directly to the instructions offered by a specific CPU instruction set, and they can't be run on CPUs that don't support that set of instructions.

HIGH-LEVEL LANGUAGE PROGRAM
OK!
OK!
ONE CPU
A DIFFERENT TYPE OF CPU
ASSEMBLY LANGUAGE PROGRAM
MNEMONICS
OK!
HUH?
ONE CPU
A DIFFERENT TYPE OF CPU

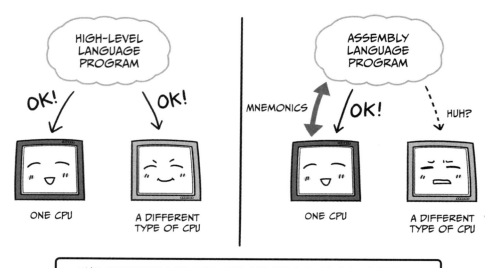

THE DIFFERENCE BETWEEN HIGH-LEVEL LANGUAGES AND ASSEMBLY LANGUAGES

Hmm. I see how high-level languages are super useful. . . . But what are the advantages of using the assembly languages you've been teaching me, then?

I mean, if high-level languages are this useful, why did you bother teaching me about the CPU structure and assembly in the first place? I kind of get the feeling that using high-level languages is the new way to do things and assembly languages were the old way. . . .

No, that's not true! Especially in scenarios where execution speed is paramount, assembly languages are very useful since they can push the CPU closer to its potential limit.

Assembly languages are essentially using mnemonics for a specific CPU instruction set, right? This means that assembly languages are easy to convert to machine language and don't waste much CPU time.

110101···
ASSEMBLY LANGUAGE PROGRAM
OKAY!

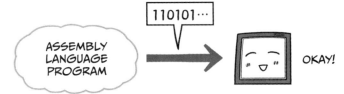

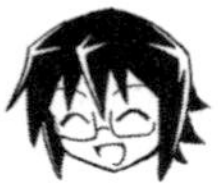

EASY TO CONVERT TO MACHINE LANGUAGE!

Some human-readable programming languages, like C, need to be *compiled* to convert them into machine language that the CPU can understand.

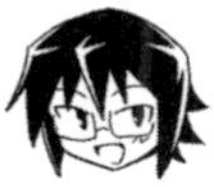

Even though the code might be easy for us to understand, it comes with a price. Because the code is being translated from a high-level language into a form the CPU can understand, it might end up executing slower* than if you had crafted it yourself in assembly code. The calculations will turn out correct, but the way that the translation system ends up performing the calculation might not be the most efficient. In the end, this means you might not be able to use all of the CPU's potential if you use a high-level language!

110101···
A BIT INEFFICIENT...
HIGH-LEVEL LANGUAGE PROGRAM
OH MY~

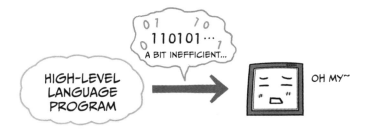

WHEN A HIGH-LEVEL LANGUAGE IS TRANSLATED INTO MACHINE LANGUAGE, UNNECESSARY PARTS OR INEFFICIENCY ARE INTRODUCED INTO THE PROGRAM.

Ohh, I see. Using assembly languages, you can write more efficient code that uses the CPU to its full potential! Assembly languages are so incredible, they are still in use today.

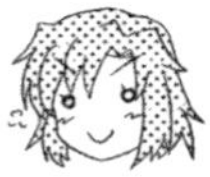

* But it's worth mentioning that modern CPUs are so fast that the delay doesn't really affect us much in most cases, even if some operations do take slightly longer.

LARGE-SCALE SOFTWARE DEVELOPMENT

The computer programs that we use every day include word processors, chat programs, and spreadsheets. We call these *application programs*, or just *applications*. Creating applications requires an incredible amount of work from many programmers over an extended amount of time. We call programs like this *large scale*, and the languages used to create them are generally high-level languages. Some examples include C, the slightly newer C++, and other languages such as Java and Python.

When developing with a high-level language, you don't have to be aware of the CPU's machine language instructions in the same way that you would if you were developing with an assembly language. You also don't have to pay attention to the different addressing modes we talked about before.

Program source code that's written in a high-level language has to be compiled so it can be converted into the machine language that the CPU can execute. Since this process is automatic and tries to optimize the use of addressing modes, among other things, the developer doesn't need to rack their brains paying attention to the CPU's instruction set or the different registers or even the addressing modes, themselves.

But when writing smaller-scale device software, it is still not uncommon to use *assembly languages*. In these situations, if you don't know everything there is to know about the CPU's peculiarities, its addressing modes, and more, writing correct software will be more or less impossible.

The mnemonics you use when writing assembly code in a particular CPU's instruction set are automatically converted into binary opcodes through a process called *assembly*. In effect, you are assembling the assembly language source code into a CPU's machine language.

Today, even basic software like your operating system (Windows, for example) is mostly developed using high-level languages like C. But parts that are critical for performance may still be developed using assembly languages. This is also true for software such as simulation applications, where assembly code might be used to optimize certain parts of the program that need to be blazing fast.

THE DIFFERENCE BETWEEN PROGRAMS AND SOURCE CODE

Let's see. We talked a bit about programs and source code before. The two words might seem to mean the same thing, but they are different, strictly speaking.

Hmm, it might be cool to know the difference. I'm all ears!

Sure. A *program* usually refers to the chain of instructions fed to a computer to make it do something. A program combined with all the other resources it needs to perform its task is referred to as *object code*, while the word *source code* is usually reserved for the code (machine or high-level) used to create the program.

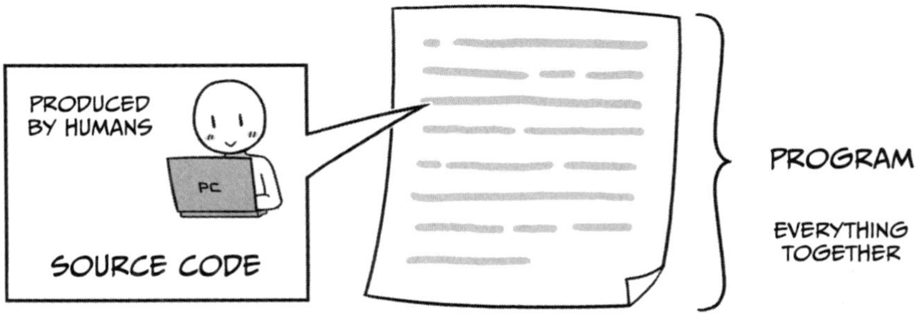
PRODUCED BY HUMANS
PC
SOURCE CODE
PROGRAM
EVERYTHING TOGETHER

Source code includes all of the instructions and text produced by humans, while the object code is the machine code that is produced when the source code is compiled, which is then executed by the CPU. Some recent AI (artificial intelligence) can even automatically produce source code.

Huh. I think I get it. Programs are the work instructions and their resources. Source code, on the other hand, is the instructions and text produced by humans to generate the work instructions.

You might also run into the term *source program*, but for simplicity's sake, you can just think of this as being the same thing as source code.

Program Basics

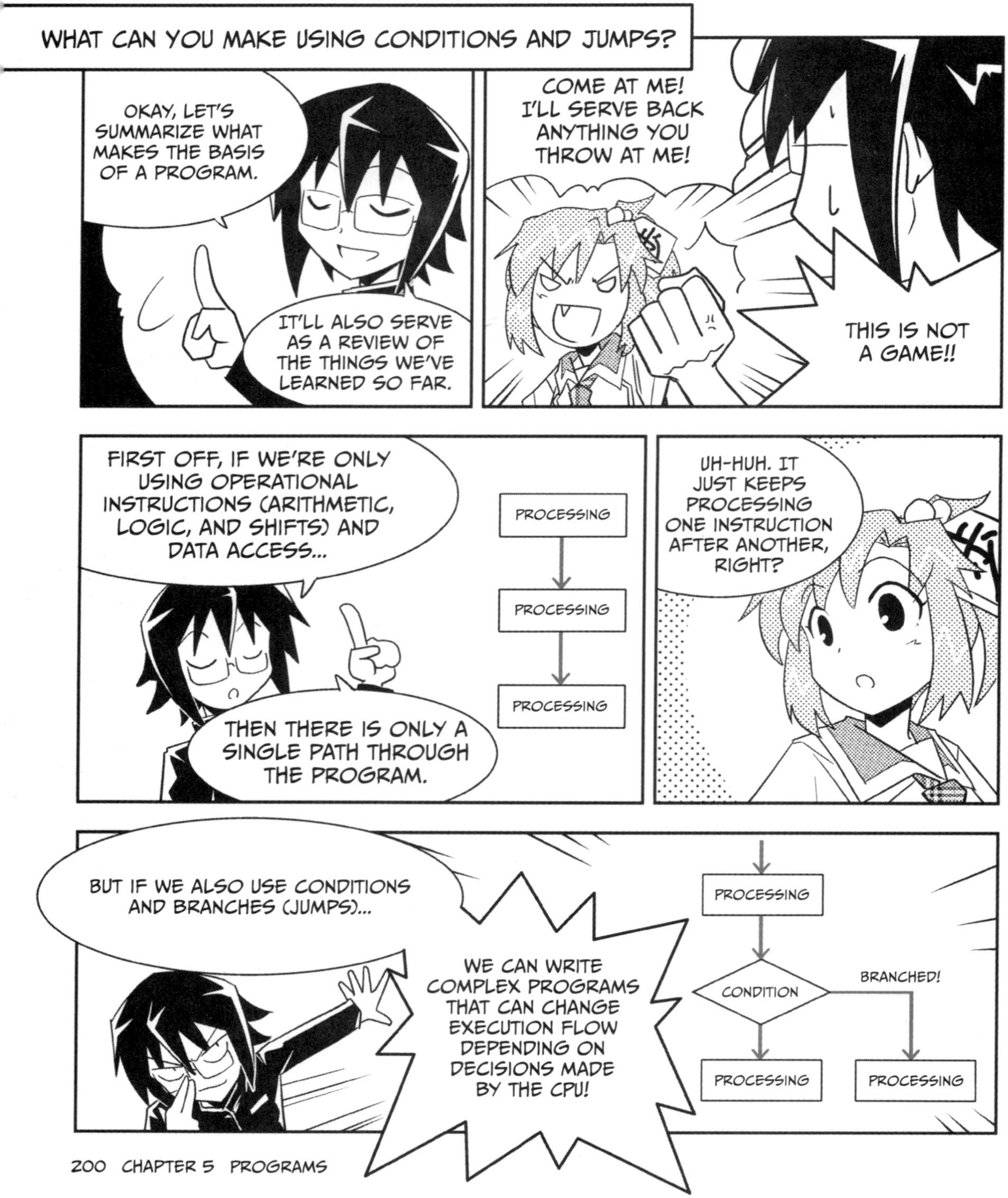
WHAT CAN YOU MAKE USING CONDITIONS AND JUMPS?
OKAY, LET'S SUMMARIZE WHAT MAKES THE BASIS OF A PROGRAM.
IT'LL ALSO SERVE AS A REVIEW OF THE THINGS WE'VE LEARNED SO FAR.
COME AT ME! I'LL SERVE BACK ANYTHING YOU THROW AT ME!
THIS IS NOT A GAME!!
FIRST OFF, IF WE'RE ONLY USING OPERATIONAL INSTRUCTIONS (ARITHMETIC, LOGIC, AND SHIFTS) AND DATA ACCESS...
PROCESSING
PROCESSING
PROCESSING
THEN THERE IS ONLY A SINGLE PATH THROUGH THE PROGRAM.
UH-HUH. IT JUST KEEPS PROCESSING ONE INSTRUCTION AFTER ANOTHER, RIGHT?
BUT IF WE ALSO USE CONDITIONS AND BRANCHES (JUMPS)...
WE CAN WRITE COMPLEX PROGRAMS THAT CAN CHANGE EXECUTION FLOW DEPENDING ON DECISIONS MADE BY THE CPU!
PROCESSING
CONDITION
BRANCHED!
PROCESSING
PROCESSING

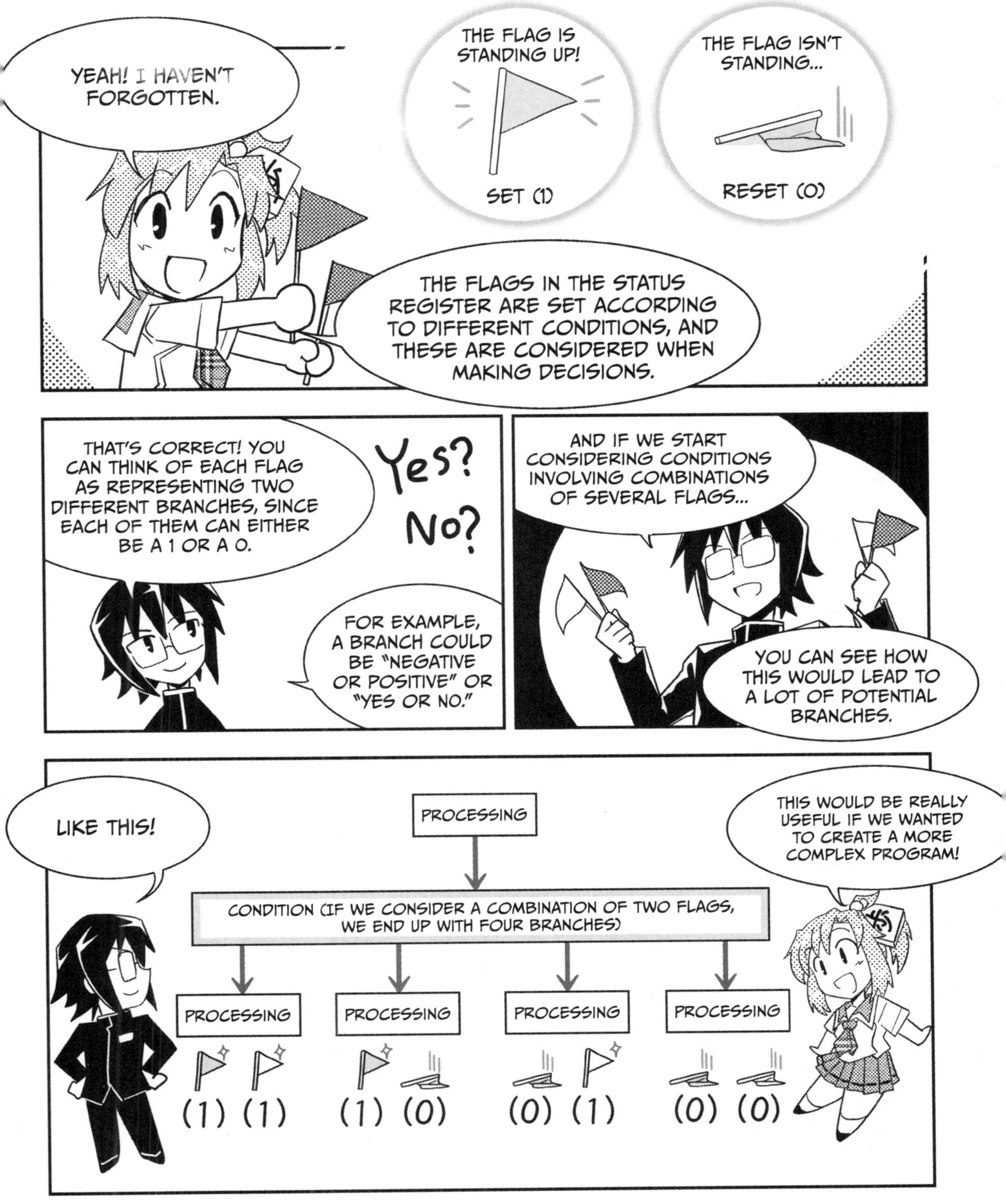
YEAH! I HAVEN'T FORGOTTEN.
THE FLAG IS STANDING UP!
SET (1)
THE FLAG ISN'T STANDING...
RESET (0)
THE FLAGS IN THE STATUS REGISTER ARE SET ACCORDING TO DIFFERENT CONDITIONS, AND THESE ARE CONSIDERED WHEN MAKING DECISIONS.
THAT'S CORRECT! YOU CAN THINK OF EACH FLAG AS REPRESENTING TWO DIFFERENT BRANCHES, SINCE EACH OF THEM CAN EITHER BE A 1 OR A 0.
Yes? No?
FOR EXAMPLE, A BRANCH COULD BE "NEGATIVE OR POSITIVE" OR "YES OR NO."
AND IF WE START CONSIDERING CONDITIONS INVOLVING COMBINATIONS OF SEVERAL FLAGS...
YOU CAN SEE HOW THIS WOULD LEAD TO A LOT OF POTENTIAL BRANCHES.
LIKE THIS!
PROCESSING
CONDITION (IF WE CONSIDER A COMBINATION OF TWO FLAGS, WE END UP WITH FOUR BRANCHES)
PROCESSING
(1) (1)
PROCESSING
(1) (0)
PROCESSING
(0) (1)
PROCESSING
(0) (0)
THIS WOULD BE REALLY USEFUL IF WE WANTED TO CREATE A MORE COMPLEX PROGRAM!

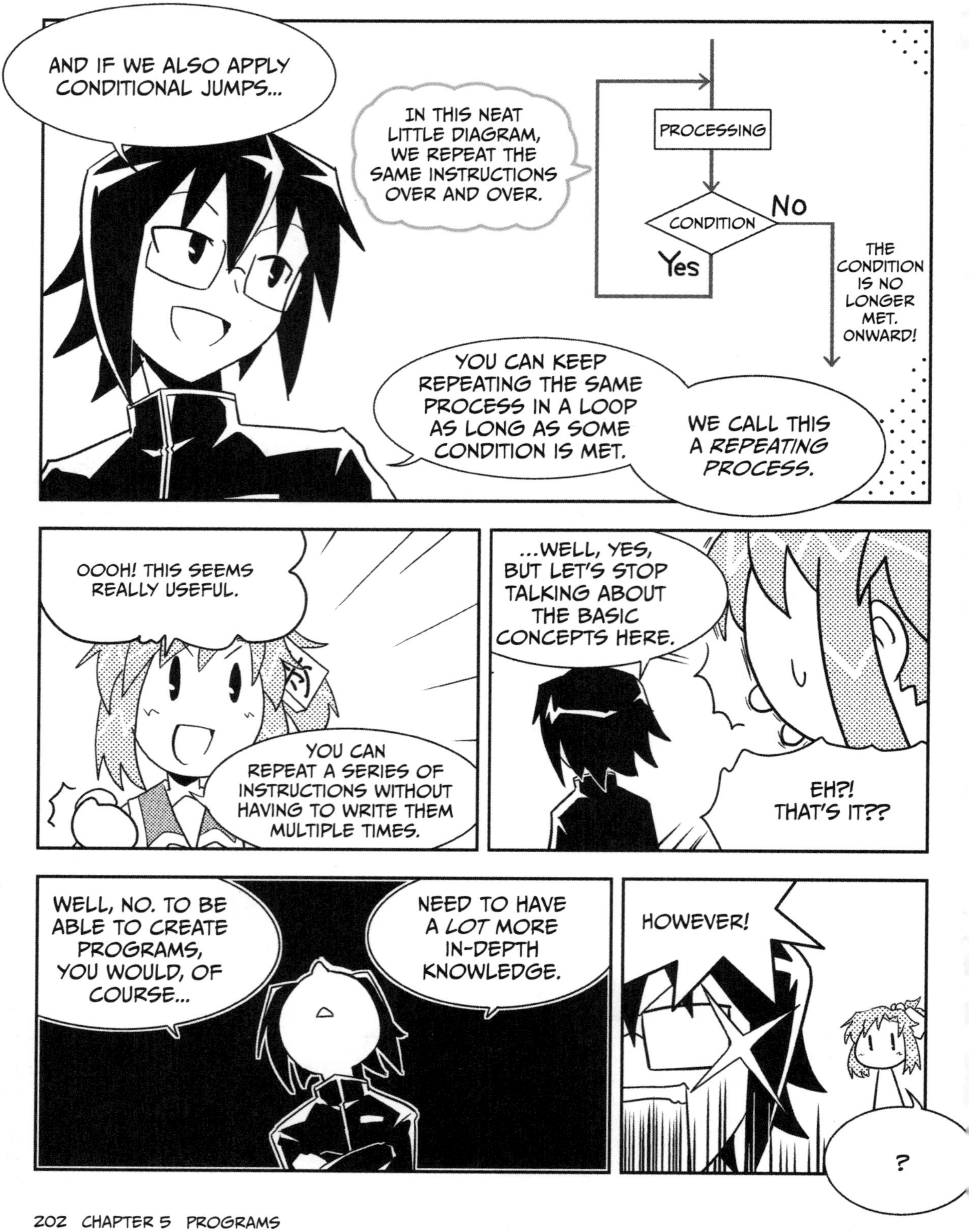
AND IF WE ALSO APPLY CONDITIONAL JUMPS...
IN THIS NEAT LITTLE DIAGRAM, WE REPEAT THE SAME INSTRUCTIONS OVER AND OVER.
PROCESSING
CONDITION
No
Yes
THE CONDITION IS NO LONGER MET. ONWARD!
YOU CAN KEEP REPEATING THE SAME PROCESS IN A LOOP AS LONG AS SOME CONDITION IS MET.
WE CALL THIS A *REPEATING PROCESS*.
OOOH! THIS SEEMS REALLY USEFUL.
YOU CAN REPEAT A SERIES OF INSTRUCTIONS WITHOUT HAVING TO WRITE THEM MULTIPLE TIMES.
...WELL, YES, BUT LET'S STOP TALKING ABOUT THE BASIC CONCEPTS HERE.
EH?! THAT'S IT??
WELL, NO. TO BE ABLE TO CREATE PROGRAMS, YOU WOULD, OF COURSE...
NEED TO HAVE A *LOT* MORE IN-DEPTH KNOWLEDGE.
HOWEVER!
?

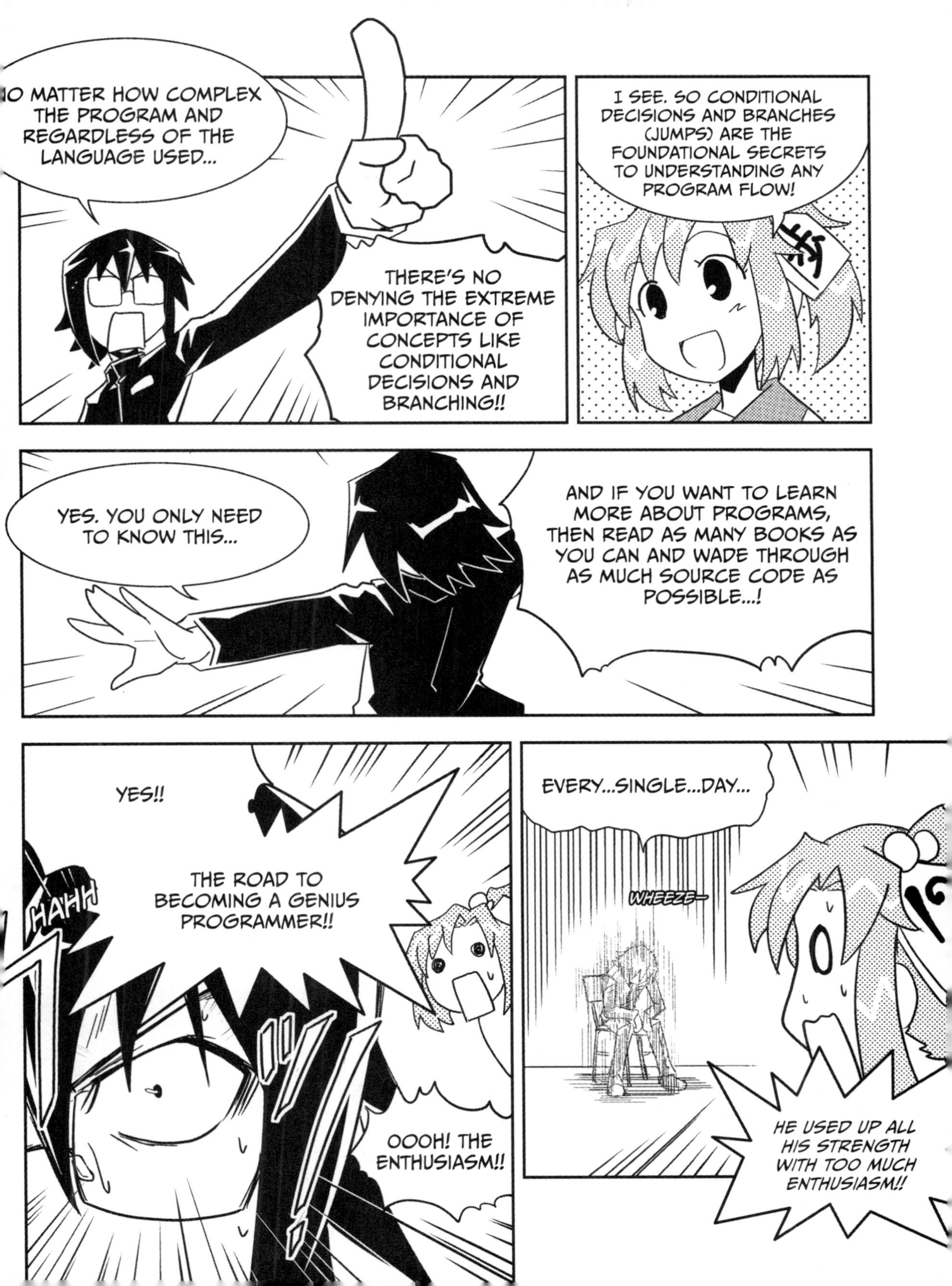
NO MATTER HOW COMPLEX THE PROGRAM AND REGARDLESS OF THE LANGUAGE USED...
THERE'S NO DENYING THE EXTREME IMPORTANCE OF CONCEPTS LIKE CONDITIONAL DECISIONS AND BRANCHING!!
I SEE. SO CONDITIONAL DECISIONS AND BRANCHES (JUMPS) ARE THE FOUNDATIONAL SECRETS TO UNDERSTANDING ANY PROGRAM FLOW!
YES. YOU ONLY NEED TO KNOW THIS...
AND IF YOU WANT TO LEARN MORE ABOUT PROGRAMS, THEN READ AS MANY BOOKS AS YOU CAN AND WADE THROUGH AS MUCH SOURCE CODE AS POSSIBLE...!
YES!!
HAHH
THE ROAD TO BECOMING A GENIUS PROGRAMMER!!
OOOH! THE ENTHUSIASM!!
EVERY...SINGLE...DAY...
WHEEZE—
HE USED UP ALL HIS STRENGTH WITH TOO MUCH ENTHUSIASM!!

WHAT SHOULD WE MAKE THE COMPUTER DO?

By the way, we've been learning about programs today, but try to remember when we talked about digitization of information. In modern society, by digitizing things like music, images, video, and any other type of information, it becomes a lot easier to process information using a computer.

Ah, I remember us talking about something like that. Now that I think about it, it's actually kind of amazing!

I mean, if computers can handle any type of information, then you could do all kinds of things if you just created an amazing enough program!

Yeah. It's just as you say. Things that weren't even conceivable in the past are gradually becoming reality today.

One good example is the facial-recognition software used in some modern security applications. These programs convert human facial features (such as the distance between the eyes, the position and size of the mouth and nose, and so on) into numerical values and use them for calculations. Some programs can then differentiate among human faces by using this information.

I see. It feels a bit like science fiction that computers are actually able to tell people's faces apart. It might even be a bit scary. But on the other hand, it could be used for fighting crime.

It seems like it might be a lot of fun to create a really cool program. I wonder what I would have it do. Maybe stock market or horse race predictions . . . ? Some program that would automatically make me a lot of money. . . .

Ah! Let's put your personal desires aside for now. But thinking about what you want to make your computer do and what people would find useful are two very important aspects of creating a program.

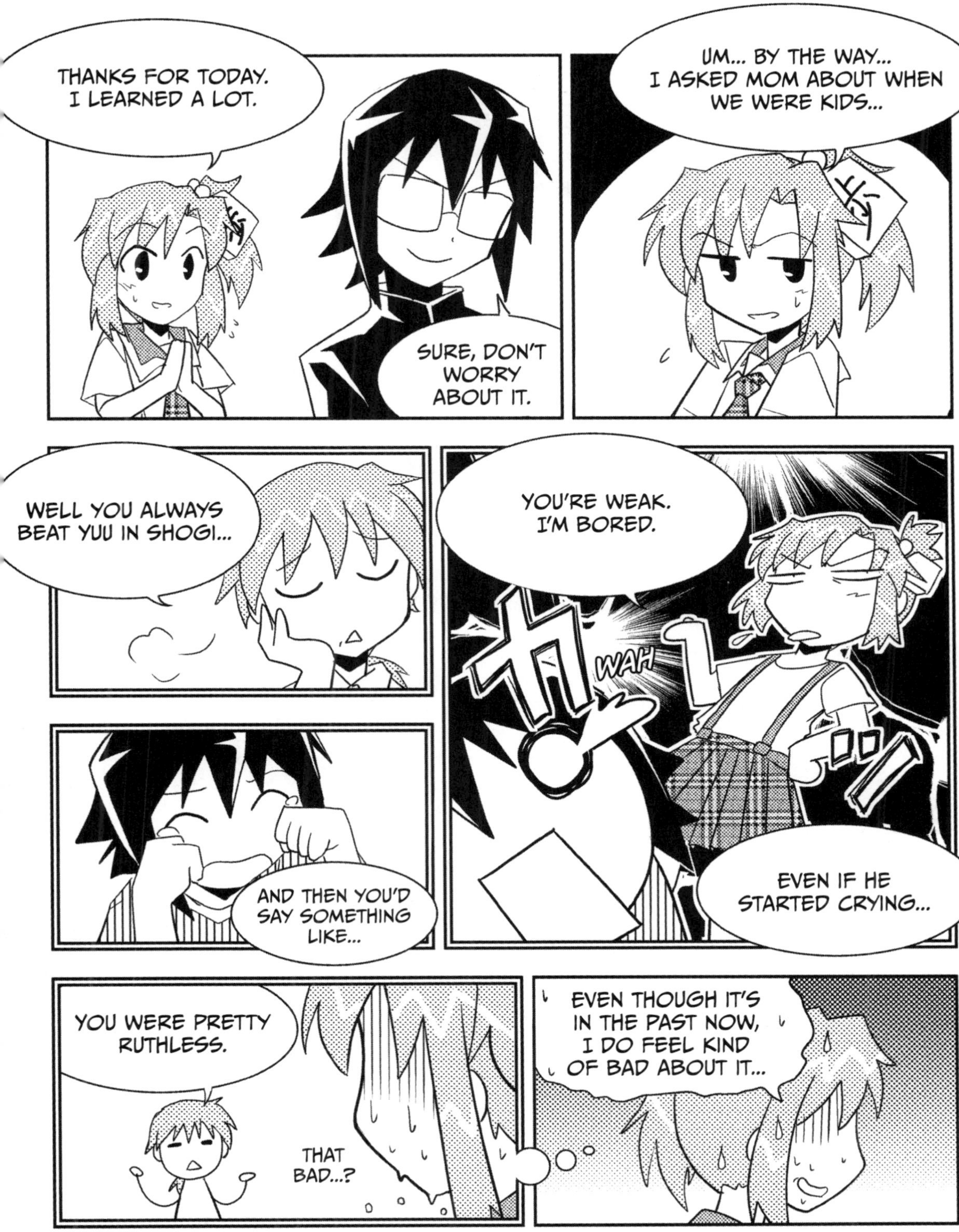
THANKS FOR TODAY. I LEARNED A LOT.
SURE, DON'T WORRY ABOUT IT.
UM... BY THE WAY... I ASKED MOM ABOUT WHEN WE WERE KIDS...
WELL YOU ALWAYS BEAT YUU IN SHOGI...
AND THEN YOU'D SAY SOMETHING LIKE...
YOU'RE WEAK. I'M BORED.
WAH
EVEN IF HE STARTED CRYING...
YOU WERE PRETTY RUTHLESS.
THAT BAD...?
EVEN THOUGH IT'S IN THE PAST NOW, I DO FEEL KIND OF BAD ABOUT IT...

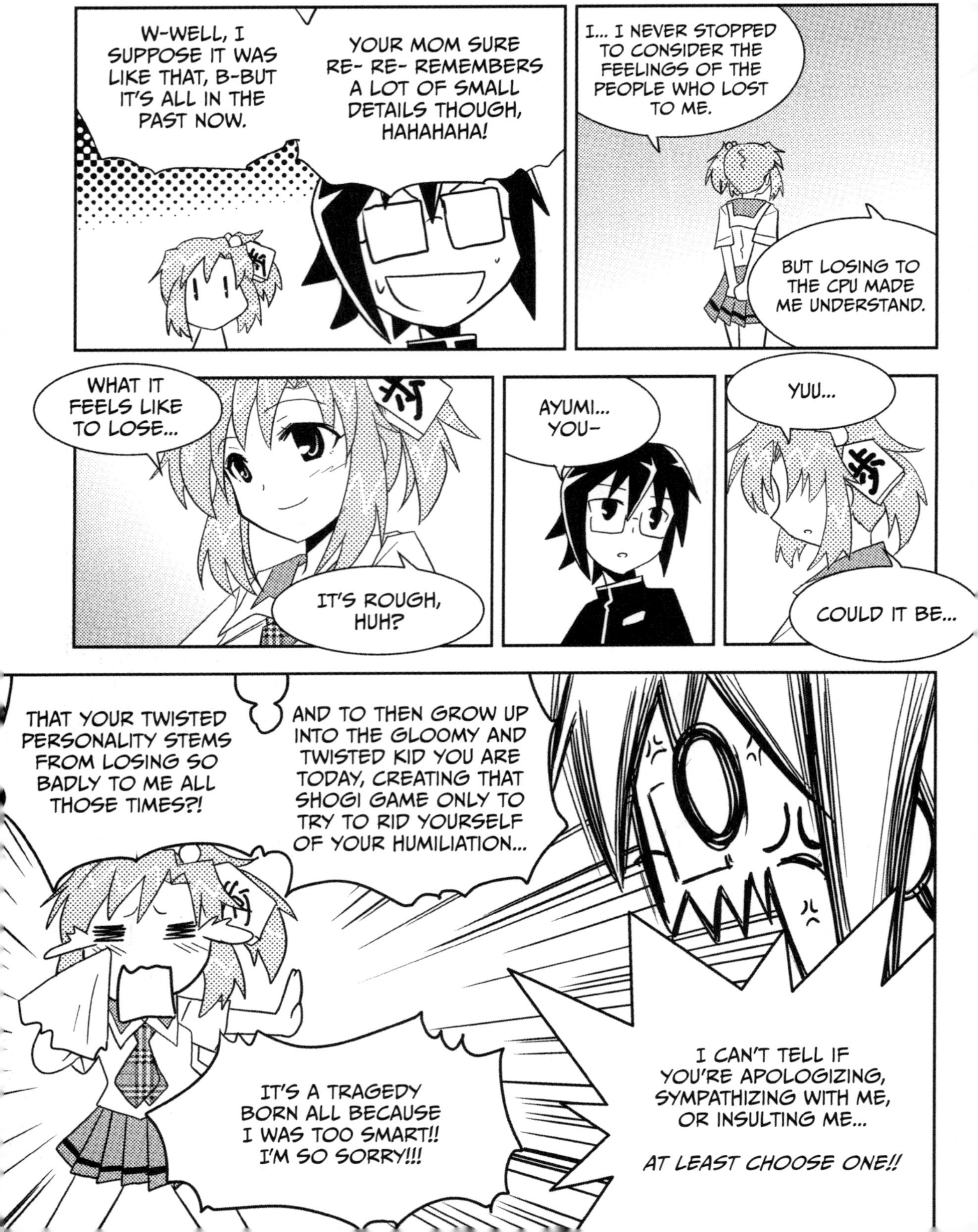
W-WELL, I SUPPOSE IT WAS LIKE THAT, B-BUT IT'S ALL IN THE PAST NOW.
YOUR MOM SURE RE- RE- REMEMBERS A LOT OF SMALL DETAILS THOUGH, HAHAHAHA!
I... I NEVER STOPPED TO CONSIDER THE FEELINGS OF THE PEOPLE WHO LOST TO ME.
BUT LOSING TO THE CPU MADE ME UNDERSTAND.
WHAT IT FEELS LIKE TO LOSE...
IT'S ROUGH, HUH?
AYUMI... YOU-
YUU...
COULD IT BE...
THAT YOUR TWISTED PERSONALITY STEMS FROM LOSING SO BADLY TO ME ALL THOSE TIMES?!
AND TO THEN GROW UP INTO THE GLOOMY AND TWISTED KID YOU ARE TODAY, CREATING THAT SHOGI GAME ONLY TO TRY TO RID YOURSELF OF YOUR HUMILIATION...
IT'S A TRAGEDY BORN ALL BECAUSE I WAS TOO SMART!! I'M SO SORRY!!!
I CAN'T TELL IF YOU'RE APOLOGIZING, SYMPATHIZING WITH ME, OR INSULTING ME...
AT LEAST CHOOSE ONE!!

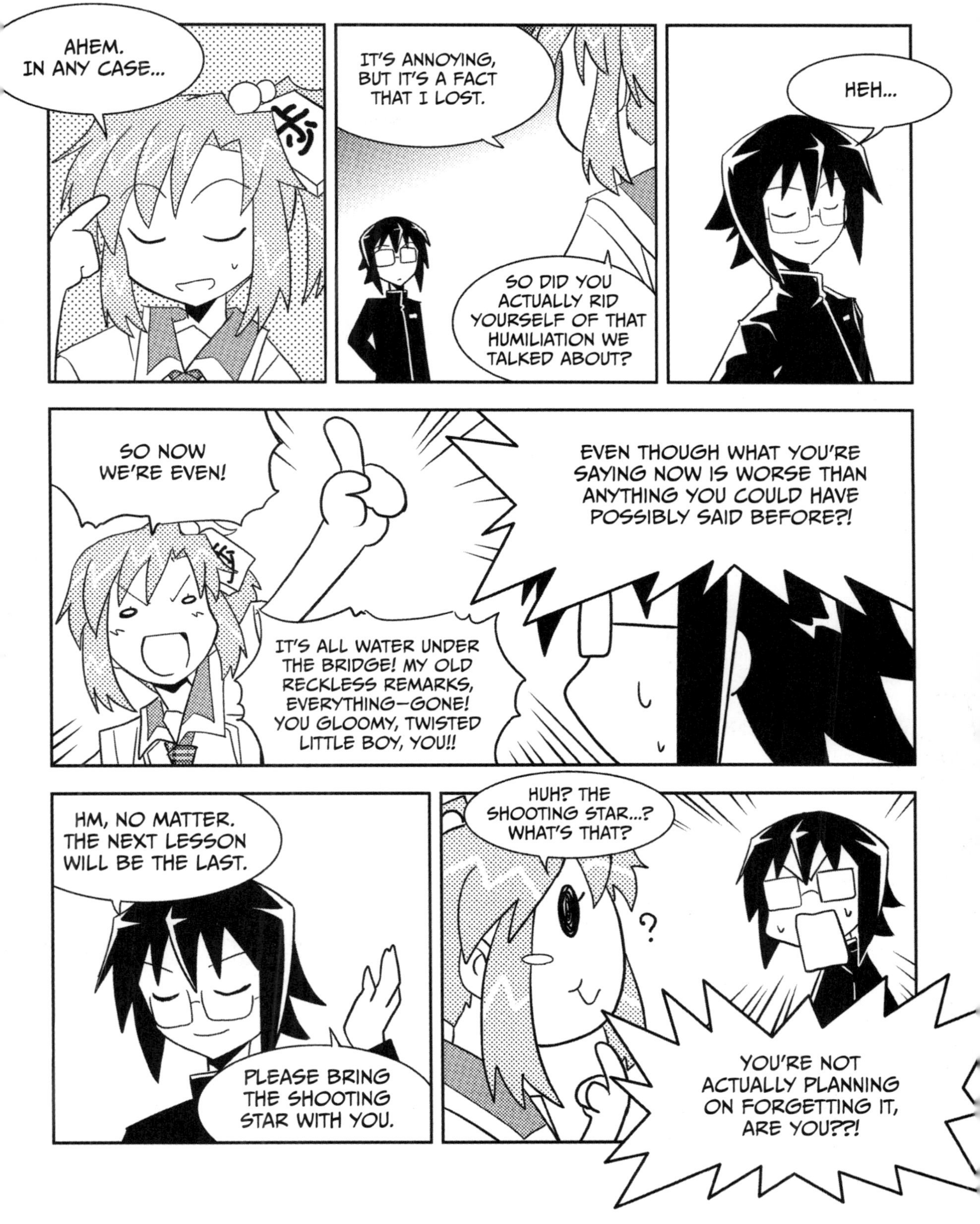
AHEM. IN ANY CASE...
IT'S ANNOYING, BUT IT'S A FACT THAT I LOST.
SO DID YOU ACTUALLY RID YOURSELF OF THAT HUMILIATION WE TALKED ABOUT?
HEH...
SO NOW WE'RE EVEN!
IT'S ALL WATER UNDER THE BRIDGE! MY OLD RECKLESS REMARKS, EVERYTHING—GONE! YOU GLOOMY, TWISTED LITTLE BOY, YOU!!
EVEN THOUGH WHAT YOU'RE SAYING NOW IS WORSE THAN ANYTHING YOU COULD HAVE POSSIBLY SAID BEFORE?!
HM, NO MATTER. THE NEXT LESSON WILL BE THE LAST.
PLEASE BRING THE SHOOTING STAR WITH YOU.
HUH? THE SHOOTING STAR...? WHAT'S THAT?
?
YOU'RE NOT ACTUALLY PLANNING ON FORGETTING IT, ARE YOU??!

WHERE ARE PROGRAMS STORED?

Programs for small devices that use microcomputers are usually stored in ROM. In personal computers, only the BIOS (the Basic Input/Output System) is stored in ROM, which in turn is used to load the operating system (OS) from an external device (such as a hard drive) into RAM. Programs are also loaded into RAM before execution.

At the dawn of the CPU era some decades ago, miniature OS-like systems called machine code monitors were used when developing assembly code line by line.

Nowadays, even assembly programming is done on personal computers. Each CPU maker provides development tools to allow programmers to more easily develop assembly language programs for their CPUs. You can create your program using these tools on your computer, attach a ROM writer to the system to embed your program into ROM, and finally integrate the ROM into your target system.

A more recently developed method allows programmers to transfer the program from a computer to the device's non-volatile memory. This saves a lot of time because you can check how the device performs without having to rewrite the ROM every time.

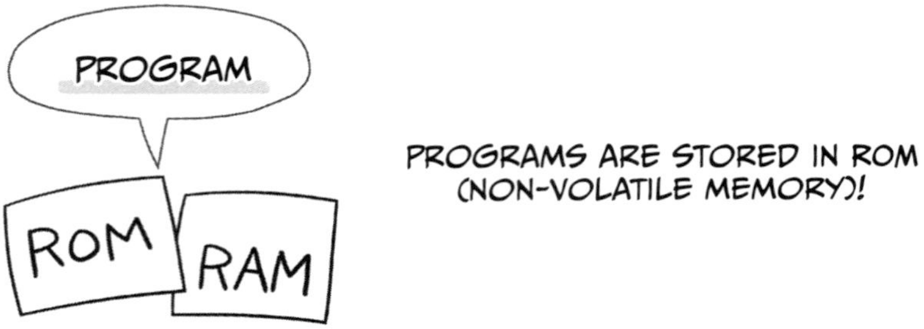
PROGRAM
ROM
RAM
PROGRAMS ARE STORED IN ROM (NON-VOLATILE MEMORY)!

It's also worth mentioning that the method of rewriting a program on CPU ROM without detaching it from the system is called *on-board programming*.

WHAT HAPPENS BEFORE A PROGRAM IS EXECUTED?

Let's talk a bit about what happens when you load a program you've written into ROM. What does the CPU do as soon as you turn on the power?

Simply turning on the power doesn't actually do anything, as there is a significant risk that the system will not perform as expected before the voltage has climbed to a certain level. To ensure that the CPU will operate properly, the circuitry on the CPU board must keep the reset pin low until the power supply voltage stabilizes and the CPU's clock generator starts functioning normally.

The clock generator normally starts operating before the power supply voltage stabilizes, so when the power supply voltage reaches the correct level, the CPU board's reset circuit sets the reset pin to high, and the CPU can begin executing instructions. The voltage needed for this is generally specified in the CPU's documentation.

At this point, all the preparations are done for loading the first line of the program. After releasing the reset state, the first thing the CPU does is load a *reset vector*.

The reset vector is usually written to the first or last part of the memory the CPU manages, and it tells the CPU where to find the first instruction of the program to run after a reset. For a PC, this would be the BIOS.

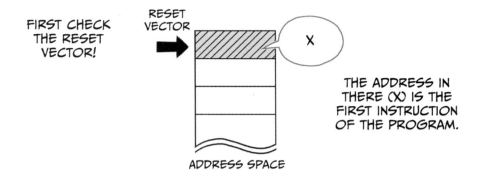

FIRST CHECK
THE RESET
VECTOR!

RESET
VECTOR

X

THE ADDRESS IN
THERE (X) IS THE
FIRST INSTRUCTION
OF THE PROGRAM.

ADDRESS SPACE

The CPU will then run the instruction at the address specified by the reset vector and proceed normally from that point. It would execute the program the instruction belongs to, perform calculations, and process data in accordance with the program flow. If the reset pin were to become active for any reason, the CPU would instantly cease all activity, no matter what it was currently working on, and return to its initial state.

A reset is actually a type of interrupt, like the ones we learned about in earlier chapters. Although we learned previously that interrupts can stop a CPU from running its current set of instructions and make it run instructions at another address, we haven't learned how the CPU knows which address to jump to. Each type of interrupt has an address associated with it, and the data structure that stores the addresses to execute depending on which type of interrupt occurs is called the *interrupt vector table (IVT)*. The reset vector is at a set location in memory, and it is the first value in the interrupt vector table. That's how it works at a very high level, but IVTs vary from CPU to CPU, so the location of the reset vector will depend on the CPU's specifications.

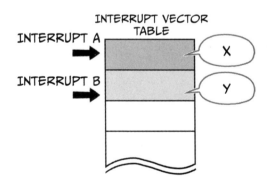

IF WE TAKE A LOOK AT
THE INTERRUPT VECTOR
TABLE, WE CAN SEE
THAT WE SHOULD...

EXECUTE X IF WE GET
AN A INTERRUPT!

EXECUTE Y IF WE GET
A B INTERRUPT!

INTERRUPT VECTOR
TABLE

INTERRUPT A

INTERRUPT B

X

Y

6

MICROCONTROLLERS

What Are Microcontrollers?

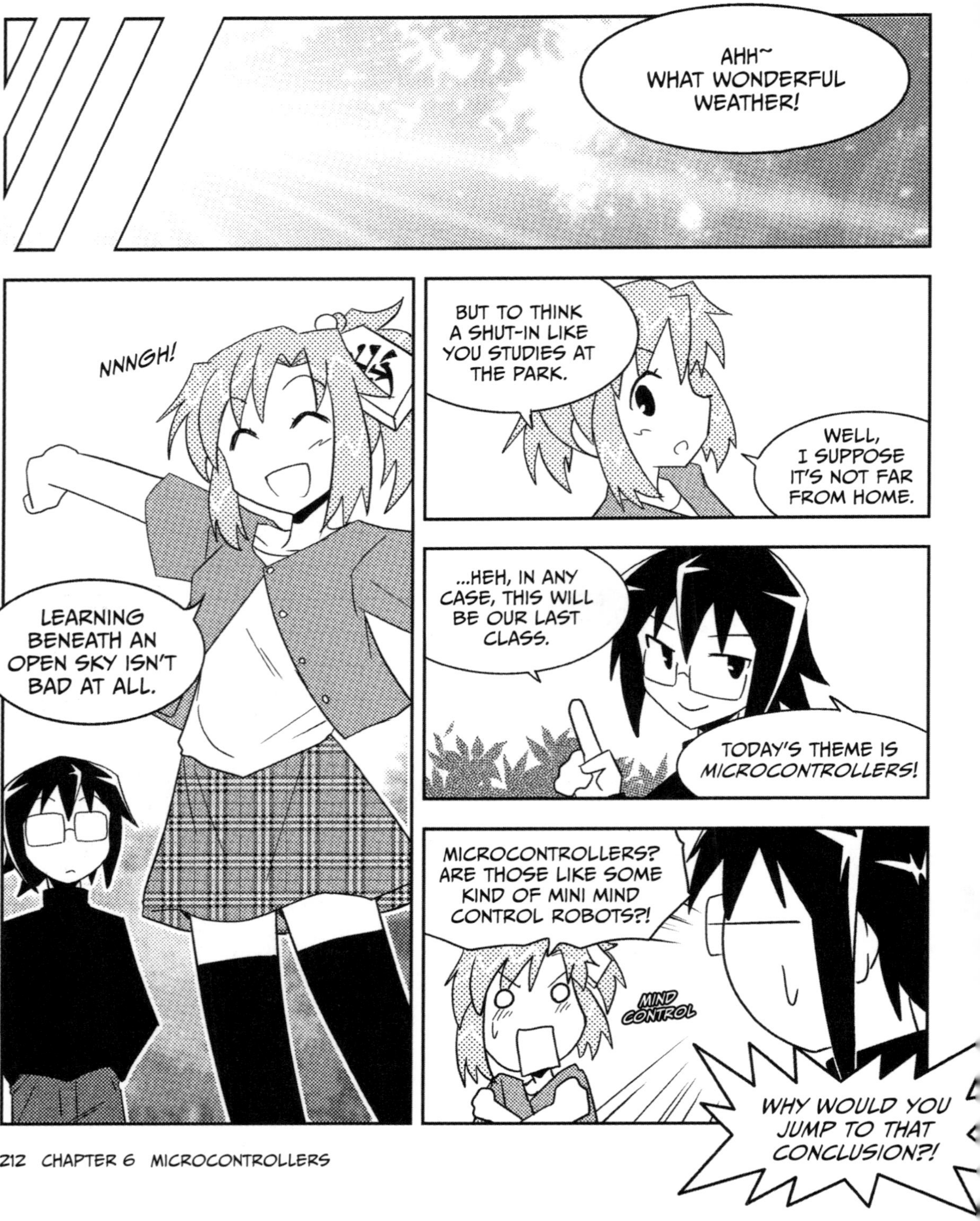
AHH~ WHAT WONDERFUL WEATHER!
NNNGH!
LEARNING BENEATH AN OPEN SKY ISN'T BAD AT ALL.
BUT TO THINK A SHUT-IN LIKE YOU STUDIES AT THE PARK.
WELL, I SUPPOSE IT'S NOT FAR FROM HOME.
...HEH, IN ANY CASE, THIS WILL BE OUR LAST CLASS.
TODAY'S THEME IS *MICROCONTROLLERS*!
MICROCONTROLLERS? ARE THOSE LIKE SOME KIND OF MINI MIND CONTROL ROBOTS?!
MIND CONTROL
WHY WOULD YOU JUMP TO THAT CONCLUSION?!

MICROCONTROLLERS ARE IN ALL KINDS OF PRODUCTS

AHEM.

"MICRO"
+
"CONTROLLER"

(THERE ARE ALSO MICROCOMPUTERS!)

AS THEIR NAME SUGGESTS, MICROCONTROLLERS ARE SMALL CONTROLLER CHIPS.

I'M NOT SURE I UNDERSTAND FROM JUST THE NAME.

WHAT DO THEY CONTROL EXACTLY?

ARE THEY DIFFERENT FROM THE CPUs IN COMPUTERS?

?

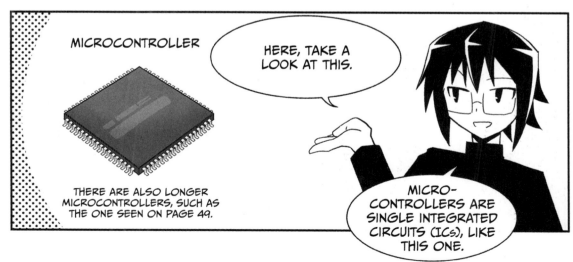

MICROCONTROLLER

HERE, TAKE A LOOK AT THIS.

THERE ARE ALSO LONGER MICROCONTROLLERS, SUCH AS THE ONE SEEN ON PAGE 49.

MICRO-CONTROLLERS ARE SINGLE INTEGRATED CIRCUITS (ICs), LIKE THIS ONE.

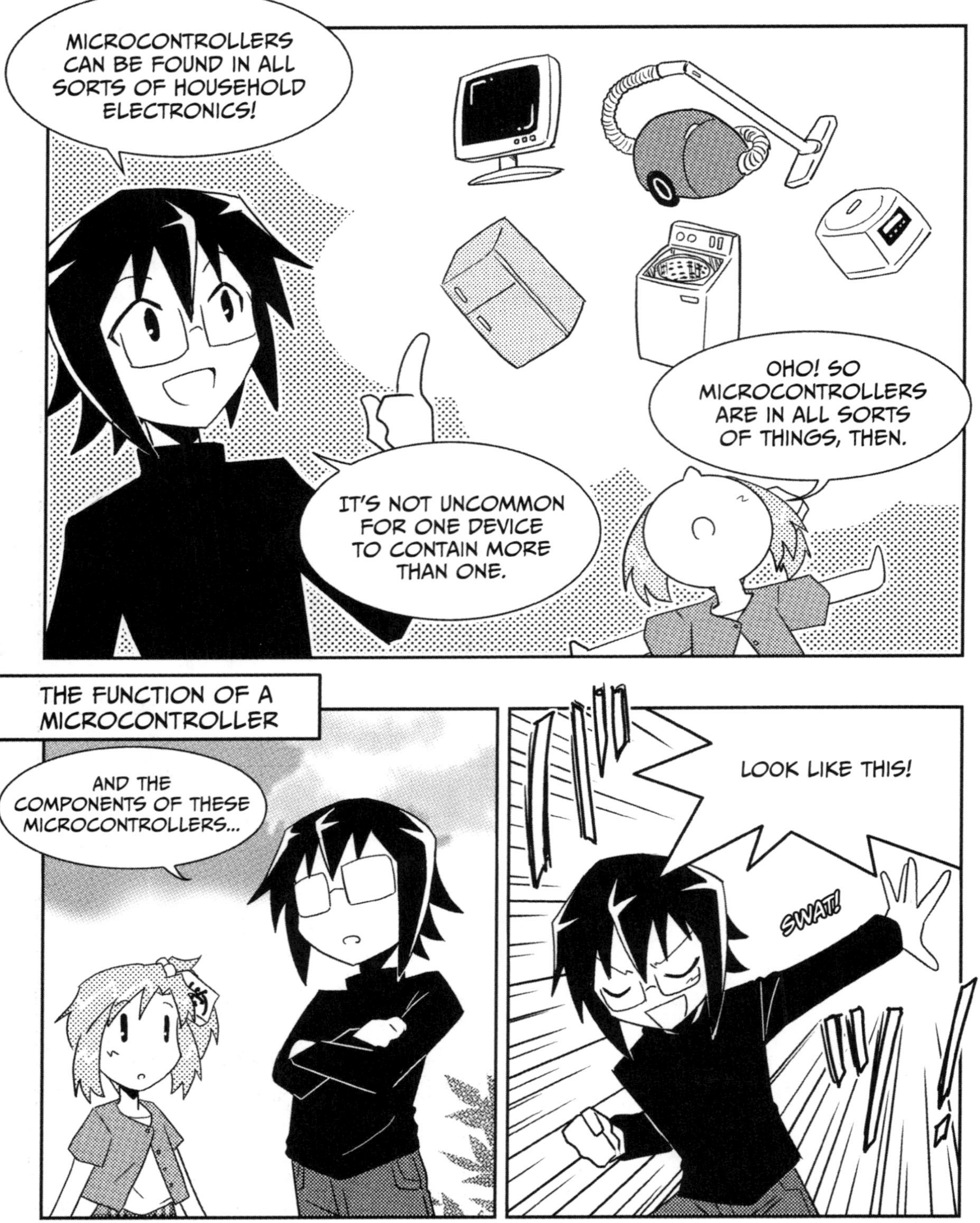
MICROCONTROLLERS CAN BE FOUND IN ALL SORTS OF HOUSEHOLD ELECTRONICS!
OHO! SO MICROCONTROLLERS ARE IN ALL SORTS OF THINGS, THEN.
IT'S NOT UNCOMMON FOR ONE DEVICE TO CONTAIN MORE THAN ONE.
THE FUNCTION OF A MICROCONTROLLER
AND THE COMPONENTS OF THESE MICROCONTROLLERS...
LOOK LIKE THIS!
SWAT!

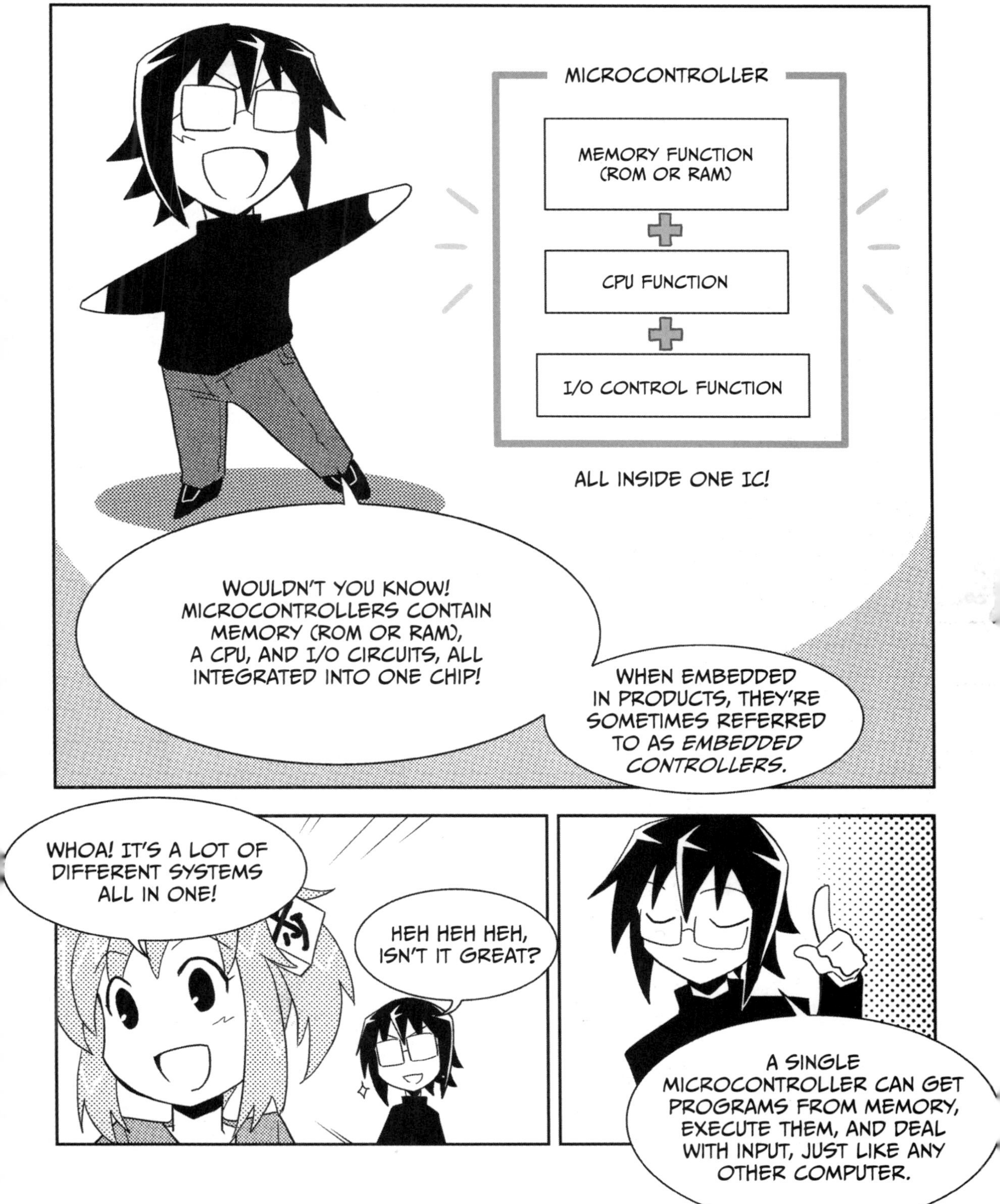
MICROCONTROLLER
MEMORY FUNCTION (ROM OR RAM)
CPU FUNCTION
I/O CONTROL FUNCTION
ALL INSIDE ONE IC!
WOULDN'T YOU KNOW! MICROCONTROLLERS CONTAIN MEMORY (ROM OR RAM), A CPU, AND I/O CIRCUITS, ALL INTEGRATED INTO ONE CHIP!
WHEN EMBEDDED IN PRODUCTS, THEY'RE SOMETIMES REFERRED TO AS *EMBEDDED CONTROLLERS*.
WHOA! IT'S A LOT OF DIFFERENT SYSTEMS ALL IN ONE!
HEH HEH HEH, ISN'T IT GREAT?
A SINGLE MICROCONTROLLER CAN GET PROGRAMS FROM MEMORY, EXECUTE THEM, AND DEAL WITH INPUT, JUST LIKE ANY OTHER COMPUTER.

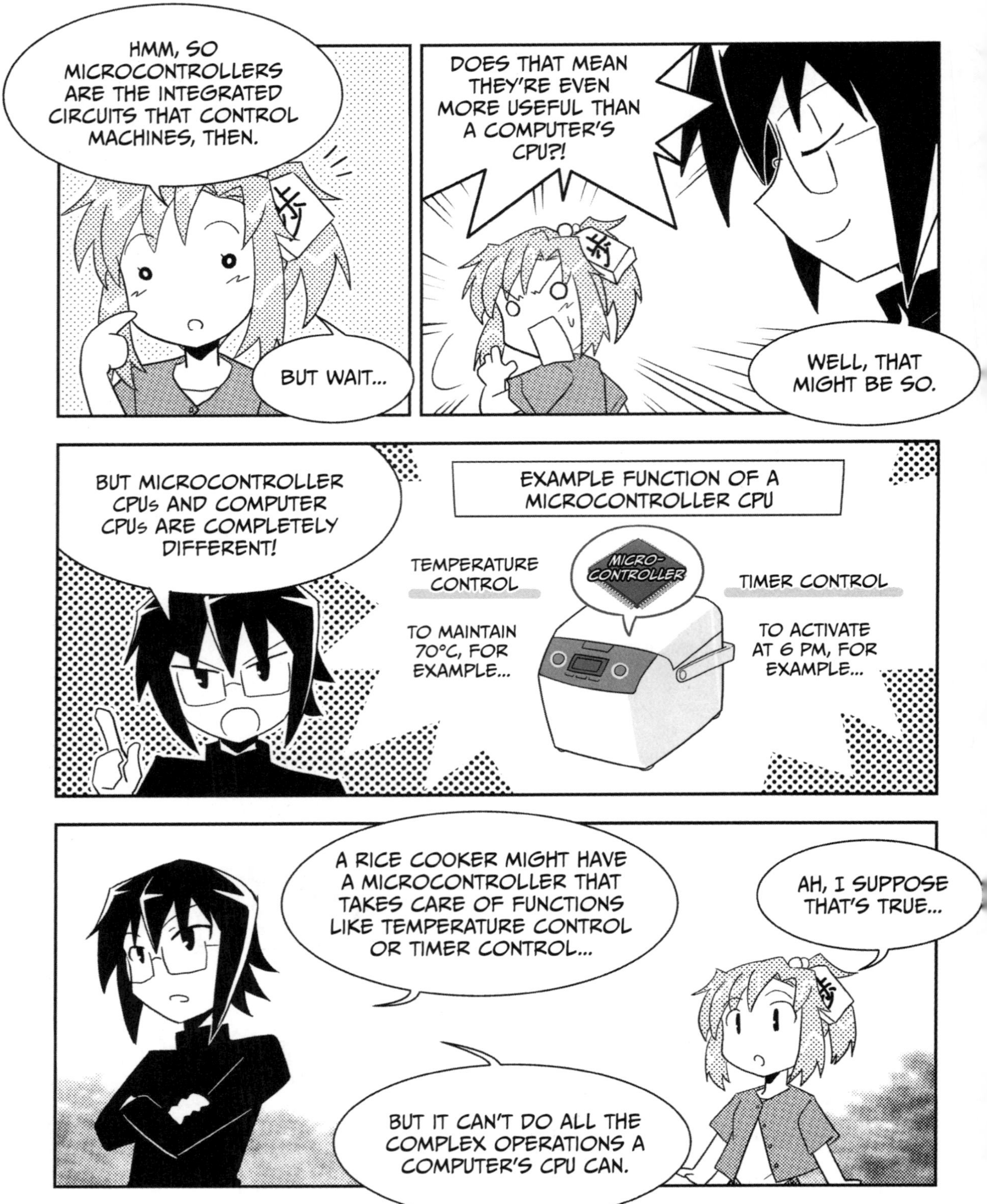
HMM, SO MICROCONTROLLERS ARE THE INTEGRATED CIRCUITS THAT CONTROL MACHINES, THEN.
BUT WAIT...
DOES THAT MEAN THEY'RE EVEN MORE USEFUL THAN A COMPUTER'S CPU?!
WELL, THAT MIGHT BE SO.
BUT MICROCONTROLLER CPUs AND COMPUTER CPUs ARE COMPLETELY DIFFERENT!
EXAMPLE FUNCTION OF A MICROCONTROLLER CPU
TEMPERATURE CONTROL
TO MAINTAIN 70°C, FOR EXAMPLE...
MICRO-CONTROLLER
TIMER CONTROL
TO ACTIVATE AT 6 PM, FOR EXAMPLE...
A RICE COOKER MIGHT HAVE A MICROCONTROLLER THAT TAKES CARE OF FUNCTIONS LIKE TEMPERATURE CONTROL OR TIMER CONTROL...
BUT IT CAN'T DO ALL THE COMPLEX OPERATIONS A COMPUTER'S CPU CAN.
AH, I SUPPOSE THAT'S TRUE...

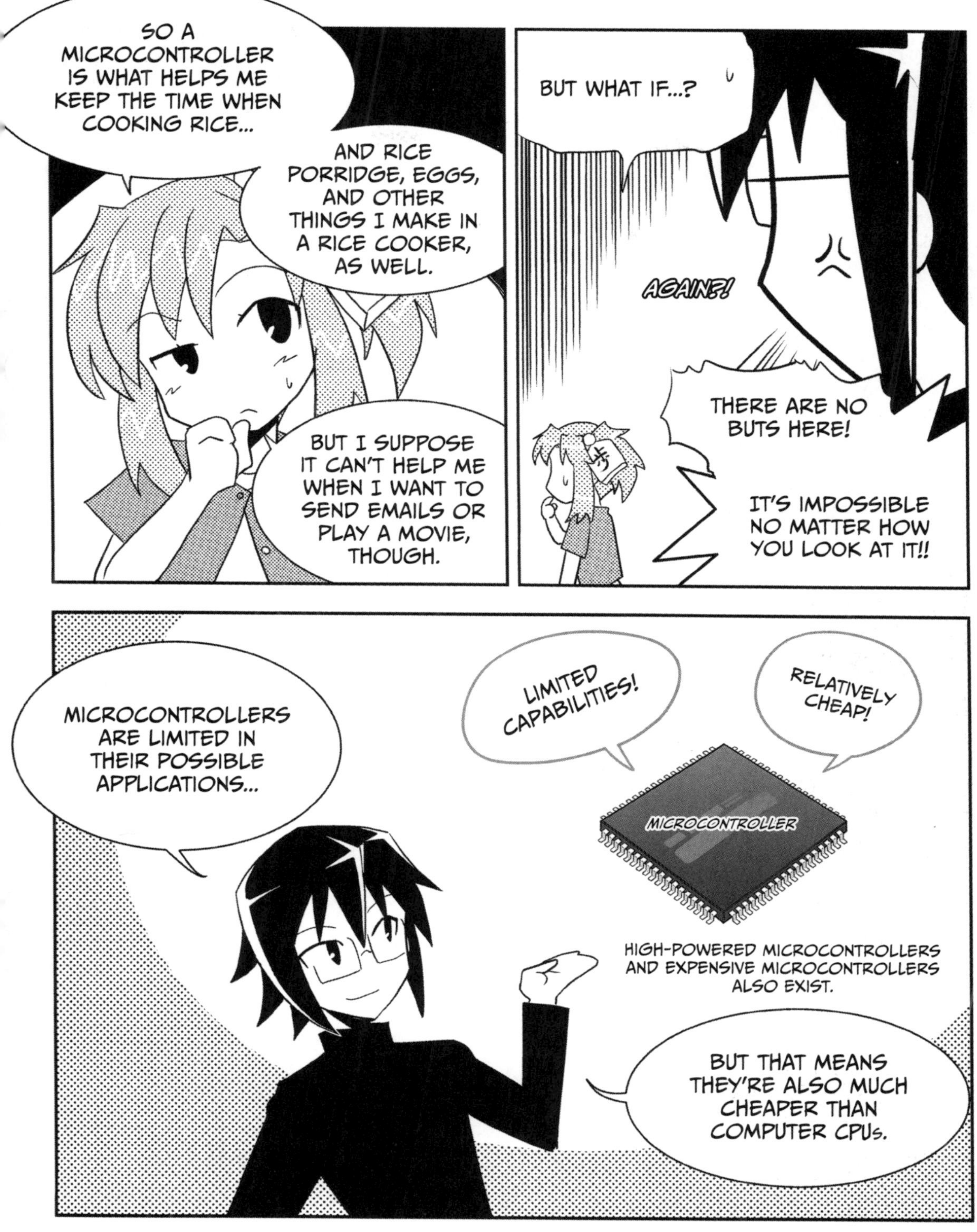
SO A MICROCONTROLLER IS WHAT HELPS ME KEEP THE TIME WHEN COOKING RICE...
AND RICE PORRIDGE, EGGS, AND OTHER THINGS I MAKE IN A RICE COOKER, AS WELL.
BUT I SUPPOSE IT CAN'T HELP ME WHEN I WANT TO SEND EMAILS OR PLAY A MOVIE, THOUGH.
BUT WHAT IF...?
AGAIN?!
THERE ARE NO BUTS HERE!
IT'S IMPOSSIBLE NO MATTER HOW YOU LOOK AT IT!!
MICROCONTROLLERS ARE LIMITED IN THEIR POSSIBLE APPLICATIONS...
LIMITED CAPABILITIES!
RELATIVELY CHEAP!
MICROCONTROLLER
HIGH-POWERED MICROCONTROLLERS AND EXPENSIVE MICROCONTROLLERS ALSO EXIST.
BUT THAT MEANS THEY'RE ALSO MUCH CHEAPER THAN COMPUTER CPUs.

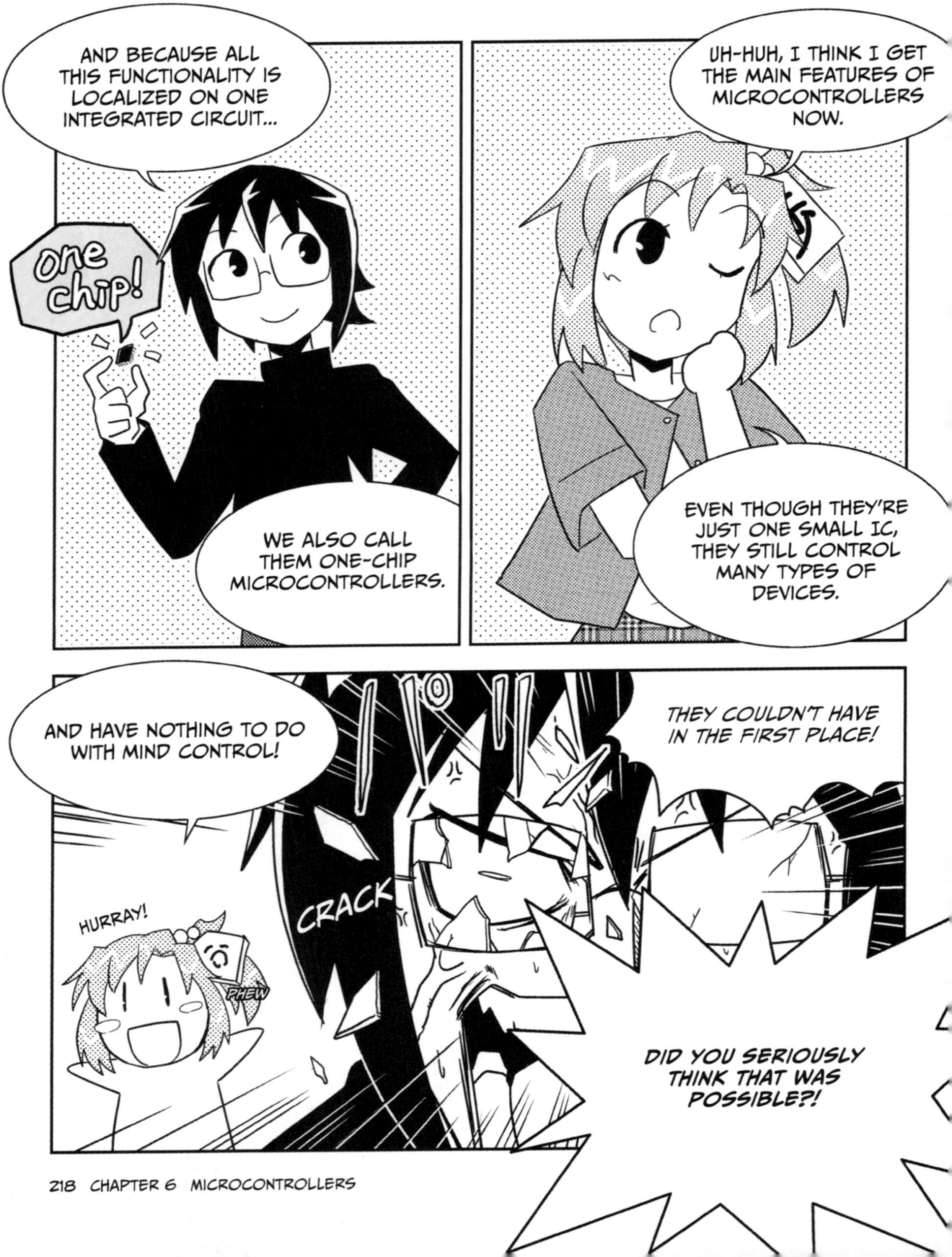
AND BECAUSE ALL THIS FUNCTIONALITY IS LOCALIZED ON ONE INTEGRATED CIRCUIT...
one chip!
WE ALSO CALL THEM ONE-CHIP MICROCONTROLLERS.
UH-HUH, I THINK I GET THE MAIN FEATURES OF MICROCONTROLLERS NOW.
EVEN THOUGH THEY'RE JUST ONE SMALL IC, THEY STILL CONTROL MANY TYPES OF DEVICES.
AND HAVE NOTHING TO DO WITH MIND CONTROL!
THEY COULDN'T HAVE IN THE FIRST PLACE!
CRACK
HURRAY!
PHEW
DID YOU SERIOUSLY THINK THAT WAS POSSIBLE?!

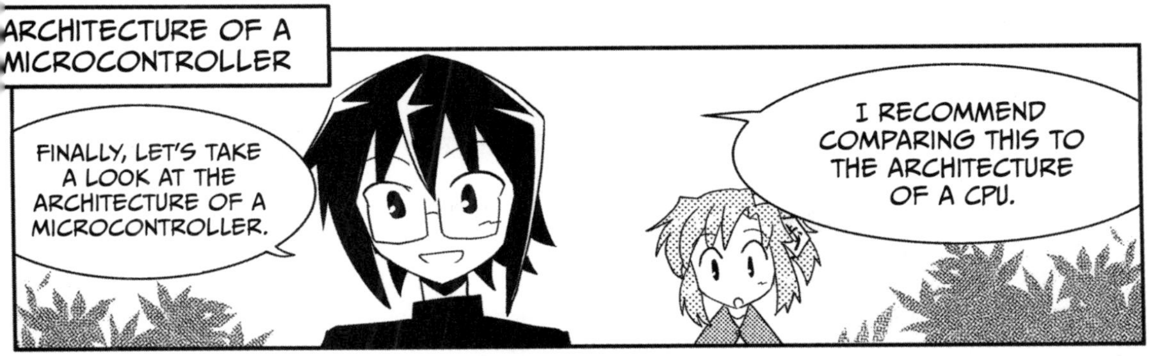
ARCHITECTURE OF A MICROCONTROLLER
FINALLY, LET'S TAKE A LOOK AT THE ARCHITECTURE OF A MICROCONTROLLER.
I RECOMMEND COMPARING THIS TO THE ARCHITECTURE OF A CPU.

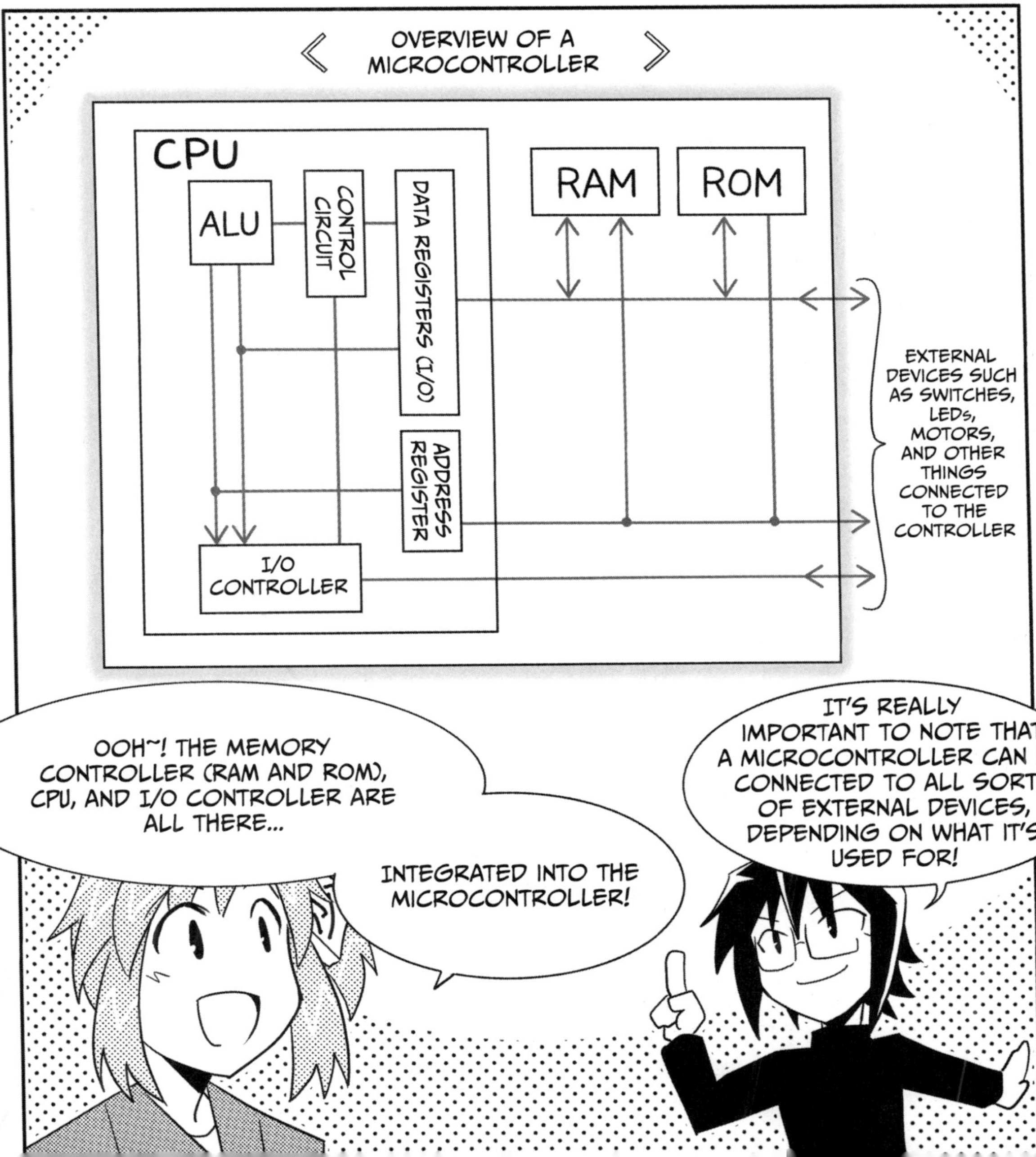
OVERVIEW OF A MICROCONTROLLER
CPU
ALU
CONTROL CIRCUIT
DATA REGISTERS (I/O)
ADDRESS REGISTER
I/O CONTROLLER
RAM
ROM
EXTERNAL DEVICES SUCH AS SWITCHES, LEDs, MOTORS, AND OTHER THINGS CONNECTED TO THE CONTROLLER
OOH~! THE MEMORY CONTROLLER (RAM AND ROM), CPU, AND I/O CONTROLLER ARE ALL THERE...
INTEGRATED INTO THE MICROCONTROLLER!
IT'S REALLY IMPORTANT TO NOTE THAT A MICROCONTROLLER CAN BE CONNECTED TO ALL SORTS OF EXTERNAL DEVICES, DEPENDING ON WHAT IT'S USED FOR!

HISTORY OF THE MICROCONTROLLER

Microcontrollers have a very interesting history. The very first electronic calculator used an ALU made with electron vacuum tubes. It was very large by today's standards, taking up an entire room the size of a volleyball court. This was around the time of World War II, in the 1940s. England and other countries were in the middle of developing electronic calculating machines to decipher the codes that the German army was using. Unlike modern computers, these were not developed in an open international marketplace but instead in top-secret military research laboratories. Because of this, it's not clear whether the American ENIAC computer, presented to the world in 1946, was truly the first computer or not.

The first transistor was invented in 1947, displacing electron vacuum tube calculators with semiconductor-based technology. And with the invention of the integrated circuit in 1958, the miniaturization of electronic calculators progressed significantly.

Even so, the 16-bit minicomputer seen in Chapter 4, which used four 74S181 chips, was not developed until 1972. Removing all external devices, it had a width of 60 cm, a height of 30 cm, and a depth of 45 cm. It could handle an address space of 16KW (kilowords, where 16 bits of data is equal to 1 word), which is what we would call 32KB today. (Compare this to modern SD cards, which are able to store 32GB of data or, in terms of memory size, about a million times more data.)

In the second half of the 1970s, Intel introduced its one-chip CPU as a mass-produced commodity. This product instantly dominated the market, lowering costs across the board.

The one-chip CPU also heralded a new age from 1976 onward in which amateur electronics enthusiasts could afford learning kits (for example, the Altair 8800 microcomputer). With these, they could learn how to program in machine language with the one-chip CPU as a base.

This is also around the time when the term *personal computer*, or *PC*, came into popular use, since you could finally have one of these technical marvels for yourself.

But progress did not stop there! One-board controllers that fit the CPU, memory, and I/O controllers onto a board about the size of an A4 sheet of paper were developed. Eventually, these components fit onto a single IC chip that could be used to control all sorts of devices.

Because these ICs had CPUs that were inseparable from their ROM or RAM memory and integrated I/O ports, they could store programs, perform calculations, and handle input and output. These ICs were called microcontrollers since they were comparatively small and controlled other devices

After this, there was a desire for larger memory, which stimulated a demand for larger computers, as well. But the small-scale devices that use integrated one-chip microcontrollers are still in very high demand today and are used in everything from household electronics to toys.

And so microcontrollers contain everything from a CPU to memory to I/O controllers.

SO WE FIRST HAD COMPUTERS USING ELECTRON VACUUM TUBES...

AND THEN TRANSISTORS MADE FROM SEMI-CONDUCTORS.

NOW, COMPUTERS IN THE FORM OF MICROCONTROLLERS ARE IN EVERYTHING FROM RICE COOKERS TO AUTOMOBILES!

WHAT ARE DSPs?

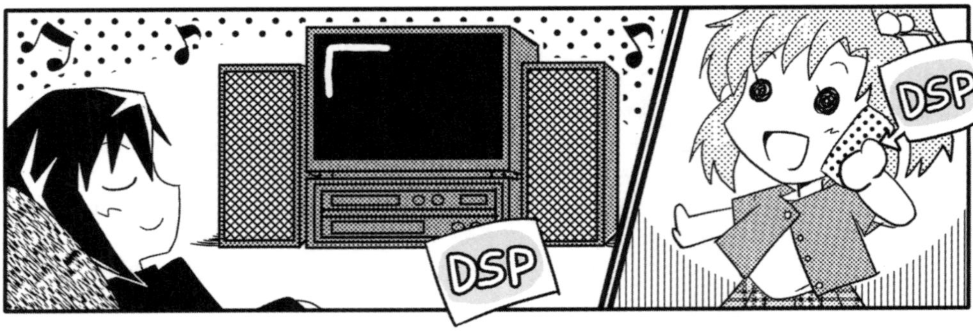
DSP
DSP

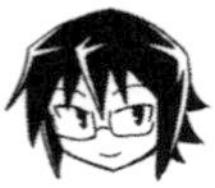

We should take this opportunity to talk a bit about DSPs, as well.

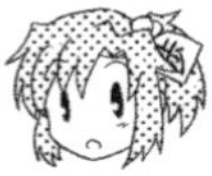

DSP? Yet another strange acronym. So, what are they?

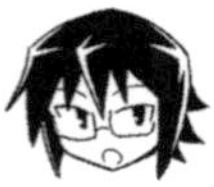

DSPs, much like CPUs, are ICs that perform operations. But compared to CPUs, they're extremely fast.

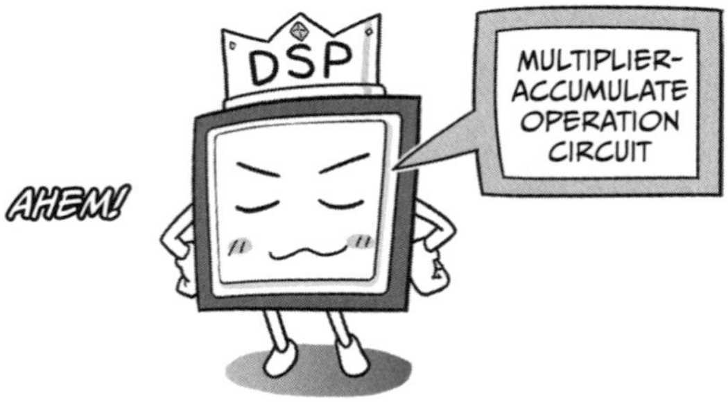
DSP
MULTIPLIER-ACCUMULATE OPERATION CIRCUIT
AHEM!

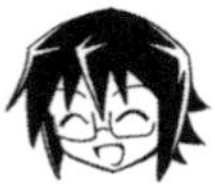

Their "brain" is made up of what is called a *multiplier-accumulate operation circuit*. This essentially means DSPs are really good at doing multiplication and addition at the same time!

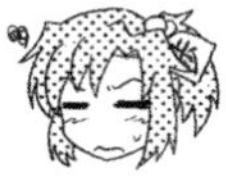

Whoa! So what's that good for? I suppose it has to be good for something.

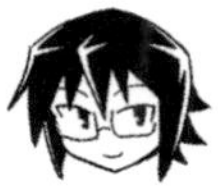

Yeah. It turns out you have to do a lot of multiplication and addition when processing digital signals, especially for audio recordings. In fact, that's what DSP is short for—*digital signal processor*.

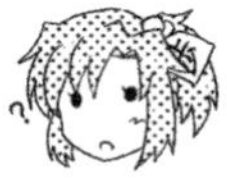

Audio . . . so . . . when I'm talking on my cell phone, for example? I suppose my analog voice has to be converted to digital form somehow for it to be transmitted to my friend on the other end of the line.

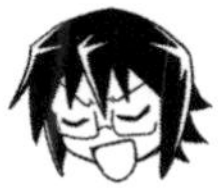

That's correct! Most modern mobile phones have DSPs. They're also being used more often for digital filtering in audio devices and for the operations required to improve acoustic effects.

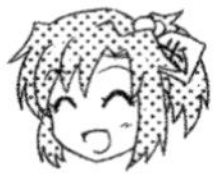

Wow, so they're all around us, these DSPs!

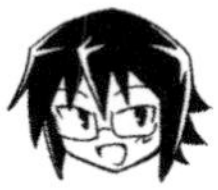

Currently, development for a one-chip DSP with large RAM at the level of a microcontroller is underway.

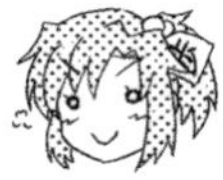

I see. So they're good at doing multiplication and addition at the same time, which is useful for digital signal processing.

While CPUs are really important, I get the sense that DSPs are, too. I'll make sure to remember them!

DSPs AND MULTIPLIER-ACCUMULATE OPERATIONS

During the development of the CPU, there was a growing need for increasing the processing speed of calculations—in particular, division and multiplication were a lot slower than desired.

As we've seen, the CPU's ALU was mostly geared toward performing addition and subtraction at this time. Using these older ALUs, you had to repeatedly perform addition to multiply two numbers and repeatedly perform subtraction to divide two numbers. At the time, computers were becoming more popular in scientific applications, which meant that demand for high-performance multiplication was very high. This is when development of the circuits that were capable of floating-point multiplication really took off, and the result was the digital signal processor, or DSP.

To process digital signals, DSPs perform fast Fourier transforms (FFTs) on them. This requires a lot of simultaneous additions and multiplications. To perform these multiplications and additions efficiently, DSP ICs have a multiplier-accumulator circuit.

Shortly after DSPs were developed, mobile phones started to use digital transmissions, and digital voice signal processing and filtering became more common. The transmission stream could also be compressed, and the receivers started using systems with DSPs at their core to convert the raw voice data using vocoders (a voice encoder/decoder).

Later, microcontroller-like DSPs with larger RAM molded into the chip started to show up, making voice data processing even faster.

MICROCONTROLLERS IN INDUSTRIAL MACHINES

CPUs, microcontrollers, and DSPs are in many of the devices we use in our daily lives. Some examples include today's wall clocks, alarm clocks, and even wristwatches, all of which are likely to contain a one-chip microcontroller. Other household devices like refrigerators, air conditioners, and washing machines are likely to contain more than one. And the remote controls used to send commands to these devices also contain a microcontroller IC.

Automated robots and conveyor belts in large-scale industry also have to be controlled in some fashion and therefore require either a CPU or DSP.

MANY DEVICES IN OUR HOMES HAVE MICROCONTROLLERS,
AND THEY EVEN HAVE INDUSTRIAL USES...

Up until now, we've had single-chip CPUs as well as microcontrollers that contain a CPU, memory, and I/O controllers all in one. The amount we can pack into a single chip is determined by tradeoffs among our capacity to produce semiconductors, their production cost, and the market's demand and margins.

Advancements in IC production technology have led to the development of FPGAs (field-programmable gate arrays). Using an FPGA, you can create any logical circuit you desire and bring it into reality with hardware. The basic structure can contain lookup tables of anywhere from several thousand to several million units in a single IC. These tables can be prepared beforehand by the IC maker and provided as is.

The initial state of the IC consists of a lookup table memory section and logic blocks that can be wired together in different ways, resulting in many possible applications. The raw IC is then configured by the user with specialized tools to write the modeled design into the circuit, creating the desired IC. Development is normally done on a computer, but the specialized tools needed can also be stored on a USB, making the creation of even large-scale logic circuits an easy task.

In the past, CPUs were different from FPGAs, but in recent years, FPGAs containing CPU functionality have started to appear. There are two ways to make an FPGA into a CPU. The first is to simply create an existing CPU design in the wiring of your logic circuit using the development tools provided, and the other is to embed a CPU in one part of the gate array as a separate IC.

In either case, the CPU as a single IC is becoming gradually less common over time. But even though we have DSPs, there is still a need to control tasks other than multiply-accumulate operations, and as such, the principles underlying the CPU will remain important concepts no matter how ICs continue to develop.

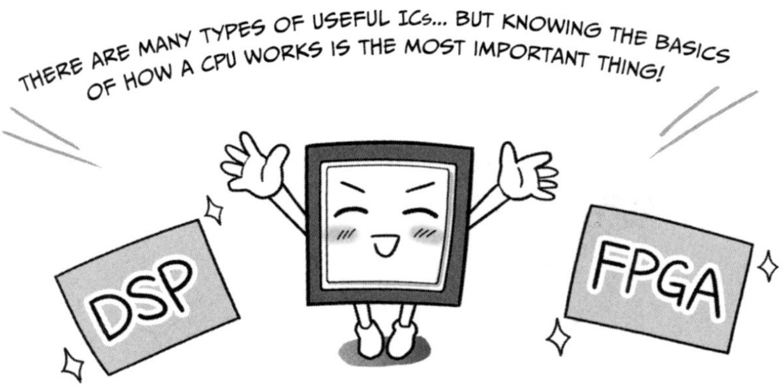
THERE ARE MANY TYPES OF USEFUL ICs... BUT KNOWING THE BASICS OF HOW A CPU WORKS IS THE MOST IMPORTANT THING!
DSP
FPGA

EPILOGUE

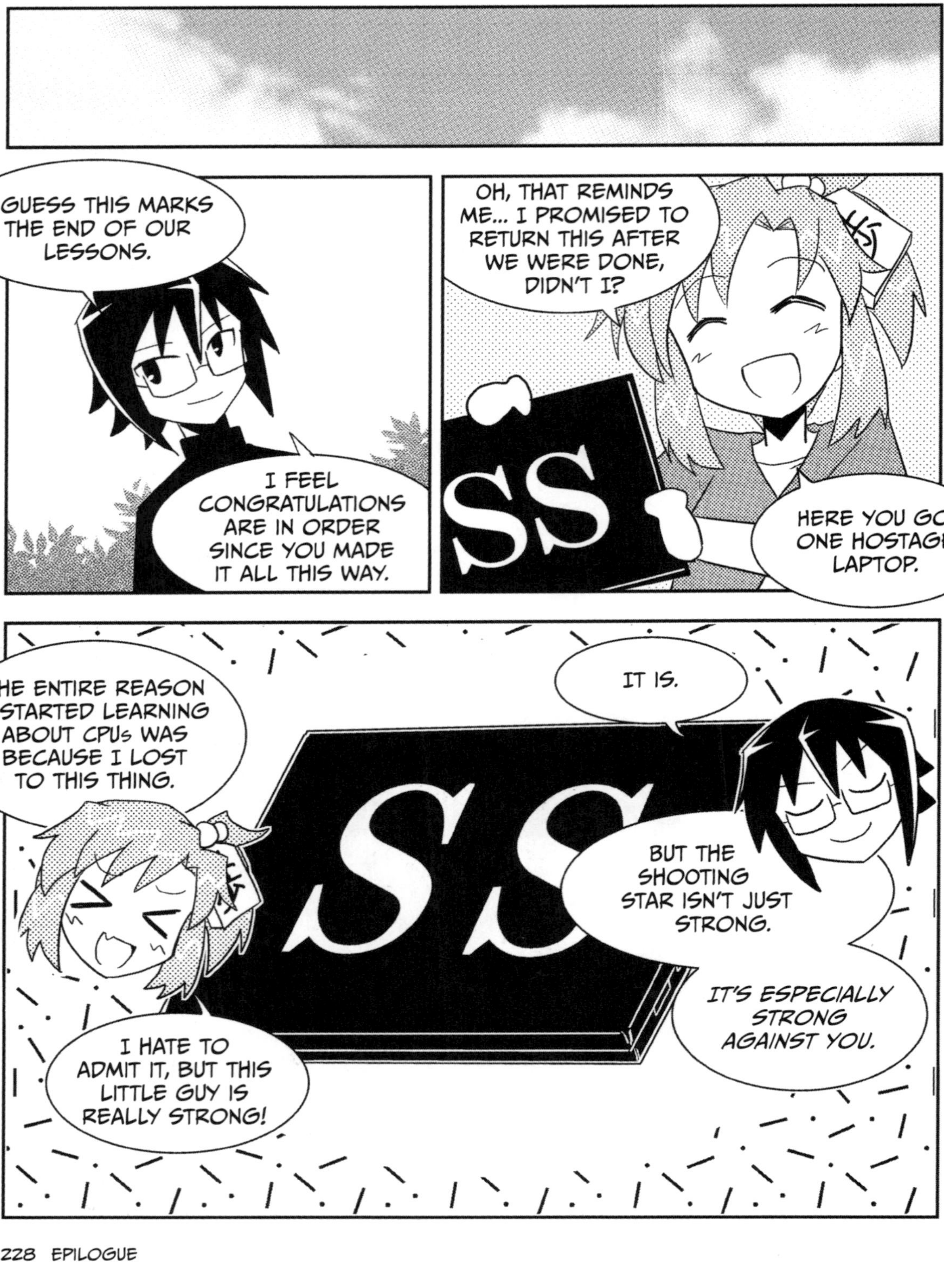
I GUESS THIS MARKS THE END OF OUR LESSONS.
I FEEL CONGRATULATIONS ARE IN ORDER SINCE YOU MADE IT ALL THIS WAY.
OH, THAT REMINDS ME... I PROMISED TO RETURN THIS AFTER WE WERE DONE, DIDN'T I?
SS
HERE YOU GO, ONE HOSTAGE LAPTOP.
THE ENTIRE REASON I STARTED LEARNING ABOUT CPUs WAS BECAUSE I LOST TO THIS THING.
I HATE TO ADMIT IT, BUT THIS LITTLE GUY IS REALLY STRONG!
SS
IT IS.
BUT THE SHOOTING STAR ISN'T JUST STRONG.
IT'S ESPECIALLY STRONG AGAINST YOU.

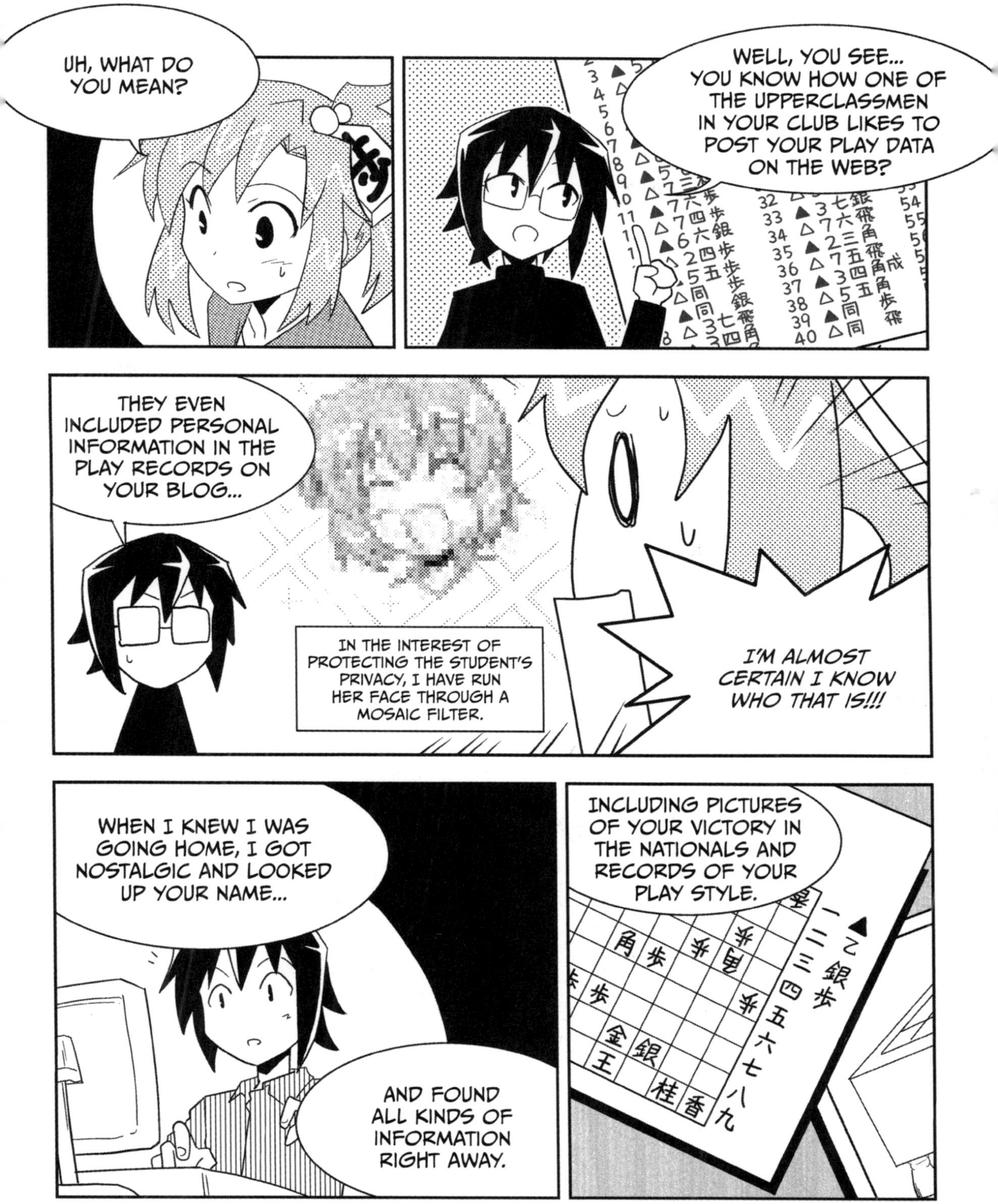

UH, WHAT DO YOU MEAN?
WELL, YOU SEE... YOU KNOW HOW ONE OF THE UPPERCLASSMEN IN YOUR CLUB LIKES TO POST YOUR PLAY DATA ON THE WEB?
THEY EVEN INCLUDED PERSONAL INFORMATION IN THE PLAY RECORDS ON YOUR BLOG...
IN THE INTEREST OF PROTECTING THE STUDENT'S PRIVACY, I HAVE RUN HER FACE THROUGH A MOSAIC FILTER.
I'M ALMOST CERTAIN I KNOW WHO THAT IS!!!
WHEN I KNEW I WAS GOING HOME, I GOT NOSTALGIC AND LOOKED UP YOUR NAME...
AND FOUND ALL KINDS OF INFORMATION RIGHT AWAY.
INCLUDING PICTURES OF YOUR VICTORY IN THE NATIONALS AND RECORDS OF YOUR PLAY STYLE.

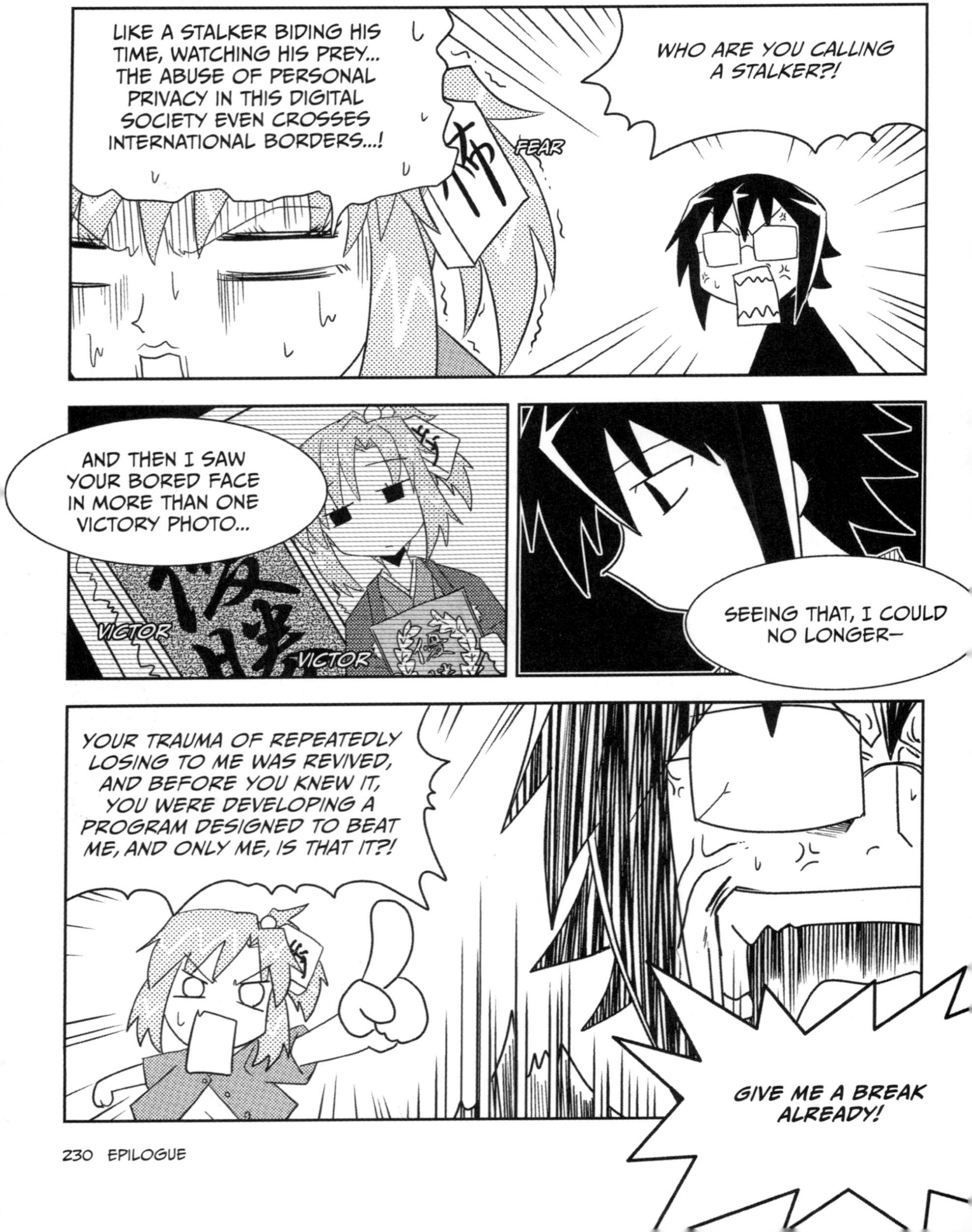

LIKE A STALKER BIDING HIS TIME, WATCHING HIS PREY... THE ABUSE OF PERSONAL PRIVACY IN THIS DIGITAL SOCIETY EVEN CROSSES INTERNATIONAL BORDERS...!
FEAR
WHO ARE YOU CALLING A STALKER?!
AND THEN I SAW YOUR BORED FACE IN MORE THAN ONE VICTORY PHOTO...
VICTOR
VICTOR
SEEING THAT, I COULD NO LONGER—
YOUR TRAUMA OF REPEATEDLY LOSING TO ME WAS REVIVED, AND BEFORE YOU KNEW IT, YOU WERE DEVELOPING A PROGRAM DESIGNED TO BEAT ME, AND ONLY ME, IS THAT IT?!
GIVE ME A BREAK ALREADY!

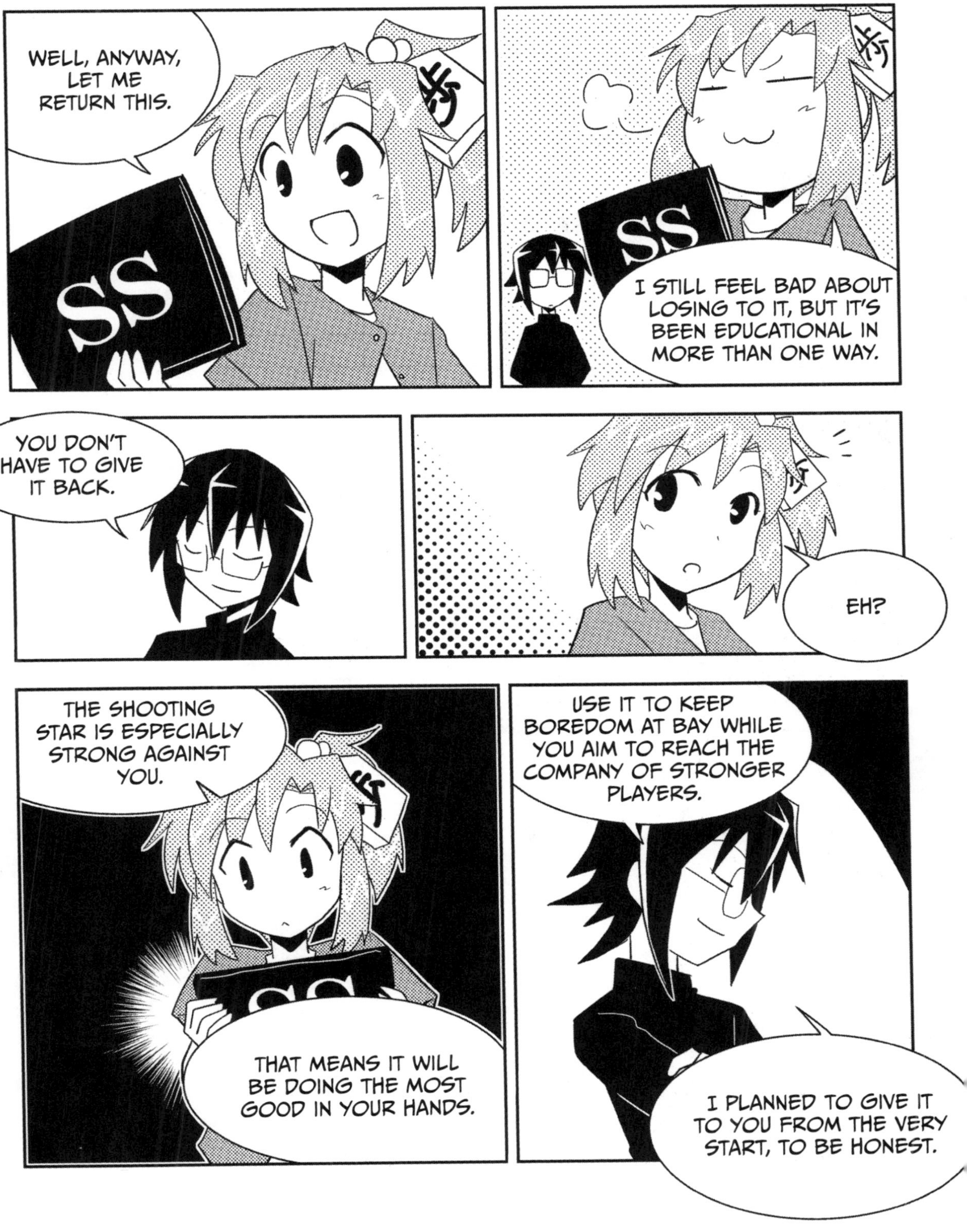
WELL, ANYWAY, LET ME RETURN THIS.
SS
I STILL FEEL BAD ABOUT LOSING TO IT, BUT IT'S BEEN EDUCATIONAL IN MORE THAN ONE WAY.
YOU DON'T HAVE TO GIVE IT BACK.
EH?
THE SHOOTING STAR IS ESPECIALLY STRONG AGAINST YOU.
THAT MEANS IT WILL BE DOING THE MOST GOOD IN YOUR HANDS.
USE IT TO KEEP BOREDOM AT BAY WHILE YOU AIM TO REACH THE COMPANY OF STRONGER PLAYERS.
I PLANNED TO GIVE IT TO YOU FROM THE VERY START, TO BE HONEST.

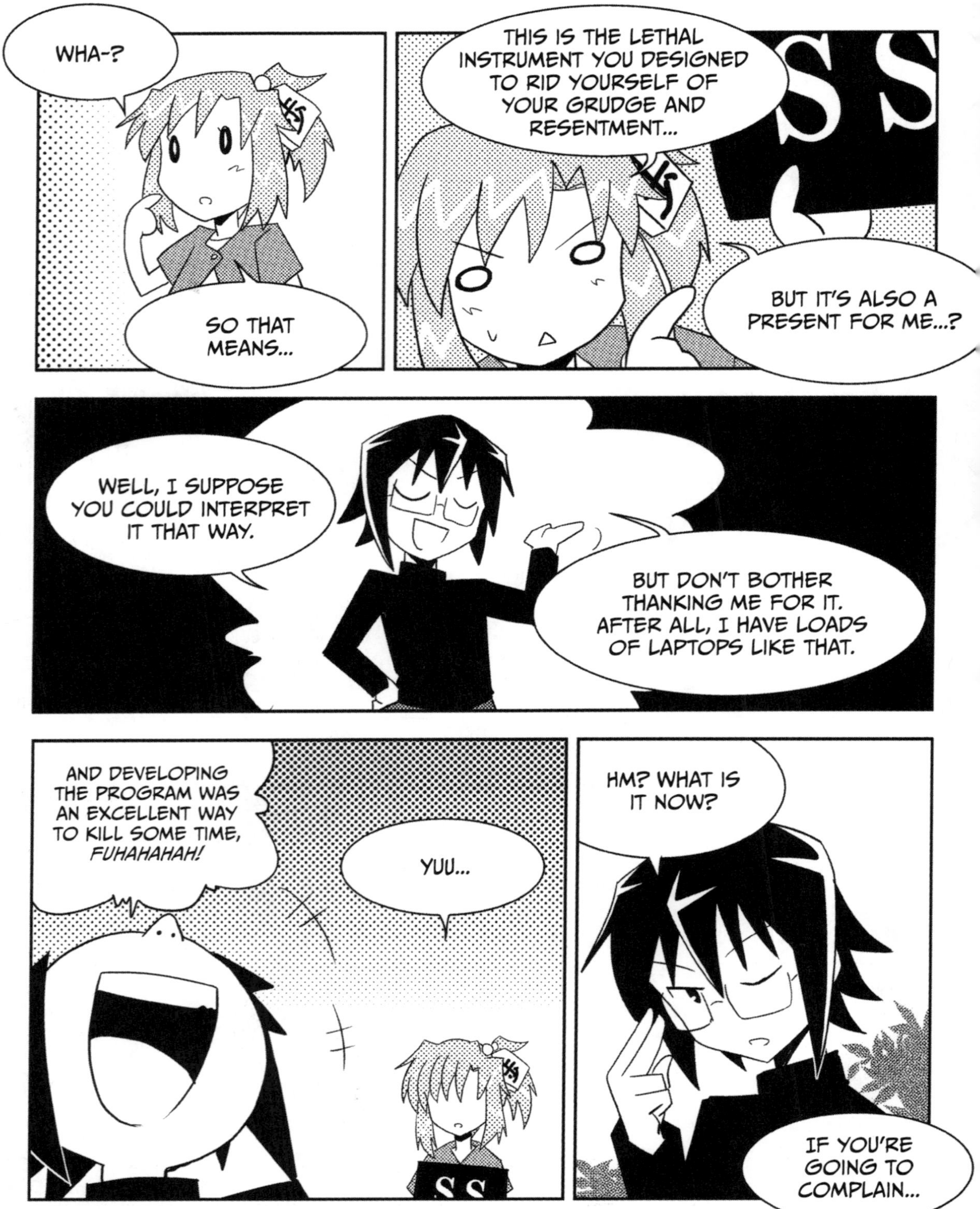
WHA-?
SO THAT MEANS...
THIS IS THE LETHAL INSTRUMENT YOU DESIGNED TO RID YOURSELF OF YOUR GRUDGE AND RESENTMENT...
BUT IT'S ALSO A PRESENT FOR ME...?
WELL, I SUPPOSE YOU COULD INTERPRET IT THAT WAY.
BUT DON'T BOTHER THANKING ME FOR IT. AFTER ALL, I HAVE LOADS OF LAPTOPS LIKE THAT.
AND DEVELOPING THE PROGRAM WAS AN EXCELLENT WAY TO KILL SOME TIME, *FUHAHAHAH!*
YUU...
HM? WHAT IS IT NOW?
IF YOU'RE GOING TO COMPLAIN...

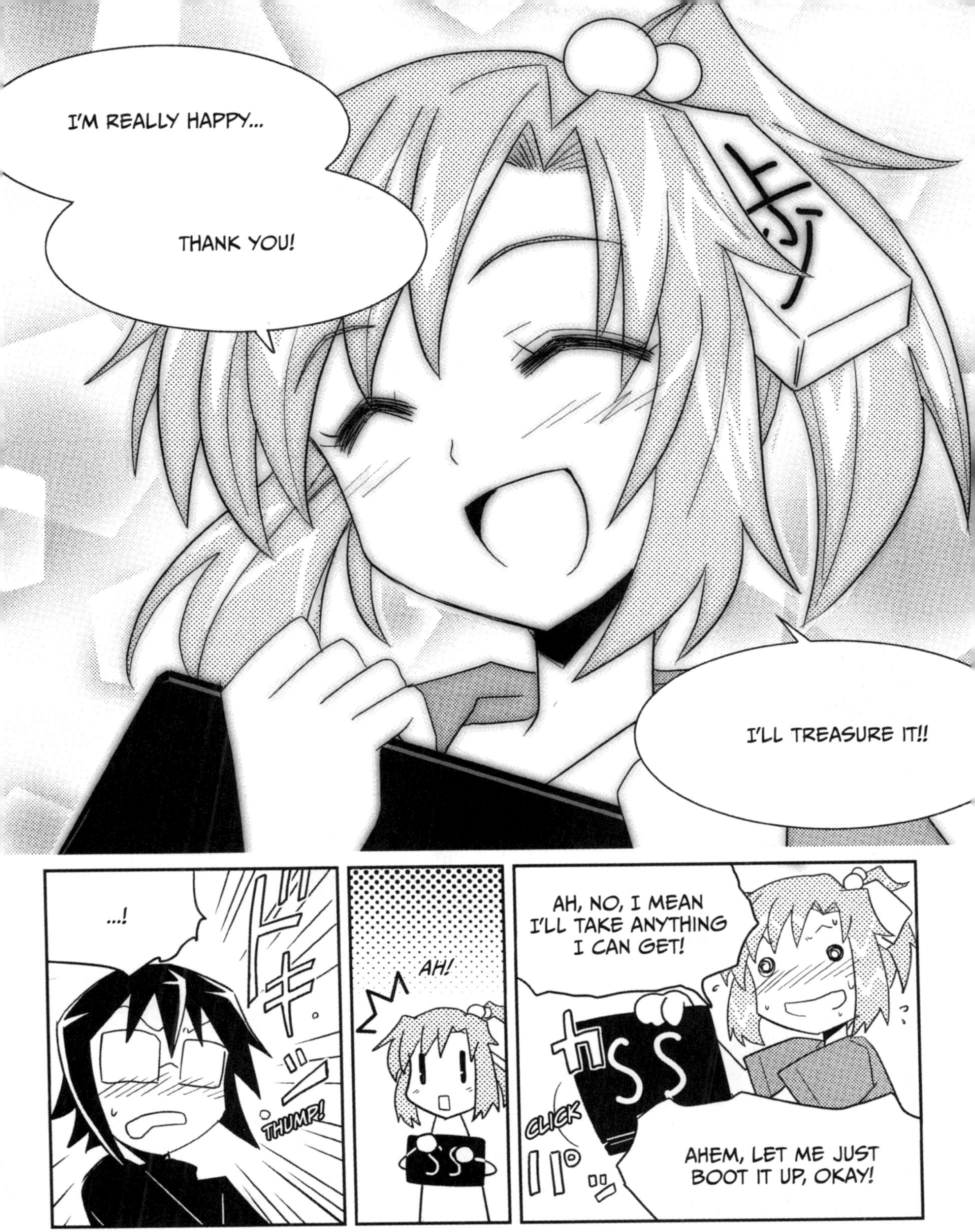
I'M REALLY HAPPY...
THANK YOU!
I'LL TREASURE IT!!
...!
THUMP!
AH!
AH, NO, I MEAN I'LL TAKE ANYTHING I CAN GET!
CLICK
AHEM, LET ME JUST BOOT IT UP, OKAY!

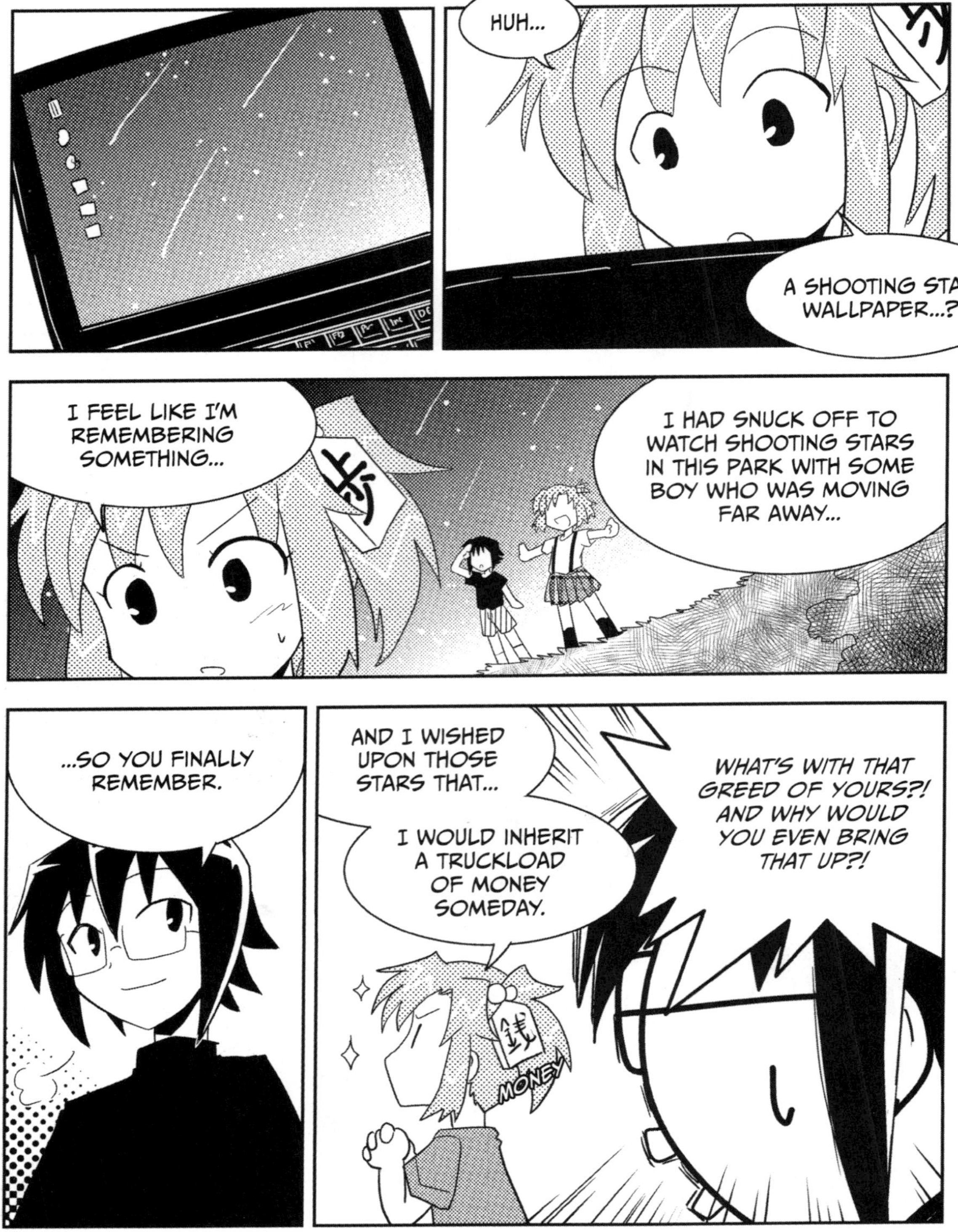
HUH...
A SHOOTING STAR WALLPAPER...?
I FEEL LIKE I'M REMEMBERING SOMETHING...
I HAD SNUCK OFF TO WATCH SHOOTING STARS IN THIS PARK WITH SOME BOY WHO WAS MOVING FAR AWAY...
...SO YOU FINALLY REMEMBER.
AND I WISHED UPON THOSE STARS THAT...
I WOULD INHERIT A TRUCKLOAD OF MONEY SOMEDAY.
MONEY
WHAT'S WITH THAT GREED OF YOURS?! AND WHY WOULD YOU EVEN BRING THAT UP?!

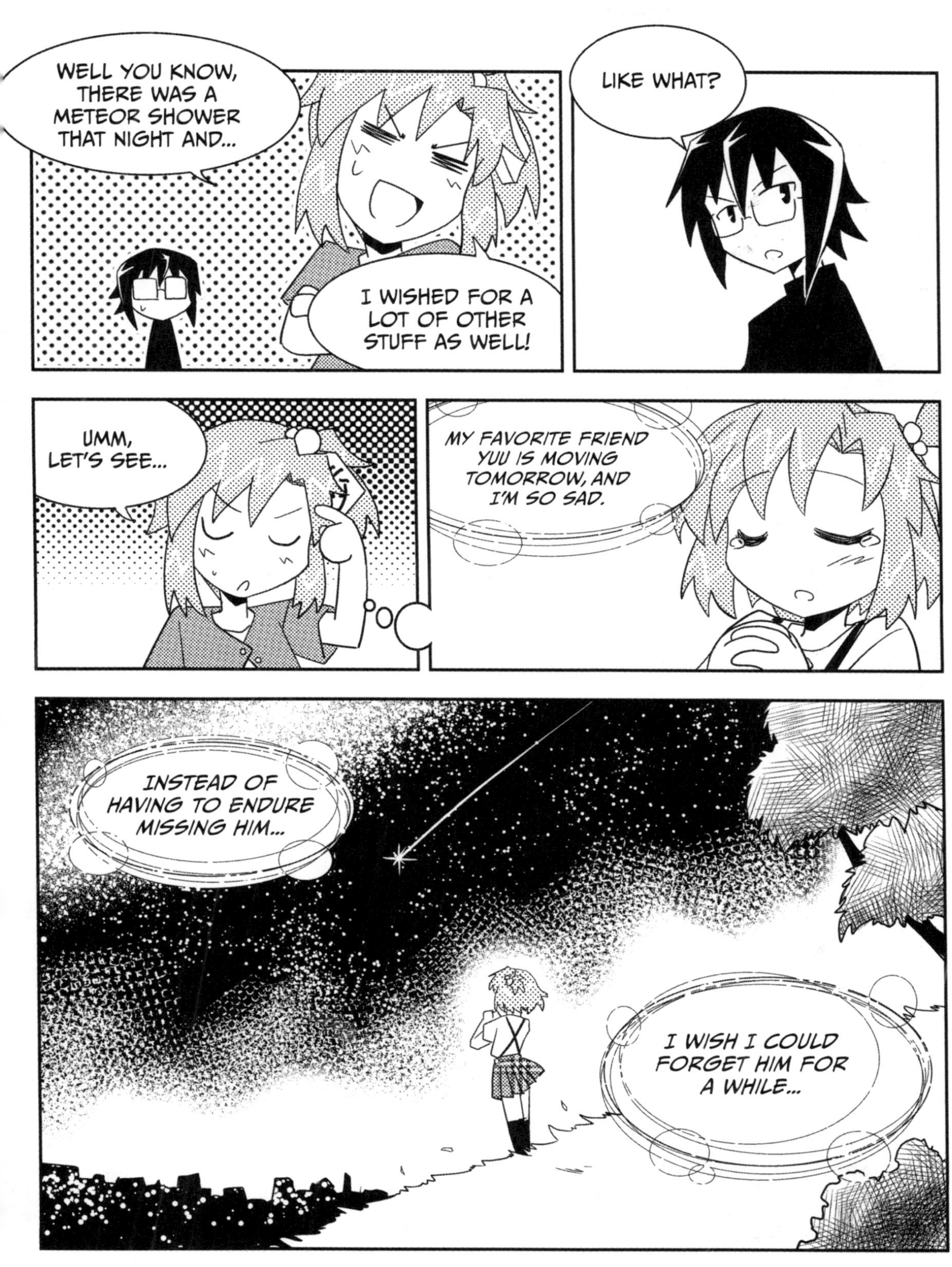
WELL YOU KNOW, THERE WAS A METEOR SHOWER THAT NIGHT AND...
I WISHED FOR A LOT OF OTHER STUFF AS WELL!
LIKE WHAT?
UMM, LET'S SEE...
MY FAVORITE FRIEND YUU IS MOVING TOMORROW, AND I'M SO SAD.
INSTEAD OF HAVING TO ENDURE MISSING HIM...
I WISH I COULD FORGET HIM FOR A WHILE...

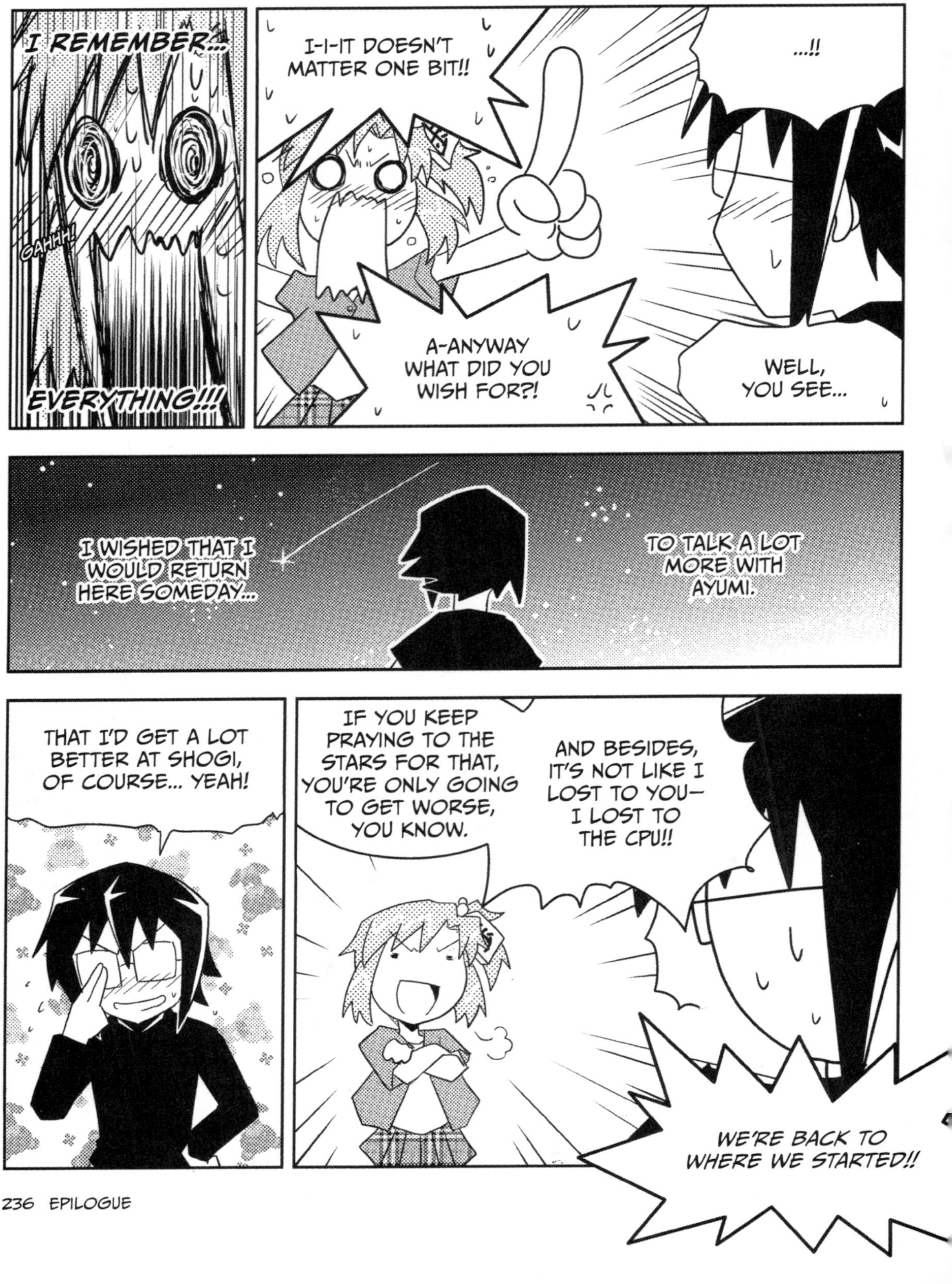
I REMEMBER...
GAHHH!
EVERYTHING!!!
I-I-IT DOESN'T MATTER ONE BIT!!
...!!
A-ANYWAY WHAT DID YOU WISH FOR?!
WELL, YOU SEE...
I WISHED THAT I WOULD RETURN HERE SOMEDAY...
TO TALK A LOT MORE WITH AYUMI.
THAT I'D GET A LOT BETTER AT SHOGI, OF COURSE... YEAH!
IF YOU KEEP PRAYING TO THE STARS FOR THAT, YOU'RE ONLY GOING TO GET WORSE, YOU KNOW.
AND BESIDES, IT'S NOT LIKE I LOST TO YOU— I LOST TO THE CPU!!
WE'RE BACK TO WHERE WE STARTED!!

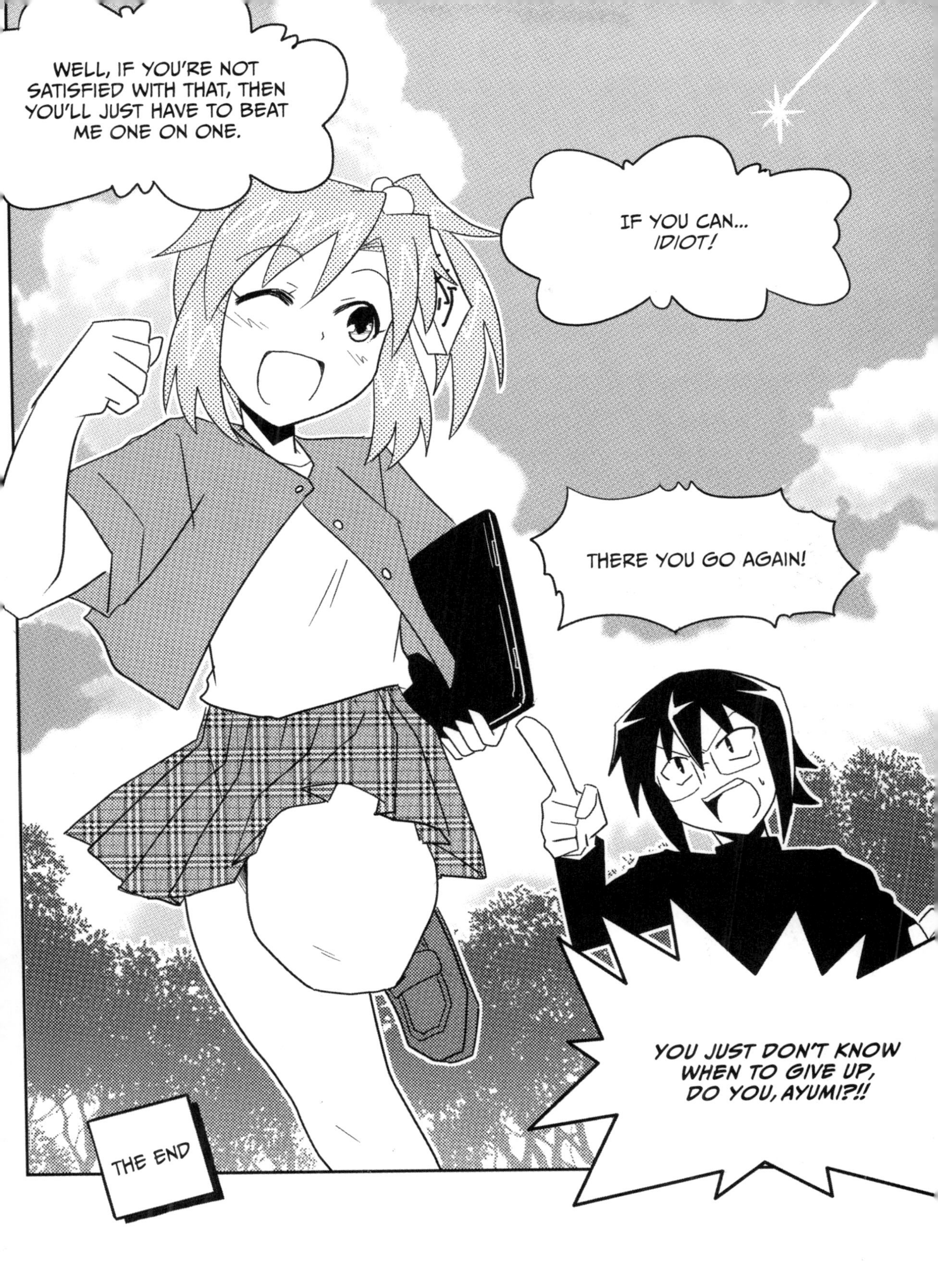
WELL, IF YOU'RE NOT SATISFIED WITH THAT, THEN YOU'LL JUST HAVE TO BEAT ME ONE ON ONE.
IF YOU CAN... *IDIOT!*
THERE YOU GO AGAIN!
YOU JUST DON'T KNOW WHEN TO GIVE UP, DO YOU, AYUMI?!!
THE END

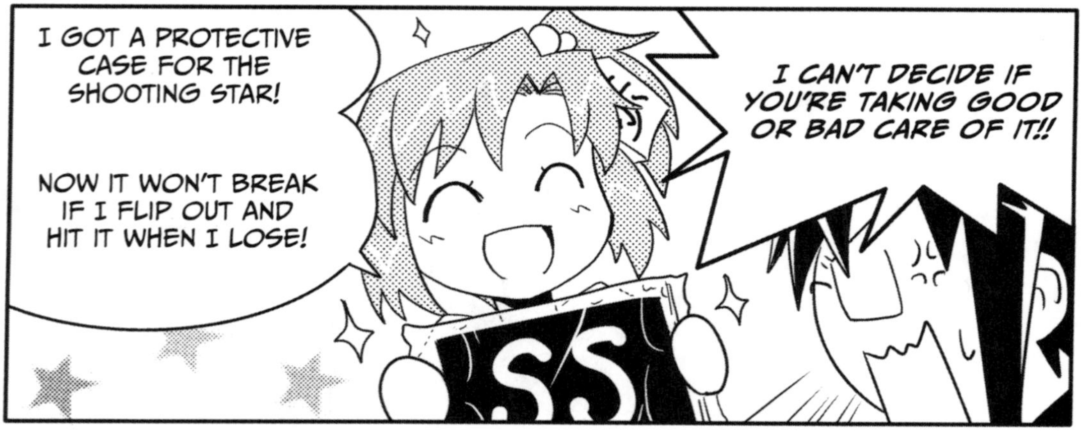
I GOT A PROTECTIVE CASE FOR THE SHOOTING STAR!
NOW IT WON'T BREAK IF I FLIP OUT AND HIT IT WHEN I LOSE!
I CAN'T DECIDE IF YOU'RE TAKING GOOD OR BAD CARE OF IT!!

AFTERWORD

Up to this point, we have only talked about very old and primitive CPUs. The ones we have shown could only really be used for things like toys or simple AC remote controls. They are too simple to be used in most modern microcomputers or CPUs today. Currently, the speed of progress is so fast that everything I say here will quickly become obsolete. But even so, I wrote this book in an attempt to help anyone who might want to learn some lasting basics—even in these fast-changing times.

In other words, I would like to emphasize that this book has concentrated on the very basic principles governing CPUs, forgoing any information relating to general computer architecture. But even so, I would like to leave you with a small impression of the current state of progress.

It is unfortunately quite hard to illustrate modern complex circuits in the type of diagrams we used at the start of the book to show the different parts of the CPU, so I'm going to have to talk in very superficial terms here.

There are many techniques used to make modern CPUs execute programs more quickly. An older one of these techniques is the *prefetch instruction*. Instead of trying to get the next instruction after the current one has finished processing, prefetching tries to extract the next instruction from memory before the current one has completed to shorten any wait times that might otherwise occur.

Since the CPU is a lot faster than main memory, it makes a lot of sense to let prefetch decode the next instructions and store them in a cache in preparation for the next calculation. Repeating this prefetching process of reading and decoding instructions ahead of time can lead to continuous execution speed increases across the board.

There is another instruction called *pipelining* in which the instruction cycle is broken into several dependent steps. These steps are usually fetch, decode, execute, access memory, and finally write back to register/memory. The goal here is to keep all parts of the CPU busy at all times by executing these steps in parallel. So while one instruction might be running its execute step, another instruction would be running its decode step, and yet another instruction would be fetching.

CPU researchers found some tendencies toward inefficiencies when using certain instruction and operand combinations. Attempts to remove these inefficiencies by simplifying the instruction set led to the development of the *RISC (reduced instruction set computer) architecture*. Processors that use this instruction set are called RISC processors.

Many worried that reducing the instruction set would make complex calculations require more instructions and therefore slow down execution. In reality, however, many applications saw a performance boost on the RISC architecture. It turns out that reducing the instruction set's complexity leads to simplifications in the hardware design that allow for higher single instruction execution clock speeds.

Because of this, RISC processors have started to be used in many different areas. Processors that don't use RISC principles have been dubbed *CISC (complex instruction set computer)*, riffing off the RISC name. This acronym was created purely as an antonym of RISCs, and there is no particular architecture associated with the CISC name.

Recent Intel and other CPU chips contain not just one but many cores, which are distributed between different processes on the system. This is something that falls in the domain of computer architecture, so as I mentioned at the start of the book, this is not something I will explain in much detail.

However, there is no requirement that all complex calculations must be performed in order. It is fine for the CPU to split up different parts of a task and run the individual parts on separate cores simultaneously, exchanging data between cores only when absolutely necessary. Letting the CPU multitask like this can improve execution speed a great deal. Using the CPU in such a way, however, poses problems not only for the hardware but also for the OS, memory access, and code execution scheduling.

INDEX

D

E

F

G

H

I

J

L

M

MFLOPS (million floating-point operations per second), 138
microcontrollers, 213
  architecture of, 220
  vs. CPUs, 216–217
  DSPs, 222–224
  function of, 214–215
  history of, 220–221
  in industrial machines, 224–225
million floating-point operations per second (MFLOPS), 138
MIPS (million instructions per second), 137
MMUs (memory management units), 114
mnemonics, 163, 192, 196–198
mode pin, 177, 179
modification registers, 175, 186
motherboards, 120
multiplexers (MUX), 93
multiplier-accumulate operation circuits, 222, 224

N

NAND gate (logic intersection complement gate), 57–58
negative flag (N-flag), 187
noise (information), 30, 33
non-maskable interrupts (NMI), 129
non-volatile memory, 132, 208
NOR gate (logic union complement gate), 57–59
NOT gate (logic negation gate), 51, 53, 56
number systems, 38–41

O

object code, 199
ODD flag, 187
on-board programming, 208
opcodes, 102–103, 110, 142, 162–163, 180
operands, 102–103, 110, 142
  addressing modes, 165, 168–174
  address modification, 174–175

address references, 167
immediate value processing, 166
  number of, 163–164
  types of, 162–165
operation execution speed, 137
operations and instructions, 14. *See also* arithmetic operations; bit shifts; digital information and operations; logic operations
  ALUs and, 22–24
  branch instructions, 155–157, 161, 200–203
  data transfer operations, 153
  I/O instructions, 154
  jump instructions, 155–157, 161
  memory and, 18–19, 70–71, 89–90, 103–105
  processing and decision making, 25–27
  programs and, 19
  skip instructions, 157
  SLEEP instruction, 188
  types of, 15
OR gate (logic union gate), 51–52, 55
output devices, 16–17
overflow, 45, 150–151
overflow flag (overflow bit; OV-flag), 151, 187

P

parallel transmission, 185
PC (program counter), 107–108, 112–114, 187
personal computers (PCs), 220
pins, 49–50
pipelining, 238
prefetch instructions, 238
primary memory, 16, 18–19, 70, 115, 116–118
primitives, 32
processing speed, 118
program counter (PC), 107–108, 112–114, 187

programs, 19, 101, 192, 199
  assembly languages, 192–194, 196–197
  with conditions and jumps, 200–203
  control unit and, 20–21
  high-level languages, 194–197
  large-scale software development, 198
  machine language, 194
  pre-execution process, 208–209
  vs. source code, 199
  storage of, 208
propagation delay, 68
Python, 198

R

RAM (random access memory), 119–121, 132, 208
read-only memory (ROM), 119–121, 132, 208
read/write (R/W) signals, 98–99
read-write memory (RWM), 132
reduced instruction set computer (RISC) architecture, 238–239
registers, 70–71, 83, 103–104
  accumulators, 104–105, 110, 143, 186
  address registers, 108
  base registers, 175, 186
  index registers, 175, 186
  instruction decoders, 109, 186
  instruction registers, 105, 109, 186
  program counter, 107–108, 112–114, 187
  shift registers, 185
  stack pointer, 126–127, 187
  status registers, 160, 186
  temp registers, 186
relative addressing, 173
repeating processes, 202
resets, 128–129
reset signals, 136–137

ABOUT THE AUTHOR

Michio Shibuya graduated from the electrical engineering department of Toukai University in 1971. Among other occupations, he has worked as an NMR researcher in a private medical institution, has spent 12 years working as a MOS product designer and developer for a foreign company, and has since pursued a career in IC design at technical departments of both domestic and foreign trading companies. Since May of 2007, Shibuya has worked for the semiconductor trading company Sankyosha, first as a field application engineer and currently as a special advisor. He is also the author of *Learning Signal Analysis and Number Analysis Using Excel*, *Learning Fourier Transforms Using Excel*, *The Manga Guide to Fourier Transforms*, *The Manga Guide to Semiconductors*, and *Learning Electrical Circuits Using the Circuit Simulator LTspice* (all published by Ohmsha).

PRODUCTION TEAM FOR THE JAPANESE EDITION

Production: Office sawa

Office sawa was established in 2006 and specializes in advertisement and educational practical guides in medicine and computers. They also take pride in their sales promotion materials, reference books, illustrations, and manga-themed manuals.

Email: office-sawa@sn.main.jp

Scenario: Sawako Sawada

Illustrations: Takashi Tonagi

HOW THIS BOOK WAS MADE

The *Manga Guide* series is a co-publication of No Starch Press and Ohmsha, Ltd. of Tokyo, Japan, one of Japan's oldest and most respected scientific and technical book publishers. Each title in the best-selling *Manga Guide* series is the product of the combined work of a manga illustrator, scenario writer, and expert scientist or mathematician. Once each title is translated into English, we rewrite and edit the translation as necessary and have an expert review each volume. The result is the English version you hold in your hands.

MORE MANGA GUIDES

Find more *Manga Guides* at your favorite bookstore, and learn more about the series at *https://www.nostarch.com/manga/*.

UPDATES

Visit *https://www.nostarch.com/microprocessors/* for updates, errata, and other information.

COLOPHON

The Manga Guide to Microprocessors is set in CCMeanwhile and Chevin. This book was printed and bound by Sheridan Books, Inc. in Chelsea, Michigan. The paper is 60# Finch Offset, which is certified by the Forest Stewardship Council (FSC).